Prospects for Peace in South Asia

ASIA-PACIFIC RESEARCH CENTER

The Asia-Pacific Research Center in the Stanford Institute for International Studies sponsors interdisciplinary research on the politics, economies, and societies of contemporary Asia. This monograph series features academic and policy-oriented research by Stanford faculty and other scholars associated with the Center.

Prospects for Peace in South Asia

Edited by Rafiq Dossani and
Henry S. Rowen

Stanford University Press

Stanford, California 2005

Stanford University Press
Stanford, California
www.sup.org

The editors acknowledge financial support from Anil and Gautam Godhwani, Asim Abdullah, Atiq Raza, Farooq Kathwari, Kanwal Rekhi, Sabeer Bhatia, the U.S. Army War College's Strategic Studies Institute, and Zia Chishti.

Library of Congress Cataloging-in-Publication Data

Prospects for peace in South Asia / edited by Rafiq Dossani and Henry S. Rowen.
    p.   cm. — (Studies of the Asia-Pacific Research Center, Stanford University)
    Includes index.
    ISBN 0-8047-5084-x (cloth : alk. paper)
    ISBN 0-8047-5085-8 (pbk. : alk. paper)
    1. South Asia—Politics and government.   2. Pakistan—Foreign relations—India.   3. India—Foreign relations—Pakistan.   I. Dossani, Rafiq, 1954–
II. Rowen, Henry S.   III. Series.
DS341.P755 2005
327.5491054—DC22

                             2004029601

Original Printing 2005

Last figure below indicates year of this printing:

14   13   12   11   10   09   08   07   06   05

Designed and typeset at Stanford University Press in 11/14 Adobe Garamond.

Contents

Prospects for Peace in South Asia

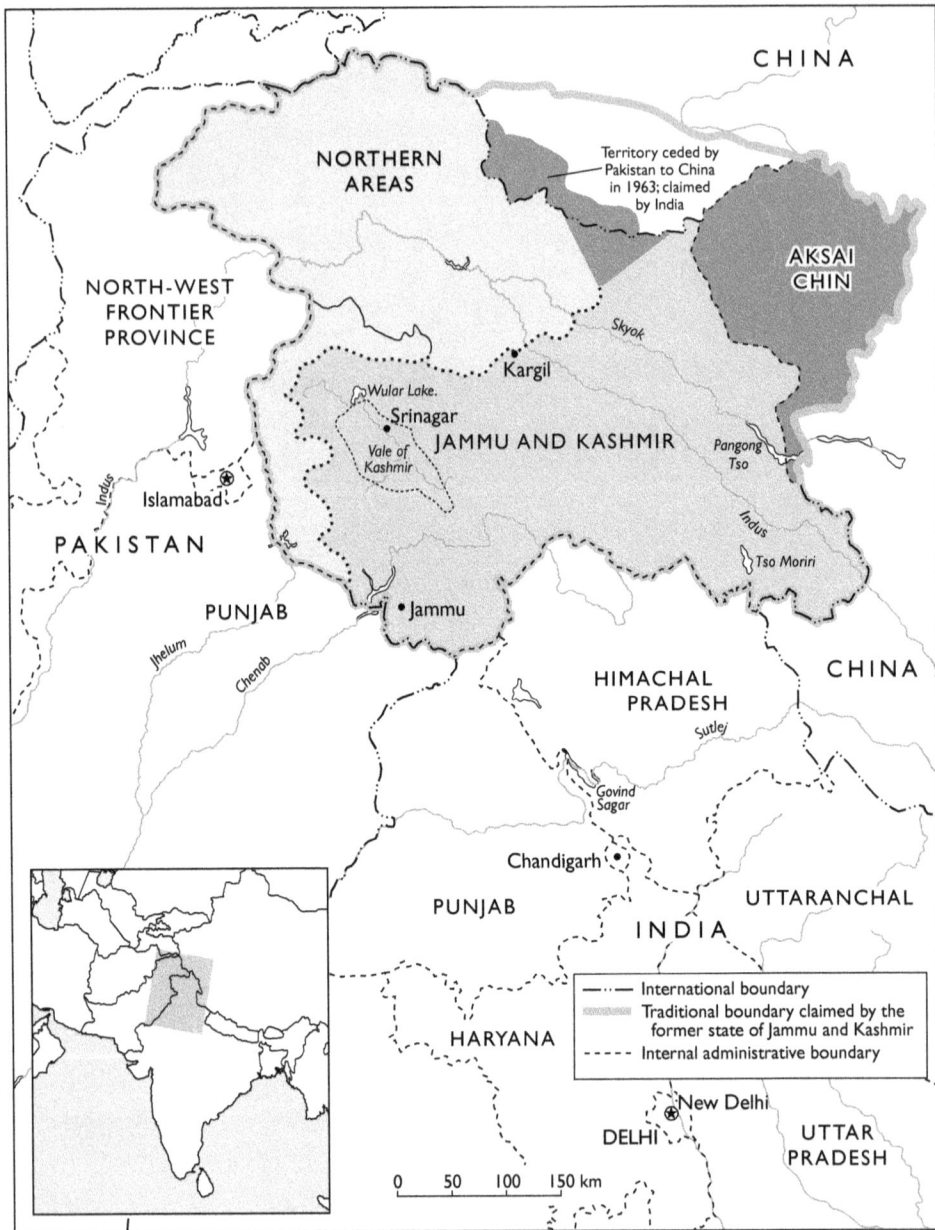

CHINA

NORTHERN
AREAS

Territory ceded by
Pakistan to China
in 1963; claimed
by India

AKSAI
CHIN

NORTH-WEST
FRONTIER
PROVINCE

Skyok

Kargil

Wular Lake.

Srinagar

JAMMU AND KASHMIR

Vale of
Kashmir

Pangong
Tso

Islamabad

Indus

PAKISTAN

Indus

Tso Moriri

PUNJAB

Jhelum

Jammu

Chenab

HIMACHAL
PRADESH

CHINA

Sutlej

Govind
Sagar

Chandigarh

UTTARANCHAL

PUNJAB

INDIA

— · — International boundary
Traditional boundary claimed by the
former state of Jammu and Kashmir
— — — Internal administrative boundary

HARYANA

New Delhi

0   50   100   150 km

DELHI

UTTAR
PRADESH

TAJIKISTAN

AFGHANISTAN

Thui An Pass

Darkot Pass

Mintaka Pass

Khunjerab Pass

CHINA

Chumar Khan Pass

Baltit

Shandur Pass

Gilgit

Dadarili Pass

PAKISTAN

Chilas

Babusar Pass

Astor

Skardu

Baltoro Glacier

Sia La

Bilafond La

Karakorum Pass

Goma

Kel

Jammu

LINE OF CONTROL

Muzaffarabad

Tithwal

Sopur

and

Kargil

Zoji La Pass

Dras

Domel

Chakothi

Baramula

Shrinagar

Kashmir

Leh

Uri

Rawala Kot

Haji Pir Pass

Campbellpore

Punch

Anantnag

Karu

Islamabad

Banihal Pass

Kotli

Rawalpindi

Rajauri

New Mirpur

Naushahra

Bhimbar

Riasi

Jhelum

Chhamb

Akhnur

Udhampur

Gujrat

Jammu

Samba

Sialkot

Kathua

INDIA

Gujranwala

Lahore

Amritsar

—·—	International boundary		
- - -	Provincial boundary		
●	Major city		
•	Town or Village		

0   25   50   75 km

0   20   50 km

ONE

Introduction

Rafiq Dossani and Henry S. Rowen

Ever since 1998, the year of India's and Pakistan's nuclear tests, an increasingly common conclusion is that the two nations, which have long been contending over Kashmir, will get into a nuclear conflict.[1] The United States has not involved itself very much in this conflict. It has influence on this dispute largely through its support of President Musharraf of Pakistan, who is regarded as an essential supporter of America's anti-terrorist operations in Afghanistan. His domestic situation is a difficult one, especially regarding the forces of religious radicalism that are the source of Pakistan's actions in Kashmir. The situation is compounded by older problems of ethnic tensions and a poorly performing economy, and the more recent crisis regarding its role in spreading nuclear-weapon-related technology and materials. Further, continuing Pakistani support for the Kashmir insurgency may no longer be tolerated by a newly resurgent India. These developments have implications for U.S. policy: American support for Pakistan is viewed as critical and includes bolstering its weak economy and supporting a Kashmir solution that is consistent with Pakistani ambitions. At this writing, it is encouraging to observe that high-level discussions are taking place between the two countries on their differences. However, we do not know what the outcome will be.

It is the objective of this book to examine the assumptions underlying the above arguments and to reevaluate the inference of likely conflict. Three key forces are analyzed: religion and its influence on civil society and politics; the role of the army as a political force, a factor relevant for Pakistan; and both countries' nuclear weapons capabilities. Following is a summary of the findings of the book's authors with respect to these assumptions.

Pakistan

Islamic radicalism in Pakistan was seeded by the army in the 1960s and has played a major role in fomenting and sustaining the Kashmir problem. Pakistan's rulers, both civilian and military, have not only sent terrorists across the Line of Control but have used them to support a domestic insurgency in Indian Kashmir that might otherwise have remained small and easily contained. Using survey data, Chris Fair and Karthik Vaidyanathan show, however, that Pakistan's urban elite—from whom the ranks of the political and military classes are drawn—is not attracted to Islamic radicalism. Despite the importance of religion in daily life, urban Pakistanis overwhelmingly support the secularization of politics, the curbing of extremism, the reforms of *madrasahs,* and the building of relations with the West. Further, in national votes, extremist parties have tended to receive negligible support.

Elections in 2002 marked a rise in support for religious parties, particularly the alliance Muttahida Majlis-e-Amal (MMA), but Fair and Vaidyanathan suggest that this may be for reasons unrelated to MMA's radical agenda. First, the MMA succeeded because it capitalized on anti-U.S. sentiment in the North-West Frontier Province (NWFP) and Baluchistan, the regions closest to Afghanistan. Further, the MMA was one of the few groups to oppose Musharraf on several issues of democracy and good governance. The MMA was also lucky: a baccalaureate was required (from this election on) in order to enter the contest, and the MMA had several *madrasah* graduates who qualified.

This does not mean that Islamic radicalism has no future in Pakistan. It relies (and has always relied) primarily on the army to survive, being insufficiently popular to influence state policy through political parties or popular agitation. The army has supported it when it needed a tool to wedge its way into power but has suppressed it otherwise. In doing so, an unmanageable monster may have been created. In his chapter, Vali Nasr describes the rise of Islamic radicalism, concluding that

[Until 9/11,] Islamization justified and supported Pakistan's regional strategic objectives and, increasingly, the ebbs and flows of its domestic politics. The failure to create a tenable structure for the role that Islam played in Pakistan led to the gradual unraveling of the concordat between Islamism and the state, just as it pushed Islamism in the direction of greater radicalism. The coup of 1999 underscored this problem. But it was the events of September 11 that placed the greatest pressure on the arrangement that had first come about in the Zia years. . . . The regional justifications for Islamization are no longer there.

The future of Islam in Pakistani politics can no longer be predicted, especially since Musharraf appears to be the most secular leader that the country has ever had. Equally, the regional and domestic politics that made Islam central to realizing Pakistan's state interests cannot be dismissed. Further, economic failures, with the resulting poverty, have made problems worse by providing a social context in which radicalism can flourish.[2]

The army has come to occupy the central role as the guarantor of Pakistan's territorial and social integrity in crises (despite some important past failures). This role will continue, primarily because of popular support. Outside of crises, army rule has been unsustainable, raising the question of how it manages so frequently to retake power. The answer, as described by Kennedy in his chapter, is that it has developed a sophisticated playbook for reentry and legitimation that has served it well over the decades. Kennedy argues that the army's inability to hold on to power suggests that what Pakistan needs is a stable constitutional system that accommodates both military and civilian leadership. He argues that the framework for such a system exists in the modified 1973 Constitution under which civilians ruled Pakistan from 1988 to 1997.

A third key factor is Pakistan's nuclear weapons capability. Little is known or declared about this capability—its extent, command mechanisms and controls, and strategic objectives—but its acquisition apparently fulfils objectives beyond deterrence, including to support insurgency in Kashmir, nation-building, and regional leadership in the Islamic world. In his chapter, Peter Lavoy discusses these objectives. Within Pakistan, nuclearization is already considered a great success, most recently in defusing the 2002 standoff with India. Given the domestic popularity of Pakistan's nuclear weapons program—to the extent that the population seems willing to bear the costs involved—the program will grow with time. The growth will occasionally occur covertly and occasionally more openly, and at varying speeds, depending on the state of relations with India and the West, on what India does with its own nuclear weapons program, and on relations between Pakistan's army and its civilian politicians.[3]

India

For the past two decades, India has seen rising popular support for Hindu radicalism. This has led to increasing intolerance of Pakistan's use of Islamic radicalism in Kashmir and to less central government support for autonomy for Kashmir—as harsher reprisals (that have earned the federal government the ill will of most of Indian Kashmir's residents) to local uprisings show. How did Hindu radicalism gain prominence in a country as pluralistic—in religion, culture, and ethnicity—as India? Much has been written about its rise.[4] In his chapter, Ainslie Embree considers the role of Hindu radicalism in the evolving definition of Indian nationalism. At independence, the Congress Party, with its stress on territorial integrity combined with religious neutrality, won the opening battle for identity over its principal opponent, the Rashtriya Swayamsevak Sangh (RSS) and its affiliates (which now includes the Bharatiya Janata Party, the leading party of the ruling coalition up to 2004), which saw independence as an opportunity to reconstruct the Hindu nation.[5] The identity war has not yet been lost by the RSS, however, as the 2003 riots in Gujarat showed. As Embree notes:

There is no question that there are many groups and individuals in civil society speaking for India, giving assurance of the reality of a national project affirming such a plural society, with special concern for secularism, with at least the minimum meaning that the nation's commitment to religious freedom, with no particular religion being privileged, represents a consensus. Looking at modern India's historic experience, however, there is no avoiding the conclusion that within civil society there is really no such consensus, and that very powerful groups are not enthusiasts for a pluralistic society but insist that a valid nationalist project be framed in terms of an Indian culture that is synonymous with Hindu culture.

As Robert Hardgrave shows in his chapter, the rise of Hindu radicalism has been accompanied by a softening of its ambitions, representing a political compromise. In 1939, the president-elect of the Hindu Mahasabha (a key RSS affiliate), M. S. Golwalkar, could write that, within India, "the foreign races must either adopt the Hindu culture and language, must learn to respect and hold in reverence Hindu religion, must entertain no ideas but those of glorification of the Hindu race and culture . . . or may stay in the country, wholly subordinated to the Hindu nation, claiming nothing, deserving no privileges, far less any preferential treatment—not even citizens' rights." Even the 1958 election manifesto of the Bharatiya Jan Sangh (BJS), the precursor of today's Bharatiya Janata Party (BJP), sought unity by "nationalizing all non-Hindus by inculcating in them the ideal of Bharatiya (Indian) culture." Since then, the BJS / BJP has experimented with a variety of strategies that could help it achieve power, including favoring socialism (in the early 1980s). It appears to have found a winning formula in building coalitions with secular parties that unite in their opposition to the Congress Party and in deflecting the more extreme elements of Hindu radicalism to the states where it rules on its own. Thus, while its own election manifesto favors the construction of a temple at the disputed site of Ayodhya, the manifesto agreed to with its coalition partners does not mention Ayodhya. As the country's ruler (in coalition) from 1998–2004, the BJP at the center was more moderate than was expected from its earlier record in the states. However, in all state elections, including those after 1998, it has invariably propounded and, when elected, practiced a radical Hindu agenda consistent with its early roots. At the very least the BJP has succeeded in bringing Hindu radicalism into the mainstream of Indian politics, thus fulfilling RSS founder Savarkar's dream of "politicizing Hinduism." "Hinduism," Hardgrave observes, "is being transformed, and, albeit slowly, Hindu nationalists are the likely beneficiary."

In her chapter, Barbara Metcalfe analyzes the declining role of Muslim Indians as a potentially countervailing socioeconomic and political force. She argues that two factors underlie this decline, which were in evidence prior to independence but have accelerated since. The first is that the general body politic's commitment to secularism has turned out to be a struggle against the widely held assumption that the real citizen in India is a Hindu. The second is the focus on moral jihad (i.e., nonviolent commitment to the ideals of Islam), which has been propagated by Muslim leaders since independence as a tactic to survive in a hostile environment. This focus has served to reinforce perceptions of Muslims as culturally defensive, inward-looking, and unable to contribute to India's socioeconomic progress. Reversing the decline will not be easy. Metcalfe notes that "until the larger society in India undertakes its own 'jihad' against anti-Muslim prejudice and the conditions that underlie it ... the moral jihad of the minority and the secularism of the entire polity will continue in uneasy tension."

The second factor in India is its nuclear capability. Protecting India's territorial integrity is a key objective of nuclearization. Rajesh Basrur's chapter discusses a recent test of this objective. In 2002, triggered by an attack on India's Parliament on December 13, 2001, blamed on Pakistan, India initiated a massive military buildup at its borders and deployed submarines and missiles in an effort to coerce Pakistan into halting support for terrorism, but underlying this was the unstated threat of nuclear war. India also hoped that the United States would view this buildup as a sign of its seriousness and would intervene to prevent Pakistan from supporting terrorism. This costly strategy ended in near failure when the initiative was withdrawn in October 2002 without its goals being achieved.

The Indian strategy of coercive diplomacy failed because the threshold for retaliation was not—and could not be—spelled out. Second, the strategy wrongly assumed that Pakistan would have to cap its costs. India knew that the cost of its own buildup would be high, but hoped that the cost of response would be more than Pakistan was willing to bear. This turned out to be untrue because Pakistan believes that its claims over Kashmir are legitimate, are related to Pakistan's very existence as a state, and, therefore, are worth a high price. Finally, Washington's intervention to defuse the situation allowed Pakistan to continue its behavior, now shielded by a powerful ally.

As a strategy to contain Pakistan, especially its support for the Kashmir insurgency, India's acquisition of a nuclear capability appears to have been a strategic blunder. Pakistan was sure to follow India's lead. However, India had other reasons for developing its bomb, primarily as a long-delayed response to China's testing of nuclear weapons since 1964, but also as part of its long-held ambition to achieve great-power status.

Meanwhile, India's improved economic growth prospects have enabled a serious consideration—for the first time, perhaps—that its ambitions to join the global elite may be realizable in the medium term. India now realizes that it must solve the Kashmir problem, by accommodation with Pakistan if necessary.

United States

The third important player is the United States. Howard Schaffer argues that the United States is largely uninterested in South Asia, with limited independent enthusiasm for resolving the Kashmir problem. With nuclearization of the subcontinent, the United States is keen to prevent a war and will intervene only as needed to avoid that outcome. The United States has also developed a strong interest in the fate of Afghanistan, which is closely linked to that of Pakistan. These factors are likely to cause South Asia to be high on the American agenda.

As Schaffer shows, U.S. disinterest is not new, the superpower having generally been a reluctant participant in South Asian affairs. Over the years, Washington's assessment of U.S. interests in South Asia has changed more markedly and taken more different directions than in almost any other region. In the 1960s, the subcontinent's preoccupation with its own problems led Washington to conclude that neither Pakistan nor India would further U.S. interests in containing the Cold War, which led to a long period of neglect of the region. Interest was rekindled with the Soviet occupation of Afghanistan, only to recede again when the Soviet occupation ended. Similarly, interest has recently been rekindled with nuclearization and Pakistan's frontline role in the battle against terrorism.

Kashmir

Kashmir is a natural locus for Indo-Pak hostility, given its location as a border state, its Muslim majority, and a history of non-Kashmiri Hindu rule that was considered oppressive by its Muslim subjects. At the time of partition, and facing an armed Muslim insurrection supported by Pakistan, its Maharaja acceded Kashmir to India on special terms. Kashmir would have its own constitution and governance, except for foreign policy, defense, and communications. It was further stipulated that Kashmir's future status as part of the Indian Union would be mutually determined by both the Indian and Kashmir sides. A war ensued between India and Pakistan over this issue, which ended with the establishment of a cease-fire line[6] brokered by the U.N. Both sides agreed that a future plebiscite by the Kashmiri people would decide their fate. None of these undertakings have been carried out.

Today, Kashmir is a divided state that reflects the outcome of the 1947 war: one-third of its area is controlled by Pakistan, and India controls most of the rest. China also owns a small stake, ceded to it by Pakistan. Both sides of Kashmir have a Muslim majority, although the Kashmiri language predominates only in the Kashmir Valley on the Indian side (among both Muslims and Hindus), while Pakistan-controlled Kashmir is mostly Punjabi-speaking. This difference between ethnicity and religion poses a problem for any attempted future unification between the two halves.

Little is known on the outside about Pakistan-controlled Kashmir, or Azad ("Independent") Kashmir. In his chapter, Rifaat Hussain discusses the origins and status of Azad Kashmir and its relationship with Pakistan. He shows that the region nominally has greater autonomy than Indian Kashmir but is in reality a satrapy of Pakistan.[7] He concludes, however, that Pakistan has been able to manage its relations with Azad Kashmir better than India has managed its relations with Indian Kashmir. Further, owing to India–Pakistan conflicts, Azad Kashmir is an important part of the calculation of the militants in the Kashmir Valley.

Indian-controlled Kashmir has gone through several phases in its relationship with India, as discussed by Chandrashekhar Dasgupta. Beginning with a period of high autonomy, the state has successively been brought closer to the Indian Union, sometimes by popular will and sometimes at Delhi's will. A key breakdown in the process was the local elections of 1987, widely believed to have been rigged, that seeded the insurgency. Pakistan quickly supported the insurgency, which had some early successes. But the army crackdown that followed the unrest was at times brutal and indiscriminate, and destroyed any popular support that might have remained for the Indian government and the idea of permanent union with India. At the same time, local support for militant activities was limited, and had ebbed by the mid-1990s, although the armed insurgency continues to the present. In 2002, the first fair elections in fifteen years were held and brought the People's Democratic Party—led by an erstwhile congressman and Kashmiri, M. M. Sayeed—to power.

India's readiness to negotiate Kashmir's future reflects recent changes in Kashmir and in Pakistan's attitude. Delhi has constantly struggled to integrate Kashmir into the Indian Union. But authoritarian governance by duly elected politicians in the early days, rigged elections, and the army's misbehavior have combined to convince most Kashmiris that India will never negotiate a fair plebiscite on Kashmir's future. This will continue to make Kashmir a difficult area to govern, even without Pakistan's support for armed insurgency and even if Delhi allows Srinagar to govern without interference. However, there is reason for hope, primarily because the populace in the Kashmir Valley has shown itself tremendously and repeatedly willing to participate in a democratic political process, rigged or otherwise. This faith may finally redound to India's favor. The elections of 2002 were popularly believed to have been fair and have brought into power a group of politicians that is trusted by local people. The local government has asked the people of Kashmir to be patient while it works to restore peace, restart economic growth, rid the valley of armed militants, and bring Delhi to agree to begin discussions of autonomy. The Indian government's readiness to negotiate over Kashmir is also linked to its great-power ambition, as earlier noted. Further, the government believes that over the longer term, India's superior economic progress is likely to make it a more desirable partner for Kashmir than Pakistan.

Although Pakistan has declared its support for a plebiscite, certain events—such as the partial success of the 1989 armed insurgency supported by Islamist militants and Pakistan's successful management of its relations with Azad Kashmir—have convinced it that the people of both sides of Kashmir do not want to be part of the Indian Union. In its view, a plebiscite would probably lead to independence, with a preference for closer relations to Pakistan than to India. In our view, this is not a realistic perspective in the absence of economic and political reform in Pakistan. The Kashmiris in the valley would face a hard choice between a democratic, politically stable, and increasingly prosperous India and a religiously compatible Pakistan that looks both poor and unstable. If the Indian government behaves better toward the Kashmiris, including granting them more control over local matters, they might come to believe that being part of India is better than being part of Pakistan, or even being independent. Second, the Indian government is most unlikely to permit a plebiscite it judges would lead to independence. Of course, this is conjectural, but our main point is that one should not assume that present attitudes will remain frozen forever.

Now that Indian Kashmir has its first fairly elected government in fifteen years, both the Indian and Kashmir governments have onerous and delicate responsibilities ahead, even if Pakistan stays out of the picture. The Kashmir government first needs to convince the local people that it is firmly on their side and that, in return, they should not resort to armed militancy. For this, it will need the support of the Indian government, through administrative action that transfers administrative and legal powers back to local government, perhaps leading to a return to the levels of autonomy under the 1952 Delhi agreement. The Indian and Kashmir governments will also need to cooperate on a calibrated withdrawal of the army from Kashmir in synchronicity with the hoped-for reduction in insurgency. This entails significant risk, since the reduced possibility of an army crackdown might spur militancy. Both governments need to agree on a timetable for discussions on autonomy, one that is benchmarked by peace-linked milestones so that the Kashmiri people are assured that their wishes will be heeded once enough peace returns.[8] Delhi will also need (perhaps surreptitiously) to surrender its five-decade-long strategy of whittling away at the concept of Kashmiri independence through administrative and legal actions.[9]

Nuclear Weapons

The advent of nuclear weapons on the subcontinent introduced a potentially catastrophic factor. Although various reasons can be constructed as to why nuclear war will not happen, or why such a war might not produce huge damage, the capacity for war is now present.

India, Pakistan, and China share (along with Russia and—presumably—North Korea) the distinction of having three-way nuclear-weapon borders. This pattern makes for complications that are poorly understood, certainly for outsiders and perhaps also for the participants. India's weapon program doubtless received much impetus from the sequence of India having been defeated by China in the Himalayas in 1962, which was followed by the first Chinese atomic test two years later. India effectively announced its nuclear weapon status in 1974 when it tested a "peaceful device," a.k.a. a "bomb." Pakistan was sure to follow suit. The only surprise is that it took from 1974 until 1998 for India to resume testing and to declare the "devices" bombs.

India's public nuclear doctrine is unclear, including who is the main enemy: China, Pakistan, or even the United States. There has been no official pronouncement, but its National Security Advisory Board calls for, among other things, forces designed for "punitive retaliation": a triad of aircraft, mobile land-based missiles, and sea-based assets; a robust command-and-control system controlled by the Prime Minister; a no-first-use pledge; and having a strong conventional force. The operational implication of some of these concepts is not clear. In any case, the development of short-range weapons, which implies being able to use them on the battlefield, suggests a focus on Pakistan rather than China.

Although there is a question about the primary orientation of India's nuclear program, this is not true of Pakistan's. It is designed to deter or defend against a stronger India. Unsurprisingly, Pakistan has not adopted a no-first-use pledge. There remain many important questions about the Pakistan program, including the control of the weapons today and, even more, in an uncertain future. The military has been in charge of the program, not heads of government. There are also questions about who might get hold of these weapons in a period of turmoil.

Michael Krepon argues in his chapter that the combination of harsh rhetoric, provocative action, and the absence of trust and channels of communication (especially in the early stages of nuclearization) invite destabilizing actions and escalation. In the early stages of these programs, the size and disposition of each side's nuclear deterrent tends to be opaque to the other, which can prompt worst-case assessments. Secure second-strike capabilities, in particular, might not exist and are difficult to assess during the early days. One side may believe that the other side is racing ahead in this respect, and so may be tempted to use nuclear weapons sooner rather than later. Finally, behavior might not be rational during moments of intense crisis arising from a miscalculation on the effect of, say, insurgency. Both sides might misread the extent of outside support. For example, India and Pakistan have engaged in brinksmanship—ratcheting up support for insurgency in Kashmir in the case of Pakistan, or coercive diplomacy on the part of India—on the assumption that the United States will intervene to prevent nuclear war anywhere in the globe. If the United States does not intervene as expected, nor does China, especially with Pakistan, the situation could escalate out of control.

One might hope that at least the possession of nuclear weapons would cause Pakistan to be more cautious about supporting terrorists in India and that both sides would think twice about engaging in conventional military operations. The caution with which the United States and the Soviet Union dealt with their confrontation in Europe over many decades supports that inference. But it is no guarantee.

Prospects for Peace

A conclusion of the above analysis is that the causes of India's and Pakistan's largely hostile relations toward one other originate not in religious radicalism but in other domestic concerns: a concern with territorial integrity in India, and the interaction of the military with civilian politicians in Pak-

TABLE I.I

Share of the Vote in National Elections for BJP and Congress, 1951–2004

	BJP vote share	Congress vote share
1951	3.1	45.0
1957	6.0	47.8
1962	6.4	44.0
1967	9.3	40.8
1971	7.4	43.7
1977	n/a[a]	34.5
1980	n/a	42.7
1984	7.8	49.1
1989	11.4	39.5
1991	20.0	36.7
1996	20.2[b]	28.8
1998	25.6[b]	25.8
1999	23.8[b]	28.3
2004	22.16	26.69

SOURCE: http://www.eci.gov.in/infoeci/key_stat/keystat_fs.htm (accessed October 21, 2003).
NOTES: a. For the 1977 elections, the Bharatiya Jana Sangh (earlier name of the BJP) merged with other parties to form the Bharatiya Lok Dal (BLD) or Janta party. The BLD contested in the national elections after the Emergency as a single party, and took 41.3 percent of the vote. The Janta Party split after its failure in the 1980 elections, when it received 18.9% of the vote. Its BJS elements regrouped to form the BJP.
b. BJP-led coalition formed the government.

istan. Religious radicalism has been invoked to support these concerns. Despite the continuing risk that both countries may have created monsters that they cannot tame, the likelihood of war remains low. As Table 1.1 shows, in India, although the Ayodhya agitation of 1989 seems to have benefited the BJP, the destruction of the Babri Mosque at Ayodhya in 1992 and the wildly popular nuclear tests of 1998 have had diminishing electoral returns.

The BJP's largely centrist, mainstream approach in power and its aggressive pursuance of economic reforms suggested that it had found the formula for success and that it would continue with the combination of the soft-central and hard-state approaches that paid off in Gujarat and subsequent local elections in 2003 and 2004. However, having unexpectedly lost the national elections in 2004, the BJP may reexamine this strategy—even though the election results do not imply anything about which of the two approaches failed it at the polls. It is possible that the party may remain in no hurry to disturb the status quo in its agenda of mainstreaming radical Hinduism, at least until it can work out a strategy of coming to power on its own in the center. Alternatively, it may turn to a more hardline stance, although the electoral arithmetic argues against such an approach. At the very least, it is likely to experiment with different approaches in local elections in the interregnum to the next round of national elections, scheduled for 2009.

In Pakistan, too, religious radicalism faces long-term decline in popular support (while managing to survive on the support of the army and civilian leaders). The religious parties' vote share peaked at 20 percent in the 1970 elections and remained below 5 percent for subsequent elections up to 2002. In 2002, the MMA improved on the performance of religious parties in the 1997 elections, when they had won only 2 percent of the votes. The MMA won 11.3 percent of the vote but took 15 percent of the seats in the National Assembly.[10] It also came to power in the NWFP and shares power (with the army-backed Pakistan Muslim League [Quaid-i-Azam]) in Baluchistan. Nationally, the PML-Q leads the government.

Although the 2002 national elections in Pakistan saw renewed support for religious parties, the conclusion that this reflects a swing toward radicalism by Pakistan's population, as portrayed in the Western press,[11] is probably inaccurate, as already noted above in our discussion of Fair and Vaidyanathan's work. For one thing, the still modest vote share of the religious parties and the electoral failure of its most orthodox constituents makes such a conclusion suspect.[12] For the 2002 elections, the religious parties fought under a common front, termed the United Council for Action (the Muttahida Majlis-e-Amal, or MMA). Its constituent parties included all the main religious parties: the Jamaat-e-Islami (JI), two factions from the Deobandi Jamiat-e-Ulema-e-Islam (JUI), the Brelvi Jamiat Ulema-e-Pakistan (JUP), the Shiite Islami Tehrik Pakistan (ITP), and the Wahhabi Jamiat Ahle Hadith (JAH). Despite severe doctrinal differences,[13] the MMA has held together subsequently, under pressure from the army.[14] The MMA's performance could also be viewed, as Fair and Vaidyanathan show in their chapter in this book, as a vote against state support for U.S. actions among Pakhtoon populations, due to ethnicity shared by the Pakhtoons of NWFP and Baluchistan with the majority Afghan population. This inference may be justified by looking at where the religious parties did well. All the MMA's seats in Baluchistan, where it won 14 out of 51 seats, were in Pashto-speaking areas.[15] By contrast, in Sindh, whose capital, Karachi, is considered to be the "emerging epicenter of extremist organizations,"[16] the MMA won only

11 of the 130 provincial seats. Overall, the Pakistan People's Party (PPP)[17]—which openly supported Pakistan's alliance with the United States—received the most votes.

While the Western press has tended to portray the election results as a challenge to Musharraf's ability to keep religious forces at bay, the reality is that it was Musharraf who managed to create a most improbable combination of doctrinally opposed religious parties that contested the elections on a common platform and that have subsequently held together. The MMA has also obliged the army by participating in governing alliances constructed by the army with secular parties such as the PML-Q. The 2002 elections thus once again illustrated the dependency of the religious parties on the army[18] and the latter's willingness to use them as a counterweight to feudal parties—though, once again, with limited success.

The election results were thus much better for Musharraf than commonly perceived. To whit: (1) the civilian population is pleased (as are Pakistan's Western allies) that democracy (albeit an imperfect one) is being reestablished in Pakistan; (2) the feudally oriented PPP and the Nawaz Sharif faction of the Pakistan Muslim League (the PML-N) are counterbalanced by the constitutional supremacy of the presidency and the alliance between the religious parties and the ruling PML-Q (even though this party is composed of feudal interests similar to those of the PML-N); (3) the domination of religious parties in the areas bordering Afghanistan is the best possible outcome to tackle the difficult issue of rebuilding Pak-Afghan relations that have been adversely affected by Pakistan's previous support to the Taliban; and (4) India faces a Pakistan ruled by persons close to the Pakistani army, thereby presenting as close to a united front as possible.

How will this post-election situation affect Pakistan's actions in Kashmir? This partly depends on the army's future role in Pakistan, partly on Pakistan's perceptions and ambitions on Kashmir (which differ from India's), and partly on the Indian threat.

The army's perception of its role has not changed since the time of Ayub and has perpetuated a vicious political cycle: given its perception of the immaturity of civilian politics, the army will voluntarily stay "in the barracks" only during normal times, returning to a prominent stabilizing role during crises.[19] In the past, Pakistan was considered by the army to be precipitously close to some type of crisis at all times.[20] Hence, the army stayed at or near the center of power at all times; that is, it was never in the barracks. By doing so, it fostered the immaturity of civilian politics since, at the very least, civilian politics takes a few uninterrupted electoral cycles to mature. Each time the army withdrew from power, it observed that corrupt, feudal parties came to power.[21] The army then invariably tried to delegitimize civilian rule, including using religious parties,[22] or by supporting sectarian disturbances as preludes to a coup d'état. As a longer term strategy, it tried to create anti-feudal forces through the religious parties.

Nuclearization and its successful test in defusing the Indian threat in 2002, combined with Indian Kashmir's local elections, have changed the environment to the point that there is now no domestic or external prospect of imminent crisis and, hence, no reason for the army to sponsor a revival of Islamic radicalism. The vicious cycle can finally be broken, a fact reflected in Indo-Pakistani negotiations since 2003. The focus of the army will now be on fostering and participating in a process of civilian–military engagement—currently informal and covert, but this could soon become formalized—to find common ground between popular will and the army's aspirations.

Although the latter has been the key domestic challenge that every civilian government since Bhutto has had to face, the difference this time is the removal of both the external threat and the external opportunity. The challenge for civilian parties is now to buy time from the army. They will need to make concessions on several fronts: the management of foreign policy will have to be shared, for example. They also need to steer the economy to a higher growth path in order to lessen the possibility of internal crises and to keep the army fully provisioned. The latter is needed to reassure the army that civilian politicians are friendly to the army's vision of the country's future as one ruled by politicians who will not weaken the army's ability to respond in a crisis.

These are difficult tasks, given the poor levels of economic and social development and the failure consistently to pursue pro-growth policies. The incentive for the participants is that both will gain long-term popular credibility. The side-benefits are the suppression of religious radicalism and that Pakistan will stay out of Indian Kashmir.

Despite the complexity, some important conclusions may be drawn. First, Pakistan is likely to become a less important actor in the near term in Kashmir. Instead, as we have suggested above, Kashmir will revert to a struggle for autonomy, at least initially nonviolent, between the Kashmiris and the Indian government. However, given the recent history of this struggle, a return to high levels of violence in the future cannot be ruled out. Much will depend on the willingness of both sides to perform on key issues: the Kashmiri government on the promotion of stability and growth, and Delhi on long-expected concessions on autonomy. Second, and despite a smaller role for Pakistan in Kashmir and the reopening of negotiations in early 2004, relations between India and Pakistan are likely to remain volatile. This will be due to both India's ongoing identity battle and the likely tortuous state of relations between the army and civilian politicians in Pakistan. Given their nuclear weapons capabilities and the strategic options that these afford both countries, the possibility of a nuclear conflict remains a serious worry.

U.S. interests in South Asia are closely tied to preventing a nuclear war while protecting Pakistan so that it may continue to play an effective role in helping U.S. forces operate in Afghanistan. Having accepted the subcontinent's nuclearization, U.S. interests in South Asia are likely to remain in the background, preserving the status quo and preventing the spread of a nuclear arms race between India and Pakistan and its spread via Pakistan to North Korea and possibly elsewhere—an aspect on which Pakistan appears to be vulnerable. Its independent interest in solving the Kashmir problem remains limited, despite India's appeals for U.S. pressure on Pakistan to reduce its support for insurgents in Kashmir and despite Pakistan's appeals for U.S. involvement in obtaining proper status for the region. The United States—at least while Pakistan remains a frontline state in the war against terrorism—will work actively to prevent conventional war between the two states, as well as the escalation of any conflict into a nuclear confrontation. The growing economic ties that the United States has developed with India are likely to outstrip those with Pakistan; in the long term, political relations between India and the United States will become closer.

Pakistan: Politics and Kashmir

TWO

Islamic Extremism and Regional Conflict in South Asia

Vali Nasr

Over the course of the past decade Pakistan has become increasingly important to global security and stability in South and Southwest Asia. Since 1988 the conflict over Kashmir has steadily intensified and during 2002 portended to an all-out nuclear war.[1] Pakistan was an integral part of the radicalization of Afghanistan's politics in the 1990s, and since the fall of the Taliban, has held the key to its stability.[2] Finally, Pakistan's myriad extremist groups and renegade tribal forces were an important part of the rise of al-Qaeda—as well as the efforts to demobilize it. Thus, Pakistan has become the critical center in an arc of extremism that stretches from Central Asia to India, creating concatenations of extremist forces that envelop each other's activities to provide an impetus for radicalism in the region.

The conflicts that Pakistan has been engaged in—in Afghanistan, Kashmir, and also domestically—have been interrelated and have fed on one another. As such, these conflicts cannot be understood separate from one another. They are all animated by the fundamental relationship between Islamic extremism and Pakistan's national interest, and its project for asserting those interests in the region.[3] Hence, to analyze developments in Kashmir since the mid-1990s and to identify a path to peace, it is important to understand how and why the Kashmir conflict reflects these interests and relates to the larger issue of the place of extremism in Pakistan's foreign policy.[4]

Understanding the way in which Islam works in Pakistan's domestic and regional politics is also important to U.S. policy making. Pursuant to the events of September 11, U.S. policy makers relied on the Pakistani government to control Islamic extremism in the South Asia region. This policy was built on the assumption that Pakistan's government is "secular" by nature and can be persuaded to aggressively clamp down on Islamist activists. The policy, however, did not take into account the extent to which Islamism is embedded in Pakistan's national interest and serves as an instrument of power for the Pakistan military.

Islamization and the Pakistan State

Islam has come to play an increasingly important role in Pakistan's domestic and international politics. Islamic ideology provides the framework through which Pakistan defines its national interests and the cadence between its domestic politics and regional ambitions. Islam supplies Pakistan with a powerful political language and policy-making framework to bring Pakistan's domestic and international interests and engagements into alignment. In Islam, the state has found a powerful means to shore up domestic authority and to project power regionally, to make Pakistan a stronger state.[5] Islam has also opened new foreign policy possibilities to Pakistan, most notably in Afghanistan and Kashmir.

The evolution of Islam's role in Pakistan's political and geostrategic thinking has evolved over the course of the past two decades, beginning with the confluence of ideological impulses with domestic and foreign policy challenges. It got its impetus from the dividend that it paid to the Pakistan state in serving its interests. This paper will trace the trajectory of this process and how it has affected that country's regional interests.

Riding the Domestic Tiger: Islam and the State since 1971

The civil war of 1971 and the secession of East Pakistan were momentous events in Pakistan's history. The division of the country seriously undermined the viability of the idea of Pakistan as a homeland for the Muslims of South Asia. As conceived, the idea of Pakistan had proved inadequate, at least to East Pakistani Bengalis.[6] To many in Pakistan, this was not only a sign of failure but also a warning of further secessions to come. The response was a turn to Islam.[7] Average Pakistanis looked to Islam for solace, but more important, they sought to redefine the idea of Pakistan to more closely approximate an "Islamic" ideal. Pakistanis saw the failure of the idea of Pakistan in that it had not been sufficiently "Islamic." This owed much to the propaganda of Islamic parties, but it also reflected the mood of the country, which saw "Muslimness" as an insufficient reason to keep culturally diverse Muslims together. Muslimness had proven to be weaker than ethnic nationalism.[8] The same, it was argued, would not be true of Islam. For, whereas Muslimness was an ethnic identity, Islam—defined as an ideology—pertained to values and to a worldview that was seen as a solution to Pakistan's predicament—what would empower the country. In addition, emphasis on Islam would have the effect of creating a uniform national culture, social, and political language, and a medium of public interaction that could sublimate parochial loyalties.

Islamist parties articulated the form of Islam that came to dominate the political discourse from this point forward. It was conservative in outlook, political in orientation, and activist in tone.[9] It quickly defined the framework of public debates and placed the government and its secular leftist agenda on the defensive. In fact, the 1970s were marked by the continued adherence of the Pakistan state to a secular definition of Pakistan, and by society's increasingly "Islamic" view of the country.[10]

The Islamic orientation was also aided by the flow of funds from the Persian Gulf to Islamic parties in order to stave off the prospects of the Left in Pakistan. The governments of Saudi Arabia and the United Arab Emirates had viewed the turn of Pakistan's politics toward the Left in the late 1960s and early 1970s with alarm and had supported all kinds of Islamic activities with the aim of strengthening Islamic institutions and ideology as a bulwark against the Left.[11] By 1973, Prime Minister Zulfiqar Ali Bhutto (d. 1979) was able to assuage those fears as he cultivated close ties with Persian Gulf rulers and purged his party of its leftist elements.[12] Still, support for Islamic activism in Pakistan continued unabated, mainly because that support had found its own momentum, and the linkages between Islamic organizations and groups in the Persian Gulf monarchies and those in Pakistan had become entrenched, operating independent of government control.

The Persian Gulf support began with the investment in mainstream Islamist parties, but soon became the main impetus behind the rise of those educational and social institutions that would promote extremism.[13] Most important in this regard were *madrasahs* (seminaries) that trained religious leaders (ulama and preachers). Here, the links between Saudi and Pakistani ulama and Sunni activists produced strong religious and intellectual bonds that became embedded in institutional contacts and networks of patronage. Saudi funding generally promoted conservative interpretations of Islam, in keeping with the views of the Kingdom's own Wahhabi school of Islam. Some of the funding, however, as will be discussed below, was attached to the war in Afghanistan and to containing Iran's influence in the region. That funding helped fuel extremism. In 1996, of the 2,463 registered *madrasahs*, 1,700 were receiving financial support from outside Pakistan.[14]

The linkages also fit into Saudi Arabia's larger agenda of controlling Islamic intellectual and cultural life across the Muslim world through such institutions as Rabitah Alam-i Islami (the Islamic World League), and of promoting its own vision of Sunnism through patronage of Islamic education in the Muslim world. As a result, the growing Islamism in Pakistan developed a Wahhabi orientation and gained a foothold in the seminaries. Both of these trends would nudge it toward extremism.

By the end of the 1970s, Islamic resurgence rooted in society had the upper hand. Key regional events converged to make its victory final. The most important developments here were the Iranian revolution of 1979 and the Afghan war of 1980–88.

The Iranian revolution placed a great deal of pressure on the relations between Islam and the state that emerged during the Zia ul-Haq (1977–88) period. The regime of General Muhammad Zia ul-Haq (d. 1988) had co-opted moderate Islamism in the framework of an Islamic state in which the state served as the senior partner and Islamist forces as junior partners. The Zia formula adopted an evolutionary approach to Islamization and sought to Islamize existing social structures rather than replace them. The success of the Iranian revolution, and its ability to replace the old state without compromising on its demands—and especially without yielding any ground to other actors—made the gains made by Islamic activists under Zia less than ideal. As such, the revolution questioned the legitimacy of the Zia formula and placed pressure on the Islamic actors to ask for more and not accept the Zia formula as the Islamic end for their struggle for power.

The Iranian revolution had a profound impact on the balance of power between Shi'is and the state, and more to the point, Shi'is and Sunnis in Pakistan. The revolution set in motion, first a power struggle between the Pakistan state and its Shi'i community, and later a broader competition for power between Shi'is and Sunnis. These struggles for domination coincided with competition for influence in Pakistan between Saudi Arabia and Iraq on the one hand and revolutionary Iran on the other—an extension of the Persian Gulf conflicts into Pakistan. The confluence of these struggles for power mobilized and radicalized Islam.[15]

The ideological force of the revolution, combined with the fact that the first successful Islamic revolution had been carried out by Shi'is, emboldened the Shi'i community and politicized its identity. Soon after the success of the revolution in Tehran, zealous emissaries of the revolutionary regime actively organized Pakistan's Shi'is.[16] The leadership of the revolution was also unhappy with Zia, the military ruler of Pakistan, for having traveled to Iran in 1977–78 to shore up the Shah's regime. In addition, after the Soviet invasion of Afghanistan in 1980 General Zia's government would become closely allied with the United States, with which Iran was increasingly at loggerheads.[17]

Pakistan's government began to invest in strengthening various Sunni institutions. In particular, it poured money into existing Sunni *madrasahs* and established new ones.[18] Curriculum reforms in the *madrasahs* allowed their graduates to enter the modern sectors of the economy and join government service.[19] The government believed that expansion of the role of the *madrasahs* in national education would entrench Sunni identity in the public arena, just as *madrasah* graduates would help establish the place of Sunni identity in various government institutions. Furthermore, the *madrasahs* and their students were viewed as important to the government's efforts to contain Shi'i activism. The Zia regime thus helped entrench Sunni Islamism in Pakistan in order to contend with the political and geostrategic threat of Shi'i Islamism.

Also, Saudi Arabia and Iraq were concerned about Shi'i activism in Pakistan and what they saw as Iran's growing influence there. At the time, the two Arab countries were involved in a bitter campaign to contain Iran's revolutionary zeal and limit its power in the region—since then, Saudi Arabia has sought to harden Sunni identity in the countries surrounding Iran, a policy which extends into Central Asia and which in turn depends on the efforts of Pakistani sectarian groups.[20] As one observer remarked of the pattern of funding of *madrasahs* in Baluchistan and southern NWFP (North-West Frontier Province) after 1980: "If you look at where the most madrassahs were constructed you will realize that they form a wall blocking Iran off from Pakistan."[21]

Pakistan was an important prize in the struggle for control of the Persian Gulf, as well as for erecting the "Sunni wall" around Iran. Saudi Arabia and Iraq therefore developed a vested interest in preserving the Sunni character of Pakistan's Islamization. In so doing, Saudi Arabia created close ties with Deobandi ulama, parties, and *madrasahs* to create a strong anti-Shi'i Sunni political and organizational front. Therefore, Saudi Arabia's regional interests—containing Iran in particular—converged with its interests to keep Pakistan from the Left. Both policies relied on Islamism. In the process, Saudi Arabia created close ties between Pakistani Islamists and Wahhabism, and produced organizations that would systematically intermesh politics and religion. Most important, the Saudi policy meant that the response to any threat to Saudi Arabia's interests in Pakistan would be more intense Wahhabi-led Islamist activism.[22]

The Saudi policy helped anchor Pakistan's domestic and regional policies in Islamism—as defined and funded by Saudi Arabia. This process also brought the two countries' regional policies into alignment. The convergence of Saudi–Pakistani regional interests then created an open field for the growth of Islamist extremism, which in turn further entrenched the policy of using Islam to realize regional objectives.

The onset of the Afghan war (1980–88) further deepened Saudi Arabia's commitment to its Sunni clients in Pakistan. In fact, the funding that Saudi Arabia provided Afghan fighters also subsidized militant Sunni organizations in Pakistan—often through the intermediary of Pakistan's military.[23] Afghanistan's Taliban and the Sipah-e-Sahaba-e-Pakistan (SSP) (and its offshoot that has been active in Kashmir, the Movement of the Companions of the Prophet [Harakat ul-Ansar, or HUA], which later became the Movement of Mujahedin [Harakat ul-Mujahedin, or HUM]) all hail from the same seminaries and receive training in the same military camps in NWFP province and southern Afghanistan. Those camps all operate under the supervision of the Pakistan military. The most famous of these was the al-Badr camp in southern Afghanistan, which was destroyed by the United States in 1998 in retaliation for the bombing of American embassies in East Africa. Since 1994, al-Badr had served as a principal training facility for the Taliban, SSP and Harakat ul-Ansar. Similarly, Ramzi Ahmed Yusuf, convicted for bombing the World Trade Center in New York, was affiliated with a Saudi-financed seminary in Baluchistan that was active in the Afghan war but had also been prominent in anti-Shi'i activities in Pakistan. Yusuf is alleged to have been responsible for a bomb blast that killed twenty-four people in the Shi'i holy shrine of Mashad in Iran in June 1994.[24]

The Afghan war also had the effect of necessitating that the Pakistan government reinforce its own commitment to Islam. If Zia's Islamization had initially been premised on the need to ride the "Islamic" tiger domestically, the Afghan war required that Pakistan also ride the Islamic tiger regionally. The Afghan war was billed as a jihad. The recruitment, training, organization, and waging of the anti-Soviet campaign was Islamic in every aspect. To successfully manage the war, the Pakistan state reinforced its own commitment to Islamization and the Islamic ideology. In so doing, Pakistan strengthened its ties to Saudi Arabia, which was both the main source of funding for Islamism regionally and a source of ideological legitimacy for Pakistan.

Also important was that Pakistan's strategy created a seamless continuum between Islamism in Afghanistan and Islamism in Pakistan. Pakistan's rulers believed that this would enable them to efficiently rule over Islamism regionally. Pakistan's Islamist forces were co-opted by the Zia regime. Their ties to their Afghan cohorts would in turn co-opt Afghan Islamism. If Islamism was the ascending ideology in the 1980s, Pakistan was determined to co-opt and control it—to both divert its threat to the state and to harness its energies to promote Pakistan's interests. Playing the Islamic card eventually anchored Pakistan's national interests in Islamism, creating a close nexus between the state and its Islamist clients.

The Afghan war also created institutions whose interests were closely tied to the Afghan war, Islamic activists, and the use of jihad in foreign policy. The most important of these was Inter-Services Intelligence (ISI). ISI grew to be an effective intelligence agency capable of managing a guerrilla war against Afghanistan. However, it also became the main defender of Islamic activism (and has retained its ties with activists). ISI also served as the conduit for extremists' impact on Pakistan's politics. The power and organizational momentum of ISI accounts for the inertia that is evident in Pakistan's use of extremism to serve its goals.[25]

Pakistan's Islam strategy was initially closely tied to the Jamaat-i-Islami, the main representative of mainstream Islamism in Pakistan.[26] The Jama'at was the oldest and most outspoken Islamist party in the country. It played an important part in the rise of Islamism in the 1970s, which culminated in the fall of the Bhutto regime in 1977. The Jama'at had then closely collaborated with General Zia ul-Haq in defining the direction that Pakistan's Islamization would take in the 1980s.[27]

The Jama'at's Afghan role was led by the party's Pashtun leader, Qazi Husain Ahmad. The Jama'at used its organizational muscle in the North-West Frontier Province to manage refugee camps, recruit fighters, and to interact with Afghan Mujahedin groups.[28] The Jama'at worked particularly closely with Gulbedin Hikmatyar's Hizb-i Islami, which throughout the war remained Pakistan's closest ally among the Mujahedin.[29] The Jama'at also used its organizational base in Pakistan and its ties across the Muslim world to mobilize resources—recruits as well as money—in support of the Afghan war and to legitimate Pakistan's Islamization drive and role in Afghanistan. So central was the role of the Jama'at in Afghanistan that the military left the management of training camps such as the al-Badr camp to the Jama'at.

The Afghan war also opened new strategic vistas for Pakistan. Since its creation, Pakistan had faced irredentist claims by Afghanistan against its northwestern territories. Pashtun nationalism had continued to pose challenges to consolidation of the Pakistan state. Throughout the 1960s and much of the 1970s Pakistan had used its close ties with Iran to offset the pincer challenges of the Afghan–Indian alliance. The Afghan pressure on Pakistan grew with the rise of Daoud Khan to power in 1975. Daoud's Pashtun nationalism directly threatened Pakistan. This threat grew with the communist coup in Kabul in 1978 and later with the Soviet invasion of Afghanistan. The Soviet Union's close ties with India meant that its growing control of Afghanistan would sandwich Pakistan between a tight alliance of Delhi and Kabul.

Pakistan saw the Afghan war as an opportunity to undo the Afghan–Indian alliance. The war's Islamic ideology was conveniently anti-communist—and as such would challenge communism for ideological dominance in the region, thus weakening Delhi's position—which was close to the USSR. Moreover, the war had brought the Mujahedin fighters, many of whom were Pashtun tribesmen, under Pakistan's control. In fact, for a time Pakistan looked to Qazi Husain and Gulbedin Hikmatyar to serve as Pashtun nationalist leaders. The Islamic tenor of the war conveniently sublimated Pashtun nationalism under the banner of Islam, which was now controlled by Pakistan.

Throughout the Afghan war Pakistan sought to divide and rule Mujahedin groups even as it promoted Islamic ideology among them.[30] Gradually, its interest in containing Pashtun nationalism gave place to the goal of controlling Afghanistan in order to provide Pakistan with "strategic depth." This concern became more important after the Kashmir conflict flared up in the late 1980s and the war in Afghanistan wound down after 1988.[31] Pakistan's military was particularly interested in providing Pakistan with a safe backyard to better absorb an Indian blitzkrieg.

This aim led Pakistan to look beyond rolling back Soviet gains in Afghanistan to controlling Kabul. The possibility of using the Afghan–Pakistan corridor to open Central Asia's riches to the world further added to the need to control the scope of war in Afghanistan. By 1994, however, it was clear that the Jama'at/Hizb-i Islami combine was unable to control Afghanistan, as the growing power of Shah Ahmad Masud and his northern troops seriously challenged Pakistan's position in Afghanistan. After the Tajik alliance of Burhanuddin Rabbani and Masud sidelined Hikmatyar, Pakistan accepted that it was losing control over Afghanistan, and potentially over Pashtun nationalism. In addition, the ferocity of the infighting among Afghan groups placed a great burden on the Pakistan army causing it to lose control over one of its factions and thus providing an opening to India to enter the fray.

It was in this context that in 1994 Pakistan turned to the Taliban.[32] Interestingly, it was the government of Prime Minister Benazir Bhutto, led by her secular Minister of Interior, General Nasirullah Babur, that opened the door to an alliance between the state and Islamist extremism. At that time, the military, and also Benazir's arch rival, Nawaz Sharif, the leader of the Pakistan Muslim League—relied on the Jama'at and its brand of Islamic activism. Benazir had forged an alliance with the Deobandi Jam'iat-i Ulama-i Islam (JUI), which had close ties to extremist sectarian forces and seminaries from which the Taliban hailed. General Babur and JUI's chief, Mawlana Fazlur Rahman, orchestrated an alliance between the government and extremist Deobandis to both undermine the army's power in Afghanistan and weaken its—and Nawaz Sharif's—position in domestic politics. General Babur was instrumental in launching the Taliban, which quickly became the rising force in Afghanistan. The growing prominence of the Taliban and their Deobandi allies in Pakistan soon led the military to look to them as serious partners for managing Afghanistan and Kashmir. This in turn necessitated greater support of the institutional basis of Deobandi ascendancy—the *madrasahs*—and the network that recruited and supported these forces and projected their power, and that extended from Afghanistan into Kashmir.

Although the Taliban were initially organized to open trade routes and bring law and order to Afghanistan—what foreign investors and common Afghans hoped for—Pakistan looked to the Taliban to protect Pashtun interests and preserve Pakistan's position in Afghanistan. General Babur, himself a Pashtun, remarked to this author that it was not acceptable for Tajiks to rule over Kabul and that the Taliban were their boys—that is, defenders of Pashtun interests that he and other Pakistani Pashtun military and civilian elite subscribed to.

General Babur and the military also looked to the Taliban to replace Hikmatyar and Qazi Husain Ahmad as Islamic spokesmen for Pashtun nationalism. Hikmatyar's failure at Kabul had proved that he and his brand of Islamism—and that of its main Pakistani ally, the Jama'at—could not contain Pashtun nationalism in the long run. The Taliban, further, held the promise of fully Islamizing Pashtun nationalism, and then making it subservient to Pakistan's interests. Through the Taliban Pakistan would first divert the attention of the Pashtuns from ethnic nationalism to religion, and then contain it within Pakistan's relations with Afghanistan. To achieve this, however, Pakistan had to bring the role of Islam in its own society and politics into greater alignment with changes that were afoot in Afghanistan.

Hence, during the 1994–96 period the Pakistan government, led by General Babur, launched a campaign to contain domestic extremism and initiated "Operation Save Punjab," which led to the arrest of some forty sectarian activists.[34] During the same time period, Babur was also instrumental in organizing militant Sunni *madrasah* students into Taliban and Harakat ul-Ansar/Harakat ul-Mujahedin (HUA/HUM) units for Pakistan-backed operations in Afghanistan and Kashmir. Training bases in Afghanistan and Kashmir were taken from the Jama'at and Hizb-i Islami and handed over to the Taliban and HUA/HUM.

This change also meant that domestically the Deobandi and sectarian extremist groups that were closely tied to the Taliban replaced the Jamaat-i-Islami and mainstream Islamism as the main allies of the military. Sectarian groups such as Sipah Sahaba (SSP) and Lashkar-i Jhangvi—both later banned for their ties to al-Qaeda—that had close ties with the Taliban and HUA/HUM thrived during General Babur's tenure of office. In fact, since the advent of the Taliban and HUA/HUM, Islamist extremism and mili-

tancy became more prominent. These links have become increasingly entrenched, creating organizational ties as well as ideological ones. According
to a Pakistan government report, eight hundred SSP and Lashkar-i Jhangvi
fighters received training at HUA/HUM's Khalid Bin Waleed military training camp in Afghanistan in 1998–99.[35] It was reported that Lashkar activists
who were responsible for the massacre of Shi'is at Maninpura as well as an
attempt on Nawaz Sharif's life were trained in HUA/HUM camps, and that
the SSP leader Riaz Basra, who masterminded most of the attacks against
Shi'i targets, was closely tied to Osama Bin Laden.[36] Increasingly, young activists turned to the Taliban as a model. During a demonstration in Karachi,
young activists taunted government leaders, proclaiming: "Do not think of
us as weak. We have ousted Soviet troops and infidels from Afghanistan, we
can do the same in Pakistan."[37]

The military, initially ideologically opposed to the Taliban, came to see
an added benefit to this change. It allowed the military, which was gradually
becoming more secular, to be more Islamically effective without becoming
any more Islamic itself. This became most clear during General Parvez
Musharraf's command of the army and later control of Pakistan.

The army's support for the Taliban and HUA/HUM was initially driven
by regional considerations. Domestic extremism was initially directed only
to make Pakistan's management of its extremist allies possible. However, by
the late 1990s, the military began to look to domestic extremist forces—SSP,
Lashkar-i Jhangvi, and the like—as a means of controlling the domestic political scene as well.

Given the growing centrality of Islam to the military's position, and its
role in strengthening Pakistan internally and regionally, it became clear that
the state would continue to rely on Islam to serve its interests. It also became
obvious that it would likely rely on increasingly extremist versions of Islamism to increase the gains that it was accruing from its Islam policy. This
proclivity has been an important factor in the growing extremism in South
Asian Islam.

The Democracy Factor

The end of the Zia regime ushered in a period of transition. The regime that
was most closely associated with Islamization, and which had the most le-

gitimacy to speak for and embody the growing Islamic identity in Pakistan, gave place to a more secular democratic order that was initially led by the most secular element in Pakistan's politics, the Pakistan People's Party (PPP). The passing of the Zia regime had not occurred through political defeat, and as such, the Islamic coalition that led Pakistan in the 1980s retained notable power. The continuation of the war in Afghanistan, too, necessitated that Pakistan remain true to its Islamic ideology.

As a result, the democratic period that followed the Zia years, 1988–99, was marked by a tug-of-war between military and civilian politicians and Islamic forces and secular political institutions.[39] The result was not only debilitating struggles for power that ultimately undermined democracy, but a more subtle competition for the soul of Pakistan. Just as democratic forces sought to recalibrate Pakistan's ideology, moving it away from Islamization to better support development and modernization, the coalition of military forces and Islamic parties sought to resist this trend by ever more tightly weaving Pakistan's foreign policy and regional interests with Islam and thus continuing to anchor domestic politics in the debate over Islamization.

In 1994 a change of events in Afghanistan led to Pakistan's greater support for extremism. This led to a palpable growth in prominence of the extremist forces in Pakistan's domestic politics as well. The empowerment of the Taliban meant giving free reign to those forces in Pakistan that shared its ideology and provided it with recruits and resources. Hence, the SSP and its offshoots became more prominent and their rhetoric began to define the tempo of Islamist discourse. The rise of the Taliban also coincided with the greater prominence of Jam'iat-i Ulama-i Islam (JUI) in national politics. JUI used its position to ensure a seamless linkage between the Taliban and domestic extremist forces centered in the *madrasah* system and military training and war in Afghanistan.

The military also concluded that, just as the Taliban's brand of Islamism had proven more productive on the battlefield in Afghanistan, extremism was likely to serve the military's objective of controlling domestic politics more effectively. General Musharraf, in particular, proved adept at using extremist forces in Punjab and also Kashmir to undermine civilian governments. In the months leading to the military coup of 1999 there were two attempts on the life of Nawaz Sharif, by Lashkar-i Jhangvi (Jhangvi's Army) and Lashkar-i Tayibah (Army of the Pure), both of which had close ties with the military.[40] Similarly, the military used militant activists to precipitate a crisis with India in Kargil, with the aim of weakening Nawaz Sharif's government. Kargil undermined Sharif's international position, depicting him as unable to deliver on regional issues and also weakening him before the military at a time of heightened nationalist feelings in Pakistan.

The government of Prime Minister Nawaz Sharif that came to power in 1997 sought to chart a new path for Pakistan.[41] The elections of 1997 were the first since 1988 to give a party a clear mandate. The Muslim League, led by Nawaz Sharif, won 63 percent of the seats in the National Assembly. The elections produced the smallest contingent of Islamist representation in the Parliament on record (a contrast with the elections of 2002). The results permitted Nawaz Sharif to vie for control of Pakistan's politics, defining the relationship between civilian rule and Islam and creating a tenable relationship between Islam and the state—the first since the Zia period. To achieve this, Sharif openly fashioned the Muslim League as simultaneously a modern democratic party that was committed to the development of Pakistan and the champion of the cause of Islamization.

In effect, he positioned the Muslim League as a democratic party with Islamic credentials, similar to European Christian Democratic parties. Sharif was known to be a pious Muslim. He used this to argue that he would deliver on the demands of Islamization just as he would pursue development. The Muslim League was to form a stable right-of-center government that would not be beholden to Islamist parties and would be able to govern Pakistan with a strong claim to represent popular and national religious aspirations.

Sharif modeled the Muslim League after Malaysia's UMNO. That party had in the 1980s successfully co-opted Islamic forces and had advocated both Islamization and capitalist development. As senior Muslim League leader, Mushahid Husain, put it: "Nawaz Sharif will be both the Erbakan [leader of Turkey's Islamist Refah Party] and Mahathir of Pakistan."[42] The Muslim League's claim was bolstered by the fact that it had taken over seats that were once held by Islamist parties and defeated those Islamist candidates that had participated in the elections. It argued that it could better serve the interests of the Islamic vote bank.

The military under General Musharraf viewed Nawaz Sharif's gambit as a threat. Had Nawaz Sharif succeeded in establishing a viable right-of-center and Islamist coalition he would have dominated the middle in Pakistan. Moreover, then it would have been a democratic party rather than the military that would have defined and controlled the nexus between Islam and the state.

The military, under General Musharraf, turned to extremist forces to undermine Sharif. This was a policy that was first adopted by Benazir in 1994 but now was perfected by the military under Musharraf. By encouraging increasing radicalization of the Islamist discourse, and by supporting the extremist forces, the military sought to destabilize relations between the Muslim League and its Islamist constituency, and to more generally radicalize Islamism to the extent that a viable center-right coalition would not be feasible. The military also used extremist forces in Kashmir to undermine Sharif, most notably in Kargil in 1999, when an incursion by militants into Indian-held Kashmir brought the two countries to the brink of war and greatly weakened Nawaz Sharif.

The growing tensions between the military and the Muslim League government eroded Sharif's authority and eventually led to the military coup of 1999. The new regime was based on an untenable relationship between a secular-leaning military elite that promised secular development and Islamist extremist forces. The military sought to manage this situation by encouraging Islamist extremism to spend its energies in Afghanistan and Kashmir. Keen to ride the tiger of radical Islam at a time when the military's ideological cadence with Islamism was waning, the military was hardpressed to react to the fact that the Afghan campaign was producing Islamic radicalism more rapidly than the military could manage. By encouraging the Afghan Jihad to extend to Kashmir, the military not only hoped to utilize the successful Afghan strategy to change the balance of power in Kashmir, but also to find a new preoccupation for the growing radicalism.

Still, the coup destroyed Pakistan's chances to contain Islamism through its co-optation of the political process under a strong secular but right-of-center party. The result of this catastrophe became clear in the elections of 2002, when the Islamist parties, facing no competition from a viable right-of-center party, captured fifty seats (the third largest bloc in the Parliament) to score their biggest victory ever. Islamist leaders such as Qazi Husain Ahmad of the Jama'at, who had been excluded by Nawaz Sharif in 1997, emerged as new national leaders.

The events of September 11, 2001, were also critical, in that al-Qaeda's adventurism led to the destruction of the Taliban and to Pakistan's loss of Afghanistan. Overnight, Pakistan lost its most important strategic objective, upon which it had anchored its Islamization drive. The fall of the Taliban coincided with a significant shift by the Pakistan military in the direction of the United States, underscoring the dissonance between its objectives and its Islamist pretenses. Thus, by the time the elections of 2002 came about, the military had lost control of the extremist forces, and having destroyed the center-right, had left the political process open to Islamic resurgence.

Since the elections of 2002, the Musharraf government has sought to marginalize civilian political forces in Pakistan—Benazir Bhutto's PPP and Nawaz Sharif's Pakistan Muslim League (PML) also performed respectably in the elections. These results were obtained despite the fact that both parties were under considerable pressure from the military, their leaders were banned from the elections and were in exile, and the elections themselves were far from free and fair. The election results convinced the Musharraf regime that civilian politicians continued to pose the greatest danger to military rule. This led General Musharraf to increasingly look to Islamist parties to manage the political process—as the military's civilian partners. The military had helped cobble together the Islamist alliance Mutahhidah Majlis Amal (MMA, United Action Front), which performed unexpectedly well in the elections. After the elections, rather than an arena for the struggle between Islam and secularism, Pakistan's politics became shaped by the competition between the military and civilian political forces. The military increasingly relied on Islamism to win this competition. In many regards Pakistan's politics under Musharraf greatly resembles the Zia period, except that under Zia the military enjoyed ideological conformity with its Islamist allies, whereas under Musharraf there exists a tacit alliance of convenience between the two without any common ideological vision. The relationship is therefore more unstable. This fact places pressure on the military to back away from its overt secularism and to move closer to MMA. Since the 2002 elections, the military has been tolerant of MMA and has gradually given in to many of its demands. For instance, the military has shied away from reforming the *madrasah* curriculums which it had once viewed as the main source of militancy in Pakistan.

These developments have placed General Musharraf in a quandary. First, the secularizing vision of his regime was compromised, as he was forced to look to the MMA rather than to civilian parties to bolster his regime. Second, the military soon found the MMA itself was a thorn in the military's side, which it was not able to easily deal with, given its desire to marginalize the PPP and PML. The MMA, far from being a convenient instrument of the military, has its own political agenda, which is not necessarily always in tune with the military's objectives—especially in the foreign policy arena.

The rise of the MMA has had a moderating effect on Pakistan's regional policy. The events of September 11, 2001, had compelled Pakistan to temper its support for jihadi activism in the region. The MMA's electoral success in the elections of 2002, contrary to expectations, did not reverse this trend but, rather, accelerated it. With the PPP and PML under pressure from the military, the MMA saw before it the opportunity to emerge as a serious contender for controlling the center in Pakistani politics. With this objective in mind, the MMA deliberately distanced itself from the Taliban fighters in southern Afghanistan and the jihadi fighters in Kashmir. Braving the storm of criticism from jihadi groups, MMA leader Mawlana Fazlur Rahman visited India in July 2003. During that trip, Rahman presented a pragmatic image of the MMA, meeting with BJP leaders and suggesting that the alliance would accept the Line of Control between Pakistani and Indian forces in Kashmir as the basis for a peace process. Rahman went even further to assure his Indian interlocutors that the MMA had no interest in jihadi activism, blaming the military for all cross-border militant activities. The MMA has thus backed away from militant posturing in order to pave the way for its own rise to power in Pakistani politics. The MMA's pragmatism has limited the military's room for maneuverability—especially the blaming of Islamists for cross-border attacks into India and for resisting the normalization of relations with Delhi. This was, in part, the reason why General Musharraf embraced the peace process with India—which he had a few years earlier undermined—to prevent the MMA from completely outmaneuvering the military on Kashmir. The MMA's policy has created an environment that augurs well for greater peace in the region. For the first time, Islamists—at least the larger Islamist parties—in Pakistan are seeing greater political benefits in peace than in conflict with India. Whether or not this trend continues will depend on the dynamics of Pakistan's domestic politics and relations between the Musharraf government and the MMA.

In conclusion, a confluence of regional and domestic developments set Pakistan on the path of greater Islamization. This Islamization justified and supported Pakistan's regional strategic objectives and, increasingly, the ebbs and flows of its domestic politics. The failure to create a tenable structure for the role that Islam played in Pakistan led to the gradual unraveling of the concordat between Islamism and the state just as it pushed Islamism in the direction of greater radicalism. The coup of 1999 underscored this problem. But it was the events of September 11 that placed the greatest pressure on the arrangement that had first come about during the Zia years.

Pakistan is today in the throes of change. The relationship between Islam and the state is in flux. The regional justifications for Islamization are no longer there. The place of Islam in Pakistan's strategic direction has to be re-defined. The pattern of relations between Islam and state interest that emerged during the Zia period, and that was embodied in the strategic and ideological links between the military and Islamist forces—to shape the war in Afghanistan and influence domestic politics—has come undone. Still, the trajectory of regional and domestic politics since 1977 has made Islam far more central to realizing Pakistan's state interests. Islam as national identity became Islam as harbinger of state interest. It is for this reason that the height of military use and abuse of Islamism to realize regional and domestic interests occurred at a time of growing secularism in the military, during the tenure of its most secular leader since Zia.

During General Musharraf's regime the public space in Pakistan has become more secular. There is today less emphasis on things Islamic in popular culture, and the government no longer looks to Islamism to provide it with legitimacy, ideas, or the language with which to articulate the interests of the state. This, however, does not mean that Islamism is a spent force in Pakistan. Islamist forces, as represented by the MMA, are cultivating support in new areas in the country's body politic. They are looking less to Islamic sentiments to propel them to power and more to what they call "sovereign issues"—namely, national security and constitutional demands. With the civilian parties under pressure, Islamist forces have emerged as the principal voices of dissent against the military's foreign and domestic policies. In this regard, Islamist force are becoming more powerful and entrenched, even if their imprint on popular culture appears to be less evident.

The fact that the current political setup in Pakistan is dependent on one man, and is perilously narrow in its base of support, means that Islamists are well positioned to take advantage of sudden regime change in Pakistan. Moreover, whereas Islamists are developing roots among new constituencies based on their political position, the secularism advocated by the Musharraf regime lacks an institutional basis of support in political parties and is vulnerable to public rejection owing to the unpopularity of the military regime. As such, Islamism is likely to remain a force in Pakistan.

This, however, does not mean that Islamist forces are likely to revert to the kind of politics they advocated during the Zia period. There is evidence that Islamists are eager to build on the gains of the past five years and, rather than representing the demand for Islamization, to capitalize on the demand for good government and for government that will serve Pakistan's national interests. As a result, they will follow policies that are likely to expand rather than limit their base of support. As Mawlana Fazlur Rahman's diplomacy with India indicates, this may mean greater pragmatism on the part of Islamists than had been previously expected. Pakistan during the post-Musharraf period may well be a more Islamic place, but that may not mean that it is likely to be more inimical to pragmatic policies in dealing with India.

THREE

Constitutional and Political Change in Pakistan: The Military-Governance Paradigm

Charles H. Kennedy

Pakistan's record as an independent nation-state is not a happy one. The litany of failures includes the following: the inability to compose a constitution until nine years after independence; the abrogation of that constitution and two others during the next twenty years; the failure to gain Kashmir; the inability to form stable democratic institutions; the failure either to sustain economic development or to effect meaningful redistribution of wealth to the impoverished masses; the loss of a majority of the population when the state of Bangladesh was formed; the inability to silence regional and sectarian disputes; and, finally, the inability to sustain a clear concept of and direction to Pakistan's nationalism.

Moreover, constitutional government in Pakistan has been more sham than substance. Pakistan has had five constitutions in its brief history: one inherited at independence (the Government of India Act of 1935, as modified by the India Independence Act of 1947), and four indigenous creations, in 1956, 1962, 1972, and 1973. Pakistan has also been governed at times without the benefit of a written constitution (1958–62, 1969–71), under a suspended constitution (1977–85), and under a "modified" though "restored" constitution (1985–97), the latter of which was wholly altered by the passage of the Thirteenth Amendment (1997–99). Between 1999 and November 2002 the state was governed under a "Provisional Constitution Order," from November 2002 to January 2004 under a "Legal Framework Order," and since then under a constitution which has been wholly revised by the operation of the Seventeenth Amendment.

At the core of these "failures" has been the chronic political dominance of

Pakistan's military. Subsequent to the military's direct intervention in 1958, Pakistan's military has been the most significant institutional actor in the political system. During the forty-six years since Pakistan's first military coup, civilian governments have only been in control for twenty-two years, and during those twenty-two years such civilian governments have been typically weak and have served, with few exceptions, at the sufferance of the military. In the two instances in which civilian governments gained majorities sufficient to amend the constitution (1977 and 1997), military coups soon followed.

This paper will approach the constitutional and political development of Pakistan first by providing an overview of Pakistan's nine constitutional phases from independence until 1999.[1] Then, in greater detail, it will chronicle the ten-stage cycle of Pakistan civil–military relations, a cycle that, unfortunately, is remarkably resilient. Indeed, it is so resilient that it may define a distinctly Pakistani style of governance—a military-governance paradigm.

An Overview of Pakistan's Political and Constitutional Structures, 1947–99

1947–56

At partition in 1947 Pakistan was declared a free sovereign dominion to be governed until a constitution could be formulated by the Constituent Assembly acting under the Government of India Act of 1935, as amended by the Indian Independence Act. Until the new constitution could be drafted, the Constituent Assembly (CA) doubled as a National Assembly, and in this role it was empowered to enact legislation. Therefore, the combination of pre-partition enactments and CA legislation constituted the effective law of the state. The duties of the governor-general, however, were ambiguous. At the core of the ambiguity were two questions: whether the CA could pass laws without the consent of the governor-general, and whether the governor-general had the legal authority to disband the CA. This ambiguity remained unchallenged until 1954.

The task of constitution making facing the CA proved to be very difficult. It was so difficult, in fact, that Governor-General Ghulam Muhammad tested the aforementioned constitutional ambiguity by disbanding the CA on October 24, 1954. He argued that since the CA was unable to produce a constitution, it was prolonging its existence at the expense of the nation. Ghulam Muhammad's action was upheld by the Federal Court of Pakistan in 1955.[2] The court argued that the governor-general had the power not only to disband the CA but also to veto any legislation passed by it. Therefore, when the second Constituent Assembly was convened, it could do little more than follow the framework established by the governor-general. Instead of a decentralized, legislature-dominated system, a form of presidential government emerged.

1956–58

Pakistan's first indigenous constitution was promulgated on March 23, 1956. It established Pakistan as an Islamic republic and replaced the governor-general with a president. The Constitution was described as "federal in form and parliamentary in composition," but objective circumstances in the state made both claims dubious. First, as a means of muting the question of representation for East Pakistan,[3] Iskandar Mirza, the new governor-general, amalgamated the provinces of West Pakistan into one unit in October 1955. This arrangement (the One Unit Plan), which was to persist until 1970, negated any federal solution to Pakistan's regional problem. With only two units in the federation, and with one holding effective control, the possibility of meaningful federalism was nil. Second, by 1956, the prospects of parliamentary democracy had become bleak. The Muslim League, the only party of national unity, was in disarray. It commanded almost no support in East Pakistan, and its platform was virtually nonexistent. The only other significant party was the Awami League (its strength limited to East Pakistan), a party that ultimately repented its decision to support the 1956 Constitution. Such party weakness led to extreme governmental instability. From August 1955 to October 1958, Pakistan had four separate and wholly ineffective governments. None of these governments was able to stay in power longer than thirteen months, and none of them could manage to hold general elections under the terms of the 1956 Constitution. Indeed, no elections were ever held under the 1956 Constitution. Given such failures of state structure, President Iskandar Mirza, in collaboration with the military and particularly Commander-in-Chief of the Army, General Ayub Khan, suspended political activity, disbanded the legislative assembly, and declared martial law on October 8, 1958, thus abrogating the Constitution less than three years after its promulgation. On October 27, General Ayub, with the support of the military, had President Mirza arrested and later exiled, thus completing Pakistan's first military coup.

1958–69

Pakistan was governed under martial law, without the benefit of a written constitution, from 1958 to 1962. From Ayub's vantage point as a soldier, the politicians had brought Pakistan to the brink of collapse. He believed that a centralized government with strong leadership was required. These views were embodied in the institutions he created, as well as in Pakistan's second indigenous constitution, a document he largely created.

Ayub's Constitution, promulgated on March 1, 1962, established a presidential form of government. Pakistan's president (Ayub) was to be both head of state and head of government. Essential decisions were to flow to and from his office, implemented by powerful civilian bureaucrats (members of the executive branch). The Constitution also established the Basic Democrats (elected and appointed local officials) as an electoral college to select the president and members of the National Assembly and provincial legislatures. The 1962 Constitution created a National Assembly, but its powers were weak; it was designed more to legitimize the decisions made by the executive than to act as an independent legislature.

1969–71

Ayub, a victim of political disturbances and ill-health, was forced to resign in March 1969.[4] General Agha Muhammad Yahya Khan, his military-appointed successor and former Chief of Army Staff (COAS), suspended the 1962 Constitution, ended the electoral role of the Basic Democrats, and reestablished martial law. Yahya also held national elections in December 1970. But the results of these elections, in which Bengali Sheikh Mujibur Rehman won an absolute majority, proved unacceptable to West Pakistan's ruling elite, and martial law, now termed "emergency rule," remained in force. Eventually, General Yahya sent additional troops to East Pakistan, thereby precipitating the horrors of the civil war and the dismemberment of the state.

1972–77

After Pakistan's defeat in the civil war, it was realized by the top leadership of the military that Yahya Khan, discredited as immediately responsible for the disaster, must go. Accordingly, on December 17, 1971, he was encouraged to resign. Three days later, the military appointed Zulfiqar Ali Bhutto as President and Chief Martial Law Administrator (CMLA). The Pakistan People's Party (PPP) which Bhutto led had come in second in the 1970 elections, winning a majority of seats in West Pakistan.

Within four months, Bhutto was elected president by the National Assembly (consisting of the 146 members who had opted for Pakistan), lifted martial law, and arranged the drafting of an "interim" constitution, which was adopted in April 1972. Under the terms of this latter document, Bhutto, as president, was granted extensive powers. For instance, the governors of the provinces were to be appointed by the president and were solely responsible to him, and the powers of the unicameral National Assembly were left weak.[5]

Once secure in office, Bhutto presided over the drafting of Pakistan's fourth constitution, which was promulgated on April 10, 1973. Unlike the interim constitution, the 1973 Constitution called for the establishment of a parliamentary system. The prime minister, a post Bhutto assumed after resigning his position as president, would be the effective head of government, with the president serving in the role of a figurehead. Although the 1973 Constitution established that the prime minister was to be elected by a majority of the National Assembly, many restrictions were placed on this provision. For instance, votes of no confidence could not be passed unless the assembly had already named the prospective successor to the prime minister, and for a no-confidence vote to be accepted, a majority of the prime minister's party had to cast votes of no confidence. It is also important to note that the 1973 Constitution established a federal form of government, with authority devolved to the four provinces of the state. The Constitution accordingly established federal and concurrent lists. Unlike earlier constitutions, the 1973 Constitution also provided for a bicameral legislature, with a House representing the provinces, and a Senate, as well as the populist National Assembly. However, the National Assembly, which elected the prime minister and in which money bills had to originate, remained the predominant legislative body. Functionally, the powers granted to Bhutto under the

1973 Constitution were as broad as those delegated to Ayub under the 1962 Constitution.

1977–85

Bhutto was removed from office after mass disturbances led by the Pakistan National Alliance (PNA) following the 1977 general election, in which Bhutto's PPP won a landslide victory. The PNA claimed that the "landslide" was the result of wholesale rigging. Before Bhutto could reach a political accommodation with the opposition, General Zia-ul-Haq, the chief of army staff, orchestrated a military coup, on July 5, 1977. The successor regime under Zia-ul-Haq, however, chose not to abrogate the 1973 Constitution. Rather, Zia's government suspended the operation of the Constitution and governed directly, through the promulgation of martial law regulations. Such regulations were defined by the courts as non-justiciable and functionally equivalent to constitutional precepts.[6] Between 1977 and 1981, Pakistan did not have legislative institutions. In 1981 Zia appointed the Majlis-i-Shura (Federal Council), but its functions were wholly advisory to the chief martial law administrator. In December 1984 Zia was elected, through a referendum, to the position of president. Nonpartisan elections (political parties were not allowed to compete, although members of the "defunct" parties could do so as individuals) were held in February 1985 to choose the members of the newly established national and provincial assemblies.

1985–88

Before the newly elected assemblies could meet, President Zia announced long-expected modifications in Pakistan's Constitution. Accordingly, on March 2, 1985, Zia promulgated the Revival of the Constitution of 1973 Order (RCO). This document ushered in the seventh phase of Pakistan's checkered constitutional history. Although nominally a revival of the 1973 Constitution, the presidential order fundamentally altered the terms of that Constitution. Most important, the RCO dramatically increased the powers of the president. First, it reversed the lines of functional authority between the prime minister and the president. The president was given the power to appoint and dismiss the prime minister; and the prime minister's role was defined as largely advisory to the president. Second, it gave the president authority to appoint and dismiss the governors of the provinces and the federal ministers. Third, the president was given the functional authority to dissolve the national and provincial assemblies.

In November 1985 the National Assembly passed the Eighth Amendment.[7] This conferred validation of Zia's revival of the Constitution and indemnified the actions of the military since assuming power in 1977. Therefore, the RCO, coupled with the Eighth Amendment, substantially modified the 1973 Constitution by concentrating predominant political authority in the hands of the president.

Despite such constitutional safeguards, the government under Prime Minister Muhammad Khan Junejo (a Zia appointee) proved too independent for President Zia's liking, and on May 29, 1988, Zia dissolved the National Assembly and the provincial assemblies and promised to hold new elections by November. Before such elections could be held, however, Zia died in an airplane crash, on August 17. Zia's sudden death thus left Pakistan without a president, prime minister, National Assembly, chief ministers, or provincial assemblies. The chairman of the Senate (not dissolved by Zia's order), Ghulam Ishaq Khan, became interim president. Under Ghulam Ishaq, elections were held in November 1988 and resulted in Benazir Bhutto's emergence as prime minister. In December, Ghulam Ishaq was elected to a five-year term in office as president.

1988–97

The election of Benazir Bhutto did not in itself change Zia's constitutional system. Although Benazir campaigned on a platform calling for the restoration of the 1973 Constitution, her electoral mandate was too narrow to engineer the two-thirds majority necessary to amend the Constitution or to rescind the Eighth Amendment. Moreover, Ghulam Ishaq Khan pursued policies that jealously safeguarded the powers of the presidency.

For instance, on August 27, 1990, the president, exercising his powers under Article 58(2)(b) of the Constitution, dismissed Benazir Bhutto's government and called for new elections to be held under the caretaker administration of Ghulam Mustapha Jatoi. Pakistan's four provincial governments were also dismissed. The superior courts upheld the actions of the president,[8] and elections were held that resulted in the Islami Jamhoori Ittehad (IJI) and Mian Nawaz Sharif's victory.

Relations between President Ghulam Ishaq Khan and Prime Minister Nawaz Sharif soured during the next three years, and on April 17, 1993, the president dismissed Nawaz Sharif's government. This time, however, in a landmark decision, the Supreme Court accepted the appeal by the ousted prime minister and ordered that his government be restored.[9] The court reasoned that the president's power to dissolve governments was limited to cases in which there were compelling reasons to dismiss a standing government. That is, it drew a distinction between the 1990 and 1993 dissolutions. The 1990 dissolution was a proper exercise of presidential authority because it had been prompted by the extra-constitutional actions of Benazir Bhutto's government, whereas the 1993 dissolution had been prompted solely by a personal rift between the prime minister and the president. The Nawaz Sharif case established the important principle that the president's power was limited by the Supreme Court. This was a profound departure from the president-dominated system envisioned by President Zia and marks a new phase in Pakistan's confusing constitutional history.[10]

The remedy afforded to the Nawaz Sharif government proved short-lived. Barely three months after the restoration of his government, the military establishment, concerned with the deteriorating law-and-order situation in the state, brokered (some say forced) the resignation of both Ghulam Ishaq Khan and Nawaz Sharif. An interim government was established, and general elections were held in December, as a result of which Benazir Bhutto returned to power, and shortly thereafter Farooq Leghari, a PPP loyalist, was elected as president.

Although relations between Benazir Bhutto and the new president were cooperative at first, they deteriorated in 1996, particularly after the death of Mir Murtaza Bhutto in September. In a widely publicized speech, Benazir charged that Leghari was behind the plot to "murder" her brother. In fact, there was no evidence linking Leghari in any way with the death. Reluctantly, Leghari moved on Benazir's government, dissolving the National Assembly on November 5.[11] Again, such actions were challenged before the Supreme Court. But the court, citing numerous examples of misrule by the Benazir government, upheld the actions of the president.[12] Elections were held in February 1997, and Nawaz Sharif and the Pakistan Muslim League–Nawaz Sharif Faction (PML-N) routed the PPP.

The period between 1988 and 1997, then, can be characterized as a period of checks and balances, of competing institutional authority. The prime minister effectively ran the administration; however, the president retained the ultimate power to dissolve the national and provincial assemblies. But such presidential authority was circumscribed by the superior judiciary, which could reverse the actions of the president and restore the assemblies. However ingenious and/or democratic this system was, it was clearly untidy. Between 1988 and 1997, Pakistan had eight prime ministers and four presidents. The system also proved short-lived.

1997–99

Nawaz Sharif and the Pakistan Muslim League (PML) had received a convincing majority of seats in the 1997 election, far more than the two-thirds necessary to revise the Constitution. This he did in a rapid and forceful manner. In April, he orchestrated the unanimous passage of the Thirteenth Amendment. This amendment repealed Articles 58(2)(b) and 112(2)(b) of the Constitution, which had respectively empowered the president to suspend the National Assembly and the governors to suspend the provincial assemblies. These articles served as the basis of presidential control of the government. Obviously, the passage of the Thirteenth Amendment was an attack upon the authority of the president, but it was also a frontal assault on the authority of the superior judiciary as well. Before the introduction of the Thirteenth Amendment (1988–97), the Supreme Court had served (for all intents and purposes) as the power broker between the president and the prime minister.

In one stroke, the passage of the Thirteenth Amendment had undone years of work by the superior judiciary. If this wasn't enough, Nawaz Sharif further signaled his intention to consolidate power by pushing through the Fourteenth Amendment to the Constitution in July. This amendment prohibited "floor-crossing" (changing party affiliation or voting against party policy) by members of Pakistan's Parliament. Combined, the two amendments left the office of prime minister (read Nawaz Sharif) functionally insulated from challenges from any direction. The president had been reduced to a figurehead, the Fourteenth Amendment had left the opposition powerless to introduce a vote of no-confidence, and the Supreme Court had been stripped of its powers to referee the succession process.

The superior judiciary was obliged to strike back; it found its vehicle in writ petitions filed before the Supreme Court that challenged provisions of the Fourteenth Amendment. Accordingly, on October 29, 1997, a three-judge bench of the Supreme Court, headed by Chief Justice Sajjad Ali Shah, admitted a petition challenging the amendment and suspended the operation of the amendment.[13] Nawaz Sharif, angered by the Court's action, issued an intemperate public diatribe against the Supreme Court, and particularly against its Chief Justice.[14] On November 2, Sajjad Ali Shah responded in kind, by citing Nawaz Sharif for contempt of court.

Earlier, two other judges of the Supreme Court (Sharif appointees) had issued an order declaring that the original appointment of Sajjad Ali Shah as Chief Justice (made by Benazir Bhutto) was illegal, as Justice Shah at his time of appointment to the position was not the senior-most jurist on the bench.[15] Upon learning of this order, Sajjad Ali Shah issued his own order (November 26), directing that no more cases be sent to the two offending judges. The next day, the two latter justices, joined by one of their colleagues, issued a counter order contending that as Sajjad Ali Shah was not competent to hold the post of Chief Justice, any orders made by him in that capacity were null and void. Before there was a resolution of this war of judicial orders, a mob (encouraged, if not directed, by Nawaz Sharif and the leadership of the PML) occupied the Supreme Court Building, disrupting the first day of the contempt hearing of the prime minister. The hearing was postponed.

Subsequently, a full bench of the Supreme Court passed an order (December 23) declaring that the original appointment of Sajjad Ali Shah was illegal and unconstitutional. Justice Ajmal Mian, the then most senior judge was duly sworn in as the new Chief Justice. During the factional wrangling, Sajjad Ali Shah had also issued an order which called for the suspension of the Thirteenth Amendment. This latter action undoubtedly had the support of President Leghari. There was considerable speculation at the time that a constitutional crisis was imminent and that the military would be obliged to intervene in order to reestablish the pre–Thirteenth Amendment system, that is, to reintroduce Article 58(2)(b). However, the military chose not to intervene. Left hanging, President Leghari resigned and was replaced in December by Nawaz Sharif's choice, Rafiq Ahmed Tarar. With Sajjad Ali Shah out of the picture, the Ajmal Mian–led Supreme Court dismissed the contempt charges against the prime minister and rejected the petitions challenging the constitutionality of the Fourteenth Amendment.

Therefore, by the end of 1998 when the dust had finally settled, Nawaz Sharif stood triumphant. In effect, he had staged a successful "civilian" coup d'état. The Thirteenth and Fourteenth Amendments were law and had withstood legal challenge; the Supreme Court (without Sajjad Ali Shah) was behaving itself; Farooq Leghari had been replaced by the more Nawaz-friendly Rafiq Tarar; and the military had decided, at least for the time being, to stay in the barracks. But they wouldn't stay there for long.

Parvez Musharraf and the Pakistani Military-Governance Paradigm

With this politico-historical background in mind, we can now turn our attention to the regime of Parvez Musharraf, who assumed power through a bloodless military coup on October 12, 1999. His assumption of power, and the political course his regime has followed since, is eerily similar to the paths followed by his military predecessors. Perhaps this is owing to the limited options available to Pakistani military rulers; perhaps it is owing to a collective lack of imagination; perhaps it is owing to a Grand Strategy formulated within the General Headquarters staff (GHQ). In any case, Musharraf's government has followed very closely the familiar patterns of military regime development within Pakistan. In the pages that follow, an explicit attempt will be made to analyze Musharraf's first four years in power in terms of the "Pakistani military-governance paradigm." This paradigm has ten sequential or nearly sequential steps. We will look at each in turn.

STEP ONE: EXPLAIN YOURSELF

The first step following a military coup is to establish a plausible, ideally, compelling excuse for subverting the political process. After all, military coups should not be entered into lightly. Pakistan's first coup, staged by President Iskandar Mirza and General Ayub Khan set a precedent by justifying their actions in terms of countering what they typified as a wholesale breakdown of the process of governance in the state. Evidence for such a "breakdown" was provided, in that each of the four previous post-1954 governments (headed by Chaudry Muhammad Ali, Hussain S. Suhrawardy, I. I. Chundrigar, and Feroz Khan Noon) were pathetically weak. Such weakness, it was alleged, had led to the growing civil unrest in East Pakistan, which threatened to deteriorate into chaos. Mirza's and Ayub's case was strong; and Ayub's case for subsequently ousting Mirza (the latter had presided over the 1954–58 mess and he had subverted his own government) was compelling.[16]

Perhaps not as compelling in retrospect were the motives of Zia-ul-Haq's "Operation Fair Play." Zia claimed that the political system of Pakistan had come unglued following Bhutto's rigging of the 1977 general election. The PNA was leading a nationwide campaign calling for Bhutto to step down and for a new election to be held, and Bhutto had for all intents and purposes admitted electoral misdeeds by promulgating the Seventh Amendment to the Constitution. The latter amendment allowed for the holding of a national referendum—ostensibly to seek popular support for continued confidence in the Prime Minister. Before such a referendum could be held, and before Bhutto could reach an accord with the PNA, the military struck. To Zia and his apologists, they had no choice but to intervene.

Parvez Musharraf's motives for staging the October 12, 1999, coup were several. The immediate motive was to counter Nawaz Sharif's dismissal of Musharraf as Chief of Army Staff and the appointment of General Khawaja Ziauddin in his stead. On its face, this is a less than compelling rationale, as the Prime Minister possessed the competent authority to dismiss a COAS—indeed, in 1998 Nawaz Sharif had done just that by dismissing Jehangir Karamat and replacing him with Musharraf. A more compelling motive was the growing concern that Nawaz Sharif was systematically overstepping his bounds and challenging the corporate interests of the military—interests that included sharing in Pakistan's governing structure. As mentioned above, Nawaz Sharif's successful abrogation of Article 58(2)(b)—the passage of the Thirteenth Amendment—had left his government immune from civilian dissolution. Such civilian presidential dissolutions had been greatly influenced by the military. Also, a compelling motive was the military's rift with Nawaz Sharif over what many in the military viewed as the latter's capitulation in Kargil.

In any case, the test of a successful excuse is if it is accepted by its recipient—if it can be sold to the public. When measured by this yardstick, it seems apparent that Ayub's and Musharraf's coups were more "successful" than Zia's. There was virtually no public outcry against the dismissals of Iskandar Mirza, nor those of Nawaz Sharif. Zia's dismissal of Bhutto was a far more difficult sell. It is also important to note that the 1999 coup followed in the tradition of being bloodless. Coups, in Pakistan, are fairly polite occasions; they are the result of consensual decision making by the officer corps. Violence would mar the proceedings, upset the paradigm.

STEP TWO: AVOID LEGAL CHAOS

Following the presentation of plausible excuses, the next step is to provide continuity of government—to avoid legal chaos. Each of Pakistan's coup-makers has followed a similar path.

On October 10, 1958, Ayub Khan promulgated the Laws (Continuance in Force) Order. The general effect of this was to validate laws, other than the 1956 Constitution, that were in force prior to the October 7 coup. It also restored the jurisdiction of all courts including the Supreme Court and High Courts, and directed that the government of Pakistan should act as nearly as possible in accordance with the abrogated Constitution. But the order made clear that "no court or person could call or permit to be called into question (i) the proclamation of 7 October, (ii) any order in pursuance of the proclamation or any martial law order or martial law regulation, (iii) any finding, judgment or order of a Special Military Court or a Summary Military Court."[17]

A nearly identical pattern was followed in Zia's Laws (Continuance in Force) Order, 1977. It repeated Ayub's formulary. "Pakistan shall, subject to this order and any order made by the president and any order made by the Chief Martial Law Administrator (CMLA) be governed as nearly as may be, in accordance with the constitution." The courts were also allowed to function normally except they would have no jurisdiction to challenge the actions of the CMLA or Martial Law Administrators or any person exercising authority on behalf of either.[18]

General Musharraf (by then the self-styled "Chief Executive") followed suit in his promulgation of the Provisional Constitution Order of 1999 (PCO):

Notwithstanding the abeyance of the provisions of the constitution of the Islamic Republic of Pakistan, . . . Pakistan shall, subject to this Order and any other Orders made by the Chief Executive, be governed as nearly as may be, in accordance with the constitution. Subject as aforesaid, all courts in existence immediately before the commencement of this Order, shall continue to function and to exercise their respective powers and jurisdiction provided that the Supreme Court or High Courts and any other court shall not have the powers to make any order against the Chief Executive or any other person exercising powers or jurisdiction under his authority.[19]

STEP THREE: MAKE THINGS LEGAL

Military coups and the abrogation or suspension of relevant constitutions are likely to draw the attention of and engender opposition from among the members of the judiciary. Pakistan's coupmakers have proven adept at encouraging the superior judiciary to be compliant and to mandate their "extra-constitutional" practices.

Ayub Khan inherited a cooperative superior judiciary. In the *Moulvi Tamizuddin* case, the Federal Court had upheld the dissolution of the Constituent Assembly by the Governor-General. More importantly, in a subsequent case (1955) the court relied upon the "doctrine of state necessity" to validate laws made invalid by the court's earlier decision.[20] With such recent legal precedents, Ayub did not risk serious legal challenge against his declaration of martial law. Indeed, when his declaration of martial law was challenged, the Supreme Court (the "Federal Court" became known as the "Supreme Court" under the terms of the 1956 Constitution) in the *Dosso* case ruled that a successful coup d'état is an internationally recognized legal method of changing a constitution.[21] Justice Muhammad Munir wrote the leading decision in all three cases.

Zia-ul-Haq faced a more complex situation. Zia's coup had displaced a populist prime minister at the peak of his power, having led the PPP to an overwhelming, albeit tainted, victory in the 1977 general elections. Moreover, Bhutto had loyalists within the superior judiciary, including the Chief Justice of the Supreme Court, Yakub Ali. Zia, nothing if not clever, seized upon the expedient of placing into abeyance the operation of the Bhutto-inspired Fifth and Sixth Amendments to the Constitution. The introduction of the latter amendments had been bitterly resented by Pakistan's superior judiciary as an infringement upon their authority.[22] The timely abrogation of these amendments also served to remove Yakub Ali from the post of Chief Justice and to elevate Anwar-ul-Haq to the position.[23]

Subsequently, in a unanimous decision written by the new Chief Justice, the Supreme Court ruled that Zia's assumption of power must be maintained as a matter of "state necessity," as Zia's actions had been necessitated in turn by a prior usurpation of power by Bhutto. Moreover, the Court ruled that Zia's actions were designed, in part, to prevent the further deterioration of the civil order. The Court drew a distinction between the current case and Ayub's coup, in that Zia's coup did not abrogate the relevant (1973) Constitution.[24]

Musharraf faced the trickiest situation of all. The "doctrine of state necessity" had fallen out of favor within Pakistan's legal circles, and the superior courts, although harmed by Nawaz Sharif's recent meddling (see discussion above) were still activist and at least episodically independent. Moreover, international public opinion by 1999 had largely dismissed the coup d'état as an acceptable means of changing government.

Accordingly, Musharraf and his advisors devised a plan to make the judiciary *ex post facto* "co-conspirators" in the coup. On December 31, 1999, he introduced an ordinance that required superior court judges to take a fresh oath of office under the terms of the PCO, *not* the 1973 Constitution.[25] Six justices of the Supreme Court and nine judges of the High Courts refused to take the new oath and stood retired.[26] The reconstituted and now ostensibly more friendly Supreme Court quickly consolidated the numerous writ petitions that had been filed challenging the constitutionality of the military coup, and on May 12, 2000, issued their landmark finding—the *Zafar Ali Shah v. Parvez Musharraf, Chief Executive of Pakistan* decision.[27] The decision, among other things, provided legal cover for Musharraf's actions. It also granted the regime a three-year grace period (until October 12, 2002) to hold general elections and to restore the national and provincial assemblies. When the dust settled following the decision, the military (and the Chief Executive) had held the field. First, Musharraf's seizure of power had not been defined as constituting an act of "martial law." An adverse finding would have occasioned a variety of domestic and international problems. Second, the military coup was defined as regrettable but justifiable. Finally, Musharraf's regime had been granted legitimacy, and given an extra-constitutional "grace period" of three years.

STEP FOUR: ELIMINATE POLITICAL OPPONENTS

By their very nature, military coups displace former political leaders who have typically been elected and who as a consequence have some degree of popular legitimacy. Clearly, it is imperative for the successful coupmaker to discredit and ideally to "get rid of" such former leaders.

Ayub's task, as has been chronicled above, proved quite simple in this regard. Iskandar Mirza had not been elected by the people to the presidency; and his legitimacy was tarnished, as he had been one of the principals in the 1958 coup. Ayub deftly had him arrested and negotiated and enforced his safe passage and exile to England.

Zia's task was far more complicated. The process that led to the legal acceptance of Zia's coup, *Begum Nusrat Bhutto v. Chief of Army Staff,* has been chronicled above. But even after the court's decision, Z. A. Bhutto remained a powerful force with which to be reckoned: Zia had promised to hold elections within ninety days of the coup; if such elections were held, Bhutto would almost certainly be reelected as Prime Minister; and Bhutto had made it clear that he intended to invoke Article 6 of the Constitution ("High Treason") against Zia once he regained his post.[28]

Zia's approach was twofold. First, he amassed extensive information detailing the misdeeds of Z. A. Bhutto and his regime and published the data in the several volume *White Papers.*[29] Second, he pursued an unlikely abetment to murder charge against Bhutto, in which Bhutto was implicated in the inadvertent murder of Nawab Muhammad Ahmad, the father of Ahmed Raza Kasuri (a political opponent of Bhutto), the actual target of the alleged "hit." Both approaches bore fruit. Bhutto's legacy was tarnished by the publication of the *White Papers.* But the legal procedures proved even more "effective." Bhutto and four co-conspirators were convicted of murder by the Lahore High Court on March 18, 1978.[30] After a lengthy appeal before the Supreme Court, the conviction was eventually upheld in a 4–3 decision on February 6, 1979.[31] Bhutto was sentenced to death. He was hanged on April 4, 1979, in the Rawalpindi Central Jail.

Chief Executive Musharraf faced a similar dilemma to that of Zia. Nawaz Sharif was a popular and elected leader. He could not be allowed to remain a viable politician. Fortunately for Musharraf, Nawaz Sharif had paradoxically provided a vehicle for his own undoing, his controversial anti-terrorism laws.[32] On December 2, 1999, Musharraf introduced two amendments to the Anti-Terrorism Ordinance. The first extended the schedule of offenses recognizable by the anti-terrorism courts to include several other provisions of Pakistan's criminal code. The courts' expanded jurisdiction would now include: (1) Section 109—Abetment of Offense; (2) Section 120—Concealing a Design to Commit an Offense; (3) Section 120B—Criminal Conspiracy to Commit a Crime Punishable by Death or with Imprisonment Greater than Two Years; (4) Section 121—Waging or Attempting to Wage War against Pakistan; (5) Section 121A—Conspiracy to Commit Certain Offenses against the State; (6) Section 122—Collecting Arms with the Intent to Wage War; (7) Section 123—Concealment with Intent to Facilitate Waging of War; (8) Section 365—Kidnapping; (9) Section 402—Being One of Five or More Persons Assembled for the Purposes of Committing Dacoity; and (10) Section 402B—Conspiracy to Commit Hijacking.[33] The second amendment promulgated on December 2 established two new special courts, one to be located at the Lahore High Court, the other at the Karachi High Court. Each of these new courts would be headed by a High Court judge, and each would have the power to "transfer, claim, or readmit any case within that province." These courts would also serve as appellate tribunals for the anti-terrorism courts.[34]

With these two amendments in place, the government turned its attention to the disposal of the case brought against Nawaz Sharif and his co-conspirators. The government's case against the former Prime Minister was designed to bring both criminal charges against Nawaz Sharif, which if successful would effectively end his political career, and to absolve Chief Executive Musharraf from any liability associated with staging the military coup of October 12. The actual charges brought by the government seem, on their face, to have been problematic at best. Essentially, the facts presented were that Prime Minister Sharif had made the decision to remove General Musharraf from his position as Chief of Army Staff, but delayed the execution of that decision until Musharraf was out of Pakistan. Therefore, when Musharraf went to Sri Lanka in order to attend a conference, Nawaz Sharif struck. Allegedly, Sharif was hopeful that by the time Musharraf had returned the unpleasantness associated with the dismissal of the COAS would have subsided. However, Nawaz Sharif's plans were foiled when key personnel within the military remained loyal to Musharraf and refused to accept the orders of the Prime Minister. When Nawaz learned that his orders were not being followed, and in light of Musharraf's imminent return to Karachi (the latter had boarded a commercial Pakistan International Airline flight destined for Karachi), Sharif struck. He ordered that the flight not be allowed to land in Pakistan. Various officials of PIA and the airport authority cooperated with the Prime Minister's directive, while others failed to cooperate. But in any case, the airplane, carrying not only General Musharraf, but also more than one hundred other passengers, was diverted from its original flight path. The diversion, in turn, "threatened the lives" of the passengers, as the aircraft was running low on fuel and as a result could not comply with the directive to land outside of Pakistan. Eventually, the relevant airport authorities relented, perhaps owing to the involvement of military personnel who had in the meantime occupied the Karachi airport. The plane landed, its passengers inconvenienced and scared, but safe. No one was hurt, let alone killed, owing to the events.

Therefore, given the charges outlined above to be brought against the ex-Prime Minister, the December 2 amendments to the Anti-Terrorism Ordinance were crucial to the government's case. The crimes for which Nawaz Sharif would be charged (Sections 109, 120B, 121A, 122, 123, 365, and 402B) were not cognizable before anti-terrorism courts prior to the amendments. Ostensibly, then, without the amendments such charges would have had to be filed with the regular courts. Moreover, the ostensible venue of such a prospective trial would have been Lahore, *not* Karachi—Lahore is Nawaz Sharif's hometown. That is, the aforementioned amendments were designed to increase the probability of the timely conviction of Nawaz Sharif. Accordingly, one of the main defense strategies of Nawaz Sharif's attorneys was to challenge the standing of the Karachi Anti-Terrorism Court, to which his case was assigned. This petition was rejected on January 12, 2000, and the trial was held. On April 6, the Karachi Anti-Terrorism Court announced its verdict—Nawaz Sharif was convicted of conspiracy to hijack the PIA flight and was sentenced to life imprisonment. Charges against his seven co-defendants were dropped.[35]

One would be safe to speculate that if this case had been brought before the regular court system that the outcome may have been different. The thread of evidence linking Nawaz Sharif to the "hijacking" was weak, at best. Certainly, a trial conducted through the regular courts would have taken far longer to complete. In any event, Nawaz Sharif appealed the decision to the Appellate Tribunal of the Sindh High Court. But the appeal was never heard, for while it was pending the government struck a deal with Nawaz Sharif and his family. In December 2000 the Sharif family were allowed to leave the country for Saudi Arabia. It was reported that the Sharif family was fined more than Rps. 20 million ($400,000) and agreed to the forfeiture of property worth in excess of Rps. 500 million ($10 million) as part of the deal.[36] This conviction and exile has likely ended Nawaz Sharif's political career. Indeed, neither he nor any of his family members were allowed to contest seats in the October 2002 general elections.

It is also important to note that the other main political threat to Musharraf—Benazir Bhutto—has been largely neutralized, owing to the earlier actions of the Nawaz Sharif government. Following the latter's landslide victory in the 1997 elections, numerous indictments were issued against both Benazir Bhutto and her husband Asif Ali Zardari, charging them with, among other things, corruption and financial impropriety. Zardari was also indicted for complicity in the 1996 murder of Murtaza Bhutto (Benazir's brother).[37] After having been convicted in absentia in 1998 and facing a five-year jail sentence, Benazir lived in self-defined exile, dividing her time between Europe and the Gulf.

STEP FIVE: ARRANGE TO BECOME PRESIDENT

Each of Pakistan's coupmakers faced a similar dilemma: how to transform and legitimize their unelected status as a CMLA or a Chief Executive into that of an elected President. Their respective remedies have been eerily similar. Each has decided to hold referenda.

On February 14, 1960, the CMLA Field Marshal Ayub Khan presented the approximately 80,000 Basic Democrats with the choice: "Have you confidence in President Field Marshal Mohammad Ayub Khan?" If he was "elected" (if a majority said "Yes"), he would then be empowered to make a constitution and to hold office for the first term under the constitution so drafted. Of the 80,000 Basic Democrats, 75,283, representing 95.6 percent of those voting, voted "Yes."[38] Voila, Pakistan had a president.

On December 20, 1984, Zia-ul-Haq followed suit, although his referendum question was a bit more complex and convoluted. Pakistani voters were asked, in keeping with Zia's then much-publicized Islamic agenda, to vote on the following question: "Whether the people of Pakistan endorse the process initiated by General Muhammad Zia-ul-Haq, the President of Pakistan, for bringing the laws of Pakistan in conformity with the Injunctions of Islam as laid down in the Holy Quran and *sunnah* of the Holy Prophet (PBUH) and for the preservation of the ideology of Pakistan, for the continuation and consolidation of that process, and for the smooth and orderly transfer of power to the elected representatives of the people."[39] When the votes were tallied, the Chief Election Commissioner announced that 62 percent of the electorate had cast their ballots and 97.7 percent of those had voted "Yes."[40] Pakistan had another president!

On May 1, 2002, Musharraf, not to be outdone, held a third referendum. This time, the Chief Executive asked the voters to elect Musharraf for a five-year term, to enable him to consolidate his "reforms and the reconstruction of institutions of state for the establishment of genuine and sustainable democracy, including the entrenchment of the local government systems, to ensure continued good governance for the welfare of the people, and to combat extremism and sectarianism."[41] Musharraf won handily, though he fell slightly short of the "margin of victory" of Zia; *only* 97.5 percent voted "Yes." However, it was reported by the Chief Election Commissioner, former Chief Justice Irshad Hasan Khan (who wrote the lead decision in the *Zafar Ali Shah v. Parvez Musharraf* case), that 71 percent of the electorate exercised their right of franchise by participating in the exercise.[42]

Of course, few, if any, have been fooled by the practice of staging presidential referenda. However, they have served their purpose. As if by magic, field marshals, generals, and chief executives have been transformed into presidents with none of the fuss of untidy electoral competition and the unpleasantness associated with opposition candidates.

STEP SIX: REINVENT LOCAL GOVERNMENT

Pakistan's system of local government has never been particularly robust. The British were far more concerned with governing their colony from the top down rather than developing grassroots democracy. Since independence, successive decision-makers have typically spent a good deal of time and political capital on constructing local governmental institutions, but their efforts have been reversed by successor regimes, who have typically seen merit in scrapping the structures of their predecessors and starting over again. There is a compelling rationale for this process. Namely, Pakistani decision-makers have seen the construction of local governmental institutions as a mechanism to enhance their respective regime's political authority and legitimacy. The main goal is not to develop representative or democratic institutions, nor to effectively govern, nor to deliver services more efficiently at the local level. Rather, the main goal of deconstruction and reconstruction of local government is linked to regime survival. To Pakistan's military leaders, the construction of local governmental institutions serves three functions: (1) to provide a source of patronage; (2) to open up an avenue for demonstrating the process of "democratization" and/or for holding "elections"; and (3) to serve as a mechanism to develop new and loyal political leaders who will challenge, if not replace, the existing political leadership. The task is to create friends and displace enemies.

Ayub Khan's scheme of Basic Democracies, introduced in 1959, is a case in point.[43] Ayub did not believe that Pakistan was ready for democracy. Therefore, the Basic Democracies program was designed to "teach democracy" from the grassroots. Under the BD program, local councils were constituted at the union, *tehsil/thana* (subdistrict), and district levels. Such councils were partially constituted by direct election, but above the union level a majority of each council's membership was appointed. The Basic Democrats also served as an electoral college for members of the provincial and national assemblies and the president. Ayub's government also introduced land reforms touted to reduce the power of landlords. The reforms placed ceilings on individual holdings of agricultural land, but most analysts agree that they were ineffective and were developed in part to target political opponents.[44] Basic Democracies was disestablished during the successor regime of Yahya Khan.

Zia-ul-Haq reintroduced local government by promulgating four provincial ordinances in 1979.[45] Like Basic Democracies, Zia established three tiers of local government in rural areas: (1) union councils—consisting of village(s); (2) *tehsil* committees; and (3) *zila* (district) councils. In urban areas, "town committees" were established for small towns, "municipal committees" for bigger towns, and "municipal corporations" for major cities. Elections based on universal adult suffrage were instituted to elect Muslim members of the union councils (80 percent of the total), while the remaining 20 percent of council seats were reserved for peasants (5 percent), workers (5 percent), tenants (5 percent), and women (5 percent). A chairman and vice-chairman were selected by the members of the respective union councils to serve as members of the *zila* (chairmen) and *tehsil* (vice-chairmen) councils. All elections were conducted on a political party-less basis. The duties of the councils were extensive, but their funding base was limited, with the bulk of their funds to be derived from federal and to a lesser extent provincial "awards." Also, similar to BD, Zia's "Local Bodies" system maintained overall control of the elected councils through relevant civil bureaucrats (federal and provincial), who served in various capacities within the councils. Unlike BD, Zia's system did not utilize the Basic Democrats as an electoral college. Elections to union councils/town committees were held in 1979, 1983, and 1987.

Zia's Local Bodies system well-served the three functions listed above: they created a vast source of patronage; provided ample scope for the staging of elections, albeit non-partisan; and, most importantly, served to develop new political leaders. Indeed, a majority of the Majlis-i-Shura appointed by Zia in 1985 had prior experience serving in Local Bodies. Also, the basis of the Islami Jamhoori Ittehad (IJI), the political party that became associated with Zia and Nawaz Sharif, drew most of its membership from those who had served in Local Bodies. As is the tradition, Zia's creation was allowed to die, a victim of malign neglect, during Benazir Bhutto's first term as prime minister.

Like his predecessors, General Musharraf saw merit in reviving a system of local government. But his intentions, at least originally, were far more ambitious. As early as October 17, 1999, Musharraf announced that one of his regime's top priorities was the "devolution of power to local government," and on November 16 he charged the high-powered National Reconstruction Bureau (NRB) with the task of developing an appropriate plan. The NRB took its mission quite seriously, releasing a draft proposal in May 2000.[46] The draft proposal was a remarkable document. Like Zia's LB and Ayub's BD, it called for the reestablishment of a three-tiered system of elected councils established at the union, *tehsil*, and *zila* levels. But, unlike the earlier programs, it suggested that such councils be given extensive authority, and comparable budgetary resources to address such additional responsibilities. Even more revolutionary, the plan called for the directly elected district "*nazims*" (mayors, or chairs, of *zila* councils) to be accorded authority to transfer or dismiss deputy commissioners (the top civil bureaucrats in the districts). It also called for the abandonment of the division level of the administrative system. Therefore, the Local Government Plan envisaged the reversal of the relationship between civil bureaucrats and elected politicians, a relationship that had been a dominant feature of local government in South Asia since the mid-nineteenth century. The LGP also called for a wholesale revision of the local governmental departments—creating new departments and eliminating or merging others. Moreover, it proposed significant revisions in the legal administration of the districts and subdistricts, and it also proposed to reserve one-half of all seats in the union councils for women. Nonetheless, it mandated that elections to the councils be held on a non-party basis.

During the next several months, some of the more radical features of the original LGP were worn away: (1) *nazims* were stripped of their prospective power to unilaterally transfer or dismiss recalcitrant DCs; (2) the election of *nazims* and *naib-nazims* (vice-mayors) was made indirect (such officials were to be elected by the members of the union councils); and (3) the reservation of posts for women in the union councils was reduced from 50 percent to 30 percent.[47] But the thrust of the reform remained intact. *Nazims* still maintained formal authority over civilian bureaucrats; district councils were provided additional funds to enable them to meet, at least partially, their expanded functions; district-level departments were significantly restructured; the division level of administration was abandoned; and women were elected, albeit indirectly, in unprecedented numbers to the union, *tehsil,* and *zila* councils. And the NRB promised additional policies which would lead to further devolution in the future.[48] The first elections to union councils were held on December 31, 2000; two subsequent phases of elections were completed by May 2001. Elections for *nazims* and *naib-nazims* were completed in July 2001.[49]

The fate of the LGP and the more recently proposed "Devolution Plan" is uncertain. The implementation of the latter directly challenges the vested interests of members of Pakistan's provincial and national assemblies; and the LGP is deeply resented by Pakistan's senior bureaucracy (particularly the members of the All-Pakistan Unified Grades). Nevertheless, the NRB won a significant battle when the Seventeenth Amendment was passed by the National Assembly in early January 2004. The latter amendment validated actions taken by Musharraf's government, including the LGP and the Legal Framework Order (LFO).

STEP SEVEN: INTIMIDATE THE CIVIL BUREAUCRACY AND THE SUPERIOR JUDICIARY

With politicians effectively weakened by the actions of the coupmakers— leaders exiled or worse, political parties banned, assemblies dissolved, etc.— the only remaining challenge to the authority of the military dictators was the civilian bureaucracy and the courts. But, unlike the services of politicians, which can be dispensed with, military governments need the services of bureaucrats and judges. The task, therefore, was more subtle—to intimidate not eliminate.

Ayub worked very closely with the civil bureaucracy, continuing a tradition that pre-dated independence. Most favored and important were the members of the Civil Service of Pakistan (CSP), the premier cadre of the bureaucracy. Officers of the CSP came to dominate virtually all aspects of Pakistan's government during Ayub's tenure. Indeed, CSP officers constituted the overwhelming majority of Ayub's political and administrative advisors. Accordingly, attempts to reform the bureaucracy, most notably the Pay and Services Commission chaired by Justice A. R. Cornelius (1959–62),[50] were successfully thwarted by the machinations of the CSP. For instance, the "Cornelius Report" was kept confidential and not released (and then it was classified) in 1969. During the course of the Disturbances in 1968–69 which led to the departure of Ayub, the Pakistani bureaucracy, and particularly its elite cadres, were targeted as corrupt and responsible for the breakdown of civil order. After Yahya Khan displaced Ayub in 1969, one of his first acts was to dismiss ("purge") 303 Class I officers of the bureaucracy—38 were members of the CSP and 78 were members of the Central Superior Services. Such a widespread purge was unprecedented and violated the well-established principle of the insulation of the bureaucracy from political control.[51]

Ayub was also favorably disposed to the judiciary. Ayub's constitutional reengineering was never seriously challenged by the courts. And the 1962 Constitution, largely a product of former Chief Justice Muhammad Shahabuddin, provided for a powerful and independent judiciary.[52]

Like Ayub, Zia did not target the civil bureaucracy directly—as had his predecessors Yahya Khan and Z. A. Bhutto.[53] But Zia extended and institutionalized the practice of military recruitment to the civil bureaucracy. In 1980, he established a 10 percent reservation of posts for retired or released military personnel in entry-level (BPS grades 17 and 18) and officer-level ranks of the bureaucracy. Such military recruits became regular members of the bureaucracy. Similarly, he introduced a reservation of 10 percent for military lateral recruitment to senior bureaucratic ranks (BPS grades 19 and above) on a three- to five-year contractual basis.[54] These policies have been continued, although the quotas have not always been filled, by each successive Pakistani government. The effects of such institutionalized military recruitment have been profound. Since Zia's initiative, retired or released military officers have become a regular part of the civilian bureaucracy, thereby directly challenging the autonomy and the career prospects of its officers. Members of the civil bureaucracy have greatly resented this intrusion into their domain.

Zia-ul-Haq's policies of intimidation were even more extensive and creative with respect to the judiciary. We have already chronicled how Zia deftly abrogated the Fifth and Sixth Amendments of the 1973 Constitution, reversing the unpopular policies of Z. A. Bhutto, and allowing Anwar-ul-

Haq to become Chief Justice. Zia was rewarded with a favorable decision in the *Nusrat Bhutto v. Chief of Army Staff* case. Zia stayed formally aloof from the Bhutto trial, but the opportunity presented to the judiciary—to stand in judgment over a prime minister who had done all in his power to weaken the judiciary—apparently proved too difficult for the superior judiciary to resist. The bizarre conviction and execution of Bhutto did incalculable damage to Pakistan's superior judiciary and made them subsequently an easy target for Zia. Following Z. A. Bhutto's trial, Zia's government went out of its way to harass and humiliate the judiciary. In 1979, Zia established military courts, which were placed beyond the jurisdiction of the regular courts. Subsequent Martial Law Orders prohibited the Supreme Court from entertaining appeals against the decisions of such courts. Also in 1979, the establishment of the Federal Shariat Court served to reduce the jurisdiction of the High Courts. In 1980, Zia started the practice of "punishment promotions." The Federal Shariat Court, situated above the High Courts, became a dumping ground for High Court judges who ran afoul of Zia.[55] Zia also introduced the practice of the rapid transfer of judges from posting to posting—the latter made particularly threatening when Zia established "permanent benches" of the High Courts in inconvenient locations.[56] In effect, judges were placed under the chronic threat of being transferred from Lahore or Karachi to remote locations like Dera Ishmail Khan or Sukkur. Finally, after introducing the Provisional Constitution Order in 1981, Zia forced superior court judges to take a fresh oath of office under the terms of the PCO, occasioning the early retirement of several judges.[57]

Zia's policies worked. The superior judiciary did not pose a significant deterrent to Zia's bold constitutional changes. He was able to wholly change Pakistan's constitutional structure, as we will see, with hardly a cautionary whimper from the superior judiciary.

One of Musharraf's first acts after assuming office was to assign standing military officers to "shadow" the activities of civilian bureaucrats. Musharraf's actions were justified as part of this accountability process—designed to reduce corruption. But their immediate effect was to demonstrate who was boss, to intimidate the officers of the civil bureaucracy. Far more significant than this to civil bureaucratic–military relations has been the Local Government Plan. The LGP gives the elected district *nazims* effective authority over district commissioners. The LGP also dissolved the administrative tier of the division. Both actions directly challenged the domain of Pakistan's federal bureaucracy, and particularly the District Management Group, the lineal descendent of the CSP. Also, Musharraf significantly increased the number of former military officers recruited to the civilian bureaucracy, filling the military recruitment quotas which had been established by Zia, but which had remained unfilled during the civilian interregnum.[58]

Also, quite early on, Musharraf showed the judiciary who was in charge by forcing superior court judges to take a fresh oath of office under the PCO. In this, he was most likely inspired by Zia's 1981 oath-taking exercise. Musharraf's actions served to factionalize the courts and considerably weakened their prospective opposition to Musharraf's constitutional engineering. *Zafar Ali Shah v. Parvez Musharraf* was decided by a court which consisted of judges who had taken the PCO oath. On January 1, 2003, Musharraf provided a further ground for discord within the superior courts by enforcing provisions of the Legal Framework Order (LFO—October 10, 2002), which had heretofore not been enforced, under which the retirement age of superior court judges was raised from sixty-five to sixty-eight years of age. The immediate effect of such changes extended the terms of all fourteen members of the Supreme Court, including the term of the then-current Chief Justice Sheikh Riaz Ahmed, who had been due to retire in March 2003. The enforcement of the provision also extended the terms of the standing judges of the four high courts and the Federal Shariat Court (FSC). Musharraf's actions could be interpreted as a transparent attempt to influence the outcome of the cases pending against the constitutionality of the LFO. Put simply, if the Supreme Court ruled that the LFO was unconstitutional, many standing judges of the superior judiciary, including the then Chief Justice of the Supreme Court, would stand retired and all superior court judges would lose three years of their prospective tenure.[59] Further, it could be argued that similar considerations may have played a role in the Supreme Court's (Shariat Appellate Bench) ruling in *United Bank, Ltd. v. Farooq Brothers* (2002), remanding the issue of prohibition of *riba* (financial interest) back to the FSC.[60] Significantly, this has effectively derailed the government's obligation to implement interest-free banking in the state.

Paradoxically, however, one of the provisions of the LFO abandoned by the Musharraf government (ostensibly as part of the "deal" with the opposition to gain passage of the Seventeenth Amendment) was to effectively "rescind" the "revision" of Article 179, which had raised the retirement age of superior court judges by three years.[61] Consequently, three judges of the

Supreme Court (Chief Justice Sheikh Riaz Ahmed, Justice Munir A. Sheikh, and Justice Qazi Muhammad Farooq) stood retired. Obviously, this process has humiliated Pakistan's superior judiciary.

STEP EIGHT: REWRITE THE CONSTITUTION

If one has successfully accomplished steps 1–7, it is time to address the actual purpose of the elaborate exercise—to construct a new constitutional system. All three of our coupmakers gave birth to a new system.

Ayub Khan went about the process of constitution-making deliberately and systematically. His task was simpler than that which faced his successors, in that he had abrogated the 1956 Constitution and could start over again with impunity. Accordingly, in February 1960, he appointed a Constitution Commission chaired by former Chief Justice Muhammad Shahauddin. The commission deliberated until April 1961, submitting their report to President Ayub.[62] Subsequently, Ayub appointed a drafting committee headed by Manzoor Qadir to put together the actual draft of the Constitution, which was finally approved on March 1, 1962.

The features of this Constitution have already been touched upon above, but it is important to note that Ayub Khan had the ultimate authority to accept or reject the terms of the Constitution throughout. Indeed, the most significant change which Ayub made to the Constitution Commission's recommendations was with respect to the method of elections. The Constitution Commission had called for the direct election of the president and National Assembly through a restricted adult franchise. The 1962 Constitution replaced direct elections with an electoral college consisting of the Basic Democrats.

Zia's rewriting of Pakistan's Constitution was far more complex and confused. This was partially owing to the fact that Zia, unlike Ayub, could not abrogate the Constitution and start from scratch. Therefore, he rewrote the Constitution in bits and pieces. New Islamic provisions, which brought about, inter alia, the creation of the Federal Shariat Court and the Shariat Appellate Bench of the Supreme Court, were introduced by a series of Presidential Ordinances promulgated between 1979 and 1984.[63] On August 12, 1983, Zia made his constitutional plans known in an address before the Majlis-i-Shura. His plans called for the "restoration" of the 1973 Constitution, but such a restoration would introduce a presidential-dominant form of government, in which the president would be empowered to appoint the prime minister, the chiefs of the armed services, the chief election commissioner, and the provincial governors. The president would also be empowered to dissolve the National Assembly. Zia also imagined the creation of a National Security Council.[64] These ideas were later incorporated into the Revival of Constitution Order (RCO) in 1985.[65]

Musharraf drew inspiration from both Ayub and Zia in his process of constitutional reengineering. Like Zia, Musharraf was confined within the parameters of maintaining the 1973 Constitution; like Ayub, Musharraf undertook his self-assigned task of constitutional revision systematically. Throughout, Musharraf has relied on his curious creation, the National Reconstruction Bureau (NRB), to formulate constitutional change. The NRB, as we have seen, also formulated the Local Government Plan and the Devolution Plans. It also produced the two-part "Conceptual Framework of Proposals of the Government of Pakistan on the Establishment of Sustainable Federal Democracy" in June–July 2002,[66] which formed the basis of the Legal Framework Order, 2002. The LFO suggests the following changes:

1. Establishment of Musharraf as president for five years;
2. An increase in the number of seats in the national and provincial assemblies;
3. An increase in the number of seats reserved for women and minorities in the national and provincial assemblies;
4. Placement of additional restrictions which could serve to disqualify would-be candidates to the national and provincial assemblies;
5. Establishment of a National Security Council;
6. Reestablishment of the power of the president to dissolve the National Assembly; and of the governors to dissolve the provincial assemblies;
7. Validation of all laws and actions taken by the government under Chief Executive Musharraf (this would include the Local Government Ordinances, the Accountability Ordinance, and the Political Parties Act). [67]

Most of these provisions were incorporated into the Seventeenth Amendment in January 2004.

STEP NINE: ORCHESTRATE ELECTIONS

With plans for constitutional reform formulated, the next step is to validate these plans—to have them endorsed officially by a competent authority. But, given the fact that the relevant competent authority (the National Assembly) has been dissolved, it is imperative to create competent authorities—that is, to hold elections.

As we have seen, Ayub, owing to his abrogation of the 1956 Constitution and the 1960 referendum, was *the* competent authority to accept the 1962 Constitution. There was no necessity to hold elections.

Zia needed to stage elections. The Majlis-i-Shura, Zia's creation, had been appointed by Zia in late 1982, but it had no real legislative function and no political legitimacy. Accordingly, following the 1984 referendum which had "elected" Zia president, Zia announced that elections would be held for the national and provincial assemblies in February 1985. The elections were to be held on a nonpartisan (party-less) basis. Candidates with partisan affiliations were prohibited from contesting the elections. The PPP and other political parties boycotted the elections. Nevertheless, the turnout was relatively high. Those elected to the 1985 National Assembly, by the very nature of their candidacy, were deemed to be generally supportive of Zia's regime—by definition, they did not belong to any political party, thus did not constitute an opposition.

With a friendly National Assembly in place, Zia placed the RCO of 1985 before that body for incorporation into the Constitution. The National Assembly complied with the passage of the Eighth Amendment. Virtually the entire text of the RCO was incorporated into the Constitution accordingly. However, two important departures from the RCO, perhaps a result of compromise, were embedded in the Eighth Amendment. First, the president's power to dissolve the National Assembly was made conditional. Before the president could dissolve the National Assembly, he was obliged to be convinced that the government could not carry out actions in accordance with the Constitution, and that following dissolution he would be obliged to hold fresh elections within ninety days. Second, the provision for the creation of the National Security Council was dropped.

Musharraf's position was even more problematic than Zia's. The *Zafar Ali Shah v. Parvez Musharraf* case had validated the 1999 PCO, but it had conditioned its acceptance upon the understanding that Musharraf would hold elections within three years of the coup (October 12, 2002). Also, Musharraf, for reasons yet partly unclear, had announced as early as August 2001 that prospective elections to the national and provincial assemblies would be held on a partisan basis.[68] Therefore, unlike his predecessors, the outcome of the prospective election was not a foregone conclusion.

Of course, Musharraf and his ever-creative NRB were not without re-sources. The NRB introduced the Political Parties Ordinance, 2002,[69] which redefined the electoral rules of the game to favor an appropriate outcome. First, it extended the scope of provisions that disqualified those who were under investigation or who had been implicated by the National Account-ability Bureau. The latter institution is a creation of, and is controlled by, Musharraf. Second, it required political parties to develop a party manifesto (a time-consuming and divisive exercise) before being deemed eligible to contest the election. But, more creatively, the NRB established educational requirements for those seeking political office. Would-be candidates for the national or provincial assemblies would now have to possess a bachelor's de-gree or its equivalent. Of course, the target of the latter were the numerous standing politicians, particularly from the PPP who did not possess the req-uisite qualifications. It is also important to note that the issuance of the Po-litical Parties Ordinance, in late June 2002, and the requirement to hold elections by October 12, placed a severe time constraint on political parties to comply with the regulations in order to contest the elections. Musharraf's government also successfully resisted the return of the Bhuttos and the Shar-ifians to Pakistan's political scene.

Musharraf's goal throughout was to ensure an outcome in which no one party would dominate and in which political parties that supported Musharraf would be able to form the government. The results of the elec-tion challenged Musharraf's goals, but the outcomes seem to have ultimately served his policy interests. Most surprising was the unexpected success of the MMA (the Muttahida Majlis-e-Amal—a six-party alliance of religious par-ties), which secured the third-largest batch of seats in the National Assem-bly; and which was able to gain a plurality in the NWFP. Also surprising was the strong showing of the PPP, despite the absence of Benazir Bhutto. Shortly after the election, but before the National Assembly was convened, Musharraf took an oath of office as President under the terms of the LFO.

Finally, on November 21, 2002, a government was formed by Mir Za-farullah Khan Jamali, Pakistan's first Baloch prime minister. Jamali is a member of the Pakistan Muslim League (Quaid-i-Azam)—a party deemed loyal to Musharraf. His coalition consisted of the PML-Q, numerous small parties, and ten defectors from the PPP, the so-called "Forward Bloc."

The reconstituted Parliament, however, found itself deeply divided over the appropriate approach to take regarding the validity of Musharraf's system and the constitutionality of the LFO. Indeed, for thirteen months (November 2002–January 2004), the activities of the National Assembly and Senate were characterized by chronic and frequent protests, walkouts, planned disturbances, and other unpleasantness occasioned by the opposition's claims that the LFO had no constitutional standing until and if the Parliament passed relevant legislation. However, the government's "hole card" was that the general election of 2002 had been conducted under the terms of various provisions of the LFO. Therefore, MPs were ultimately caught in the web of a carefully crafted Catch 22—if the parliamentarians decided that the LFO was unconstitutional, then the election which had brought them to power would, as a consequence, be null and void. Some compromise was inevitable in such a situation, although the "negotiations" with the opposition proved far more difficult for Musharraf and Jamali to accomplish than had been Zia's and Junejo's experience with introducing the Eighth Amendment. But when the dust finally settled, Musharraf and Jamali had convinced the MMA to "support" (in reality, to abstain from countering) a creative package solution of constitutional revisions which, among other things, kept the Jamali government in power and avoided a constitutional meltdown. The main features of the compromise were: Musharraf would be obliged to relinquish his position as Chief of Army Staff (COAS) by the end of 2004 (Musharraf has since backed away from this commitment); plans for the creation of a National Security Council would be scrapped; and the extension of the tenure of superior court judges (see above) would be abandoned. In exchange for these "concessions" by the government, the MMA would begrudgingly endorse (abstain from opposing) provisions of the LFO, including:

1. the reintroduction of the power of the president and governors to respectively dismiss the national and provincial assemblies;
2. the confirmation of Musharraf's election as president for five years; and
3. the confirmation of the general election of 2002 and the creation of the Jamali government.

The crowning achievement of the "deal" was the blanket endorsement of Musharraf's actions taken since assuming office in October 1999. The revised Article 270AA of the amended Constitution reads:

> All orders made, proceedings taken, appointments made, including secondments and deputations, and acts done by any authority, or by any person, which were made, taken or done, or purported to have been made, taken or done, between

the twelfth day of October 1999, and the date on which this Article comes into force (both days inclusive), in the exercise of the powers derived from any Proclamation, President's Orders, Ordinances, Chief Executive's Orders, enactments, including amendments in the Constitution, notifications, rules, orders, by-laws or in execution of or in compliance with any orders made or sentences passed by any authority in the exercise or purported exercise of powers as aforesaid, shall notwithstanding any judgment of any court, be deemed to be and always to have been validly made, taken or done and shall not be called in question in any court or forum on any ground whatsoever.[70]

STEP TEN: IMPLEMENT THE SYSTEM

However effective Pakistan's coupmakers have been at seizing power, subverting respective constitutions, and establishing new constitutional structures, they have been signal failures at institutionalizing the systems they have introduced with such effort and cost.

Ayub's attempts at institutionalization of his constitutional system were particularly awkward. The 1962 Constitution mandated that national and provincial assemblies be elected indirectly by the Basic Democrats. Accordingly, such institutions were established in June 1962, formally terminating martial law. Ayub's intent was not to significantly transfer power or authority to the newly constituted legislature but rather to maintain control through his well-developed system of civil–military authoritarianism. But Ayub's plans were foiled by the interests of politicians, even if selected indirectly, serving in the assemblies.

Accordingly, Ayub was forced to reluctantly accept the legalization of political parties, banned since the 1958 coup, through the passage of the Political Parties Act of 1962, in July. With the lid lifted on political party activity, political parties were reconvened and Ayub was "forced" to become involved and later to become president of his own political party—the "Conventionist" Muslim League. Despite such developments, however, political activity within Pakistan remained highly controlled, the press muzzled, and political opposition subject to significant restrictions. But Ayub's carefully crafted authoritarian system would eventually unravel.

Under the terms of Ayub's Constitution, presidential elections were mandated to be held within five years of the incumbent's assumption of office. Therefore, Ayub, who had been elected president in 1960 (see above), was required to seek reelection in 1965. The 80,000 Basic Democrats would serve as an electoral college for the selection of the president. Ayub's political opponents decided to join forces to contest the election, forming an umbrella group, the Combined Opposition Party (COP). The COP nominated Fatima Jinnah, Mohammad Ali Jinnah's sister, to head their party and to contest the election. The ultimate outcome of the election was a foregone conclusion—Ayub could not lose, given the nature of the indirect electoral process, the nature and self-interests of the Basic Democrats, and Ayub's profound "incumbent advantages." But Fatima Jinnah and the COP did extraordinarily well. Ayub prevailed, receiving 49,951 votes to Jinnah's 28,691.[71] More important than this electoral outcome, however, were the long-term consequences for the Ayubian system. The COP claimed that the election had been rigged, both structurally, owing to the nature of the indirect electoral process, and physically, by vote-buying and tampering. Although Ayub had won the election, the legitimacy of his system had been significantly undermined.

Subsequent to this election and until Ayub's resignation from office on March 25, 1969, Ayub's regime came under increasing pressure, both international and domestic. The misadventure of the Pakistan Army's "Operation Gibraltar" (see chapter by Rifaat Hussain), the resultant disaster of the 1965 war with India, and the humiliating Tashkent Agreement did irreparable harm to Ayub's stature as a statesman and emboldened domestic opposition. The growing secessionist sentiment within East Pakistan, as evidenced by Sheikh Mujib's Six Points, and Ayub's ill-conceived ruse of introducing the Agartala Conspiracy case, further weakened the government. But the Disturbances of 1968–69 proved to be the final straw that broke the government's back.[72]

For our purposes, what is important to note is that after Ayub resigned his carefully crafted system was easily and perhaps carelessly abandoned by his military successor. General Yahya Khan, the Chief of Army Staff who assumed power following Ayub's resignation, promulgated his own Legal Framework Order on March 28, 1970, which savaged the Ayubian system: (1) it disestablished the Basic Democrats; (2) it replaced One Unit in West Pakistan by establishing four provinces; and (3) it mandated direct popular elections under universal adult suffrage for the national and provincial elections.[73] In retrospect, Yahya's actions were perhaps the most ill-considered of all of Pakistan's LFOs: direct elections to the National Assembly were a certain recipe for the horrors of the civil war and the eventual dismemberment of the state.

Zia's constitutional system proved even more short-lived. To Zia, his selection of Muhammad Khan Junejo as prime minister in 1985, to preside
over the National Assembly, did not signal a transfer of power from the military to a civilian government. The RCO had "restored" the Constitution
but it had left Zia, as president, in charge (see above). But, as was the case
with Ayub's indirectly elected National Assembly, the best-laid plans of Pakistan's coupmakers can come unglued.

In short, Prime Minister Junejo took his role seriously, and his growing
independence from presidential (read military) dominance spelled his
downfall. The example of Junejo's "negotiation" with Zia, which resulted in
the revision of the RCO (the Eighth Amendment) curtailing the establishment of the National Security Council has already been cited. More importantly, Junejo encouraged the emergence of parliamentary groupings reflecting different political affiliations in open defiance of Zia's ban on political
parties. Also, Junejo proved none too eager to advance Zia's Islamic agenda,
nor to press for the passage of a Shariah bill in the National Assembly.[74] But
the immediate cause of Zia's decision to invoke Article 58(2)(b) and to dissolve the National Assembly seems to have been provided by Junejo's unwillingness to halt the National Assembly's investigation into the Ojheri
army munitions depot explosions. Such investigations would prove embar-
rassing to the military. In any case, on May 29, 1988, Zia issued an order dissolving the National Assembly and called upon the four respective provincial governors to follow suit in the provinces.

Zia did not fear that his order would be challenged. The framers of the
1985 RCO had consciously and thoroughly introduced a text that established a presidential-dominant system. Zia had been elected as president of
that system before the RCO was formulated. Clearly, Zia's 1988 dissolution
order was made by a chief executive confident of his powers, firm in his belief that his office and person were unassailable. One can speculate as to
what Zia's next act would have been. He was contemplating adopting another set of constitutional reforms which, if implemented, would have significantly altered Pakistan's federal structure.[75] If this had transpired, it
would have likely required new elections and a new electoral system. But
fate intervened. On August 17, Zia was assassinated. His death precipitated
a constitutional crisis of epic proportions. Pakistan was left without a president, prime minister, National Assembly, chief ministers, and provincial assemblies. The Chairman of the Senate (the Senate was not subject to disso-

lution by the president), Ghulam Ishaq Khan, was mandated by the Constitution to assume the post of president. His first official act was to schedule elections for the national and provincial assemblies.

The death of Zia effectively ended his constitutional system. Political parties were allowed to openly contest the ensuing general elections; prime ministers gained increasing authority; the military returned to the barracks.

Musharraf's current efforts can be viewed as an attempt to return to Zia's constitutional system. Musharraf has presided over the election of what he hopes will be a docile National Assembly, with a cooperative prime minister. Musharraf hopes to be able to exercise a veto power over the outcomes of the political process. But, of course, there is considerable uncertainty whether Musharraf's wishes will be fulfilled. There are many differences between Musharraf's and Zia's political situations. First, the 2002 National Assembly was elected along partisan lines—the MNA's have individual constituencies and are organized along party lines. Second, although Musharraf won a resounding victory through the passage of the Seventeenth Amendment validating his system, he still faces a very contentious National Assembly and Senate. The "alliance" between PML-Q and the MMA is likely to be short-lived and/or the MMA will insist on conditions for continued cooperation with the government which will prove very difficult for the government to accept. And the PML-N and the PPP are likely to remain wholly opposed to the government, with little to lose if they continue their disruptive opposition tactics. Third, the civilian interregnum that followed Zia's death (1988–97) established constraints, albeit flexible, on the authority of the president to dissolve elected assemblies. The threshold for the exercise of the president's power to dissolve the government of an independent-minded prime minister or fractious National Assembly is much higher in 2005 that it was when Zia faced a recalcitrant Prime Minister Junejo. Fourth, the government faces an extremely difficult international situation—the war in Afghanistan continues; relations with India remain fragile and dangerous; and the so-called Global War Against Terrorism continues to complicate Pakistan's foreign policy options. Moreover, Musharraf, like Zia, has many enemies—some of them armed.

At the time of this writing, the health of Musharraf's newly-born political system is at best fragile; the prognosis for its survival still uncertain.

Caveats and a Reluctant Conclusion

Before offering a conclusion, I have three caveats with the foregoing analysis. First is the obvious omission of foreign policy from considerations of the military-governance paradigm. Pakistan's military leaders have been more enthusiastically wedded to seeking the support of the international community (read U.S.) than their civilian counterparts. This is an important, perhaps crucial, policy consideration of Pakistan's coupmakers. I have ignored it here, as I deemed it beyond the scope of this exercise. Second, by focusing on the ten steps of the Pakistan *military*-governance paradigm, I did not mean to imply that Pakistan's civilian leaders had not engaged in similar strategies of regime survival. Perhaps this exercise should/could be revised to include the Bhuttos and Sharifians? Finally, I want to disabuse the reader of the notion that the actions of Pakistan's three military leaders have been solely motivated by cynical considerations of regime survival. Each of the three martial law regimes—Ayub's, Zia's, and Musharraf's—have significantly and sincerely engaged in the attempt to address issues of "governance" of the state. One can certainly have differences with the nature of their visions—but it is hard to find fault with the depth of their efforts. For instance, as Braibanti so meticulously demonstrated, Ayub empowered thirty-four separate commissions of inquiry between 1958 and 1964, each produced at least one report, and some of the reports still stand as definitive on their respective topic.[76] Similarly, Zia's attempts to bring Pakistan's laws into conformance with the injunctions of Islam produced an extraordinary scholarship, centered on the decisions of the superior judiciary. Finally, one has to be an admirer of the National Reconstruction Bureau. Its voluminous writings represent a very significant and serious attempt to come to grips with Pakistan's seemingly insoluble problems of governance. No comparable attempts at addressing Pakistan's political dilemmas have been undertaken by any of Pakistan's civilian regimes.

Reluctantly, I offer the following conclusion. Pakistan's failure to develop a stable constitutional system is the fault of both Pakistan's military and civilian leadership. There is plenty of blame to go around. Clearly, constitutional stability can only be achieved if there is an accommodation between the interests of the two sets of actors. Neither the corporate interests of the military nor the ideological interests and representational proclivities of political parties can be ignored in such an accommodation—neither side can be allowed to win. Given this, tidy and well-defined constitutional systems that provide no constitutional role for the military (such as Nawaz Sharif's post–Thirteenth Amendment system), or no scope for political party activity (such as Zia's RCO), cannot hope to provide long-lasting solutions to Pakistan's constitutional dilemma. Rather, what is needed are untidy constitutional accommodations, accommodations in which neither the military nor the political parties "wins" or "loses," but in which the interests of both are partially accommodated.

Pakistan stumbled upon, perhaps invented, such a system during the civilian interregnum of 1988–97—a system that can best be typified as the "58(2)(b) system." The system was based upon the 1973 Constitution, as modified by the RCO and the Eighth Amendment. In this system, the civilian president (Ghulam Ishaq Khan; Farooq Leghari) was empowered as had been the late Zia-ul-Haq to dissolve the National Assembly under Article 58(2)(b). But, unlike Zia's system, which envisaged untrammeled authority for the president, the 58(2)(b) system as it developed placed the burden of proof for the dismissal of a government on the shoulders of a civilian president. Such presidents typically had the backing of the military, but they had to show clear and convincing evidence of why they had to take the extreme action of dismissing an elected government. The referee between the president and the prime minister was the Supreme Court. Four dismissals of the National Assembly and their respective prime ministers occurred during this period—Zia of Junejo, G. I. Khan of Benazir Bhutto, G. I. Khan of Nawaz Sharif, and Farooq Leghari of Benazir Bhutto. The Supreme Court upheld the two dismissals of Benazir Bhutto; took issue with Zia's dismissal of Junejo but let it stand for want of a political remedy; and overturned G. I. Khan's dismissal of Nawaz Sharif.[77] Coupled with the attendant and numerous dismissals of provincial assemblies, the system was anything but tidy. *But*, the constitutional system had the merit of keeping the military in the barracks, *and* provided some degree of accountability to civilian governments. The system was dealt a fatal blow when Nawaz Sharif's PML was able to win a two-thirds majority in the 1997 election and was consequently able to amend the Constitution by passing the Thirteenth Amendment. Following the passage of the Thirteenth Amendment, the only recourse for the military, if its corporate interests were violated, was a military coup—hence, the unfortunate events of October 1999.

Perhaps the reintroduction of an idealized version of 58(2)(b) is a viable alternative to Pakistan's tortured constitutional history? Ideally, in such a system the president would be a duly-elected civilian; the superior courts would be free from political interference in undertaking their responsibility as referees of the process; and the president would be loathe to exercise his authority except in extreme cases. However flawed such a system may be, it seems preferable to the continuance of Pakistan's military-governance paradigm.

Ultimately, the stakes of establishing a stable constitutional order in Pakistan continue to rise. Settling this issue is a crucial precondition for addressing the numerous domestic problems and shortcomings facing the state. It is also crucial if Pakistan is to find a suitable accommodation with its neighbors. Pakistan's inability to settle its long-standing constitutional crisis continues to poison its dealings with India, and consequently remains an impediment to promoting peace in the region.

FOUR

The Practice of Islam in Pakistan and the Influence of Islam on Pakistani Politics

C. Christine Fair and Karthik Vaidyanathan

Introduction

Speculation about the trends in the practice of Islam among the Pakistani polity and the influence of Islam upon Pakistani politics has been rife, particularly in the wake of September 11, 2001, and the decision of President Musharraf to support the U.S.-led war on terrorism. Yet, little of what has been written about Pakistan is based upon empirical studies of Islam and politics. Rather, much that has been written has been based upon qualitative research methods or upon content analysis of Pakistani publications.

Both methods, while valuable, have specific shortcomings. Researchers employing these methods have little means of defining the representativeness of their findings. Those who rely upon a close reading of the Pakistani popular press are confronted with a myriad of challenges based upon the nature of the Pakistani press. At one extreme are those papers that are published in English. They are consumed by an English-literate elite, and the views that such papers espouse may not reflect the sentiments of the Pakistani populace at large. At the other extreme are the copious vernacular papers that also reflect the niche preferences of their constituents. The quality of journalism inherent in these vernacular publications is widely regarded as suspect and the publications as popular fonts of disinformation. What is conspicuously absent in Pakistan is a popular press that captures the sentiment of the wide-ranging Pakistani populace.

This paper will augment the body of literature of Islam in Pakistan and the influence of Islam upon Pakistani politics by drawing upon three recent surveys conducted by three different organizations.[1] This effort has four objectives. First, it will explore Pakistani religious commitments. Second, it will identify trends in support for religious and militant organizations. Third, it will assess public support for reform efforts undertaken by the Musharraf regime. Fourth, it will untangle the dual trends of changing religious propensity and anti-U.S. sentiment.

These empirical findings will be augmented with interviews conducted by one of the authors in Pakistan in January 2003 with serving and retired Pakistani generals and other officers, think-tank analysts, politicians, journalists, and U.S. consular personnel in Islamabad and Lahore.

In the next section, the three data sources will be described and critiqued. In the third section, we present the empirical findings. The fourth section discusses the empirical findings and synthesizes them with interview data and the literature. Finally, we conclude with a discussion of future directions.

Data and Methodology

THE SURVEYS

This paper employs data from three different surveys conducted by the Gallup Organization, the *Herald* (Karachi), and by the U.S. Department of State.

Gallup Poll

The Gallup Poll was fielded in nine countries in December 2001 and January 2002 (see Figure 4.1). The sample size across these nine states was 10,004. Of these, 2,043 were from Pakistan. The percentage of Christian respondents in the Gallup Lebanese sample was very different from the percentage of Christians in the Lebanese population base. Whereas 57 percent of the Gallup Lebanese sample was Muslim and 43 percent Christian, 70 percent of the Lebanese population is Muslim and 30 percent are Christian.[2] Rather than constructing weights to account for this distributional difference between the sample composition and the overall population, we divided the Lebanon sample into Muslim and Christian groups for purposes of analysis.

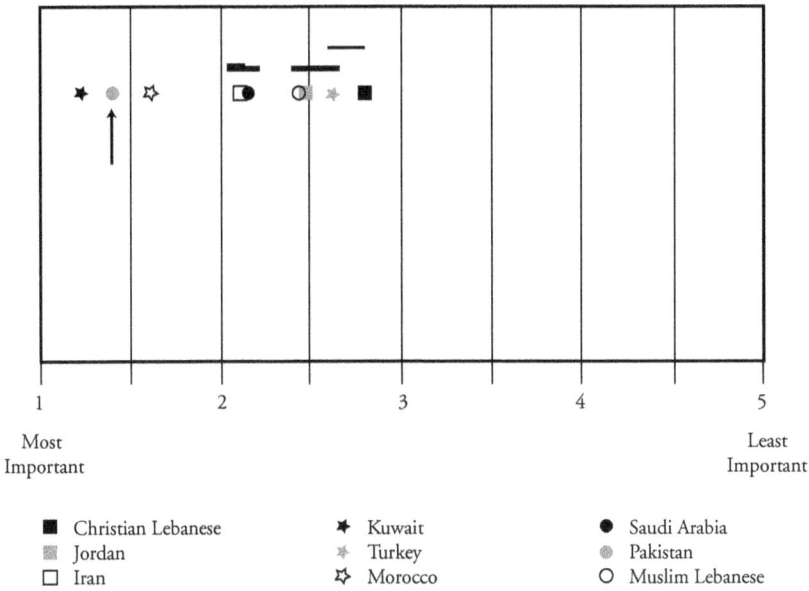

1	2	3	4	5
Most Important				Least Important

■ Christian Lebanese	✳ Kuwait	● Saudi Arabia
▨ Jordan	✴ Turkey	◉ Pakistan
□ Iran	✪ Morocco	○ Muslim Lebanese

FIGURE 4.1. Where does religion rank among these five things: family, extended family, country, self, and religion?

Therefore, in our analyses, we present findings from ten groups (two of which are from Lebanon).

According to the Gallup Organization, the sample design of the survey seeks to measure the opinions of the entire national population of each country. To achieve this, the in-country samples were derived using a multistage probability sampling technique. The first stage is comprised of selecting primary sampling units (PSUs), which are the main locations where the interviews are conducted. Notably, individual PSUs were selected from each urban and rural stratum, and, where possible, further stratified by other socioeconomic and demographic variables (for example, educational attainment and household income). To ensure that the survey samples conform to their respective national population distributions, undersampled rural areas were weighted upward.

Other stages in the sample design were devised to contend with possible biases in the selection of the households and the selection of household members. The Gallup Organization maintains that as a result of the way in which the samples were drawn and weighted, the poll results should represent the entire population of adults (aged eighteen and above) resident in the given country at the time of the interview. It is important to note that the Gallup Organization did not employ citizenship screens or screens for religion (thus the problem with the Lebanese sample). This may be particularly disconcerting for the Gulf states, given that a large percentage of their population is comprised of expatriates from South and Southeast Asia. The overall sample is given below.

Pakistan	2,043
Iran	1,501
Indonesia	1,050
Turkey	1,019
Lebanon	1,050
Morocco	1,000
Kuwait	790
Jordan	797
Saudi Arabia	754
Total Sample	10,004

Source: Gallup Organization, "The 2002 Gallup Poll of the Islamic World?" http://www.gallup.com/poll/summits/islam.asp (accessed March 12, 2003). In some countries (for example, Saudi Arabia and Indonesia), some questions were not included in the survey variant fielded for those countries. As a consequence, the countries represented for specific questions may vary.[3]

Herald Survey

The second source of data is the reported findings of a poll commissioned by the *Herald,* a news publication based in Karachi, and conducted by Oasis International Pakistan. This poll was conducted in two days (January 27 and 28, 2002). The poll included 1,239 urban respondents, of whom 634 were female. According to the description of the sampling methodology, a "stratified disproportionate sampling" was used to ensure that individuals from all socioeconomic groups were included.[4] (Had the sample been proportionately drawn on the basis of representation, there would have been relatively few respondents from higher income brackets.) The survey team included fifty-six male and fifty-six female interviewees. This enabled the survey team to conduct same-sex interviews within the respondents' homes in a standardized in-person format.

The sample is nearly evenly distributed between men and women, drawn across four age groups (18–24, 25–34, 35–44, and 45–64) and from four socioeconomic groups defined by income, profession, work experience, and education. The sample reportedly is representative of Pakistan's primary urban centers, such as Karachi and Larkana (Sindh), Lahore, Multan, and Rawalpindi-Islamabad (Punjab), Quetta (Baluchistan), and Peshawar (North West Frontier Province). Respondents are distributed roughly equally across the different cities. (Note that the sample was not drawn according to the population share of these cities.) According to the *Herald,* the survey does not cover rural Pakistan and has a margin of error that ranges from 3 to 5 percent.

U.S. Department of State

The third data source is from a survey sponsored by the Office of Research of the U.S. Department of State.[5] The survey instrument was written by the Office of Research and was executed by a "reputable Pakistani public opinion research firm." The fielding of the instrument began in the middle of March 2002 and ended in the first week of April.

The sample size was 2,058. All respondents were over eighteen years of age and were based in ten major cities in Baluchistan, Punjab, NWFP, and Sindh. The results were tabulated using weights to adjust for the educational distribution across Pakistan. These population weights were derived using official Government of Pakistan data from the 1998 Housing Census of Pakistan. According to the Department of State, the 95 percent confidence interval is plus or minus 3 percentage points.[6] Since the surveys have been repeated several times, where possible and where relevant, we present time-trend analyses.

Critical Views of the Data

While the Gallup Poll was drawn from a nationally representative sample, the other two surveys were conducted in urban environs. The Gallup data also provide extensive psychographic and demographic information about respondents, which is not available with the other two data sources. Because Gallup produced respondent-level data, we were able to analyze the data controlling for education, gender, locality of the respondent (rural vs. urban), and so forth.

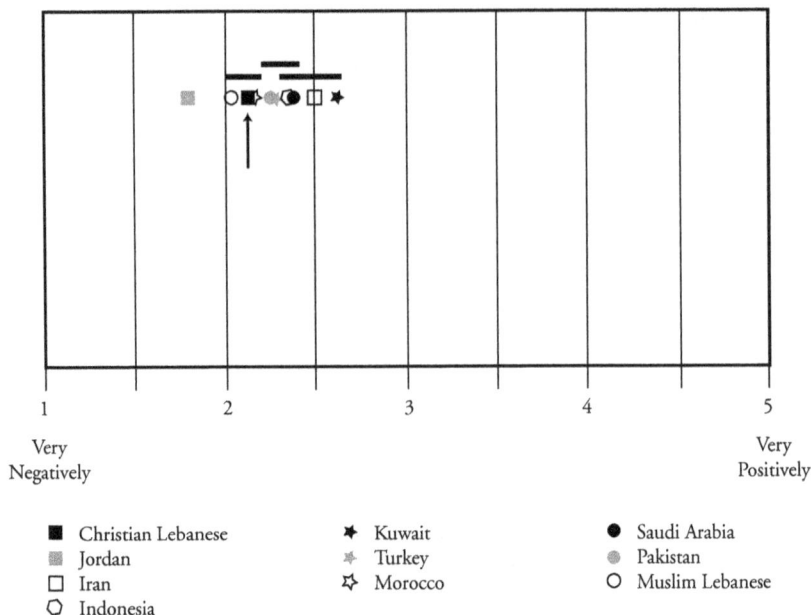

FIGURE 4.2. How positively or negatively is our value system being influenced by the West?

One of the drawbacks of the Gallup data is that some of the questions asked of the respondents are vague, allowing for multiple interpretations. For example, several questions ask respondents about their feelings toward the following countries: France, the United States, Great Britain, Russia, and China. However, it is difficult to interpret the responses. Are the respondents indicating their assessment of the people of those countries? Are they interpreting the question to be about national policies—foreign or domestic? Are participants in the survey addressing their perception of the culture of those countries? As such, such questions only convey vague information. Other problems with this survey include the deliberate exclusion of questions in sensitive markets, such as Saudi Arabia. Further, as this survey only addresses Muslim countries, it is difficult to contextualize these respondents' answers. Do respondents in Pakistan, Lebanon, or Saudi Arabia answer the various survey items in ways that are statistically different from those of, say, France? All of these concerns render interpretation of results less straightforward than they may appear at first blush.[7]

With respect to the data published by the *Herald* and the U.S. Department of State, we employed their published tabulations. Unfortunately, the

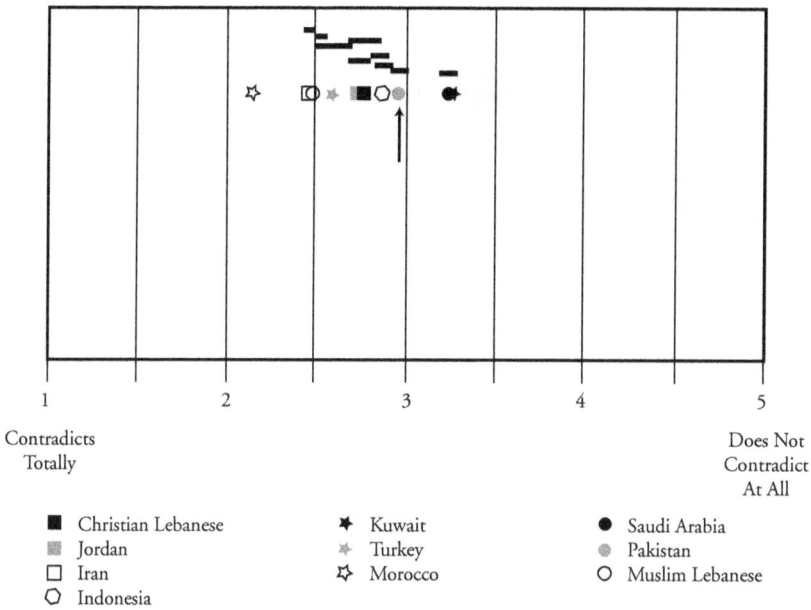

FIGURE 4.3. To what extent are aspects of modernity as we currently experience it in contradiction with our traditional value system?

estimates of the sample means did not have standard errors associated with them. Therefore, we are unable to determine whether or not a pair-wise comparison of sample means is statistically significant.

Gallup Data Handling and Methodology

Analyses of the respondent-level data from the Gallup survey were conducted by the authors. For those questions that were answered on a scale (for example, ordinal data), we deleted all answers that were either "missing" or indicated as "don't know." This was done such that we could employ the most powerful statistical tests to make pair-wise comparisons of the observed country means. We used a non-parametric analogue to the t-test called the Wilcoxon Rank-Sum Test (also known as the Mann-Whitney U Test) to compare pair-wise country means and to determine the statistical significance of the observed difference. For nominal data items (that is, questions which are answered with a "Yes" or a "No," and "Don't know"), a typical Chi-Square test was used to execute pair-wise comparisons of country means.

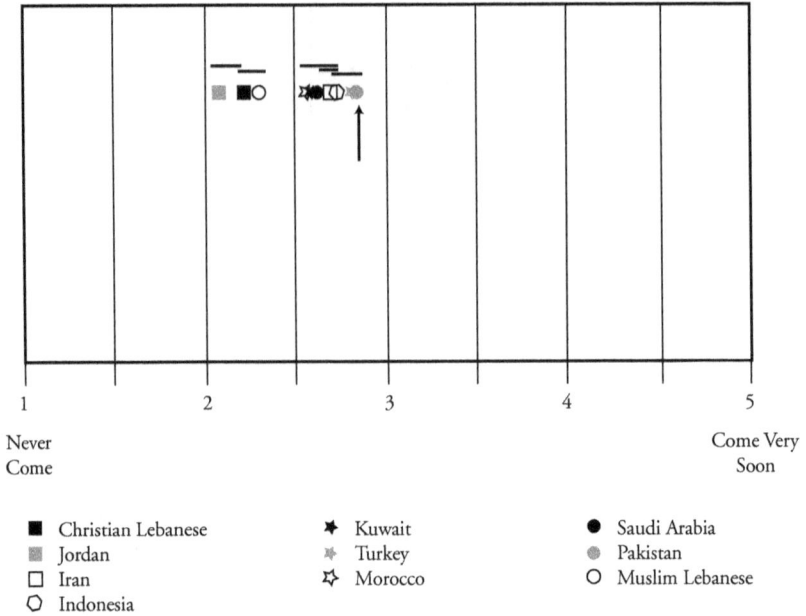

FIGURE 4.4. The time for a better understanding between the West and the Arab/Muslim world will probably . . .

The probability cutoff employed here is higher than may be usually employed to determine whether pair-wise differences of means are statistically significant. We used a probability cutoff of 0.001 or lower. This bound was determined using the Bonferroni correction method to adjust the standard 0.05 threshold. The Bonferonni-determined cutoff was calculated by dividing the 0.05 threshold by the total number of unique pair-wise country comparisons; for most questions this meant forty-five unique comparisons (by comparing eight countries, plus Muslim and Christian Lebanese). For those questions that were not fielded in specific countries, the Bonferonni cutoff was adjusted accordingly. To graphically indicate differences in responses between countries, a black bar is used to indicate which nations are statistically indistinguishable.

Findings

In this section, we report findings from the various data sets employed in this analysis. First, we employ the multicountry findings of the Gallup data

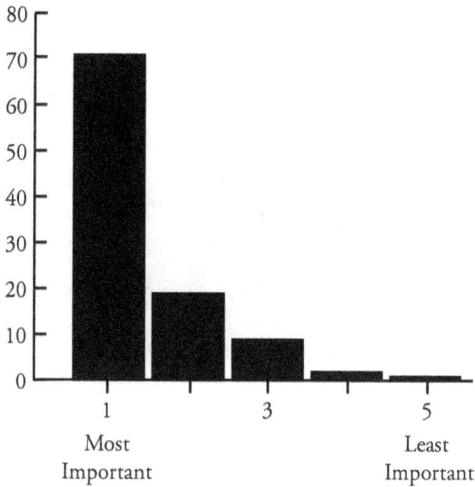

FIGURE 4.5. Importance of religion among one's family, extended family, religion, country, and self.

to contextualize Pakistan vis-à-vis the other Muslim countries included in the survey.[8] This will provide a broad overview of how Pakistani participants responded to a series of background questions on religion, family, and perceptions of the West and of modernity. Second, we explore these general findings more thoroughly by presenting results of in-house RAND analyses of Pakistani respondents in the Gallup data. In the third and fourth section, we analyze published findings from the *Herald* and from the U.S. Department of State data, respectively.

Pakistan in Context

To contextualize Pakistan and Pakistani respondents, we present findings from four questions from the Gallup poll fielded in eight Muslim countries. (Note: Indonesian respondents were not asked to respond to these questions.) These questions are intended to provide a broad overview of respondent sentiment on the importance of religion, the perceived influence of the West on traditional culture, views on modernity, and relations with the West.

To ascertain the importance of religion (however defined), Gallup re-

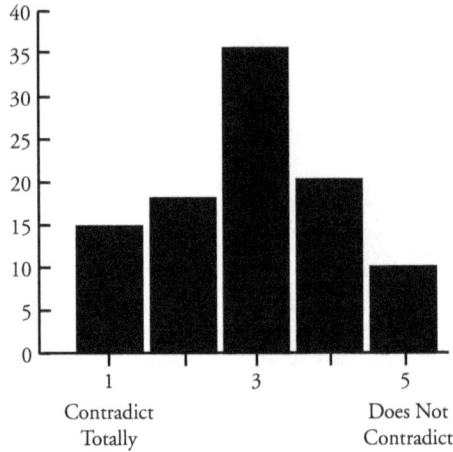

FIGURE 4.6. To what extent do aspects of modernity, as we currently experience this in our society, contradict our traditional value system?

quested respondents to rank religion within other parameters, including family, extended family, country, self, and religion. Among the participants of the eight countries (nine groups), Pakistanis are more likely to rank religion as "most important" (a value of "1"), as shown in Figure 4.1. Only Kuwaiti respondents were more likely to rank it so.

The questionnaire also asked whether respondents felt the West was negatively influencing their value system. Among participants from the eight countries, Pakistanis (along with Moroccan and Muslim Lebanese respondents, as indicated by the black bar) were most negative in their assessment. (These results are available in Figure 4.2.) The reader should note the tight distribution of responses: the country means of most countries were clustered between 2 and 2.5.

Gallup also sought to understand the various perceptions of modernity among their respondents. The survey included two variants of the same question: one asked whether respondents found "modernity as they experienced it to be in conflict with their traditional value system," and the second inquired whether or not the respondents found modernity "as experienced by the West" contradicted their value system. Consistent with their general survey methodology, Gallup did not provide any fixed definition of modernity, leaving its meaning to be determined by the subjective interpretation of the respondent.

Here, we present findings only for the first variant of the question. Pak-

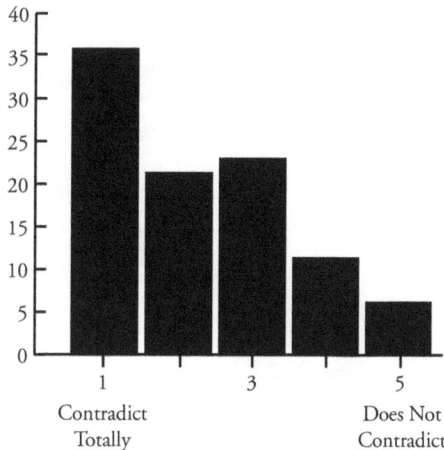

FIGURE 4.7. To what extent do aspects of modernity, as experienced in the West, contradict our traditional value system?

istani respondents were less likely than most to indicate a total contradiction and were more likely to inveigh on the subject neutrally (see Figure 4.3). This suggests that even though Pakistani respondents were more concerned than most about the influence of the West upon their traditional value system, they were among the least concerned about the corrosive influence of modernity writ large. Although, as we will see, their agnosticism about modernity is not unqualified.

On the question of how optimistic respondents were about a potential rapprochement between the West and the Arab/Muslim world, Pakistani respondents (along with Morocco, Indonesia, and Iran, as indicated by the black bar) were the least pessimistic (see Figure 4.4). For sure, the magnitude of this finding is certainly mitigated by the tight distribution of the sample means: most country means fell between the values of 2.1 (Jordan) and 2.8 (Pakistan). Thus, for most purposes, the country means suggest either ambivalence on the issue or a slight indication that a bettering of relations will not be forthcoming.

Gallup Data: Pakistani Respondents

Having situated Pakistan among the other respondent countries, we now explore findings exclusively for Pakistani respondents in the Gallup data. It

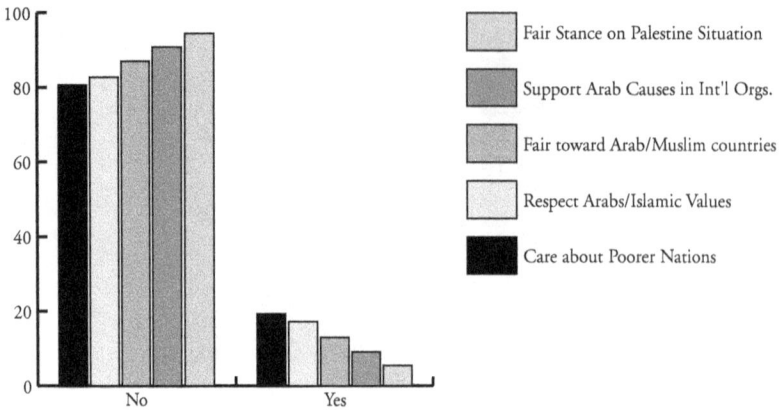

FIGURE 4.8. Which of these statements do you associate with Western nations?

should be noted that as we have respondent-level data, we were able to examine whether there were significant differences in means when broken out
by gender, urban vs. rural, age, and levels of education. Notably, none of the
pair-wise differences examined were statistically different or significant in
magnitude. As such, we only present aggregate means for the entire Pakistan
sample.

In this analysis, we present findings from four questions for the Pakistani
respondents. First, we examined the distribution of Pakistani respondents'
ranking of the importance of religion among one's own family, extended
family, religion, country, and self. As shown in Figure 4.5, more than 70 percent of Pakistani respondents ranked religion as "Most Important." Nearly
20 percent ranked religion second among these five things. It should be recalled that the connotation of "religion" was left to the subjective interpretation of the respondent. However, this metric suggests that irrespective of
how the participants interpreted "religion," they resoundingly asserted its
primacy.

We next examined Pakistani opinion about modernity. We first looked at
the distribution of Pakistani responses on whether or not their experience of
modernity contradicts their traditional value system. These data elements
were ordinal, with "1" indicating a "total contradiction," and "5" indicating
that "it does not contradict." As shown in Figure 4.6, the largest share of respondents answered with a value of "3." One way of interpreting this response is ambivalence. The distribution of responses in the direction of "total contradiction" and "no contradiction at all" is nearly symmetric.

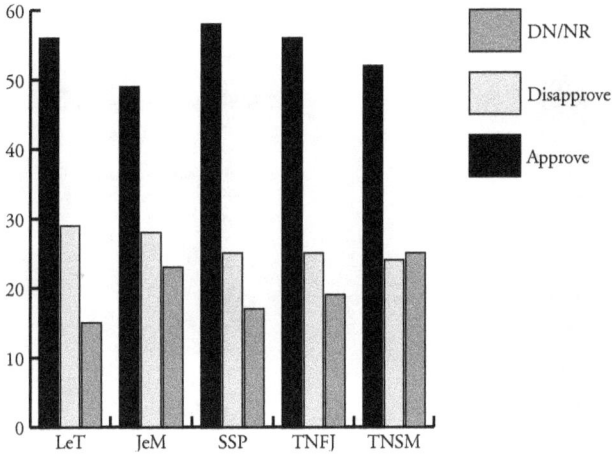

FIGURE 4.9. Do you approve or disapprove of the ban on these religious organizations?

However, when one examines the distribution of Pakistani responses about whether or not they perceive modernity, "as experienced by the West," to contradict their traditional value system, the distribution shifts. Whereas in the former question, Pakistani respondents appear ambivalent, in this question Pakistani respondents tended to be more likely to find a total contradiction, as shown in Figure 4.7.

Finally, we analyzed responses to a series of five statements, given below. Respondents were requested to indicate whether these statements applied to the countries of the West:

"Care about poorer nations"
"Respect Arab/Islamic values"
"Fair toward Arab/Muslim countries"
"Support Arab causes in international organizations"
"Fair stance on Palestine situation"

While the individual percentages are indicated in Figure 4.8, it is notable that Pakistani respondents overwhelmingly indicated that these statements did not apply to the West. Indeed, the principal findings from this question suggests that a large majority of Pakistani respondents perceive the countries of the West to be disrespectful toward and unfair and indifferent to Islamic values, states, and causes.

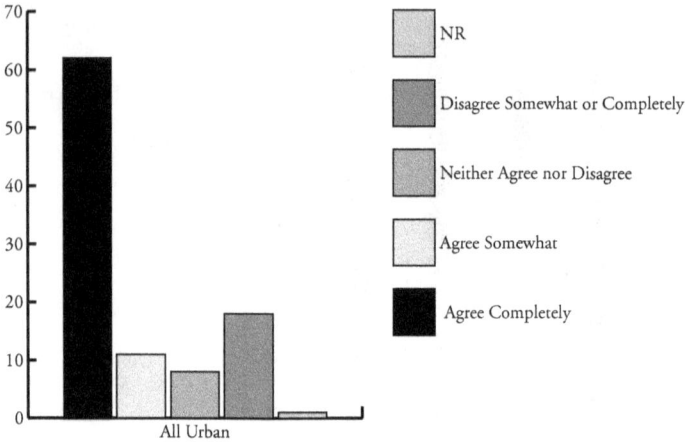

FIGURE 4.10. To what extent do you agree or disagree that religion should be kept separate from politics?

Evidence from the Herald

In this analysis, we examined three metrics from the expansive survey commissioned by the *Herald.* These data elements addressed levels of support for: reform efforts of the Musharraf regime; secularization of politics and a legal framework based on the Q'uran and Sunnah.

The first of such questions addressed the issue of support for efforts to ban religious *tanzeems* (organizations). The groups identified in this question included those groups that operate primarily in the Kashmir theater, such as the Lashkar-e-Taiba (LeT) and Jaish-e-Muhammad (JeM). It also included sectarian groups, such as the Sunni Deobandi Sipah-e-Sahaba-e-Pakistan (SSP), which targets Shi'as in Pakistan, and the Shi'a organizations that target Sunnis, such as the Tehrik-e-Nifaz-e-Fiqah-e-Jaffria (TNFJ). The question also addressed the Tehrik-e-Nifaz-e-Shariat-e-Mo-hammadi (TNSM), which fought along with the Taliban and seeks to transform Pakistan into a state similar to that of Afghanistan under the Taliban.

The largest share of respondents indicated support for the ban—even for those groups that operate in Kashmir, such as the LeT and JeM: more than 50 percent of respondents supported banning the LeT, and nearly 50 percent supported the ban on JeM. A majority of respondents also agreed with banning the sectarian groups SSP and TNFJ. Slightly more than 50 percent

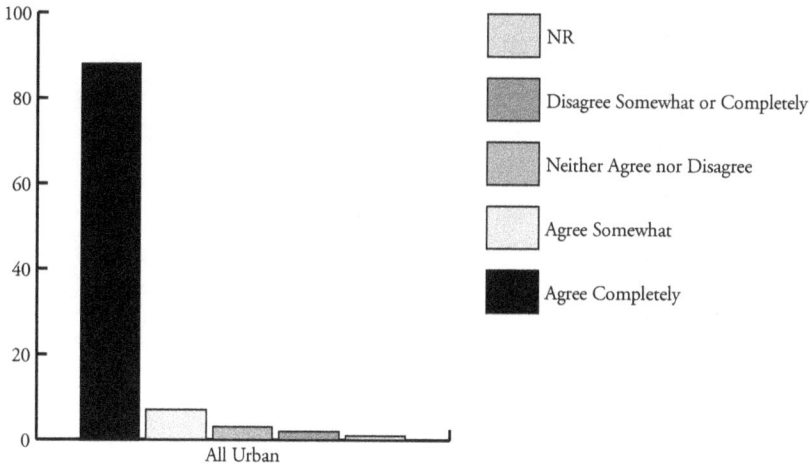

FIGURE 4.11. To what extent do you agree or disagree that Q'uran and Sunnah should be the source of all Pakistani law?

concurred with the prohibition on the pro-Taliban group TNSM (see Figure 4.9).

The next set of questions examined the level of support for the secularization of politics and the level of support for using the Q'uran and Sunnah as the basis of Pakistani law. As shown in Figure 4.10, the largest fraction of Pakistani respondents (over 60 percent) agreed completely and another 10 percent agreed somewhat that religion should be kept separate from politics. Fewer than 20 percent indicated that they disagreed with the assertion that religion should be separate from politics. Yet, despite the ostensible large-scale support for separation of Islam from politics, respondents overwhelmingly indicated widespread support for the use of the Q'uran and the Sunnah as the basis of all Pakistani law. As shown in Figure 4.11, more than 80 percent agree completely that Q'uran and Sunnah should comprise the basis of Pakistani law.

U.S. Department of State

We next examined four separate data elements from a 2002 U.S. Department of State Survey. Specifically, we present findings on public support for

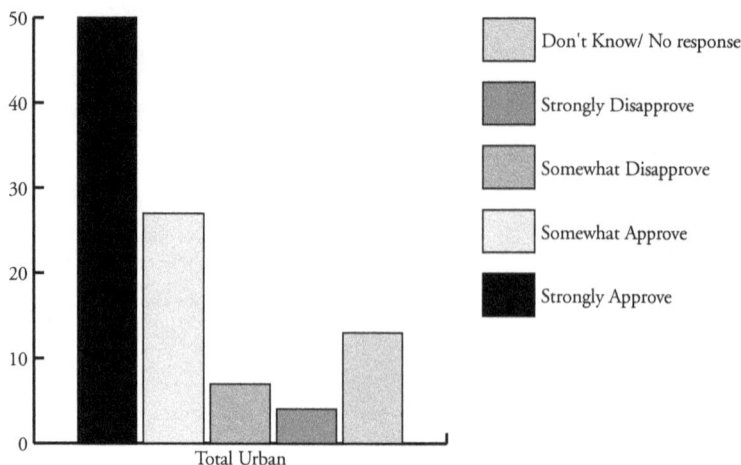

FIGURE 4.12. In general, do you approve or disapprove of our government banning those groups of religious militants? Strongly or only somewhat?

banning religious militant groups, support for decreased state tolerance of religious extremism in Pakistan, and support for *madrasah* reform. We also present longitudinal findings tracing out the support for religious leaders since January 1998.

With respect to support for banning religious militant groups, 50 percent of respondents indicated that they "strongly approved" and another 27 percent indicated that they "approve somewhat" of banning religious militant groups. Conversely, only 4 percent indicated that they "strongly disapprove," and another 7 percent "somewhat disapprove." These findings (shown in Figure 4.12) resemble the findings of the *Herald* survey data (available in Figure 4.9).

Pakistani respondents also indicated that they are generally supportive of decreased state tolerance of religious extremism. For example, Figure 4.13 demonstrates that 50 percent of the respondents indicated that they strongly support decreased tolerance for such extremism, and another 28 percent indicated "somewhat support" for the same. Conversely, only 7 percent indicated that they "strongly disapprove," and another 3 percent noted that they "somewhat disapprove" of the statement.

Moreover, Pakistani respondents indicated a strong level of support for *madrasah* reform, as shown in Figure 4.14. The largest share of respondents (66 percent) indicated that they strongly support *madrasah* reform, and an-

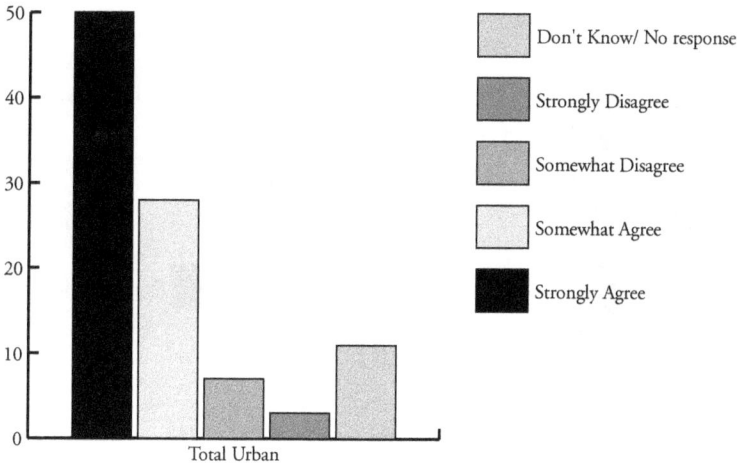

FIGURE 4.13. Do you agree or disagree that religious extremism should no longer be tolerated in Pakistan? Strongly or only somewhat?

other 20 percent said that they somewhat support such reform. Only 4 percent somewhat opposed and 3 percent strongly opposed such reform.

Finally, we examined available time-trend data on support for religious leaders. For analytical purposes, we combined categories of "A good deal of support" and "A fair amount." We also combined responses for "Not very much" and "No confidence." The third grouping of responses was formed by combining responses indicated as "Don't know" and "No response."

This is presented in Figure 4.15. It is notable that the overall trend in support for religious leaders from June/July 1998 to March/April 2002 is downward. In the beginning of the data series, 56 percent of respondents indicated that they supported religious leaders. In March/April 2002, support was at 38 percent.

Despite considerable volatility in this data series, there are a few intriguing features. First, in July 1999, there was a substantial increase in support for religious leaders (from 40 to 48 percent). Similarly, another "bubble of support" appears across September/October 2001 and persists until January 2002. While we cannot determine whether these increases are statistically significant with the available information about these data series, we will revisit these bursts in support and posit some potential explanations.

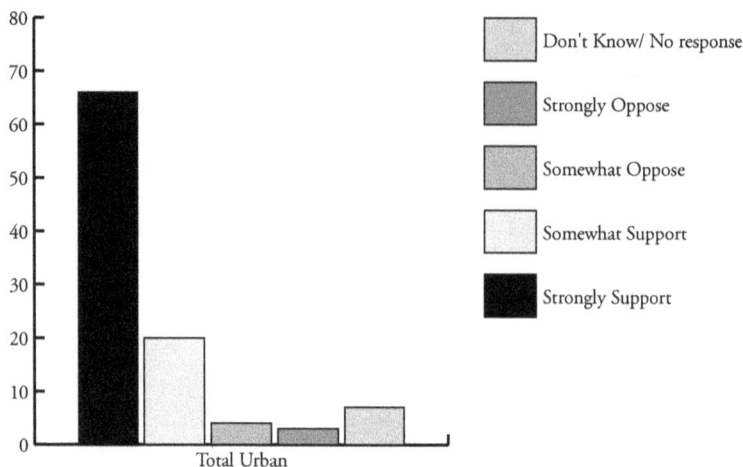

FIGURE 4.14. Do you support or oppose *madrasah* reform? Strongly or somewhat?

Discussion

DATA INTEGRITY REVISITED

Looking across these different data sources, a number of themes and ostensible contradictions emerge. This section will identify and, where possible, attempt to cast light on some of the more perplexing contradictions, drawing from data from in-country interviews and from the literature, where appropriate. Unfortunately, because of the nature of the survey instruments and some of the more vague and undefined concepts inherent in the instruments, it may not be possible to fully disentangle discordant findings. Moreover, in the final analysis, the robustness and durability of these analyses turn on the credibility of those who fielded and prepared the data for analysis. Unfortunately, there is little information that permits such an assessment of these concerns.

It must also be kept in mind that with the exception of the Gallup data, these answers reflect *urban* Pakistani respondents. We therefore know very little about the respondents of rural or even suburban areas. Moreover, while Gallup is confident of its country-level aggregate results, Gallup does not suggest that the accuracy of the polling measures holds beyond the national-level reporting. (For example, we could not safely use the Gallup data to ob-

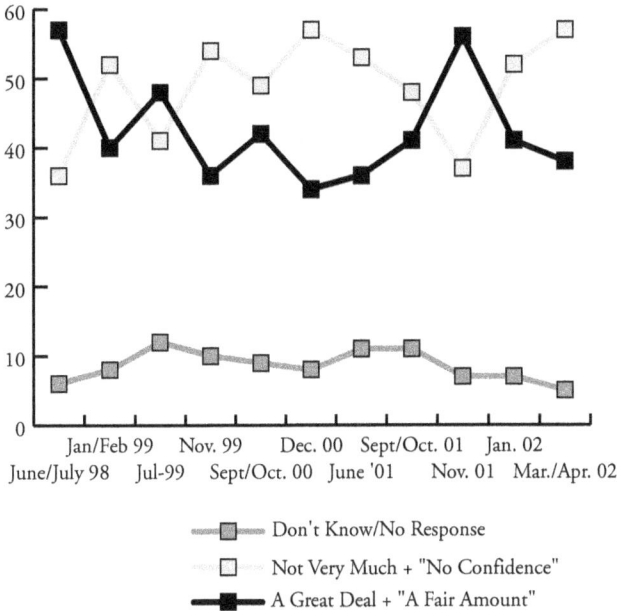

FIGURE 4.15. Please tell me how much confidence you have in Pakistan's religious leaders?

tain information about rural or urban respondents or for other demographic distributions.)

Thus, it should be kept in mind that, with the exception of the Gallup results, these findings tend to reflect a particular (that is, urban) segment of the Pakistani public populace, rather than Pakistan at large. It may be tempting to diminish the significance of the urban-focused findings of the *Herald* and the U.S. Department of State surveys on the basis that urbanites may differ in key characteristics from their rural or suburban counterparts. However, it should be noted that Pakistan is the most urbanized country in South Asia (see Table 4.1), and the trend toward urbanization continues despite a slowed pace in recent years.[9]

MODERNITY AND THE WEST

The Gallup data suggest that even though Pakistani respondents tend to be among the *most* concerned about the untoward influence upon their traditional value system, they are the *least* pessimistic about the possibility of a future rapprochement between the West and the Muslim/Arab world.

TABLE 4.1

Percentage of Population in Urban Areas. Countries of South Asia, 2001

Country	Percentage Urban (2001)
Pakistan	33.40
India	27.90
Bangladesh	25.60
Sri Lanka	23.10
Afghanistan	22.30
Nepal	12.20
Bhutan	7.40

SOURCE: *World Urbanization Prospects, The 2001 Revision: Data Tables and Highlights Table,* specifically Table "A.1. Population of urban and rural areas at mid-year and percentage urban, 2001" (United Nations Secretariat, 2002).

Another interesting finding is that Pakistanis appear to have conflicted perceptions of modernity. Even though they are likely to find modernity *as experienced by the West* to be discordant with their own traditions and values, they are less concerned about modernity *as they experience* it. Making sense of this finding is complicated by the fact that Gallup has provided no sense of what they intend "modernity" to suggest to the respondent. Nor is there any information about how the notion of modernity was interpreted by the survey participants.

Thus, this finding that Pakistani respondents view modernity in distinct ways—depending upon whether the reference is their own encounter with it or whether the reference is the West's experience of modernity—could simply be an artifact of poor polling or of a poorly crafted instrument. However, it is also possible that the different answers to the two question variants reflect some genuine interest on the part of Pakistani respondents to adopt features of modernity that conform to their value system. It may also suggest that Pakistanis may feel empowered to engage in this process of adaptation, to absorb that which is acceptable and to discard that which is not, or that they feel empowered to create their own concept of modernity altogether.

Indeed, Pakistanis have access to the amenities of modernity and they partake of and contribute to notions of a globalized culture. Even the most "fundamentalist" organizations make extensive use of technology in pursuit of their objectives. For example, the militant organization Lashkar-e-Taiba makes extensive use of the Internet to disseminate information about its operations and—particularly prior to being a proscribed foreign terrorist organization—for raising funds. They also publish extensively through the traditional means of print capital. Even among the much-vilified *madrasahs*, there are those institutions that make heavy use of electronic media. Rather than teaching their pupils to avoid engagement with modernity, these *madrasahs* are selectively appropriating its tools.[10]

Jerrold Green notes the fascination that scholars of Islam and Islamic societies have with the information revolution, which comprises only one important dimension of modernity.[11] Green cites a compelling draft analysis by Eric Rouleau of "The Use of Information Technology by Dissidents." Rouleau, according to Green, writes that in Iran, "even at the bastion of conservatism [in Qom] . . . to which this writer paid a visit, an entire floor is devoted to arrays of sophisticated computers. . . . One is thus confronted with the unusual sight of rows of mullahs in traditional garb playing computer keyboards like pianos."[12]

However, Green's comments upon Rouleau's observation are relevant to this quandary over modernity:

> The only thing that is so surprising is that it is so surprising. Mullahs drive cars, fly in planes, and use telephones. Why would they not use computers? ... All who observe the Middle East not only agree that these technologies are used and that they are important, but they also wish to point out that whomever they champion uses them.[13]

Green's observations are useful to remind us that modernity and the embrace of modernity is not the exclusive precipitant of secularization or privatization of faith. Moreover, Green's assessment echoes that of Vali Nasr, who notes that not only does modernization *not* necessarily produce secularization, but religion too can no longer be seen as "impervious to change and irrelevant to modernization. The task therefore becomes one of reconciling anachronistic values and loyalties with time-honoured assumptions about the content, nature and direction of modernizing change."[14]

Certainly, one interpretation of the Gallup results of Pakistan is consistent with these worldviews. Namely, rather than rejecting modernity out of hand, Pakistani respondents appear to be actively mobilizing modernizing changes that are consistent with their worldviews while remaining suspect of those elements which are discordant with their perceived ensemble of values and traditions.

SECULARIZATION OF POLITICS AND ISLAMIC LAW

As noted, data published in the *Herald* present the dichotomous finding that even though Pakistani respondents overwhelmingly indicated a support for a secularization of politics, they still supported the notion that the Q'uran and Sunnah should comprise the basis of Pakistani law.

A number of explanations may be offered to de-conflict these findings. First, it may simply reflect poor polling. Second, it could reflect a hesitance on the part of respondents to answer freely on one or both questions. For example, depending upon how the question is fielded, respondents may anticipate that supporting a secularization of politics is the "expected" answer or feel awkward about answering to the contrary. Similarly, respondents may have felt uncomfortable disagreeing that the Q'uran and the Sunnah should form the fundament of Pakistani law. This latter is particularly understandable, given the context of Pakistan's draconian anti-blasphemy laws and the harsh punishment that ensues if convicted. The *Herald*, which also noted this dichotomy, also expressed the concern that "few Pakistani Muslims can be expected to say publicly that they would prefer to be governed by secular legislation as opposed to laws rooted in religious scriptures."[15]

Yet another explanation may be that Pakistani respondents do not necessarily see these two issues in conflict. For example, it is often heard within Pakistan and elsewhere that Islam is not simply a religion, it is a complete system for living one's life. This view, if widely held, may explain the broad support for Q'uran and Sunnah within the context of Pakistan's legal framework. However, given the preference for such a legal framework, it is entirely possible that respondents prefer that religious organizations should not engage in politics. In fact, this view is held by many religious organizations themselves. For example, Tablighi Jamaat (see chapter by Metcalf in this book), as a principle, does not involve itself in politics.

Alternatively, it may be the case that respondents distinguish between politicians *as lawmakers* and politicians *as implementers* of law, with greater importance on the latter. Pakistani respondents may believe that an ideal politician might be someone who accepts current interpretations of the law and who spends most of her/his time in being fair, hardworking, and eschewing corruption and other untoward activities.

POPULAR SUPPORT FOR REFORM EFFORTS

Both the data from the *Herald* and the U.S. Department of State suggest that there is wide support among Pakistani respondents for banning religious organizations, *madrasah* reform, containment of religious intolerance, and so forth. Yet, despite what appears to be a broad base of support for such reform efforts, the Musharraf regime has not been aggressive in fully implementing any of these reform efforts. Even though several different ordinances have been passed on *madrasah* reform, little has actually been done. There is neither incentive to comply with the ordinance nor punishment for those who choose not to comply.[16]

Similarly, while the government of Pakistan has ostensibly proscribed militant organizations such as Lashkar-e-Taiba (LeT), Jaish-e-Mohammed (JeM), Sipah-e-Sahaba-e-Pakistan (SSP), Sipah-e-Mohammed Pakistan (SMP), Lashkar-e-Jhangvi (LeJ), etc., in practice this has not occurred. While Pakistan temporarily detained many of the leaders of the proscribed groups, they have subsequently been released. The groups also re-formed under new names. According to data obtained through interviews in Pakistan in January 2003, these groups are still operating but have been told to "keep a low profile" to minimize conflict with India and the United States.[17] In November 2003, the government of Pakistan again tried to impose new bans on the newly reorganized and renamed outfits. For example, on November 4, 2003, the government outlawed six militant groups: Tehreek-e-Islami (formerly Tehrik-i-Jafria Pakistan), Millat-e-Islamia Pakistan (former Sipah-i-Sahaba Pakistan), Khudam ul-Islam (former Jaish-i-Mohammad), Hezbul Tehrir, Jamiat ul Furqan, and Jamiat ul-Ansar.[18] Jamaat-ul-Dawa was put on a watch-list.[19] The authors have not been able to ascertain the efficacy of these more recent efforts.

There is a growing consensus that Pakistan would like to curb sectarian militant groups (including, among others, SSP, LeJ, and SMP) and the sanguineous violence associated with the Sunni-Shi'a conflict. Indeed, according to our interviews in 2003, sectarian violence has declined, in part due to the increased ability of the police to penetrate the cells and shut them down.

In practice, permanently degrading the power of these groups—much less dismantling them—is considerably more difficult. The problem principally arises from Pakistan's persistent belief that it can contain some forms of militancy (for example, Taliban and al-Qaeda remnants and sectarian groups) while sustaining those groups that claim to operate in Kashmir.

While such a clear segmentation of militant groups is alluring, it is not realistic or feasible. Sunni sectarian groups have long been tied to those groups operating in Kashmir and Pakistan. Lashkar-e-Jhangvi militants were trained in Afghanistan along with militants operating in Kashmir. The SSP has long been associated with the faction of Jam'iat-i-Ulama-Islami (JUI), led by Sami 'u 'l-Haq, and Pakistan-backed Harakat-ul-Ansar and Taliban units operating in Kashmir and Afghanistan. Similarly, the LeJ is also an off-shoot of JUI.[20]

The government of Pakistan has been hesitant to truly shut down the militant production system—in which the *madrasahs* figure prominently—because it seeks to maintain its options on the Kashmir issue.[21] Thus, even while Pakistan has generally been very supportive of the U.S.-led anti-terrorism efforts with respect to al-Qaeda and the Taliban, it has not demonstrated a robust commitment to reverse course on the Kashmir militancy at this juncture.

It also remains unclear who within Pakistan is thoroughly convinced of the strategic advantages of abandoning Pakistan's long-worn policy of using militant proxies in Indian-held Kashmir.

SUPPORT FOR ISLAMIC PARTIES

Despite the various positions articulated by Pakistani respondents vis-à-vis reform efforts, secularization of politics, and support for religious leaders, the coalition of Islamic parties still did very well in the October 2002 elections. How can this be explained? Again, the question must be asked whether the polling data systematically failed to capture the nuances of Pakistani popular sentiment or whether something more complex is operating among the Pakistani electorate.

In this paper, we offer the following hypothesis to explain the electoral outcome, *despite* what appeared to be countervailing trends in Pakistani popular sentiment. We submit that the growing anti-American sentiment, efforts of the Musharraf regime to manipulate the electoral outcome, and concordant increasing resentment of the Musharraf regime and the Army have created a political space, which the coalition of Islamic parties, the Muttahida Majlis-e-Amal (MMA), could exploit. Each of these trends will be explored and synthesized below.

Growing Anti-American Sentiment

While coalitions of religious parties are not new in Pakistan, the MMA is the first political alliance that includes both Sh'ia and Deobandi groups.[22] This is not to say that there had not been efforts to mitigate sectarian conflict and to build bridges across the various religious communities. For example, the Milli-Yakjehti Council (National Solidarity Council) first met in 1994 in Islamabad and worked for some 2–3 years. According to the Vice-Ameer of Jamaat Islami (JI), as a result of these efforts, there was a truce in sectarian strife that endured 10–12 months.

More recently, the U.S.-led operations in Afghanistan and in Pakistan provided another occasion for various groups to consider working in concert. According to the Vice-Ameer of JI, various religious groups again began collaborating during October 2001. This spirit of cooperation arose because some Deobandi groups and JI objected to the government's decision to support the U.S. by providing bases, facilities, and intelligence, and sought to mobilize public opinion around these concerns. It was for this purpose that the Pakistan Afghan Defense Council (PADC) was organized and included a wide range of groups, including both Shi'a and Ahle-Hadith organizations. According to the Vice-Ameer, much of the PADC evolved into the current MMA. Moreover, this organizational structure of the PADC facilitated the mobilization of the nascent MMA for the October 2002 elections.

Between the launch of Operation Enduring Freedom, on October 7, 2001, and the October 2002 elections, a number of developments occurred in the context of Pakistan–U.S. relations, which have caused considerable discord. Moreover, the MMA has ideally situated itself to exploit this discontent. Pakistanis resident in the North West Frontier Province and in Baluchistan were most affected by the launch of Operation Enduring Freedom. This is because the peoples of these areas share language, family, cultural, and clan structures with those across the border in Afghanistan. Not only were the residents of these areas hostile to the U.S. operation, they were also hostile to the Musharraf decision to support U.S. activities in Afghanistan.

A second issue of concern, not only for the residents of these areas, but also for Pakistan's population at large, is the reality that the post-Taliban and the pre-Taliban regimes in Kabul are virtually indistinguishable. Our interviews suggest that Pakistanis generally, and residents of the NWFP in particular, resent the fact that the nascent government of Afghanistan does not reflect the population distribution of Pakhtuns.

Further, the issue of "hot-pursuit" of fugitive Taliban and al-Qaeda remnants into the border provinces has been a source of anti-U.S. and anti-Musharraf sentiment among Pakistanis, as such raids are seen as fundamentally eroding their sense of sovereignty. The government of Pakistan has insisted that no such "hot pursuit" operations have taken place. Rather, the government of Pakistan maintains that it is Pakistani security forces that are conducting these raids, with assistance from the U.S. Federal Bureau of Investigation.

Pakistanis do not appear to believe this. And if the official governmental version were believed at face value, there would still be resistance to such raids. This is because there has not previously been a culture of Pakistani security forces operating in the tribal areas. Moreover, in Baluchistan such operations are particularly resented because of the use of Pakistani security forces in squelching a separatist movement in that province. Consequently, any sort of action in these areas is seen as highly problematic and as an affront to tribal and national sovereignty.

Another source of growing resentment with the United States has been voiced over the U.S. unwillingness to broker a negotiated settlement with India over Kashmir. Interlocutors in Pakistan widely expressed the view that Musharraf expected some U.S. exertions in this direction, and in turn, this was used to generate support among the Pakistani populace for reversing its twenty-year-old policy in Afghanistan. Despite the U.S. claims of massive aid and assistance provided to Pakistan, many interviewed in Pakistan lamented the type of assistance that Pakistan is receiving from the U.S. For example, journalists and other opinion shapers noted that the U.S. appears to be most inclined to provide Army aid. In other words, the U.S.—despite its claims to support democracies—is simply providing the Musharraf regime the resources that his institution most desires. Such critics of the basis of U.S. aid have argued that the aid should have been targeted to bolster Pakistani civil institutions—not the Army.

Finally, the U.S. decision in 2003 to selectively enforce Immigration and Naturalization Service registration requirements for some twenty (mostly Muslim) countries has generated considerable outrage. Pakistanis argue that they have been a "front line" state in the fight against terrorisms and yet, within the United States, Pakistani nationals are treated as potential security threats. It is impossible to overstate the popular resentment against the United States that this has generated.

Electoral Follies

A number of the Pakistani interlocutors we interviewed in 2003 have noted that many of the electoral rules and regulations promulgated for the October 2002 elections created an unexpected advantage for the MMA. First, Musharraf made a baccalaureate a prerequisite to contest the elections, which inadvertently redounded to the advantage of the MMA. Under Zia ul Haq, *madrasah* degrees were declared to be the equivalent of a baccalaureate. As a consequence, the MMA generally had an easier time fielding candidates with their *madrasah* degrees than the mainstream parties, the candidates of which do not generally have bachelor's degrees.

Second, the lowering of the voting age and efforts to make voting more accessible inadvertently enabled the Islamist parties to mobilize the *madrasah* youth as a voting block. Pakistanis interviewed also alleged that the various militant organizations contributed to this effort by using their manpower and organizational infrastructure to "round up the vote."

Third, it is widely reported among Pakistani interlocutors that the Musharraf regime was most concerned about containing the ability of the PPP and the PML-N to develop a platform and supporting constituencies. As a consequence, significant efforts were exerted to limit their ability to cultivate a political platform and concomitant political support. These interlocutors generally believed that the Musharraf regime did not expect the religious parties to perform well, at least in part because historically they have always had a weak electoral showing. According to one high-placed politician in the NWFP government, the Interservices Intelligence Directorate was monitoring the potential support for religious parties and did not find cause for concern. While the PPP and PML-N were denied access to the public, the religious parties, through the institutions of the mosques and the Friday sermons, were able to formulate a national platform and cultivate support for their positions.

One of the tools that has been used to reign in politicians and render them compliant accomplices of the Musharraf regime has been the National Accountability Bureau (NAB). Many in Pakistan are asking why it is that many serving ministers and parliamentarians have been convicted by the National Accountability Bureau. For example, Minister of the Interior Faisal Saleh Hayat was "awarded" this portfolio upon forming a "forward" (those that supported the current government against their parties' wishes) bloc of the PPP. Yet he had been declared by NAB to be a defaulter on a loan that was valued at 250 million rupees from the National Bank of Pakistan and was out on bail. Similarly, the federal Minister for Water and Power was a former PPP leader who was convicted of two counts of corruption. He, too, was out on bail. There are numerous other examples, such as the federal Minister for Agriculture and Livestock, the Governor of Sindh, and the federal Minister for Women's Development and Social Welfare.[23]

Pakistani observers ask why it is that the political aspirations of Benazir Bhutto, Asif Zardari, and the Sharif family have been squashed by the political cases against them when other notable politicians with pending cases and convictions currently serve in the assemblies, on the cabinet, or in the governors' houses.[24] The prevailing sentiment has been that NAB has been used as a means to disarm potential political rivals, while the dismissal of comparable cases has been employed to politically enable particular members of select parties. As a consequence, those politicians whose political futures have been resuscitated understand that their continued service hinges upon the vicissitudes of the serving regime. As such, these politicians are not likely to provide robust opposition to the policies of the center.

The collective efforts to cultivate politicians compliant with the regime and to squash any opposition from the mainstream parties, according to Pakistani interlocutors, have created a particular space for the MMA to be the lone voice protesting the policies of the center. A keen observer of internal Pakistan affairs, retired lieutenant-general, Talat Masood, in a January 2003 editorial, described the MMA's unique role as a proponent of issues that resonate with the Pakistani populace, such as democracy and good governance. According to Masood,

The present situation of the ruling party is somewhat unique. Prime Minister Jamali is a consensus candidate of the coalition but the power rests elsewhere—with the president and partly with the parliamentary leader and his associates—which makes his task very difficult indeed. For every major decision the prime minister will have to look to these power centres for approval and guidance. If he tries to assert himself then these contradictions will come to the fore and it could lead to frictions.

On the other hand, the opposition would be willing to support him provided he is seen to be distancing himself from the president and pursuing policies to strengthen the democratic institutions. Interestingly, at least as of now, it is the MMA which has emerged as the principal defender of the Constitution, the torchbearer of democracy and the promoter of good governance.[25]

Growing Contempt for Musharraf and the Army

Cartoons and editorials in Pakistani newspapers echo the growing concern that Musharraf has surrendered Pakistan's sovereignty to the United States. Moreover, Musharraf's April 2002 referendum and explicit efforts to manipulate the electoral outcome eviscerated his base of support within broad segments of the Pakistani populace. They also noted that the ISI has always had an important role within Pakistani domestic politics, but they expressed concern that whereas the ISI used to be a "lone operator" in Pakistani foreign policy, it is being transformed into an increasingly domestic-focused organization with wide-ranging impact upon the future of Pakistan's ability to develop robust democratic institutions.

Summary and Synthesis

At first blush, many of the survey findings seem discordant with the on-the-ground realities and electoral outcomes within Pakistan. Below, we offer several tentative efforts to de-conflict these different sets of findings.

MMA STEPPED INTO A POWER VACUUM

Many observers in Pakistan have noted that the MMA performed well in the 2002 elections in part because of the political vacuum created by the Musharraf regime and the unexpected backlash of efforts to manipulate the electoral outcome. However, the same observers argue that the MMA in particular was able to harness the growing anti-American and anti-Musharraf sentiment and convert this into votes. Interlocutors note that overall the MMA did not perform spectacularly, as it is not particularly strong at the center. However, it did manage to capture the NWFP assembly. It also came close to capturing the Baluchistan assembly. The group tended to field candidates where it could most expect a return on its investment. For example, it did not field candidates in rural Punjab where it had no expectation of success. The areas in which it was best able to perform were those areas most affected by U.S. actions and areas where anti-U.S. sentiment is most intense.

This analysis finds evidence that on other occasions, religious parties were able to capitalize upon anti-U.S. and anti-government sentiment. As shown in Figure 4.14, while there is an overall downward trend for support of religious leaders, there are at least two notable bubbles where support for them lurched upward.

One such spike in support for religious parties occurred in July 1999. At that time, then Prime Minister Nawaz Sharif went to Washington, D.C., to find an exit strategy from Pakistan's disastrous Kargil Operation. While the Kargil Operation was launched by Pakistan's Northern Light Infantry, Islamabad claimed that it was an entirely Mujahadeen affair. This story was eventually dismissed by India and the rest of the world. As a consequence of what was seen as a ribald aggression in the wake of the Lahore Process (launched in the months prior to national elections), India's ruling party, the BJP, reacted swiftly to recuperate lost political capital. The Indian response was aggressive (although they maintain that they did not cross the Line of Control) and included the use of airpower.[26]

During this July 4, 1999, meeting with President Clinton, Prime Minister Sharif was told without qualification to restore the sanctity of the Line of Control. As Pakistan had cloaked this operation as a "Mujahideen operation" both to its domestic and international audience, face-saving withdrawal was difficult to execute. Editorial pages were rife with criticism that the Sharif government squandered the gains of the Mujahideen in Kargil at the whim of the United States without any solid U.S. commitment to facilitate a settlement on Kashmir. Moreover, editorial pages highly criticized the U.S. position vis-à-vis Indo-Pakistan affairs.[27]

The second increase in support for religious leaders occurred in the months spanning September 2001 through January 2002—that is, during the launch and conduct of Operation Enduring Freedom. During these critical months, the Pakistan government made its facilities widely available to the U.S. in the conduct of its counterterrorism operations in the region. Residents in the areas bordering Afghanistan were outraged by the conduct of Operation Enduring Freedom, given their deep ties with Afghans across the border.

One possible explanation for these spikes in support for religious parties is that the religious parties are the beneficiaries of anti-U.S. sentiment and popular discontent with the Pakistani government's decisions to follow the dictates of Washington. Clearly, this is speculative, as the data do not provide any means of assessing whether these observed increases were simply due to chance (that is, due to "noise" in the data), or whether they are actually tracking events and the concomitant Pakistani reactions. However, the hypothesis advanced here is that U.S. policies that are abhorrent to Pakistanis may create a political space that is exploited by the religious parties in Pakistan. As this may be an important policy finding, this issue requires more rigorous exploration. For example, if this finding is generally valid, we may expect that the U.S. operations against Iraq, enforcement of INS registration requirements, and deportation of Pakistanis may create further operating space for the MMA.

Discussions with several highly placed Pakistani government officials in January 2003, and with one of Pakistan's most senior diplomats in February 2003, indicate that they share this interpretation. This diplomatic representative expressed the concern that as these policies translate into support for the MMA, they increase the survival pressures on Musharraf, who has already become a target for militant religious organizations. Another official interviewed in January (a governor of one of Pakistan's four provinces) lamented that as a representative of the Center (that is, as a member of the PML-Q, fronting for Musharraf), he has to deal with the fallout of the popular sentiment against U.S. actions and the support that this generates for the MMA. Both interlocutors indicated that the U.S. should have a more enhanced understanding of the impact of its policies on the Pakistani electorate and the survivability of the PML-Q, the democratic face of the Musharraf regime.

Irrespective of the ability of the MMA to capitalize upon anti-U.S. sentiment, interlocutors have cited other reasons for the success of the MMA. Apart from deep concerns about the abuse of the NAB to selectively recruit or banish mainstream politicians, the MMA has done much to advance several issues of democracy and good governance.

The MMA contests the Legal Framework Order and insists upon the 1973 Constitution. Members of the MMA have insisted upon taking their oath under the 1973 Constitution. Recently, during the inaugural session of the upper house, opposition members (including the MQM, the PPP, and the ANP) took their oaths "under the un-amended constitution as it existed before Gen Musharraf seized power on Oct 12, 1999."[28]

The MMA is also critical of the other extrajudicial processes used by Musharraf and his acolytes. For example, it argues that the banning of religious organizations was illegal, and it is the illegality of the proscription that forms the ballast of their opposition to it. For example, the Vice-Ameer of JI explained that there is a legal process by which a political party can be declared illegal. However, the Musharraf regime did not exercise that legal recourse. The Vice-Ameer was careful to couch his critique of the ban on militant groups within the parameters of the law.

The MMA has also noted that by Pakistani law, Musharraf cannot both be president and chief of army staff. The MMA has stated that it would be willing to support Musharraf if he were to step down from the Army. This could create confrontation because Musharraf, despite agreeing to step down by the end of 2004, has not done so. The MMA is also contesting the forming of the National Security Council, on the grounds that it will permanently enshrine the Army within the policy-making apparatus to the detriment of civilian institutions.

Thus, at the national level, the MMA has been one of the few loudly dissenting voices on issues of sovereignty, restoration of the 1973 Constitution, decreased obstruction of the army in democratic processes, and the exercise of judicial processes. As one liberal commentator noted, "Whenever the MMA opens their mouth, they make sense."

Even on religious issues, the MMA has not moved as one would expect. Within the NWFP, it has banned drinking (which has been banned for decades), banned gambling parlors (also already banned), has torn down film advertisements (but the cinemas remain open), and has confiscated audio tapes, video tapes, CDs, and DVDs. It is pursuing the abolishment of co-ed education, and it is also pushing for separate transport for men and women. However, it is pursuing these only in the NWFP.

Liberal commentators have expressed concern that even though the MMA is "making sense" in its immediate policy, the downstream effect of an enduring MMA will be corrosive on a polity that ordinarily perceives itself as liberal. Moreover, as the civilian government increasingly is revealed to be a Musharraf puppet, the MMA will increasingly look more attractive to the average voter, particularly if the MMA continues its path of articulating those concerns most relevant to the Pakistani populace. One retired brigadier from the Pakistan Army summarized this option in the following way, "Even an atheist like myself resonates with their issues, even though I don't resonate with the individuals involved."

Conclusion

This paper has identified some of the apparent disconnects between and among findings of various poll-based data, as well as discordance between positions suggested by the polls and on-the-ground reality. Where possible, we have tried to de-conflict these views through the use of qualitative data gathered during fieldwork in Pakistan.

Certain issues have emerged that require more rigorous understanding. First, to what extent do the 2002 elections reflect a move toward greater support for fundamentalist Islam and its involvement in politics *or* to what extent do they reflect growing anti-U.S., anti-Musharraf, and anti–Pakistan Army sentiment? Understanding this dynamic has significant policy implications for the U.S. government.

For example, to what extent should the United States consider the impact of its policies on Pakistan's domestic situation, and over what time horizon and with what ameliorative or palliative initiatives? What are the trade-offs that are inherent in supporting a Musharraf-specific regime versus more generalized notions of support for the State of Pakistan, its people, and its institutions? To what extent is the U.S. behooved in providing military support to continue wooing the Pakistani Army when the Pakistani populace appears leery of this type of support? To what extent should the U.S. support institution-building in Pakistan to help develop a robust culture of democracy at the expense of vexing the Pakistan Army? These are all questions that are of tremendous importance for U.S. policy toward Pakistan and for the future turns of events within Pakistan's domestic political environment.

Another concern that emerges from these survey findings is that even though both the *Herald* and the U.S. Department of State data suggest widespread support for *madrasah* reform, and for curbing militancy and intolerance, there seems to be little robust effort on the part of the Pakistani government to move on these issues. Reforms of these types are important to stave off the corrosive influences of these accoutrements of militancy upon Pakistan's social and political fabric, but they also are necessary to normalizing relations with India, Iran, Afghanistan, and other states in the region. While curbing militancy and the institutions that produce militancy (for example, the *madrasahs*) are necessary to normalize relations between Pakistan and its neighbors, it is not sufficient. Moreover, these issues pose direct and significant threats to U.S. interests in Pakistan and in the region. As such, the continued failure to enact reforms of these sorts merit concern.

Finally, Pakistani preferences for modes of governances and instruments of law remain an issue of perplexity. The poll data are contradictory. Pakistani respondents claim that they would like to see a decreased involvement of religious parties within politics, while still upholding that Pakistani law should be based upon the Q'uran and Sunnah. What will be the long-term consequences of these preferences upon the shape of the future state of Pakistan? What will these alternative futures mean in terms of Pakistan's relations with its neighbors and with the West? What are the consequences for Pakistan's own internal security?

While this paper certainly raises more questions than it can answer, it shows the need for continued and systematic data collection in Pakistan. Pakistan's salience to the policy community is not likely to diminish. Rather, Pakistan's importance to the global community is likely to increase, as its internal security and foreign policy objectives are key to South Asian deterrence stability and rehabilitation efforts in Afghanistan, among others, as well as diminishing the spread of militancy and terrorism throughout the region and indeed the world.

FIVE

Pakistan's Relations with Azad Kashmir and the Impact on Indo-Pakistani Relations

Rifaat Hussain

In visible contrast to the growing body of scholarship on India's relations with Kashmir, ties between Pakistan and Azad (Free) Kashmir (the area under Pakistani influence) have received scant scholarly attention. This intellectual "silence" is partly a function of the small size of the area comprising Azad Kashmir and the marked absence of violence in the internal politics of the territory under Pakistani control, but it is also largely due to the predominantly status quo bias of the "partition literature." Yet, the significance of Pakistan–Kashmir ties can hardly be exaggerated. Symbolically, as noted by Victoria Schofield, "as so long as Azad Jammu and Kashmir existed," Pakistan could convincingly argue that "an alternative formula other than integration within the Indian Union presented itself to the Kashmiris across the ceasefire line."[1]

Apart from keeping the possibility of an "internal settlement" of the Kashmir question open, Pakistan's relations with Azad Kashmir are a critical component of Islamabad's overall security strategy vis-à-vis India, and they lie at the heart of Pakistan's Islamic identity. As such, they have become the most vital source of recurring India–Pakistan crises. Pakistan's perceived inability to stem the flow of "terrorist" activity from across the Line of Control (LoC) that divides Azad Kashmir from Indian-held Kashmir lay at the core of the May–June 2002 "compound crisis,"[2] which very nearly provoked a catastrophic war between the nuclear-armed adversaries. The crisis was later defused only through direct American diplomatic intervention.

This paper looks at the nature, evolution, and dynamics of Pakistan's relations with Azad Kashmir in the dual context of Pakistan's Kashmir policy and the impact this policy has had on India–Pakistan ties. The central argument of this paper is that while Pakistan's relations with Azad Kashmir display many of the features of interstate inequality associated with the notion of dependent development, these ties are qualitatively different[3] from the situation of "internal colonialism" that characterizes New Delhi's rule over Indian-held Kashmir.[4] Due to the paucity of statistical data, no empirical examination of the different dimensions of the structure of ties between Pakistan and Azad Kashmir will be made.[5]

Azad Kashmir: Historical Antecedents

Lying between longitude 73–75 degrees and latitude 33–36 degrees, Azad Jammu and Kashmir (henceforth AJK) has an area of 5,134 square miles. In the 1981 census, the total population of AJK was 1.98 million, which is estimated to have grown to over 2.7 million in 1993.[6] The population is 100 percent Muslim, and 90 percent of the total population is rural. Density of population is 205 persons per square kilometer, relative to 300 for Pakistan. Thirteen percent of the land mass is cultivated, and 43 percent is covered with forest.[7]

The Northern Area (the Gilgit, Baltistan, and Diamont districts), administered by Pakistan, has an area of 27,800 square miles (82,010 square kilometers). The Karakorum Mountains surround the Northern Area, with twenty-eight peaks of more than 20,000 feet (6,100 meters). Within these mountains are a number of important passes: Chaleli, Mintka, Kilik, Shamshal, Shandour, Karambar, Thougre, Burril, and Durhit. The Northern Area has a population of about 650,000 people, who live in 645 villages and towns perched along narrow valleys. Some people live at 11,000 feet (3,350 meters) and climb in the summer to 14,000 feet (4,265 meters) with their sheep and goats.[8] India, however, does not recognize the Northern Area as part of Pakistan. It argues that it was part of Jammu and Kashmir State by virtue of the Maharaja's decision to accede in favor of India.

Since 1974, AJK has had a parliamentary form of government. The president is the head of the state; he is elected by a joint session of the Assembly and the Azad Kashmir Council and has only titular powers. The prime minister, supported by a Council of Ministers, is the chief executive.[9] The legislative assembly consists of forty-eight members, of whom forty are elected by direct franchise and eight (three male and five female) are elected by the members of the assembly. The state has its own Supreme Court and High Court. AJK is divided into two divisions—Muzaffarabad and Mirpur—and five administrative districts, namely, Muzaffarabad, Poonch, Bagh, Mirpur, and Kotli. The state's capital is Muzaffarabad. AJK also has a broad-based local (municipal) system. There are 182 union councils, 12 town committees, 30 *markaz* (center) councils, 2 municipal corporations, and 5 municipal committees with 17 subdivisions / *tehsils* and 1,646 villages.

The Interim Constitution of AJK (1974) lays down the following functions to the government of Pakistan:

The responsibilities of the Government of Pakistan under the UNCIP Resolutions are:

(a) The defense and security of AJK;
(b) The current coin or the issue of any bills, notes or other paper currency;
(c) The external affairs of AJK including foreign trade, foreign aid and communication.

The modern state of Jammu and Kashmir evolved from the Dogra heartland in Jammu, the home of many different ethnic groups and a diverse set of cultures. In 1834 Ladakh was conquered and incorporated into the state. Baltistan was conquered and annexed by the Dogras in 1840. The Valley of Kashmir was acquired in 1846, when the British sold it to the Sikh ruler Gulab Singh for the sum of 7.5 million rupees, on account of his neutrality during the first Anglo-Sikh war. The Dogras made several attempts to capture Gilgit during the period 1850–90, but never established control. In 1935 Gilgit was leased to the British for sixty years, but the lease was terminated with the subcontinent's independence in 1947. Poonch joined the state in 1936, as the result of a judicial settlement. Aksai Chin came under Chinese control in 1962 (as part of a negotiated settlement between Pakistan and China).

Dogra rule over the state of Jammu and Kashmir was "hated" by the Muslims, who constituted the majority of the population and who "were discriminated against in every way."[10] The first signs of Muslim organization and assertion came in the field of education. In 1905 the Mirwaiz of Kashmir, the spiritual leader of the Kashmiri Muslims, founded an educational forum which sought to provide schooling for poor Muslims and fund those who wished to study abroad. Its beneficiaries included people such as Sheikh Mohammed Abdullah, Ghulam Abbas, Mirza Aslam Beg, and G. M. Sadiq, all future leaders of Indian-controlled Kashmir.

Following Maharaja Hari Singh's succession to the throne in 1925, simmering Muslim resentment against their subjugation reached new heights.[11] In 1929, Ghulam Abbas, a Muslim from Jammu, reorganized the Anjuman-i-Islam ("Muslim Association") into the Young Men's Muslim Association of Jammu, to work for the betterment of Muslims. In Srinagar, the Reading Room Party led by Muhammad Yusuf, Prem Nath Bazaz, and Sheikh Mohammed Abdullah came into being to fight against Hari Singh's oppressive rule. The massacre of twenty-one Kashmiri protestors by Dogra police in the Abdul Qadir incident in Srinagar, on July 13, 1931, further intensified Kashmiri Muslim opposition to the Maharaja's autocratic rule.

In 1932 the All Jammu and Kashmir Muslim Conference was formed by Sheikh Abdullah to give an institutional voice to Muslim demands for better treatment. The All Jammu and Kashmir Muslim Conference contested the thirty-five seats open to them under the 1932 Constitutional Act and won sixteen. However, dissatisfied with the limiting focus of Muslim politics centered on demands for better pay and jobs, and deeply influenced by the socialist thinking of the India National Congress and Jawaharlal Nehru, who had fought for the rights of the people in the princely states under the aegis of the States' Peoples' Congress (a wing of the Congress Party), Sheikh Abdullah distanced himself from the All Jammu and Kashmir Muslim Conference. In 1939, he founded the National Conference and moved closer to the rising Congress Party leader, Jawaharlal Nehru, who promised a secular and socialist India.

Sheikh Abdullah's growing ideological and political affinity with the Indian National Congress made the policy platform of the National Conference "meaningless to Muslims," especially those of "ethnic Punjabi stock from Mirpur and Poonch," who found his advocacy of land-redistribution threatening to their feudal interests. Paralleling the National Conference's strategic drift toward the Indian National Congress, the weakened Muslim Conference, led by the Mirwaiz of Kashmir, Mohammed Yusuf Shah, began a close and important association with the Muslim League. The League, led by Mohammed Ali Jinnah, passed a historic resolution in Lahore in 1940 calling for the creation of independent states in "those areas in which the Muslims are numerically in a majority."[12] In 1943 the Muslim Conference invited Mohammed Ali Jinnah to Kashmir to chair its annual summit. Without hiding his dislike of Sheikh Abdullah, Jinnah asserted that the Muslim Conference "enjoyed the support of the overwhelming majority of the population of the Vale of Kashmir."[13]

In sharp contrast to Jinnah's rejectionist stance, Jawaharlal Nehru praised Sheikh Abdullah as an undisputed leader of the Kashmiri people. Speaking at the annual session of the National Conference in Sopore in 1945, where he was invited as a guest speaker, Nehru said, "Dogra government forced you to lead a subhuman existence. Thanks to Sheikh Sahib's efforts you have once again attained human dignity. In Kashmir, wherever I have gone, I have heard the resounding slogan of 'Long live the Lion of Kashmir.'"[14]

The growing links between the National Conference and the Indian National Congress, on the one hand, and the Muslim Conference and the All India Muslim League, on the other, also reflected the profound differences in the positions of the Congress Party and the Muslim League toward the princely states. Jawaharlal Nehru and the Congress Party had defined their position on the Indian States in August 1935: "The Indian National Congress recognizes that the people in Indian (princely) states have an inherent right of Swaraj [Independence] no less than the people of British India. It has accordingly declared itself in favour of establishment of representative responsible Government in the States." On the contrary, Mohammed Ali Jinnah and the Muslim League made it clear that they did not wish to interfere with the internal affairs of the princely states, which were a "matter primarily to be resolved between the rulers and the peoples of the states."[15] Jinnah's decision to "leave Kashmir alone" was motivated by the realization that "any claim to the State of Jammu and Kashmir in a future Pakistan on the grounds of its Muslim-majority population would only open the door to a Congress claim to the state of Hyderabad as part of India because of its Hindu majority, and, moreover, the Hindu majority in Calcutta might be used as an excuse to exclude that great city from an independent Muslim-majority Bengal."[16]

In 1946 Sheikh Abdullah launched his famous "Quit Kashmir" movement to protest autocratic Dogra rule. The Muslim Conference boycotted the campaign at the behest of the All India Muslim League, which charged that the Sheikh had launched the agitation in order to salvage his sagging popularity, a result of his pro-India stance. Sheikh Abdullah was arrested in 1946 after he attempted to visit Nehru in New Delhi. To demonstrate his solidarity with his incarcerated friend, Nehru attempted to visit Kashmir in July 1946, with the intention of defending Abdullah at his trial. After waiting for several hours to gain entry, he was taken into protective custody before being released. This episode further solidified the personal friendship between Sheikh Abdullah and the future prime minister of India.

At the time of the partition of British India in 1947, the State of Jammu and Kashmir was one of the 564 princely states asked by the British to join either Pakistan or India, in accordance with the twin principles of geographical contiguity and self-determination.[17]

Although the State of Jammu and Kashmir had a Muslim majority (77 percent in the census of 1941) and shared a long border with the new state of Pakistan, the Maharaja refused to opt for Pakistan. His reticence stemmed in large part from his opposition to "the communalism inherent in the League's two-nation theory" and the fact that "joining Pakistan would leave a substantial number of Hindus in Jammu as a minority, as well as Buddhists in Ladakh."[18]

Faced with the armed revolt by Muslims from Poonch in June 1947, the Maharaja retaliated with brutal force against them. He further ordered his rebellious subjects to hand over their weapons. "Feeling distinctly vulnerable, the Poonchis looked for another source of arms and found they were readily available from NWFP (North West Frontier Province in Pakistan)."[19]

The revolt then spread to the other areas of Jammu and Kashmir. To stabilize the situation, the Maharaja signed a standstill agreement with the new state of Pakistan. The situation deteriorated during August and September of 1947, as the Kashmiri Muslims openly revolted. In this armed insurrection they were joined by their fellow tribesmen from the North West Frontier Province in Pakistan, who were incited by communal riots and clashes in neighboring Punjab and stories of Hindu and Sikh attacks on Muslim villages in Jammu, where there was a large non-Muslim population. By late October 1947, the tribesmen-led rebellion had succeeded in capturing several towns, massacred large numbers of civilians, and advanced within four miles of the capital, Srinagar.[20]

To forestall his imminent overthrow by the advancing rebel troops, the Maharaja requested military aid from India on October 24. The uprising caused considerable interest in Pakistan, where Mohammed Ali Jinnah and his prime minister, Liaqat Ali Khan, hoped that it might force the Maharaja to opt for Pakistan. Exploiting the links between the Poonch rebels, individuals, and "Pakistani components of the old Indian Army," Pakistani authorities furnished "weapons and men" in "slight" quantity to the insurgents.[21] Sensing that Kashmir was ready for the taking, Nehru sent V. P. Menon to Srinagar on October 25, where he reportedly told the Maharaja "that if he did not sign the Instrument of Accession there and then Delhi would be unable to send Indian troops to help him."[22] Faced with this ultimatum, the embattled Maharaja acceded to the Indian Union. The Indian government accepted the Maharaja's accession, while stipulating that this accession of Kashmir to India should be ratified ultimately by popular consultation. India's military intervention on behalf of the besieged Maharaja led to the first India–Pakistan war over Kashmir. India took the Kashmir dispute to the United Nations, calling for the world body's intervention in the matter.

After their first war over Kashmir in 1947–48, India and Pakistan signed a ceasefire agreement on January 1, 1949. The two states again went to war over Kashmir in 1965, and the resulting Line of Control divided old Jammu and Kashmir into four political units: (1) Ladakh and Jammu and the Kashmir Valley (Indian-occupied Kashmir, or occupied Kashmir, from a Pakistani viewpoint); (2) Azad Kashmir (Pakistan-occupied Kashmir, from an Indian viewpoint); (3) the Northern Area, administered by Pakistan; and (4) Aksai Chin (which had already been ceded by Pakistan to China in 1962), controlled by China.

Evolution of Pakistan–Azad Kashmir Ties

The government of Azad Kashmir was established at Pulandri in Jammu district on October 24, 1947, under the aegis of the working committee of the All Jammu Kashmir Muslim Conference. Sardar Mohammed Ibrahim Khan, a thirty-two-year-old Sudhan who had organized an army of about "50,000" during the Poonch rebellion,[23] was confirmed as president of this new entity. The Azad Kashmir government defined its objective as the liberation of Jammu and Kashmir from the Dogra dynasty and then the Indian authorities. In a bid to assert its legality, on November 3 the Azad Kashmir government requested international recognition as a State from the U.N. General Assembly. Its international legal status, however, never went beyond what the United Nations Commission for India and Pakistan (UNCIP) described as a "territory to be administered by the local authorities under surveillance of the Commission."[24]

In March 1949 the AJK government concluded a power-sharing treaty with the government of Pakistan. According to this treaty, matters pertaining to defense, foreign affairs, negotiations with UNCIP, publicity in foreign countries, responsibilities for relief and rehabilitation of refugees, the plebiscite, activities related to the procurement of food, civil supplies, transport and refugee camps, and medical aid were to be dealt with by Pakistan. Additionally, the affairs of Gilgit and Baltistan, previously under a political agent, became the responsibility of the Pakistan government.[25] All other matters fell within the purview of the Azad Kashmir administration.

In 1948 the Pakistan government created the Ministry for Kashmir Affairs (MKA), headed by a Joint Secretary, and placed it under the general guidance of the federal Ministry of Home Affairs. In addition to supervising the foreign and financial arrangement of Azad Kashmir, the MKA was also to "assist in the appointment of leaders of Azad Kashmir."[26] In 1952 the government of Pakistan promulgated new "Rules of Business," which vested full power in the Joint Secretary of the MKA rather than in the Muslim Conference Party.[27] Both Sheikh Mohammed Ibrahim and Ghulam Abbas criticized this as an infringement on the rights of the people of Azad Jammu and Kashmir to freely choose their own government and "sought assurances that [it] would not over-ride popular sentiment within Azad Kashmir."[28]

Despite assurances by the Pakistan government that it would not be "shadowing the government in Muzaffarabad," the confidence of the Muslim Conference in the former's "integrity" remained very low. In May 1954, Sardar Mohammed Ibrahim publicly protested against bribery, corruption, and embezzlement, and accused the Minister of Kashmiri Affairs of proposing to "colonize" Azad Kashmir.[29]

Pakistan's taking of direct administrative control over the Northern Area (the Gilgit, Baltistan, and Diamont districts), on the assumption that they had never formed part of the disputed territory of the State of Jammu and Kashmir, further angered Muzaffarabad, which viewed this move as a continuation of the British colonial policy of divide and rule.

In 1955, following the publication of the Kashmir Government Act, the Pakistani authorities placed Poonch and parts of Mirpur under martial law, after the outbreak of widespread disturbances.

In April 1957 riot police broke up the meeting of the Muslim Conference, after Sardar Mohammed Ibrahim called for some form of direct action in favor of a "united and independent" Kashmir.

This growing disaffection of the Muslim Conference toward Pakistan led to the formation, in 1958, of the Kashmir Liberation Movement (KLM), with K. H. Khurshid as Acting Secretary. The KLM was a nonviolent body which repeatedly challenged Pakistani control over Azad Kashmir by attempting to cross the ceasefire line into India. The KLM's activities led to the arrest of Ghulam Abbas and further widened the gulf between the old guard of the Muslim Conference and the Pakistani authorities.

In 1961 the military regime of Ayub Khan implemented the system of indirect elections in Azad Kashmir. This was done in clear violation of its earlier assurances that the provisions of the "Basic Democracies" ordinance (see the chapter by Charles Kennedy in this book) would not be extended to Azad Kashmir. Through this system, 2,400 Basic Democrats elected K. H. Khurshid as the new head of government in Muzaffarabad.

Facing splits in its ranks caused by differences over its response to events within Pakistan, the Muslim Conference, under the leadership of Abdul Qayyum Khan, organized fresh crossings of the ceasefire line and set up groups of armed volunteers to "liberate" Indian-held Kashmir, not "for Pakistan but for a separate Kashmiri state." Such activity provoked clashes with the Pakistani authorities, who attempted to contain such agitation, in view of the sensitivities of the border areas.

These strains in Pakistan's relations with Azad Kashmir did not deter Muzaffarabad from either becoming "dependent on Pakistan for its economic survival" or from becoming an "adjunct to Pakistani politics, at times used as a launching pad for initiatives into the valley, at others, a poor relation, which because of Pakistan's claim to the whole of the State of Jammu and Kashmir, the Pakistani government never found itself in a position to acknowledge as a province of Pakistan."[30]

In 1964 General Ayub Khan appointed a Kashmir Public Committee, with Foreign Secretary Aziz Ahmed as its chairman, to keep the Kashmir situation under review.[31] The Kashmir committee then prepared two plans, one to encourage sabotage across the ceasefire line and the other to provide "all out support for guerillas to be inducted into Kashmir."[32] Both these tasks were assigned to "HQ 12 Division located at Murree."[33] In mid-February 1965 the Kashmir Committee prepared Operation Gibraltar, which was personally approved by General Ayub Khan on May 13.[34] The principal aim of Operation Gibraltar was to "disrupt the situation in the Srinagar Valley and create conditions whereby the emboldened local populace would rise against the Indian Army of occupation using weapons provided by Pakistan."[35] The Kashmir cell trained some "7,000" guerrillas who, led by Pakistan army officers crossed the ceasefire line in August and launched their attack.[36] The anticipated Kashmiri revolt, however, never materialized.[37] Operation Gibraltar turned into a military disaster for Pakistan, as India launched a counter-military offensive along the ceasefire line, which allowed the Indian military to "cut off the militant's supply lines, leaving the infiltrators short of material and completely isolated."[38] The swift Indian military response endangered the security of Azad Kashmir, as many forward Pakistani posts, including Hajipir Pass, fell to the Indian army on August 29, 1965.[39] By September 10, the Indian Army "virtually held a line from Uri to Poonch."[40]

Operation Gibraltar's manifest failure to achieve its stated aims of "defreezing the Kashmir problem" and "weakening India's resolve" so as to "bring her to a conference table without provoking a general war" caused profound disillusionment in Pakistan and Azad Kashmir.[41] Contrary to its objectives, Operation Gibraltar not only triggered a full-scale India–Pakistan war but also underscored Pakistan's inability to fight a "thousand year" war with India over Kashmir. In the wake of the 1965 war, it became quite evident that Pakistan "could not realistically expect New Delhi to give ground on Kashmir or expect the rest of the world to exert itself after Pakistan had tried and failed to resolve the issue through the use of force."[42]

Having lost hope for the liberation from New Delhi rule of an Indian-controlled Kashmir, leaders of the political parties in Azad Kashmir turned inward and began agitating for sovereign status. In 1968 Amanullah Khan led a procession of the All Parties Kashmir Committee in Karachi, which represented various political parties including the Plebiscite Front and the Liberation League. Other Azad Kashmiri leaders, such as Sardar Abdul Qayyum, Sardar Ibrahim, and K. H. Khurshid, joined forces and demanded that "Azad Kashmir should be recognized as the sovereign government successor of Maharaja Hari Singh for the whole of the state." In 1969 the Pakistan People's Party, founded by Zulfiqar Ali Bhutto in October 1967, set up its branch in Muzaffarabad. This development marked the beginning of party politics in Azad Kashmir.[43]

Faced with the rising tide of Kashmiri nationalism, Islamabad announced a new constitutional arrangement for Azad Kashmir. Under the 1970 Kashmir Government Act, a twenty-five-member Legislative Assembly, elected by full adult suffrage, was organized. Sardar Abdul Qayyum won the first presidential elections in October 1970, which, according to one analyst, proved the point that Kashmiris "were not a bunch of mountain dwelling simple folk who live on Pakistan's bounty but a dynamic people even capable of giving a lead to Pakistan despite having our wings clipped in the 1949 Karachi Agreement."[44] The introduction of electoral politics in Azad Kashmir, while removing the biggest source of unease between Islamabad and Muzaffarabad, did not lead to a complete harmony of views.

Following Pakistan's dismemberment and humiliating defeat in the 1971 India–Pakistan war, Islamabad signed the Simla Agreement with India in July 1972. The Simla Agreement was "devoid of any reference to the UN's mediation and peacekeeping roles in Kashmir." Further, "It said nothing of the UN resolutions that had enabled the original ceasefire; and there was no mention of the role that UNMOGIP (United Nations Military Observer Group in India and Pakistan) . . . might play in delimiting the new line in policing it."[45] These omissions, coupled with the conversion of the ceasefire line into the Line of Control (LoC), as a result of which the Indian and Pakistani forces deployed in Kashmir became "eyeball-to-eyeball," created an impression in Azad Kashmir that Pakistan was either no longer able or, worse, willing, to stand up for the rights of the Kashmiri people. These negative Kashmiri perceptions were reinforced by Islamabad's decision to put Gilgit and Pakistan-administered Baltistan under Islamabad's direct control. The incorporation of the former princely state of Hunza into the detached Northern Territories in 1974 further undermined hopes of a special relationship spawned by the Kashmir Government Act promulgated the same year.

Despite Muzaffarabad's public protestations, Islamabad continued the process of political integration of the Northern Areas into Pakistan. In 1977, the area was included in Martial Law Zone-E by General Zia ul Haq, when he assumed power in a military coup on July 5. In April 1982 Haq nominated three members of the Federal Majlis-e-Shura from the Northern Areas and publicly stated, "Kashmir has been a disputed issue, but so far as the Northern Areas are concerned, we do not accept them as disputed." In July 1982 General Zia declared that the northern regions of Gilgit, Hunza, and Skardu were an integral part of Pakistan.[46] In 1984 special units of the Indian Army occupied three key passes (Sia, Bilafond La, and Gyong La) in the Saltoro range, thus dominating the approaches onto the massive Siachin Glacier.[47] The Pakistan Army's efforts to get the area vacated proved futile due to the extraordinary hazards of altitude and climate.[48] Indian military incursion into Siachin further strengthened the Zia regime's resolve to accelerate the process of integration of the Northern Areas into Pakistan.

These moves by the military regime provoked a strong reaction in Azad Kashmir. On May 4, 1984, four of the major political parties (the Jammu and Kashmir Muslim Conference, the Azad Kashmir People's Party, the Jammu and Kashmir Mahaze-e-Raiy Shumari–Plebiscite Front, and the Azad Muslim Conference) sent a jointly signed letter to President Zia explaining their position on the issue of the Northern Areas. While claiming that the Northern Areas had belonged to Azad Kashmir, they charged that Zia's statements "were depriving around six to seven hundred thousand inhabitants of the area of their right to vote in the plebiscite, which will be a great loss to Kashmir and to Pakistan."[49]

Ignoring Muzaffarabad's assertions, Islamabad announced a "reform package" for the Northern Areas in April 1994, the implementation of which turned this contested territory into a de facto fifth province of Pakistan.[50] To further extend Islamabad's administrative and legal writ to the Northern Areas, the federal government, for the first time, decided to appoint a Chief Secretary and four Secretaries in the area.

To underscore Azad Kashmir's opposition to Islamabad's moves to absorb the Northern Areas into the administrative structure of Pakistan, the full bench of the Azad Kashmir High Court held, in a ruling on March 18, 1993, that the "Northern Areas (Gilgit and Baltistan) are part of Azad Kashmir, historically and constitutionally," and further pronounced that "the Azad Kashmir government should establish administrative and legal institutions in these areas." Islamabad challenged this decision in the Supreme Court in Muzaffarabad. Announcing its decision on September 14, 1994, the AJK Supreme Court said: "No doubt, that the Northern Areas are part of the state of Jammu and Kashmir—but not of Azad Kashmir. Therefore the government need not take administrative control of these areas." The Supreme Court of Pakistan, in its verdict of May 28, 1999, pronounced: "The Northern Areas were a constitutional part of the State of Jammu and Kashmir."[51] It called upon the government of Pakistan to "ensure that basic human rights and other political and administrative institutions are provided in the areas within six months. However, the action should not adversely affect Pakistan's stand concerning the Kashmir dispute."

Pursuant to the Supreme Court's decision, Islamabad prepared a constitutional reform package, announced by General (Ret.) Abdul Majeed Malik during his visit to the area on October 2, 1999. The package envisaged replacing the existing Northern Areas Council with a Legislative Council and called for the holding of elections for the Council and local bodies. Despite the takeover of power by the Army on October 12, 1999, these elections were held. On July 7, 2000, the military government announced another package of reforms, under which the Northern Area Council was renamed as the "Northern Area Legislative Council," comprising twenty-nine members. Five seats were reserved for women—one elected indirectly from each district. The moves by Islamabad to "empower" the people of the Northern Areas and to improve their depressed economic condition continue to evoke anxiety and opposition in Azad Kashmir. Muzaffarabad sees these administrative and political initiatives not only as a blatant violation of the sovereignty of AJK, but also as an effort by Islamabad to "truncate" the size of the disputed territory of the State of Jammu and Kashmir.

Impact on India–Pakistan Relations

The dynamics of Pakistan's uneasy relations with Azad Kashmir qualitatively changed under the impact of the twin events of the decade-long Soviet–Afghan war, which began with Moscow's military invasion of Afghanistan in December 1979, and the outbreak of the "Intifada" in Indian-held Kashmir in 1988–89.[52] The two events revived the age-old ties between the Kashmiris and the Afghans as "neighbours and friends,"[53] ties that had lain dormant since the time of Durrani rule over Kashmir in the later half of the eighteenth century. But they also gave Islamabad new and dangerous tools, in the form of Islamic jihad, to continue to play its "offset strategy" against India in Kashmir.[54]

The Soviet–Afghan war, which culminated in Moscow's defeat in 1988, created a nexus between Islamic militancy and Pakistan's foreign policy. As a "frontline state," Pakistan became the linchpin of CIA-backed Afghan resistance against the Soviet occupation of Afghanistan.

Besides having acted as a channel for the CIA's massive covert aid program to the Afghan "Mujahideen," the ISI (Pakistan's Inter-Services Intelligence) "got deeply involved in the training and recruitment of Mujahideen . . . to sustain the war."[55]

This mobilizing effort spawned the mushroom growth of religious *madrasahs* in Pakistan.[56] They soon "developed into sanctuaries of religious zealots and political power."[57]

The Afghan jihad also accentuated the role of Islam in Pakistan's strategic culture, giving rise to the belief that the success of the Afghan jihad could be "replicated elsewhere, and it offered an option to bring an end to non-Muslim domination of the Muslims."[58] Thus, after the withdrawal of the Soviet forces from Afghanistan in 1989, "Kashmir became the new 'Jihad' and the Hindus the new infidels."[59]

Backed by the ISI, these jihadi groups[60]—prominent among which were the Hizbul Mujahidin, the Al Badr Mujahideen, the Harkat ul-Mujahedin (previously known as Harkat ul-Ansar), the Lashkar-i-Tayyiba, and the Jaish-e-Mohammed—"found a new cause in Indian-administered Kashmir where an insurgency had erupted in 1989."[61] Their involvement in the Kashmiri Intifada transformed it from a domestic insurgency (conducted via the Jammu Kashmir Liberation Front) into a low-intensity conflict between India and Pakistan. As Islamabad's forward policy in Indian-held Kashmir began to take its toll on Indian security forces,[62] and along with them on innocent civilians, New Delhi accused Pakistan of waging a proxy war against India from Azad Kashmir. Indian and foreign media reports identified at least ninety-one insurgent training camps in Azad Kashmir, "the bulk of which lie contiguous to the Indian districts of Kupwara, Baramullah, Poonch, Rajuari and Jammu."[63]

Islamabad denied these accusations and responded that the Kashmiri insurgency was the product of decades of Indian abuses in the state. V. P. Singh, who became Prime Minister on December 2, 1989, pledged to fight fire with fire.

In January 1990 New Delhi appointed hard-liner Jagmohan Malhotra as governor of Jammu and Kashmir and sent 150,000 additional troops to restore law and order. Indian J&K Chief Minister Farooq Abdullah resigned, and tensions between the militants, mostly Kashmiri youth, and the Indian security forces exploded into mass violence, in which over one hundred people were killed.

The bloody events of January 1990 transformed the Kashmiri uprising into a renewed Indo-Pakistani confrontation. As the hostile rhetoric, along with conventional firing, across the Line of Control in Kashmir mounted, India and Pakistan made threatening military moves with nuclear overtones.[64] Mindful of the Brasstacks experience in 1987, and determined not to let India have a "running start against" it,[65] Islamabad issued orders to its scientists to assemble a nuclear weapon.

This move caused alarm in Washington, prompting American officials to send messages to the "governments of China, the Soviet Union, and European countries asking them to urge India and Pakistan to exercise restraint."[66] To prevent India and Pakistan from stumbling into war over Kashmir, President George Bush sent his Deputy National Security Robert Gates to Islamabad and New Delhi. Gates urged leaders in both capitals to avoid any action that might trigger a conflict. In Islamabad Robert Gates told Pakistan leaders, "The United States had war-gamed every conceivable scenario between you and the Indians. There is not a single way you win. The only question is how much territory and how many military forces you will lose."[67] He went on to tell his Pakistani hosts that their "resumption of the nuclear weapon program had been detected and would force the United States to invoke the Pressler Amendment, cutting off economic and military aid to Pakistan."[68]

Tensions between India and Pakistan eased, and following an exchange of "non-papers" intended to "reduce hostile rhetoric, increase contact between military commanders, share information on military exercise, prevent airspace violations by military aircraft, and open negotiations on a wide range of outstanding issues,"[69] both sides agreed to resume foreign-secretary-level talks. No agreement resulted from the three rounds of talks, but the fourth round, held in New Delhi in April 1991, did culminate in an agreement on "Advance Notification on Military Exercises, Maneuvers, and Troop Movement," and a concurrent deal on the "Prevention of Airspace Violations."

The 1990 Kashmir crisis had several important consequences for Pakistan's security outlook. One, it convinced Pakistani leaders of the efficacy of their nuclear weapons capability as a check against Indian proclivity for aggression against their country. Two, it also caused the rupture of Pakistan–U.S. strategic ties on account of the two countries' differences on the nuclear question. Following the dismissal of Benazir Bhutto's government by President Ghulam Ishaq Khan in August 1990 and the refusal of the caretaker government to "give up its existing capability," Washington announced the imposition of Pressler sanctions against Pakistan in October 1990. Three, it also forced Islamabad to "curb the independence sentiment" that clearly lay at the foundation of the Kashmiri Intifada.[70] As part of this effort, Islamabad told Muzaffarabad that "accession to Pakistan was the only option open to Kashmiris."[71]

Undeterred by the punitive American actions, Islamabad publicly acknowledged that it had the components and the know-how to assemble at least one nuclear device. Pakistan's Foreign Secretary, Shahryar Kahn, told the *Washington Post* that this capability existed prior to Nawaz Sharif's election in October 1990 and that the new government "froze the program."[72]

New Delhi reacted to Islamabad's admission to having a nuclear device by demanding greater American pressure on Pakistan and called for more robust Indian countermeasures. Indian Defense Minister Sharad Pawar publicly stated that if Pakistan was thinking of making a nuclear threat, "India's reaction would be to make Islamabad bear the burden of suffering for generations"—a clear reference to nuclear retaliation.[73]

The intensification of the Indian missile development program, especially the flight-testing of the short-range, nuclear-capable Prithvi missile in August 1992, which Islamabad perceived as "Pakistan specific," combined with the destruction of the Babari Mosque at Ayodhya by Hindu radicals on December 6, 1992, and New Delhi's unwillingness to negotiate bilateral constraints on nuclear activities with Pakistan due to India's concern with China's long-term threat, kept India–Pakistan relations in a deep freeze for the next two years.

The Indian and Pakistani foreign secretaries met in early January 1994 and agreed to exchange proposals on key issues of concern. But Islamabad's insistence on the inclusion of Kashmir as the core issue on the agenda for talks stalled the normalization process.

Indo-Pakistan relations turned acrimonious in the mid-1990s, when the Clinton administration, in a bid to improve its strained ties with Islamabad, decided to allow delivery of the $368 million worth of Pakistan-owned military equipment that had been retained in the United States since 1990 and to permit the resumption of economic aid, investment guarantees, and military training. New Delhi saw this initiative as a conscious attempt by Washington to reopen channels of military assistance to Pakistan and thereby disturb the India–Pakistan strategic balance. In deference to New Delhi's sensitivities, Islamabad was not given the F-16s that it had paid for. Instead, proceeds from their sale to a third party were to be reimbursed. The passage of the Brown Amendment and its subsequent implementation marked the failure of the American punitive strategy and sanction-oriented approach toward Islamabad. Coupled with the amendment's tacit acceptance of Pakistan as a de facto nuclear weapon state, it also signaled "the Clinton administration's desire to put relations with Pakistan on a friendlier footing."[74]

India and Pakistan resumed dialogue in 1997 after a hiatus of four years. The main impetus for the resumption of dialogue emanated from a series of opportune political developments and exploratory meetings throughout 1996 and 1997. India's national elections in May 1996 produced a new United Front Government, first under Deve Gowda and then under Foreign Minister I. K. Gujral, which tried to set a new tone for New Delhi's role in South Asia under the Gujral Doctrine.

The Gujral Doctrine sought to improve relations with India's neighbors without strict reciprocity and on the principle of accommodation to smaller powers. With regard to Pakistan, it emphasized the role of confidence-building measures, ongoing dialogue, the avoidance of hostile propaganda, and people-to-people contacts. The return to power, in February 1997, of Nawaz Sharif, who successfully campaigned on the theme of "cooperation not confrontation with India," nicely dovetailed with the goodwill of the new Indian leadership. In his first month in office, Nawaz Sharif accepted a proposal from India's Prime Minister Deve Gowda to engage in wide-ranging comprehensive talks on all issues at an "appropriate" level. The prime ministers agreed that foreign-secretary-level talks would be held in New Delhi on March 28–31, 1997. The first round of renewed talks, despite being overshadowed by political turmoil in India which led to the downfall of the Deve Gowda government, did lead to Indian acceptance of the Pakistani suggestion that "working groups" should be set up to tackle the outstanding issues at a later date.

The elevation of I. K. Gujral to the office of prime minister in April and a special "chemistry" between him and Nawaz Sharif, both from the Punjab, inspired hopes for a new beginning. The May 12 Sharif–Gujral meeting in the Maldives, led to an undertaking "to release civilian prisoners, establish a hotline to facilitate communication, relax travel restrictions, and to institute a series of working groups to address outstanding issues, including Kashmir, for the foreign-secretary-level talks scheduled for June." The June talks, held in Murree, Pakistan, resulted in a joint statement, which detailed the two countries' commitment to resolving outstanding issues in an integrated bilateral manner.

The two governments pledged to commission working groups to address a number of peace and security issues, including CBMs, Jammu and Kashmir, and the settlement of such disputes as Siachin, the Wullar Barrage/Tulbul Navigation Project, and Sir Creek. The groups would also attempt to promote economic and commercial cooperation and friendly exchanges in other fields.

The "Male spirit" dissipated after the mid-term Indian general elections held in February and March 1998, in which the right-wing Hindu Nationalist Party, the Bharatiya Janata Party (BJP) came to power. Less than a day before he was sworn in as India's fourteenth prime minister, Atal Bihari Vajpayee unveiled a policy agenda on behalf of the new thirteen-party coalition government led by the BJP. While aspiring to usher India into a "new political age" of dynamic growth, the thirty-two-point policy blueprint, among other things, called for a "strategic defense review" and committed the BJP-led government to "take all necessary steps and exercise all available options," including the "option to induct nuclear weapons," to ensure the "security, territorial integrity and unity of India." This unvarnished espousal by the BJP of its immediate nuclear ambitions evoked great unease and alarm in Pakistan.

Reacting to the new Indian government's nuclear policy, a spokesman for the Pakistan Foreign Office said, "This is a dangerous development for the region as well as for the world at large. We are very seriously disturbed at this assertion and its implications, which threaten the peace and stability of South Asia. It multiplies manifold the threat to Pakistan's security besides dealing a grievous blow to global and regional efforts at nuclear non-proliferation." The minister warned, "In this situation, if the need arises, we shall review our policy to safeguard our sovereignty, territorial integrity and national interests."

In his address to the Disarmament Conference in Geneva on March 19, 1998, Pakistani Foreign Minister Gohar Ayub Khan warned the world community that India's pledge to go nuclear could "push" South Asia "into a dangerous arms race." He said that while "Pakistan does not wish to expend its scarce resources on a conventional or a nuclear arms race," there should be no "doubt about our ability and determination to deliver a swift and telling response to any aggression or adventurism against Pakistan."[75]

On May 11 and 13, 1998, India conducted five nuclear tests code-named "Shakti" and proclaimed itself a nuclear weapon state.[76] The Indian nuclear tests created a great sense of alarm in Pakistan. Pakistan's foreign minister, Gohar Ayub Khan, described them as a "death blow to the global efforts at nuclear non-proliferation" and called upon the international community to issue a strong condemnation.[77]

Reacting to international appeals that Islamabad should exercise restraint in the face of India's provocative action, Prime Minister Nawaz Sharif stated that "being a sovereign state Pakistan has every right to undertake measures for national defense and security."[78] Belligerent statements by Indian leaders, which warned Islamabad to roll back its anti-India policy and vacate Azad Kashmir, not only aggravated Pakistani threat perceptions but convinced Islamabad that the Shakti tests had decisively tilted the strategic balance in India's favor.[79]

Characterizing Indian action as a qualitative change in its security environment, Islamabad brushed aside international urgings not to conduct a rival nuclear test. In a May 13 statement, Foreign Minister Gohar Ayub Khan categorically stated, "Indian actions pose an immediate and grave threat to Pakistan's security and these will not go unanswered."[80] Clearly Pakistan, under immense domestic political pressure, was increasingly unable to manage the pressure from overseas, particularly its closest Western ally, the United States. Notably, Chinese pressure on Pakistan was largely muted during this period. The Muslim states of West Asia and the Middle East also stayed quiet.[81]

To review Pakistan's security options in the wake of the Indian nuclear tests, Prime Minister Nawaz Sharif convened a meeting of the Defense Committee of the Cabinet. Joining strident calls for an immediate tit-for-tat response by the small but powerful pro-bomb lobby in Pakistan, the leader of the opposition, Benazir Bhutto, called upon the Nawaz government to "immediately respond to the Indian test."

Two weeks later, on May 28 and 30, Pakistan matched Indian action by conducting five nuclear tests in the Chagai Hill range in the province of Baluchistan.

The May 1998 rival nuclear tests by India and Pakistan not only underscored the continued salience of security issues in South Asia in the post-Cold War era, but also belied the expectation that the end of the Cold War would necessarily lead to the end of what Robert Lifton and Richard Falk describe as "nuclearism"—that is, the "psychological, political and military dependence on nuclear weapons . . . as a solution to . . . the dilemma of security."[82]

Following its tit-for-tat nuclear tests in May 1998, Pakistan's traditional security dilemma vis-à-vis its hostile neighbor, India, was somewhat attenuated. Nuclear weapons appear to have had three general effects on interstate relations. First, nuclear weapons provide the nuclear state with an "infrangible guarantee of its independence and physical security." Second, mutual deterrence among antagonistic nuclear states places a limitation on violence and, in turn, acts as a brake on total war. Third, by altering the "offense-defense" balance in favor of defense, nuclear weapons have made it possible for weaker states to "defend themselves effectively against large powerful countries."[83]

Pakistan faced the burden of additional American sanctions in May 1998. In response to Pakistani nuclear tests, President Clinton imposed congressionally mandated sanctions, under which all American bilateral and multilateral economic assistance to Pakistan was cut off. The United States and other shareholders in the International Monetary Fund also formed a coalition to block disbursement of the IMF credit and the parallel adjustment loan from the World Bank.

Because of its prior economic vulnerability, the Pakistani economy was severely hit by this withdrawal of international financing and by the indirect effects of this withdrawal on other capital inflows to Pakistan. As part of its three-pronged strategy of "damage control," which aimed to prevent any escalation of a nuclear and missile race between India and Pakistan, minimize damage to the non-proliferation regime, and promote bilateral dialogue between India and Pakistan, the United States called upon New Delhi and Islamabad to comply with the benchmarks set out by the Security Council in its Resolution 1172, passed on June 6, 1998. These included such steps as: signing and ratifying the Comprehensive Test Ban Treaty; halting all further production of weapon-usable fissile material and joining the negotiations on a fissile material treaty at the Conference on Disarmament in Geneva; limiting development and deployment of delivery vehicles for weapons of mass destruction; and resuming a bilateral dialogue on resolving long-standing tensions and disputes.

In pursuit of these goals, U.S. Deputy Secretary of State Strobe Talbott visited New Delhi and Islamabad on July 19–23, 1998. While failing to evoke any definitive response from New Delhi in terms of the benchmarks, Mr. Talbott's visit to Islamabad went beyond the promise of "constructive engagement" between Pakistan and the United States. In exchange for American help in getting an IMF-centered, multibillion dollar rescue economic package for the ailing Pakistani economy, Islamabad provisionally agreed to consider taking the following four steps to address the American's proliferation concerns: (1) making a public commitment on softening its position on the CTBT; (2) exercising restraint on the deployment of long-range missiles; (3) exercising restraint on fissile material production; and (4) observing export control on the transfer of missile and nuclear technology.

Mr. Talbott's July 1998 visit to India and Pakistan also led to the resumption of their stalled bilateral dialogue, albeit indirectly under the aegis of the South Asian Association for Regional Cooperation (SAARC). In keeping with the SAARC practice of "informal consultations" among member states on contentious bilateral political matters which otherwise cannot be discussed in SAARC summit meetings, Prime Ministers Sharif and Vajpayee held two rounds of "informal" bilateral talks at the tenth SAARC summit meeting, held in Colombo, Sri Lanka in July 1998. The first round, held on July 29, were described as wide-ranging, in which all issues, including the core issue of Kashmir, were discussed by both leaders.

Following the first round, it was announced that India and Pakistan would be resuming the "dialogue" process, the modalities of which were to be worked out by their respective foreign secretaries. Accordingly, India Foreign Secretary K. Raghunath met with his Pakistani counterpart, Mr. Shamshad Ahmed Khan, twice, on July 29 and July 30, to overcome the "procedural" and "substantive" impediments to the formal resumption of an India–Pakistan dialogue. These talks foundered on the rock of Indian insistence that New Delhi was no longer bound by the Islamabad Accord of June 27, 1997, under which both countries had agreed to conduct their future negotiations within the framework of "working groups" on eight specific issues, including the contentious question of Jammu and Kashmir.

To help break the impasse, a second round of Sharif–Vajpayee talks was held on the last day of the Colombo summit on July 31. This second meeting became a total failure, as it coincided with a marked escalation of hostilities between India and Pakistan along the volatile Line of Control in Kashmir, in which over three dozen people, including four Pakistani soldiers, were killed by Indian firing. Prime Minister Nawaz Sharif described the outcome of his talks with the Indian Prime Minister as "zero," and Indian Foreign Secretary Raghunath accused Islamabad of carrying out a "propagandist" exercise in the garb of conducting talks.[84]

The failure of the India–Pakistan talks at Colombo on July 31, 1998, was accompanied by a week of sustained artillery clashes between Indian and Pakistani troops across the flammable Line of Control in the disputed state of Jammu and Kashmir. Besides claiming more than a hundred lives and causing extensive damage to civilian property on both sides of the Kashmir divide, these violent military clashes evoked an exchange of harsh words between New Delhi and Islamabad.

Following press reports that Indian war planes had violated Pakistani airspace on August 1, 1998,[85] Kashmir Affairs Minister Lt. General (Ret.) Abdul Majeed Malik told a news conference in Islamabad that Pakistan was ready to "give a befitting reply to any armed conflict imposed on it by India."[86] A day later, Prime Minister Nawaz Sharif accused India of "taking South Asia to the brink of war" and called upon the international community to take notice of Indian aggression.[87]

In response, Indian Prime Minister Vajpayee warned Islamabad that "India would use a firm hand to respond to any attack on its border." He expressed the resolve of his government to "fully back" the efforts of the Indian army to "repulse the nefarious designs of Pakistan."[88]

This marked escalation in India–Pakistan verbal hostility, coupled with intensive firing by both sides along the volatile LoC, generated considerable international concern. On August 3, 1998, Washington reportedly sent "urgent messages" to Islamabad and New Delhi, asking them to "refrain from proactive actions and rhetoric," to "resume the senior level dialogue as soon as possible," and to "approach the problem imaginatively and constructively."[89]

In a similar vein, China also urged India and Pakistan to "show restraint and eliminate their differences through dialogue."[90] In its statement before the U.N. Sub-Commission on Prevention of Discrimination and Protection of Minorities, the Organization of Islamic Conference (OIC) also expressed its "deep concern" over the escalation of tensions across the LoC and voiced its apprehension that if allowed to go unchecked these activities could entail "disastrous consequences."[91]

Motivated partly by their shared interest in avoiding the risks of inadvertent escalation inherent in the prevailing explosive situation along the LoC, and partly by the need to play to the international gallery, both New Delhi and Islamabad expressed their willingness to resume the stalled India–Pakistan talks. Characterizing the situation along the LoC as "unprecedented," a spokesman for the Pakistan Foreign Office called for "serious" India–Pakistan dialogue to "de-escalate" tensions.[92]

The Chief of Army Staff, General Jehangir Karamat, while addressing officers at the Karachi, Multan, and Malir garrisons, stressed the need to "avoid unnecessary rhetoric" and "lurid headlines," as they "do not contribute to security" and "induce false bravado and euphoria."[93]

General Karamat's call for a level-headed response to the combustible situation in Kashmir was directed as much at the hawkish elements within the country as it was at those in India clamoring for seizing control of "Azad Kashmir" through military means. For its part, New Delhi also emitted conciliatory signals. On August 3, 1998, Indian Home Minister Lal Krishna Advani reportedly said that India was willing to "resume dialogue with Pakistan on all issues including Kashmir" and that these talks "would be held on the basis of Simla Agreement."[94] Indian Prime Minister Vajpayee also underscored his desire for a "purposeful" dialogue with his Pakistani counterpart during their meeting at the Non-Aligned Movement summit in Durban and at the U.N. General Assembly meeting in New York in September 1998.

The joint statement issued after the Nawaz–Vajpayee meeting in New York on September 24 said that the two leaders had "reaffirmed their common belief that an environment of durable peace and security was in the supreme interest of both India and Pakistan and of the region as a whole. They expressed their determination to renew and reinvigorate efforts to secure such an environment. They agreed that the peaceful settlement of all outstanding issues, including Jammu and Kashmir, was essential for the purpose." It further said that the two sides agreed to "operationalise the mechanism to address all items in the agreed agenda of June 23, 1997 in a purposeful and composite manner in October and November."

Encouraged by the prospects of the resumption of the India–Pakistan dialogue process, Washington announced the partial lifting of sanctions against India and Pakistan on November 7, 1998. This action enabled U.S. support for IMF assistance to Pakistan as a one-time exception to the sanctions still in place.

In October 1998 India and Pakistan resumed foreign-secretary-level talks, which paved the way for a summit meeting between the prime ministers of the two countries, which was held in Lahore on February 20–21, 1999. The Vajpayee–Sharif summit resulted in three agreements: a joint statement, the Lahore Declaration, and a Memorandum of Understanding. The MoU dealt with nuclear issues and committed both sides to adopt a wide range of confidence-building measures aimed at the avoidance and prevention of conflict.

The hopes of better India–Pakistan relations generated by the Lahore

Summit were dashed by the May–July 1999 Kargil crisis, which brought the two countries to the brink of war. Angered by Pakistan's military incursion, which endangered its vital supply routes to Leh and the Siachin region, New Delhi threatened to impose a war on Pakistan in order to restore the status quo. India also effectively mobilized world opinion against Pakistan.

Caving in to mounting international pressure for withdrawal, Prime Minister Nawaz Sharif made a dash to Washington on July 4 and signed a joint statement with President Clinton, which called for the restoration of the "sanctity" of the Line of Control in accordance with the Simla Agreement. Riding the wave of world sympathy unleashed by the Kargil episode, India adopted an uncompromising attitude toward Pakistan. In August 1999 India shot down the Pakistan navy aircraft *Atlantique*, killing all nineteen people on board, after the ill-fated plane went astray during a training flight in Baluchistan. Shunning Pakistani and international calls for the resumption of the India–Pakistan "dialogue," New Delhi declared that it would not talk to Islamabad unless the latter committed itself to severing its links with the Kashmiri militants and stopped its alleged support for "cross-border" terrorism in Indian-held Kashmir. Pakistan's retreat from democracy after the October 12, 1999 military coup intensified Islamabad's regional and international isolation.

President Bill Clinton's Indo-centric visit to South Asia in March 2000 marked a paradigm shift in American thinking toward the region. Discarding its posture of even-handedness between India and Pakistan, Clinton singled out India as the preferred partner of the United States in the new millennium and warned Pakistan against the dangers of diplomatic isolation stemming from its drift toward fundamentalism and extremism. Washington categorically told Islamabad that it needed to take concrete steps to stabilize the Line of Control before India–Pakistan dialogue could begin.

Later, in June 2000 Islamabad announced that it would enforce a unilateral cease-fire along the LoC. Under growing international pressure to defuse tensions along the LoC in Kashmir, and to address New Delhi's concern regarding "cross-border terrorism," Islamabad officially announced on December 2, 2000 that its "armed forces deployed along the LoC will observe maximum restraint."

Islamabad also called upon New Delhi to initiate consultations with the leadership of the All Parties Hurriyat Conference (APHC) to prepare the ground "for the commencement of tripartite negotiations between Pakistan,

India and the APHC."[95] Islamabad's move to observe full restraint along the LoC came in response to New Delhi's decision to observe a unilateral cease-fire against Kashmiri militants during the holy month of Ramadan.[96]

Building on these positive moves, Indian Prime Minister Atal Behari Vajpayee, in his "Musings from Kumarakom," extended an open-ended invitation to the Pakistani president to come to India. Mr. Vajpayee not only talked of his personal desire to seek "innovative approaches" toward the Kashmir issue, but also clearly stated that "India is willing and ready to seek a lasting solution to the Kashmir problem. Towards this end, we are prepared to recommence talks with Pakistan at any level, provided Islamabad gives sufficient proof of its preparedness to create a conducive atmosphere for a meaningful dialogue."

Islamabad responded positively to this offer of top-level talks, which was conveyed to General Pervez Musharraf by the Indian High Commissioner in Islamabad, Mr. Vijay Nambiar, when he met the Pakistani leader on January 14, 2001. On May 23, New Delhi sent a formal letter of invitation to General Musharraf for a visit to India to hold talks with Prime Minister Vajpayee on "all outstanding issues, including Jammu and Kashmir."

Islamabad accepted the invitation a week later, emphasizing the need for the two sides to "do their utmost to overcome the legacy of distrust and hostility, in order to build a brighter future for our people."

General Musharraf visited India on July 14–16, 2001 under the full gaze of global media. His characterization of the Kashmir dispute as the "core issue," coupled with his insistence that there could be no enduring peace between India and Pakistan unless it was addressed by both sides in a meaningful, "result-oriented" manner, led to last-minute pressure from Indian conservatives, as a result of which Prime Minister Vajpayee refused to sign a draft agreed to earlier, which, among other things, said that the "settlement of Jammu and Kashmir will pave the way for the normalization of Indo-Pakistan relations."

The missed opportunity for peace in Agra was followed by enhanced militancy in Indian-occupied Kashmir and its brutal suppression by the Indian security forces. India–Pakistan relations turned chilly, as both sides accused each other of subverting peace in Agra.

India–Pakistan ties experienced new turbulence in the wake of the September 11 terrorist attacks on the United States. New Delhi's characterization of Islamabad as the "biggest source of terrorism" in South Asia led Gen-

eral Pervez Musharraf to publicly tell India to "lay off." Following the October terrorist attack on the State Assembly in Srinagar in Indian-held Kashmir, in which forty people were killed, the Indian army shelled eleven Pakistani border posts along the LoC as a "punitive strike" for Islamabad's
perceived support for terrorist activity against India.

Two days later, on October 17, 2001, Islamabad announced that its armed
forces had been put on high alert in view of the forward movement of some
Indian troops and Air Force assets.

Alarmed, American President George Bush called upon India and Pakistan to "stand down," and his visiting Secretary of State Colin Powell told
the feuding neighbors to resume their stalled dialogue.

The relations between India and Pakistan reached their lowest ebb after
the December 13 incident of a terrorist attack on India's Parliament, in
which over a dozen people, including five security guards, were killed. Despite Islamabad's swift and strong condemnation of the attack, Prime Minister Vajpayee accused Islamabad of supporting the Kashmir militant outfits
Lashkar-i-Tayyiba and Jaish-i-Mohammed, whom he blamed for carrying
out the attack. Islamabad denied these allegations and accused New Delhi
of "stage-managing" the attack to discredit the Kashmir struggle for freedom
and to give Pakistan a bad name as a state sponsor of terrorism.

Having warned Islamabad of dire consequences if it failed to address New
Delhi's concerns regarding cross-border terrorism, especially the arrest and
handing over to India of Maulana Masood Azhar, head of Jaish-i-Mohammed (who had been released from an Indian prison in exchange for a
hijacked Indian airliner in December 1998), India announced that it had begun deploying troops along its border with Pakistan and that its short-range
missiles had been put "in position." New Delhi also rejected Islamabad's call
for an independent investigation of the December 13 attack on the Indian
Parliament and described as "cosmetic" Islamabad's decision to freeze the financial assets of Lashkar-i-Tayyiba and Jaish-i-Mohammed and to detain
the latter's leader.

Worried that a war between India and Pakistan would derail its ongoing
military campaign against the al-Qaeda terrorist network in Afghanistan,
Washington repeatedly called on India and Pakistan to exercise restraint.
Following New Delhi's decision to recall its envoy from Pakistan and the an-
nouncement of reciprocal economic and diplomatic sanctions by both sides,
U.N. General Secretary Kofi Annan called on Islamabad and New Delhi to

"avoid escalating actions and further statements that could aggravate the situation between both countries."

Despite these calls for restraint, relations between India and Pakistan remained volatile. As talk of war raged in New Delhi, President Musharraf, addressed the nation on January 12, 2002 and , announced sweeping reforms. Unequivocally condemning the radical Islamists who had set up a "state within a state," he declared his determination to rid Pakistani society of their pernicious influence. He announced a ban on all sectarian-related activity and set up speedy trial courts to punish those involved in it. Most significantly, he banned six extremist Islamic groups involved in sectarian campaigns in the country, including Lashkar-i-Tayyiba and Jaish-i-Mohammed, that had already been designated as terrorist groups by the U.S. State Department. Signaling a qualitative shift in Pakistan's involvement in Islamic militancy in Kashmir, President Musharraf said, "No organization will be able to carry out terrorism on the pretext of Kashmir."

Two days before President Musharraf's landmark speech, Islamabad announced the setting up of a National Kashmir Committee, under the presidency of the moderate Sardar Muhammed Abdul Qayyum Khan, a former president of Azad Kashmir. Its purpose was to continue the struggle for the rights of the Kashmiri people by new means. Islamabad's sweeping measures to curb Islamic militancy in Pakistan and to end armed support to the insurgents in Kashmir failed to dissipate war clouds, however.

Fearing imminent war, Pakistan redeployed more than 50,000 troops along its border with Afghanistan to the Indian border. Islamabad also informed Washington that in the event of an India–Pakistan war, it would have to reclaim some airfields that had been loaned to the United States for its military operations in Afghanistan.

To prevent a looming India–Pakistan war from playing havoc with its military campaign against al-Qaeda forces, Washington launched a diplomatic campaign to defuse the India–Pakistan crisis. Following Deputy Secretary of State Richard Armitage's visit to New Delhi and Islamabad in June 2002, both countries agreed to pull themselves back from the brink of a catastrophic war. In response to President Pervez Musharraf's pledge that he would "permanently" end his country's support for armed militancy in Indian-held Kashmir, New Delhi lifted some of the diplomatic and economic curbs imposed on Islamabad in the wake of the December 13, 2001, terrorist attacks on the Indian Parliament.

President Musharraf's decision to limit Islamabad's strategic support for the militancy in Kashmir, while greeted with howls of "sell-out" by Islamic hard-liners in the country, evoked a positive response from New Delhi in May 2003. India's Prime Minister Atal Behari Vajpayee told the Indian Parliament on May 2, 2003 that he was willing to make his "third and final" effort at peace by agreeing to hold "decisive talks" with Pakistan to resolve the India–Pakistan dispute. Two weeks earlier, during a visit to Kashmir, he had said that he wanted to extend the "hand of friendship" to Pakistan, its archenemy with whom India nearly went to war the previous summer.

In response, Pakistan's Prime Minister Jamali called Mr. Vajpayee on April 28 and thus broke the ice between the two feuding neighbors. Both sides then announced the return of diplomats to each other's capitals and agreed to reestablish communication and sporting links. Islamabad also invited Mr. Vajpayee to visit Pakistan and proposed that both sides should "begin talks from where they were left off at Agra and work out an agenda for a tiered dialogue, including summit-interaction." Pakistan also offered to discuss trade issues and measures relating to building confidence and the security of both countries' nuclear arsenals.

While agreeing to examine these Pakistani proposals "in due course," New Delhi invoked the standard caveat that real peace between the two countries would only be possible "when there is evidence of Pakistan taking firm and credible action against cross-border terrorism and to dismantle the infrastructure of support to terrorism." These Indian and Pakistani peace moves were welcomed by the world.

As peace moves continued into the summer even under the new Indian government, it should be noted that a number of factors drive the latest India–Pakistan quest for peace. First, there is a clear recognition by both sides of the inefficacy of war to resolve their differences over the central issue of Kashmir. As nuclear-armed neighbors, India and Pakistan realize that their continuing feuding over Kashmir has turned South Asia into a riskier place, not only for its inhabitants but also for accessing foreign investment.

Second, sustained American pressure on both countries to bury the hatchet over the Kashmir dispute is working. Washington realizes that without peace, South Asia will remain a nuclear flashpoint and therefore one of the most dangerous places on earth. More importantly, it threatens its strategic goal of peace and stability in Afghanistan, where the process of stabilization continues to be complex. Islamabad feels hemmed in by the growing Indian diplomatic and economic presence in Afghanistan and is therefore reluctant to let the pro-Indian, Tajik-dominated dispensation in Kabul gain ground. Further, long-standing proposals for building a trans-Asian gas pipeline would become feasible only through India–Pakistan cooperation in Afghanistan.

The third factor pushing India and Pakistan toward peace is the need to display responsible nuclear custodianship to the developed world, where the worry of terrorism is rife. Islamabad and New Delhi thus feel obligated to reassure the world community about their nuclear weapons and growing missile capabilities. Resumption of the India–Pakistan dialogue, with its focus on nuclear risk reduction measures, seems to be the only credible way of easing world concern over the safety and security of the two countries' nuclear arsenals.

Finally, the peace moves were also driven by the "Vajpayee" factor: the aging Indian Prime Minister's personal mission was to architect peace between India and Pakistan. Although Vajpayee lost the 2004 Indian parliamentary elections and, with it, the chance to secure a place in history, peace may yet occur. Despite Vajpayee's fall, the overarching structural factors may continue to foster peace, especially if the international community (most importantly, the United States) continues to support the process. It is imperative that Washington use its influence and presence in the region to advance the cause of peace between the two nuclear-armed adversaries. India and Pakistan have often failed to grasp peace because there were no credible third parties involved in the dialogue. The United States has the rare opportunity now to play that vital role. A U.S.-brokered India–Pakistan dialogue centered on the Kashmir dispute is the only realistic way out of South Asia's security conundrum.

India: Politics and Kashmir

SIX

Who Speaks for India? The Role of Civil Society in Defining Indian Nationalism

Ainslie T. Embree

Rabindranath Tagore, the most famous of India's modern poets, lamented in the last year of his life that sometimes he had ventured near the homes of the peasant, the fisherman, the weaver, but that he had lacked the courage to go in, for he knew his poetry had not entered the songless land of "those who live near us and yet remain unknown."[1] In the same vein, the young Indira Nehru, who was destined to rule India for seventeen years, wrote to her father from Oxford, "Few Indians get to know this immense space of land that is India," or to know the people, "who speak a tongue and think thoughts that are not our own."[2] Her father, Jawaharlal Nehru, as a young man had come face to face with village India, and seen what he regarded as appalling poverty, religious superstition, and the crushing burden of British rule. He had asked then: "What is this India? How does she fit into the modern world?" Why had she fallen so far behind the rest of the world, even China? Was there some hidden well of strength hidden in the people that could be used to revitalize India?[3] Mahatma Gandhi believed that there was such strength in India, but it existed where "this cursed modern civilization has not reached," and it was hard to communicate with this India. The reason was plain enough: "Those in whose name we speak, we do not know, nor do they know us."[4] All of them were seeking to find some version of a civil society that could speak for India.[5]

It would be hard to find national leaders of equal importance in other countries speaking in such a tentative, almost bewildered way about the nature of their society, and the quotations can be parsed to reveal much about India in the twentieth century as it embarked on what is surely one of the greatest experiments in human history: the transfer of power from an autocratic, imperial state that was governed, through right of conquest, by foreigners who owed their allegiance to a distant Western power, to a modern, democratic state that would be governed by representatives of its own people. None of them felt it necessary to declare to the world the causes, which impelled them to seek "to dissolve political bands which connected them with another"; they were self-evident. What they were seeking were answers for themselves about India, how they could speak for a people they did not know. To put it another way, they were seeking a definition of India as nation.

Astonishingly, in 1901, as he ended his term as Governor-General, Lord Curzon undertook to answer the question, "Who speaks for India?" An Indian nationalist had declared that Curzon would leave India as the most odious and hated of British rulers because he had forgotten the English methods of ruling and had fallen "in love with Asiatic ways of ruling," but Curzon insisted, in effect, that he spoke for India.[6] There was, he argued, no public opinion in India, only the voices of the noisy English-speaking intellectuals who had grouped themselves into the Indian National Congress. He contemptuously dismissed them as "a microscopic minority," whose views were a manufactured public opinion, "barren and ineffective because it merely represented the partisan views of a clique." If this was so, then who spoke for the real Indians, "the Indian poor, the Indian peasant, and the patient, humble, silent millions?" Although he did not use the phrase, what he described as lacking in India was what we now call civil society—groups and institutions, which responding to the needs, wishes, and opinions of the people, could speak for India, both initiating social change and providing sources of stability. Without such a civil society, only authoritarian but benevolent rulers like himself and the other British officials could speak for India, giving the people of India the law and order that the people desperately needed.[7]

In opposing ways, the Indian nationalists and the arch-imperialist were saying that India had not found a voice, that the nation that was coming into existence had not been defined, that it was a nation without a nationalism that expressed the consciousness of its people. The focus of this paper is the process of how this nationalism was defined after the coming of independence in 1947, at first mainly through the government and its agencies, and then through groups within civil society.

The definition of India as a Hindu nation by groups within civil society became of fundamental importance in the last two decades of the twentieth century as Hindu nationalism, or Hindutva, became a force in political rhetoric and electoral politics. This is of peculiar importance for the prospects for peace with Pakistan since an Islamic nation is identified as the major threat to India's external security and the vast Muslim minority in India is seen as a potential internal threat. Pakistan had long identified India as a Hindu nation, an appellation that official India had vigorously rejected, asserting its constitutionally defined status a secular state. A new dimension was added, however, when the Indian government made common cause with the United States in the war on terrorism, with a marked tendency for both countries to see Islam as its identifying characteristic. For both India and Pakistan, the accepted definitions of the nature of nationalism within civil society became obstacles to peace.

Discovering Civil Society

Civil society is understood, in its broadest terms, as an autonomous arena free from state control, sometimes cooperating with the state but often in opposition or in rivalry with some of the state's functions as it defines public issues and defends its autonomy. Each must recognize the legitimacy of the other, however, for effective functioning, including protection of the institutions of civil society by the state. This sphere of relative autonomy has generally been understood as lying between the family and the state, and includes a wide variety of groups and organizations with membership based on consent. While some definitions of civil society do not recognize a distinct sphere for civil society, Partha Chatterjee convincingly argues that it is useful, especially in thinking about twentieth-century nation-states to consider a domain of mediating political institutions between civil society and the state.[8] This is especially important in looking at Indian society, where, as Ashutosh Varshney puts it, "Civil society is not a non-political but a non-state space of collective life," so that he would include trade unions and political parties in civil life, because, although they play political roles, they also provide platforms for social interaction.[9] The word "civil" has, it is worth noting, long and specialized usage in modern India, because to a large degree executive, legislative, and administrative power was lodged with the officials, all British, in the group known since 1853 as the Indian Civil Service. They were, of course, the very antithesis of civil society in the modern sense, but the term indicated that government was in the hands of civilians, not the military, a distinction important for the future of India.

In Chatterjee's usage, civil society in India refers to those institutions of "modern institutional life originating in Western societies which are based on equality, autonomy, freedom of entry and exit, contract, deliberative procedures of decision making, recognized rights and duties of members, and other such principles."[10] This is a comprehensive listing of defining characteristics of civil society, but it appears to have limiting factors. "Originating in Western societies," for example, will probably seem provocative to organizations in India that stress their indigenous character, and, in any case, their transplantation into Indian culture often radically modified their character. While many of the institutions of civil society have immediate links with institutions in the Western world, including the concept of civil society itself, they are deeply embedded in the indigenous social structures and historical experiences of the South Asian subcontinent. Religious and quasi-religious organizations, for example, in India have often been modified by contact with Western institutions, but they find a place in the sphere of civil society. Broadly speaking, the development of democracy in India is closely related to activities of civil society, for while civil society may exist to some degree in a non-democratic political order, democracy surely cannot exist without the activities of civil society. These activities include, in no particular order, social service organizations, organized sports, aspects of popular culture such as the cinema and television, the print media, business and labor movements, women's movements, human rights groups, non-government organizations, both indigenous and foreign, the activities of religious groups, environmental concerns, cultural and educational enterprises, and, very significantly, the project of nationalism itself as nurtured by groups belonging to civil society as it merges with the political sphere. It is the achievements of some of the groups, notably the Rashtriya Swayamsewak Sangh (RSS) and the Vishva Hindu Parishad (VHP), in promoting a definition of nationalism that will be particularly noted in this essay, as they have particular relevance for the prospects of peace in South Asia. To some, these organizations may seem the very antithesis of the civility of discourse often associated with civil society, but in fact they fit its general definitional pattern.

Few serious observers would now speak of the likely breakup of the Indian state, but many did in the first decade after independence. In what remains one of the most insightful studies of the period, Selig Harrison, a friendly observer, characterized what he saw as India's struggle for national survival as a "struggle against herself."[11] Against the constitutional dream of unity and fraternity were ranged what Jawaharlal Nehru famously called "the fissiparous tendencies" of Indian society—tensions rooted in the religious identities of its people, an immense burden of poverty and illiteracy, the divisive social order denoted by caste, the claims of self-serving regional politicians, and multiple regional languages. C. Rajagopalachari, a great figure in the struggle for independence and Governor-General from 1948 to 1950, had become convinced by 1957 that the centrifugal forces latent in Indian society would prevail, and that the country would face political anarchy. At that point, India might move toward fascism, "which is Nature's way out of disorder and misrule."[12]

Although the indicators that pointed to danger for India after 1947 were numerous and daunting, the building of a new nation was attempted through a series of five-year plans to restructure the economy toward a large measure of state control, through an emphasis on the peaceful coexistence of India's myriad religious and social groupings, and through a foreign policy based on non-alignment that aimed at both asserting India's rightful position in the international community while freeing herself from foreign entanglements. To achieve these aims, the political leaders, personified in the dominance of Jawaharlal Nehru, sought to control what they were fond of calling "the commanding heights" of national life in order to preserve the unity and stability of the nation while making change possible.

Central to all these aims in the early years of the new India was "national integration," the binding together of the diversity of Indian civilization through an ideological nationalism summarized in the catchphrase, "unity in diversity." It is not certain who first used it, but it was probably popularized through the textbooks, widely used in Indian schools, by the historian Vincent Smith, who glorified the British conquest of the Indian subcontinent. One of the many ironies of modern Indian history is that Smith, in common with many British and Indian historians, found that beyond this diversity, however, was an underlying fundamental unity in Indian civilization, summed up in the term Hinduism, for, he argued, "India is primarily a Hindu country."[13] This was precisely what the nationalism of Nehru and, indeed, many modern Indian academic historians explicitly deny, but which has become, we will be emphasizing later, the dominant element in the version of Indian nationalism now known as Hindutva, or "Indianness."

To examine in any detail the claims of groups in civil society in contemporary India—that is, the public space between the strictly private and the state as manifested at various levels—would require an excursion into India's long and convoluted historical experience, as well as a detailed study of the multitude of organizations and activities that make up civil society in contemporary India. That is a larger enterprise than the one undertaken here. Attention is focused more narrowly on the role of individuals, institutions, and groups in civic society in the contested area of defining Indian nationalism, especially as it relates to the great constitutional commitments of preserving the unity and integrity of the nation in the context of a democratic, secular society. In a strong civil society, there are likely to be groups that claim to speak more authentically for the nation than their rivals or the official voices of the state, and in India these groups have often clashed, leading to violence. The institutions of civil society do not necessarily promote peace and harmony; indeed, some, like those quintessential elements of civil society, freedom of speech and assembly, may produce conflicts, when, as an interesting study suggests, "an increase in freedom of speech can create an opening for nationalist myth makers to hijack public discourse."[14] The leaders of the Indian nationalist movement were acutely aware of this danger, and from the beginning tried to formulate the nationalist project in ways that would appeal to the widest audience and would not exacerbate any of the historical, regional, class, or religious differences within Indian society. Although it can be argued that the attempt ultimately failed with Partition in 1947 and then after independence, through the success of political parties, first the Jan Sangh and then, more notably, the Bharatiya Janata Party (BJP), that defined the nationalist project in terms of a divisive Hindu cultural nationalism, nevertheless the narrative of that project is not completed.

The founding of the Indian National Congress in 1885 marks the formal beginning of the nationalist movement, and it was then, and remained for nearly fifty years, essentially a part of civil society as it gradually transformed itself in the 1930s into a political party. As it gained followers in its early years it had to provide, however tentatively, a nationalist ideology. The nature of the historical experience of the Indian subcontinent denied it the markers that had characterized nationalist movements in Europe, such as a common language, shared religious symbols, great victories that could feed the national pride, and a hated oppressor. They had, of course, the British rulers, but the attitude of the leaders of the nationalist movement to the British was always ambivalent—it was almost sixty years before the Congress leaders were willing to declare openly that they wanted the British out. There were at least three central themes of the Congress that could be used without stirring up sectarian and regional strife, and these dominated the thinking of the nationalist leaders. One was the need for constitutional representative government based on some form of democratic practice that would give Indians their rightful place in shaping the destiny of their country. Another was the overwhelming stress on the poverty of India as the result of British economic exploitation. This interpretation found its canonical texts in the "Drain theory" of Dadabhai Naoroji and in the economic histories of R. C. Dutt.[15] The third was that the political unification achieved by Great Britain was merely a replication of what had been done by India's own great rulers in the past and was therefore an integral part of the national inheritance. All three of these themes were the product of civil society in the period before the nationalist project of the Indian National Congress was politicized after the Minto-Morley reforms of 1909, which gave at least minimal electoral representation.

A useful entry into the growth and formation of the nationalist project and the role of civil society in India is the Preamble to the Indian Constitution, which provides a lawyerly summary of the views of those who spoke for India as members of the Constituent Assembly in 1950 and of the later parliamentarians in 1976 as they amended it. India, according to the 1950 document, was "a SOVEREIGN DEMOCRATIC REPUBLIC" (words are capitalized in the original document) securing to all its citizens justice, liberty, and equality, the dignity of the individual, and "the unity of the Nation." The 1976 amendment added two words to the definition of the republic by declaring it was "a SOVEREIGN SOCIALIST SECULAR DEMOCRATIC REPUBLIC," and that beyond its unity, "the unity and integrity of the Nation" would be assured.[16] The commitment to democracy seems to have been accepted in India as a given and has not been much contested, at least in public discourse, and socialism, while denounced at times, appears to be accepted as a pious platitude. No one is likely to denounce the quest for national security, only how it is to be achieved, and it has continually been linked with secularism, the other new entry in the definition of the national commitment. While these words and phrases may appear bland statements of a parliamentary consensus, in fact they reflect bitter controversies over matters of urgent national concern. The phrases resonate with awareness of India's historical experience as well as with hopes for the future.

The stated constitutional aspirations—unity, national integrity, and secularism—are the ones that have most affected Indian domestic and foreign policy as they have converged with each other in the nationalist project, that is, the attempt to articulate the essential nature of Indian national life. In customary political discourse in India, unity generally refers to attitudinal dispositions between citizens, especially relating to religion and caste affiliations, as well as to linguistic and interregional distinctions. The preservation of national integrity also has geographical and territorial resonance, for while the secessionists' movements in Kashmir and Punjab had not begun when the phrase was added to the Preamble, they had long been underway in the northeast, particularly in Nagaland.

The contested grounds of attitudinal unity and territorial integrity were demonstrated in the dispute over a national anthem, with many members of the Indian National Congress arguing for Bankim Chandra Chatterjee's evocative poem, *Vande Mataram*, "Hail to the Mother," construing it as a hymn to India as motherland, while Jinnah for the Muslim League denounced it as an idolatrous hymn of hate against Muslims.[17] What was finally chosen as the national anthem, Tagore's poem *Jana Gana Mana*, is perhaps unique among national songs in being essentially a listing of geographical areas and sites to be revered by the singer as symbols of the unity of the nation.

For everyone in positions of leadership or involved in any way with public life, necessity for concern for the unity and integrity of the nation was written across the lessons they had learned in school, in the actual political process, and, above all, in the Partition of 1947 that had traumatized the subcontinent. While the Preamble speaks as if unity and national integrity were assured realities, they were given prominence precisely because they were so far from being a reality but were greatly needed as the ancient civilization took on the form of a new nation. If the concern of Indian political leaders with the unity of the nation seems excessive, both in such legislation and in rhetoric, it should be remembered that they were reflecting what they believed to be the realities of a society divided by language, religion, and caste. This was partly their own observation of Indian society, but it was also reflecting an intellectual inheritance of every educated person of an understanding of the political history of India as shaped largely in the nineteenth century by British administrator-historians whose works were influential both in the West and in India. In the words of a sympathetic commentator, the historians they read believed, like most Victorian historians, that political power was the shaping force of civilization and they were convinced of the necessity and moral justification of British rule in India.[18] Western historians were also convinced that despite all the magnificent cultural achievements of Indian civilization, her political history was one of fragmentation and disunity. Without the strong hand of the British, Indians had been taught, and I think were convinced, India would quickly lapse into what she had always been, "a medley of petty states, with ever varying boundaries, and engaged in unceasing and internecine war."[19] For such a fragmented society without any kind of unifying civil society, democracy was an impossible dream; India could only be ruled well by an authoritarian government. And it was not just self-serving British imperialists who subscribed to this reading of Indian history. For President Theodore Roosevelt, British rule in India was "the most colossal example history affords of the successful administration by men of European blood of a thickly populated region in another continent." And, he went on, if the British withdrew, India "would become a chaos of bloodshed and violence. . . . The only beneficiaries among the natives would be the lawless, the violent and the bloodthirsty."[20]

While such talk may grate on modern sensibilities, it is a reminder to us that this interpretation of Indian history was one that Nehru, Jinnah, and their generation had as part of their own understanding of their past. In creating a nationalist project, this interpretation had to be both explained and rejected. Thus, among the many legacies of British rule to independent India was the belief in the importance of a unified India with a strong central state as the guarantor of its unity and integrity. Civil society was the domain of contending regional loyalties, languages, castes, and religion. To a very considerable degree, the new rulers after independence accepted the historical function of imperialism as it has been exemplified, in their reading of history, by the Mauryas, the Guptas, the Mughals, and the British. This is at least part of the reason why there was resistance in the Nehru years to participation by private groups or non-governmental organizations in spheres of influence that seemed to intrude upon what were regarded as nation-building activities. These were the domain of the government. For Nehru, many of India's problems arose from organizations in civil society that needed the strong hand of government control.

"Our first and most immediate objective," Nehru told the nation on August 15, 1947, "must be to put an end to all internal strife and violence, which disfigure and degrade us and injure the cause of freedom."[21] For Nehru, the unity of India was inseparable from its greatness and power as a nation, and he was convinced, after World War II broke out, that the great lesson that the war was teaching was that smaller nations cannot exist as separate entities and if India was to attain her rightful place in the world, she must do so as a large, united nation.[22] While Nehru appealed to the people to make India strong and united, it was fundamental to his understanding of the political process, as it was to Indira Gandhi, his daughter and successor, that ultimately government must have the defining voice in creating and furthering strength and unity.

The protection of the unity and integrity of the nation imply far more than territorial protection of the physical boundaries of the nation, although that is certainly included; civil society and the instrumentalities of the state in India are both embedded in the project of defining the nation and articulating a nationalist ideology. It is that task that to a remarkable degree underlies many of the concerns of contemporary India, affecting social and political development at all levels. One of these concerns, raised at the very beginning of the nationalist movement, was the rights of religious or ethnic groups in a democratic society, and this has remained the most troubling problem in India's social and political life.

Democracy, in the classic nineteenth-century liberal definition that the Indian national movement inherited, is based on majority rule, but this definition tends to ignore the claims of groups within a democratic state that, having their own defined cultural traditions, do not accept the cultural imperatives of the majority. The representatives of the Muslim League never really denied that the Indian National Congress spoke for the majority of the people of India, who were Hindus, but they insisted that they did not speak for the quarter of the population who were Muslims. In the Indian subcontinent, Muhammad Ali Jinnah insisted, two nations existed, defined by language, religion, history, and culture. The creation of Pakistan was the fruit of his commitment to this idea of two nations in the subcontinent. Whether he really wanted two nation-states is moot, for when he denied the possibility of a single nation-state based on a common culture, the Indian

National Congress said, in effect, that there would be one strong, unified, centralized state, India, even if it meant the secession of the hypothetical state, Pakistan, for which Jinnah claimed to be the sole spokesman.[23]

In independent India, a persistent and, to many, a troubling reminder of the two-nations theory remains, with citizens who identify themselves as Muslims having different personal laws, covering such vital matters as marriage, divorce, inheritance, and adoption, enforced by the state. For many non-Muslims, and probably some Muslims, the existence of laws that privilege a religious community seems to undermine the idea of civil society with all citizens under the same rules of law.

Even more urgent is the right of self-determination for groups after a state has come into existence. India had not only sympathized with the desire of the people of East Bengal in their struggle for autonomy from West Pakistan but had actively supported its secession with military aid. It is worth remembering that when this was happening in 1971, India had not yet faced the issue of secession in Punjab and Kashmir. By 1975, however, fears, apparently quite genuine, about the unity and integrity of the nation led to the declaration of what is known as the Emergency, under Article 352 of the constitution, that gave the president the right to suspend civil liberties, including freedom of speech and assembly, if he judged grave internal dangers threatened the state. The advocacy of secession had already been made a criminal offence in the Sixteenth Amendment in 1963, and this was strengthened by a law in 1967. This action, which made punishable any speech or writing that seemed to support "cession" or "secession" of any part of Indian territory, was characterized by Granville Austin in his careful study of the Constitution as "undemocratic, intellectually wrong-headed."[24]

The inheritors of British rule in the subcontinent thus had the daunting task of revising that imperial state and converting it into a democratic nation that gave justice and freedom while securing its unity and integrity. It was a task that had never before been attempted in history. It was this necessary commitment to national unity, more than anything else, that decided the internal and external policies of India. Throughout his long career as a leader of the struggle for independence, Jawaharlal Nehru had been quite certain that the great danger to India's unity, and hence to its greatness, were the divisiveness and violence rooted in religion.[25] Characterized by obscurantism and bigotry, religion was a reactionary force preventing needed change. "Religion in India," he wrote, "has not only broken our backs but stifled and killed almost all originality of thought and mind."[26] In 1926 he had expressed his hope that the passage of time would "scotch our so-called religion and secularize our own intelligentsia" and that, just as in Europe mass education had weakened the power of religion, so the process was bound to be repeated in India.[27] The official statement on the relation of religion to the state, however, that he drafted on the subject for the Indian National Congress meeting in Karachi in 1931 lacks this emphasis, probably recognizing that his views did not sit well with most of the other congressmen, notably Mahatma Gandhi. The document expresses instead the minimal hope that the independent India for which they were fighting would "observe neutrality in regard to all religions."[28]

That was, in effect, restating the colonial compromise of neutrality that guided relations between religion and the state under British rule and that was renewed and codified in the Constitution. There were, however, very considerable differences between the colonial state in the nineteenth century and the nation-state after 1947. In British India, the declaration of religious neutrality served a complex purpose. On one level, it was an answer to powerful groups in Great Britain that demanded, as the representatives of a Christian nation, that the British rulers of India should express the national faith in its governance of India; on another level, it expressed the intention of the foreign government to act as arbitrator to keep the peace between sectarian groups in India. In independent India, the government represented the will of the people both in fact and theory. The new nation-state had to provide a definition of India; it had to speak for India, permitting itself neither the self-assured dogmatism of the imperial Curzon nor the acknowledgment of Gandhi that "those in whose name we speak, we do not know, nor do they know us."[29] India now had a far more lively and aggressive civil society than it ever had before. The religious neutrality of non-interference came under attack as groups in civil society insisted on having a leading role in giving substance to the nationalist project.

Two issues concerning the relation of the state to institutionalized religion emerged very prominently during the constitutional debates that showed the power of groups in civil society to challenge each other and the state. One was the right given in Article 25 not only to practice and profess but to propagate one's religion, that is, to seek to make converts. There were very few opponents of the granting of freedom to all religious groups in India to practice their religion, but serious objections were raised then, and even more in the late 1990s and the early years of the twenty-first century, against the right of conversion. The other issue that troubled many Hindu leaders was that religious neutrality, or secularism, seemed to equate all religions, giving them equal status in Indian society when this was manifestly not true. Hinduism, in all its varieties, not only represents an overwhelming percentage of the people, but Indian culture is inextricably bound up with it. Nehru himself, the arch-secularist, underlined this when he spoke of the Ganga. He carefully refrained from saying that it was sacred, but he called it the river of India, "round which are intertwined her racial memories, her hopes and fears, her songs of triumph."[30]

Within civil society, a fateful contest developed over the meaning and scope of secularism as it related to what I have called the nationalist project. Many individuals and organizations saw secularism, and a nationalism defined without reference to religious authority, as the only foundation on which an inclusive nationalism could be based; others, while not asking for India to be declared a Hindu state, saw Hindu culture and Indian culture as convertible terms. Cultural nationalism, not a Hindu state was their aim. Secularism had imposing support in civil society from academics, journalists, public intellectuals, and the Indian National Congress, as well as the parties of the Left. For all of them, secularism seemed the only realistic and practical basis of nationalism in a country made up of so many diverse cultural, religious, ethnic, and linguistic groups. Further, and this may be the most important aspect of the nationalist project, Indian history provided no great national heroes who cut across the boundaries of region and religion. Shivaji, the great Maratha warrior, for many Hindus was a champion of India against the invading foreigners and a defender of the faith. In textbooks written by Muslims he is seen as a perfidious traitor to the Mughal emperor whose salt he had eaten.

Secularism, constructed with an ideology of liberal democracy, social justice, and neither interfering in religious institutions nor seeking their support, seemed suited to the complexity of Indian social life. It had fervent support from Christians and Muslims, who saw it as the bulwark against the pervasive power of Hindu culture and the demands of Hindu organizations for the removal of the right of conversion from the Constitution. Amartya Sen, the Nobel Prize–winning economist, was expressing what was probably a very common view among intellectuals, when, having examined with considerable care and fairness contemporary Indian criticism of secularism, he defended its utility for Indian social and political life, arguing that secularism is basically what he calls "symmetric political treatment of different religious communities," leaving open the possibility of different choices that the forms of symmetry can take.[31]

Secularism under government patronage was seen, however, by many of its supporters, not just as a utilitarian necessity, but also as a profound expression of the nature of Indian culture. In public speeches, textbooks, and also in popular culture, there was continual emphasis on the unity of all religions and on toleration as the characteristic virtue of Indian society. Two great icons of religious toleration were found in the Indian past. One was the Mauryan emperor, Ashoka (c. 272–233 BC), whose famous Rock and Pillar Edicts seemed to proclaim religious toleration and the duty of a ruler to care for the welfare of his subjects. His great empire, in some fashion touching most of India except the extreme South, also proclaimed that the territorial unity of India was the mark of a virtuous ruler. A symbol associated with his reign, the Wheel of Righteousness, on the Indian flag conveniently avoided the use of artifacts associated with either Hinduism or Islam. The other icon of religious toleration was the Mughal emperor, Akbar (r. 1556–1605), who was also seen as promoter of religious toleration and a unifier of India. Both of these rulers, incidentally, were also regarded by the British as their exemplary precursors, displaying the same virtues they claimed for themselves of toleration and concern for their people and for having unified India.

It is this reading of Indian history and society that is behind the amendments of 1976 declaring India was a secular state characterized by unity and integrity. The speeches of Indian leaders that year in Parliament and elsewhere insist on this interpretation of India's past and present, while stressing the reality of internal and external threats. The internal threats have the familiar label of communalism, symbolized by the opposition party, the Jan Sangh, with many of its leading figures drawn from the RSS, the most outspoken proponents of Hindu cultural nationalism. Mrs. Gandhi warned the people, in almost apocalyptic terms, that if the Jan Sangh came to power, its leaders would not merely jail opponents (as she had been forced to do), but they would lop off their heads. The Congress President, D. K. Barooah, spoke of the forces both within the country and without, who were angered at India's commitment to territorial integrity, secularism, democracy, and socialism; while unnamed, the context made clear that the external enemies were Pakistan and the United States, aided by their agents within the country. These enemies merged with the secessionist demands of groups claiming the right to self-determination, backed by foreign powers.

In 1976, with the Emergency in full force, Mrs. Gandhi insisted that it was threats to the unity and integrity of the nation, from both internal and external enemies, that had forced her to take drastic action. This was the argument used by Siddhartha Shankar Ray, the Chief Minister of West Bengal, who was apparently the major architect of the Emergency declared on June 25, 1975.[32] Among the most vigorous defenders of the unity of India during these particular debates was Atul Bihari Vajpayee, later the Prime Minister, who attacked the weakness of the government in clinging to Article 370 of the Constitution, which gave special status of autonomy to Kashmir, as an invitation to separatism and secession. He reminded Mrs. Gandhi that it was her father who had declared in 1963 in the Lok Sabha that Article 370 was not a permanent part of the Constitution, and that it would gradually be eroded.[33]

Civil Society and the Right of Self-determination

The critics of secularism as an integral element in the nationalist project were strengthened when groups within civil society began to make claims for the right of self-determination in which a religious vocabulary was mixed with the language of political subnationalism. Typically, leaders within regions that the government of India had declared to be territorial India began with demands for redress of alleged grievances within the framework of existing laws and political conventions, then moved on to include a demand for a large measure of autonomy within a revised constitutional framework, finally moving from legally contained agitation by organizations within civil society to armed militancy against the state with a demand for independence. Nagaland, the Khalistan movement in Punjab, and some of the groups in Kashmir after 1989 followed this pattern.

Indian leaders of the Indian nationalist movement in the 1920s would surely have given assent to President Wilson's resounding declaration that "no people must be forced under sovereignty under which it does not wish to live," but at the end of the century they would probably have agreed with his Secretary of State Robert Lansing that it was a calamity that the phrase was ever uttered, as it would breed discontent, disorder, and rebellion.[34]

For India, an interesting and important aspect of the right of self-determination began with the debates in the United Nations on the covenants on human rights and self-determination. In the debates, there was always an implicit ambiguity in India's position. India was unequivocally in favor of self-determination for all peoples under the control of the European empires—the French, the British, the Portuguese. In 1960 the landmark resolution known as the Declaration on the Granting of Independence to Colonial Territories and Countries was passed. "All peoples," it declares, "have the right to self-determination; by virtue of that right they freely determine their political status and freely pursue their economic, social, and cultural development," and no territory must change hands, the instrument stressed, except for the purpose of securing those who inhabit it a fair chance of life and liberty. India's stance had been given almost canonical status in Prime Minister Nehru's memorable speech at the United Nations in November 1948. "Great countries like India," he insisted, "who have passed out of the colonial state do not conceive it possible that other countries should remain under the yolk of colonial rule."[35]

In India, the ambiguities and conflicts of the U.N. resolutions on self-determination became apparent. Critics of India were quick to point out that India, which had so often excoriated European imperialism, did not seek the opinions of the territories it took over after 1947. Hyderabad was taken over by India without any consultation with its people; so was Goa; and the French ceded their enclaves to India. Most fatefully, Kashmir was divided militarily between India and Pakistan. Prime Minister Nehru disposed of the ambiguities of self-determination by stating that, "We are not prepared to tolerate the presence of the Portuguese in Goa even if the Goans want them to be there."[36]

After the U.N. Declaration of 1960 on the right of people to self-determination, almost every year the right was reaffirmed in some fashion, but in 1966 two international human rights covenants were passed, one on social and economic rights and another on civil and political rights. Both covenants are unequivocal on the subject of self-determination, emphasizing that by virtue of this right people can determine their political status in order to attain their social and cultural goals.[37] Quite clearly, the doctrine of self-determination was raising some very tricky problems for India. Do minorities within a state have the right to self-determination? The issue was the right of groups within an existing, independent state to self-determination, and India now saw in such resolutions a threat to its national integrity.

Looking back to India's former unwavering stance toward the right of self-determination, the Indian delegate declared that the right of self-determination was restricted only to people under foreign domination and not to "sovereign independent states or to a section of a people or a nation." To make it applicable to an existing nation would undermine the very essence of its national integrity.[38]

Explicit assertions that some peoples included within the territories claimed by contemporary India are not Indians, and therefore have the right of self-determination, came from three areas—all very different from each other in culture and historical experience. All are at the heart of India's concern for its territorial integrity and for the nationalism project, the defining of the nature of Indian as a nation. The first of these areas, the state of Nagaland in the mountain borderland between Assam and Myanmar, is the homeland of a tribal people, the Nagas; the second is Punjab; and the third is Kashmir.

The rejection of India was not new in the Naga area, for as long ago as 1929 a Naga Group had submitted a memorandum to the Simon Commission, when new arrangements were being contemplated for the governing of India, arguing that their territory had never been conquered by an Indian power, and that the British, while they asserted control over the area, had not extended their laws to it. Their culture was entirely different from that of India; they were neither Hindu nor Muslim, with many of them being Christians.[39] Then, on August 14, 1947, the day before India became independent, Zapu Phizo, the leader of a secessionist movement in the Naga Hills, declared the independence of Nagaland, the only region, with the exception of Pakistan, to do so. This marked the beginning of what the Indian government called a period of insurgency and terrorism and what Phizo and his followers called a war for self-determination and liberation against the ruthless might of the Indian army. The area was more or less pacified, but there is no indication that the people have been brought into the mainstream of Indian national life.

An aspect of the Nagaland insurgency that links it directly with an important strain in Indian nationalism is the identification of the rebels and their leaders as Christians. The Indian government very early in the struggle asserted that the sense of Naga nationalism and their sense of difference from the people of India, "the Hindus of the plains," was a modern construct which had been forged by Christian missionaries. The most likely explanation is the one given by S. C. Dev, the Indian official in charge of the area: the Christians start schools, send students to college, open dispensaries for medical help; in other words, he suggests, the poor tribals accept Christianity, "not out of religious conviction but from hopes of material gain."[40] If Hinduism has made less impact, it is because with its "emancipated tolerance" it has not sought to force a single culture on the people. In 1997 a cease-fire was worked out between the rebels and the government of India. This began to break down, however, when the Naga leaders laid claim to all territories where Nagas live, not just the area that the Indian government had created as the state of Nagaland. The Indian government insists that Naga identity is a construct created by Christian leaders, which the Nagas do not deny, but they argue that their religion is part of their national identity. According to a well-informed student of the region, saving the faltering Naga peace process will require "confronting the constructionism of modern identities by the political actors themselves."[41] To argue, as the spokesmen for the Indian government often do, that the nationalism of Nagaland has no historic basis but is a modern construct, is to ignore the reality that all modern nationalisms are constructs, including that of India itself, as the nationalist project indicates.

The insurgency by Sikhs in Punjab in the 1980s, unlike that in Nagaland, was not on the territorial or historical periphery of the Indian nation, but close to its heartland, and, up to that time, was the most serious threat to the unity and integrity of the nation. On one level, the insurgency can be understood as a subnationalist movement by the Sikhs, a well-recognized group, who, against the encompassing nationalist claims of India, were asserting the right of self-determination.[42] By all the conventional markers of a shared culture—religion, language, traditional geographic homeland, and a history of which they were very proud—the leaders of the Sikh insurgency could claim that the Sikhs were a nation. The insurgency was contained through the superior military power of the Indian government, and there can be little doubt that one important outcome was that it strengthened the opponents of secularism, who saw the claims of nationhood of the Sikh radical insurgents as based on a denial of a common Indian culture rooted in Hindu civilization.

The most painful present issue involving the right of self-determination as far as India is concerned is, of course, Kashmir. The insurgency is more or less confined to the relatively small area of Kashmir Valley, a region within a larger political entity, the old princely state of Jammu and Kashmir. Kashmir is an easy fit for the template of self-determination. Multiple identities are available, based on shared history, language, religion, culture, a sense of a territory that is peculiarly theirs, all focusing on a grievance against India viewed as an illegitimate occupying power. Adding to all this is the assistance, material and moral, given by the people of Pakistan. Ever since the issue was taken to the U.N. Security Council, Pakistan has emphasized that the insurgency is rooted in the fierce desire of the Muslims of Kashmir to be free from Hindu oppression, thus asserting that it is motivated by pan-Islamic sentiments. The other actor is India, with the government and the media increasingly relating the violence to Muslim terrorism. The third actor is the United States, drawn into the situation by the need for support from both Pakistan and India in its war on terrorism, which, even if the administration tries to avoid speaking of Islamic terrorism, is popularly seen as such. The insurgency in Kashmir has thus become a central symbol of forces working against unity, national integration, and sovereignty, and has easily been appropriated as a symbol of their struggle by the proponents of Hindu nationalism. From another point of view, it has become the symbol of a fight of a minority whose homeland has been overrun by a powerful external force, an *intifada* comparable to that of the Palestinians. As in Palestine, appeal at first was not made to religion, but to a political liberation struggle against an external power.

The analyst, Bharat Wariavwalla, surveying the insurrections and secessionist movements in India, argues that they have resulted from the attempt to impose a concept of "nation" upon India's many ancient communities, leading to disunity instead of the unity that was sought. Kashmir and Punjab are the price paid for trying to create "an imaginary nation" out of South Asia's deeply rooted multiculturalism, which is very different from the multiculturalism of the United States, where the diversity comes from recent immigrant groups coming into a well-established nation-state.[43] The loose federalism which he suggests as a solution may be unacceptable to India's leaders after half a century of striving to create a unitary, centralized state and to impose nationhood upon it. There is a contradiction in the Indian Constitution's assertion of liberty, equality, social justice, and fraternity, and the unbending assertion of national unity and integrity that categorically denies the elements of the civil polity to some groups that place their liberty above the territorial integrity of the nation.

Civil Society: Its Dense Networks and the Definition of India

The autonomous activities characteristic of civil societies are integral to the process of democratization, and Graeme Gill in an interesting analysis suggests the relationship is best understood in terms of three types of orders or groups of these activities.[44] The first of these, common to most societies, whatever their political structures, are unorganized substructures of groups through which individuals order their private lives, interacting with others but having little interaction with the ruling authorities. The second order represents the groups that form "the dense networks," the core of civil society. The third order consists of groups that have definite aims for controlling the levers of power but gain their influence and power from acting within civil society.

The assumption that pre-modern India had few institutions comparable to the Western idea of civil society was made canonical by many interpreters of Indian civilization, including the great Germans, Hegel and Marx. For Hegel, there could have been no civil society and no freedom in India because there was no political state; for Marx, its village communities were the foundations of an Oriental despotism that had prevented progress and change. In his dramatic phrase, they had restrained the human mind, transforming "a self-developing social state into never changing natural destiny"[45]—in fact, a form of civil society, which, while it should not be romanticized, existed independently of the rulers, preserving the cultural and religious traditions.[46] Religious festivals of all kinds provided a form of civil society, as did the wandering singers and small troupes that presented dramatizations, however crudely, of the great mythological stories. The eighteenth century, for example, often thought of as culturally barren and characterized by chaotic warfare, provides, in both North and South India, flourishing and varied expressions of poetry, painting, architecture, and forms of religious devotion centered on religious leaders and places of pilgrimage.

In this primary order of civil society, moreover, one sees economic life, primarily agricultural, but also trade and commerce, both regional and interregional, as well as outside the subcontinent, that was not dependent upon the state. As economic historians constantly remind us, economic and social changes took place throughout the centuries for which there is inadequate documentation, but they were probably linked to alterations in the organization of state power, shifts in commercial relations with other parts of the world, and slow and largely invisible developments in the technology of production.[47]

This little-known, and perhaps unknowable order of civil society in India, is the basis of the second order, what Gill calls "the dense networks" or the main currency of civil society.[48] One example is the elaborate system of credit that existed in the Mughal empire and which apparently had its roots in far earlier times, with specialized caste groups controlling the system of the *hundi,* or bill of exchange. This business, which included arrangements for insurance, was not connected with the state, but apparently was an autonomous structure.[49] In the South, traders and merchants accrued great wealth, and in one case at least, a great trader, Jamal-ud-Din, had an army of 6,000 men and a fleet of fifty ships, which he used to set himself up as ruler in the Honavur district on the west coast south of Goa. Another Muslim trader monopolized the trade in Cannanore and the Maldive Islands so successfully that he was able to keep out Portuguese intruders.[50] The most famous of these great entrepreneurs from a rudimentary civil society who enmeshed their affairs with rulers was the enormously wealthy Jagat Seth of Bengal, who had a central role in the transfer of power from the Nawab of Bengal to the East India Company. Although he had no official position in the Nawab's court, he was, Robert Clive explained in a letter home to the East India Company, "the properest person to settle the affairs of this government."[51]

Many aspects of the activities of civil society can be related to the political and economic changes associated with the British conquest, but it is a misreading of modern Indian history to see the changes as imposition of British power on a conquered race. Much has been made, for example, by historians of modern India, more perhaps in the West than in India itself, of the effects on Indian society of many of the innovations of British rule, such as the vast amount of material collected in the great decennial censuses, beginning in 1871, on castes, religious divisions, and language. Bernard Cohn's work has been particularly influential in directing attention to the importance of the classifying and counting of the characteristics of the population of India in many of the political, cultural, and religious battles of modern India. It was not just that the foreign rulers used these collections of data to determine their approach to governing India, but, perhaps more important, that they played a key role, Cohn asserts, "in making objective to the Indians themselves their culture and society."[52] As far as India is concerned, Edward Said's very influential emphasis on Western dominance through accretion of knowledge of Indian society overlooks the deliberate acquisition of knowledge from the West by Indians. This was not because Western imperialism forced its knowledge on Indians, but because from the very beginning of the nineteenth century Indians saw what was useful in Western culture and sought to obtain it.

One of the earliest expressions of this attitude is found in the travel writings of Abu Talib Khan, who had been attached to the Court of Awadh and who visited Europe in 1799–1803. He was struck by the importance of what we would now call civil society in Great Britain, in contrast to India. He attributed British economic and military superiority over Europe and Asia to their great advances in technology and the discipline and order which industrial processes had imposed upon society. He was also greatly impressed by the large number of societies and social activities that were enjoyed in common by the people, and especially by their large scale, which in contrast to the personalized charities of India, created and supported educational and humanistic institutions of all kinds.[53]

The avidity with which the Indian elites sought to learn from the English is exemplified in the career of Rammohun Roy (1772–1833), who made the argument for Indians learning from the English with startling simplicity. Since much of India had been subject for centuries to Muslim rule, he wrote in 1823, the civil and religious rights of the original inhabitants had been trampled upon. That the British had been able to conquer India was due to the "dissensions and pusillanimous conduct of the native princes and chiefs, as well as to the ignorance existing in the East, of the modern improvements in the art of war." British wars of conquest were fought for them mainly by Indian soldiers, since in India "the notion of patriotism has never made its way." Backing the victories of the British, moreover, was the kind of knowledge that the natives of Europe had acquired in "Mathematics, Natural Philosophy, Chemistry, Anatomy and other useful Sciences." Indian students, meanwhile, spent their time debating, within their own tradition, such useless questions as, "In what manner is the soul absorbed into the Deity?" Acquisition of useful knowledge could only come through the study of English, and with such knowledge Indians could advance in social and intellectual improvement.[54] Calcutta would then be on its way to becoming the center of civil society, with, as a later Bengali writer put it, "a front seat before the window of the West."[55]

That view of the West did not lead Indians, except in a very few cases, to the rejection and abandonment of their own tradition, but rather to a pattern of selection, accommodation, and adaptation from which they constructed their dense network of institutions, movements, societies, and ethnic groupings that comprised civil society. They were able to relate them to the complex mosaic of their society through interpretations that, while sometimes forced, served to maintain civilizational links with the past as well as with groups that were not participants in the network.

Some of the elements that make up the second order of dense networks of civil society in contemporary India can be classed under two very broad categories, all of which are interrelated and all of which connect in various ways with the third order. All these aspects of civil life are concerned with the nationalist project of defining the nation and defending its unity and national integrity. The first of these categories, a product of democratic pluralism, is the activities of non-governmental organizations, many of which are involved in social and economic development projects. They have a special importance in contemporary India, where the state had made a claim for control and supervision in these areas. They include social welfare projects, organized religious movements, women's movements, business organizations, professional societies, educational institutions of a remarkable variety, and environmental causes.

Globalization is related to all of these, sometimes seen as an adversary, sometimes as the ally of democracy in furthering social and economic development, for many aspects of civil society in India are linked with what has been called "the global associational revolution . . . a massive upsurge of organized private, voluntary activity in literally every corner of the world."[56] Being involved in the whole economic and social process of globalization, has, however, introduced new tensions into Indian civil society, for as Joseph Stiglitz has argued "the benefits of globalization have been less than its advocates claim, the price paid has been greater, as the environment has been destroyed, as political processes have been corrupted, and as the rapid pace of change has not allowed countries time for cultural adaptation."[57] The effect of globalization has, however, been much less in India than in some other countries, however, partly because of the policies of the government in the first four decades of independence that opposed foreign investment, but also because of the opposition from groups in civil society, both from the Left and Right, which see it as distorting India's attempts at social justice and asserting Indian cultural values. The great multinationals also seem to pose threats to India's sovereignty, with the memory of the East India Company often being evoked.

The second broad category of aspects of civil society engaged in the nationalist project to encourage unity and national integrity is popular culture, although I am not using this term in quite the same way that Breckenridge and Appadurai have used it in their seminal studies.[58] Popular culture, under almost any definition, however, includes organized sport, cinema, television, radio, cassettes and videos, and the print media.

The use of the term "popular" is not in any way judgmental in terms of aesthetics, moral values, or class, but has only a quantitative reference to organized social activities that have a wide appeal throughout the nation. Cinema, the most ubiquitous form of popular culture in India, is an aspect of civil society that has been so thoroughly indigenized that it is as absurd to speak of cinema in India as "foreign" as it would be to speak of it in the United States as foreign. India has been producing films almost as long as the United States; the most familiar statistics regarding the Indian cinema is that it produces more full-length features annually than any other country, and that perhaps thirteen million people a day see one of those films in some sort of permanent theatre, plus hundreds of millions more who watch them on television.[59] Governments, both before and since India became independent, have been greatly concerned about the effect of this mass media on this enormous audience, resulting in censorship and attempts to control its content. In addition, academics and journalists have argued over its influence in shaping a sense of national identity through the ideas and values it transmits, and while there is no agreement in detail, some broad conclusions relate to the question, "Who speaks for India?"

Indian cinema, it is plausibly argued, more than any other art form, confronts in a direct way issues of individual identity in relation to traditional values and behavioral and cultural patterns, which differ so markedly from region to region and class to class, underlining the difficulty in knowing other Indians that Tagore and others emphasized.[60] Thus, M. V. Kamath, the journalist, can claim that the cinema does speak for India, that it cuts across class and regional differences, giving access to the organizing principles by which the society attempts "to order and conceptualize its experience."[61] An illustration of this is the argument that the variety of Hindi used in many films is an important factor in national integration, helping to fulfill the constitutional requirement that Hindi become the national language.

At the same time, Hindi films use nationalistic themes, glorifying the freedom struggle, as in the early Technicolor film of nearly fifty years ago, *Jhansi ki Rani.* Even before independence, in the 1930s and 1940s, films were made based on familiar stories from the immense storehouse of Hindu mythology that were easily recognizable allegories of the struggle against the British. Traditional values are exemplified in films that are built around struggles that are resolved within the moral order and that shows respect for family and kinship ties, particularly that of the mother, the incarnation of goodness. In the other direction is the film villain, lecherous, greedy, nasty, who "breaks the most sacred taboos of the moral order."[62]

This reading of the meaning and metaphor of films may seem to ignore the violence and vulgarity of many films, but they are framed within the borders of the tradition as good overcomes evil, qualities that are self-defined within all cultures. That violence is at times necessary was a common excuse for the barbarities of the massacre in Gujarat in the spring of 2002: the evildoers, the Muslims, had to be taught in an unmistakable fashion that crimes against Hindus would not go unpunished in a moral universe.[63]

Television, cinema's close relative, has been the most potent medium for conveying the combined message of nationalism, religion, and the glory of the nation through the extraordinary success of the presentation of the two great epics of the Hindu tradition, the *Mahabharata* and the *Ramayana.* The popularity of the two series is partly explicable simply because they told stories everyone knew in the familiar idiom of the cinema screen, but there is more to it than that. Secularists denounced them as heavy-handed Hindu propaganda that should not have been subsidized by the government-controlled network, but their enthusiastic acceptance by all classes indicates that they had activated a deeply felt need. Hindu nationalists had long complained that the educational system had denied the children of India a knowledge of their heritage by expunging from the history texts, in deference to secularism, all reference to the great heroes of the Indian past. While the history taught in other nations had taught children to respect the creators of their nations, the Washingtons and the Lincolns, Indian texts were silent about the Pandavas, the great war that had defined the history of India, and the deeds of the eponymous heroes of the race, Krishna and Rama. Now, before their eyes, India's true history, its *heilig geschicte,* was being made vivid. That history had, of course, never been forgotten, but the most modern of inventions was now bringing it to life. This was part of the process Tanika Sarkar describes when she argues that foreign rule had forced exposure to a radically new civilization, with a way of looking at the past that made Indian history seem inferior and primitive, but that at the same time, there was among the intelligentsia "a need to escape from it to one's own past, to one's own roots."[64] The TV spectaculars were part of the dense webs of civil society that were reflecting the values of Indian society.

Cricket, a ubiquitous feature of Indian popular culture, deserves mention for its somewhat mystifying place, at least to an outsider, in the nationalist project of unity and national integrity. The game passed from being an elitist pastime of the British in India to being a national sport that promotes "aggressive nationalism, reinforces hostilities, exacerbates tensions, and polarizes communities."[65] Lord Harris, the governor of Bombay, was the president of the Marylebone Cricket Club, and promoted the game among the British in India, but he considered the Indians too effete, too lacking in the qualities the game demanded. An Indian tournament was created in Bombay early in the twentieth century, however, with the formation of teams along communal lines—a Hindu one in 1907 and a Muslim one in 1911. In 1937, a team was formed with Christians and Anglo-Indians. The game seems not to have been attacked as "un-Indian" during the nationalist movement, but Gandhi denounced the tournament's communal structure as divisive when the nationalist movement was trying to promote national unity.

It was not until after the coming of independence that cricket became a vehicle of aggressive nationalism, especially on the not very frequent occasions when Indian and Pakistani teams met. At one test match in Delhi in 1998, the Indian fans shouted anti-Muslim as well as anti-Pakistan slogans at the Pakistani players, and in a game at Calcutta fans hurled stones at the Pakistanis. Indian Muslims were berated for cheering the Pakistan team; this was used as proof by Hindu nationalists that Indian Muslims were potential traitors. The Indian government then banned test matches between the two countries for several years (lifting it only in late 2004), on the grounds that they arouse national sentiments and inflame passions. Cricket, mourned a fan, may never be just a game again, since it now "has to bear the burden of national expectations."[66] The quintessential sport of the foreign rulers had become an icon of cultural nationalism.

Civil Society: Cultural Nationalism and the Nationalist Project

In a remarkable letter to leading members of the Indian National Congress in 1954, Prime Minister Nehru argued that secularism did not just mean freedom of religion but it was a way of thinking, an attitude of modernity, which would prevent religion from interfering with social and political development. Secularism was, in effect, an ideology, conveying "the idea of social and political equality."[67] It is not surprising that this understanding of secularism as an ideology hostile to institutional religion was a denial of the verities of the Indian way of life, as expounded since time immemorial in the structures of Indian society, as well as in its philosophical and literary tradition. Both the secularists and their opponents had a common agenda of seeking the unity and integrity of the nation, but they had radically different views of how this was to be achieved. For the secularists, the good society would be based on autonomous individuals within civil society finding their sources of authority in human reason and rational calculations; for their opponents, authority was derived from the corporate traditions of an organic social order. The spokesmen for India, they argued, were those who defined that nation, and protected its integrity and asserted its unity through Hindu nationalism, Hindu being understood not as a particular religion but a living, ancient culture of which religious beliefs and practices were one, but only one, component.

The best known, and most influential, of groups that defined the Indian nation in terms of Hindu cultural nationalism are the Rashtriya Swayamsewak Sangh (RSS) and the Vishva Hindu Parishad (VHP). Even though to their opponents they seem in their message and methods to deny everything that "civil" stands for, they fall within the definition of civil society as an autonomous arena free from state control, sometimes cooperating with the state but often in opposition or in rivalry with some of the state's functions as they define public issues and defend their own autonomy.

Criticism of secularism, it is important to note, does not come only from supporters of the RSS and VHP; increasingly, in the last decades of the twentieth century, leading intellectuals began to question the validity of the definition of India as a secular state. The criticisms of two of them, Ashis Nandy and T. N. Madan, well known in both India and the West as eloquent spokesmen for liberal democracy, are especially important in understanding the popular success of the open and vigorous opponents of Nehruvian secularism, as they prefer to call Nehru's vision of a modern society un-burdened by the demands of religion. They argue that this is fundamentally foreign to the Indian ethos, as it expels religion from public life with its pub-lic/private distinction drawn from modern Western social thought. Nandy argues that the attempt to expel religion from public life does not make sense to believers in any religion, for, to them, "religion is what it is precisely because it provides an overall theory of life, including public life."[68] For Madan, secularism as a credo of life is impossible, it is impracticable as a ba-sis for state action, and it is sterile as a blueprint of the future. "Secularism is the dream of a minority which wants to shape the majority in its own im-age."[69] Rajeev Bhargava, an Indian political scientist, suggests that such ar-guments show that secularism no longer has the attraction it once had as a peculiarly Indian example of toleration and fair play, and that "criticism of secularism is fast becoming part of the common sense of the Indian middle class as distinct from the scholarly forays of the intellectuals."[70]

What appears to be increasingly attractive as common sense to many people is some version of the ideology of Hindu nationalism, known as Hindutva, as championed by various individuals and organizations. As noted above, all components of civil society do not necessarily lead to har-monious relations, but may engender strife, and, for better or worse, it must be acknowledged that the opponents of secularism have formed organiza-tions, as exemplified in the RSS and the VHP, that are far more successful in winning support in many segments of society than has secularism. This in-dicates the superior organizational skills of their leaders, as well as their abil-ity to articulate an appealing version of the nationalist project, which they can translate into electoral support and mobilization of crowds to demon-strate and, very frequently, to take violent action.

When an official publication of the RSS declared in 1985 that the organ-ization was spearheading a national renaissance, that a popular wave of sup-port for its activities was rising all over India, and that "the whole world has come to recognize it as a most potent force in shaping the future destiny of this great and vast country,"[71] this seemed a bombastic boast from the fringes of Indian civil society. While it had been in existence since 1925, be-fore 1947 the general public, if aware of it at all, associated the RSS with lit-tle groups of men and boys in khaki shorts, exercising with long sticks and reciting pledges. The members were known to be pro-Hindu and anti-Mus-lim and anti-Christian, but the organization gained a more sinister reputation in 1948 when it became known that the assassin of Mahatma Gandhi was a former member, and the RSS was banned for suspected complicity in the plot, although this was never proven. Nana Deshmukh, one of the RSS leaders, summarized what he regarded as the vicious lies and slanders that the secularists, chief of whom was Nehru, spread against the RSS when they accused them of being "fascist, obscurantist, chauvinistic, supporters of dictatorship, a secret organization, enemies of socialism."[72]

Recognition of the political importance of the RSS began with the strong showing in electoral contests in the 1950s and 1960s by the Bharatiya Jana Sangh, a political party that drew many leaders from the RSS, but its influence grew when it became a major opponent of Mrs. Gandhi during the Emergency of 1975–77. Its role in Indian politics increased with the formation of the Bharatiya Janata Party (BJP), the successor of the Jana Sangh. Its success is indicated by electoral statistics: in the elections of 1984, it won two seats; in 1991, it won 122; and in 1998 it became the major party in India's ruling coalition. The RSS and its membership could now truly claim that its nationalist project had become central in the mainstream of India's political discourse.[73]

Five aspects of the RSS are important for explicating its complex influential role as a component of the civil society of contemporary India: leadership; organization of the movement; ideology; identification of the enemies of the nation; and the *sangh parivar*, or family of related organizations. All five are deeply rooted, as the leadership insists, in familiar patterns of Indian culture, but at the same time they are all immediately involved in the changing patterns of modernity in contemporary India. The symbols and the vocabulary of the movement can be instantly related to Indian culture, as they are conveyed through all the artifacts of modernity—newspapers, journals, radio, television, the Internet. The difficulty for an outsider in considering the RSS is not to bring to the discussion a deep distrust based on some of the results of its alleged influence in attacks on Muslims and Christians, but one can escape bias to some extent by acknowledging at the outset that the RSS and its affiliated organizations have legitimacy within the contemporary understanding of civil society. Their attempt to define the nation in cultural terms that include religion as a component is an ambition that will resonate with many groups in other countries in the past and in the present, including the United States.

LEADERSHIP

The RSS was founded in Nagpur, a city in central India, in 1925 by K. B. Hedgewar (1889–1940), but not much is known about its early years, partly because Hedgewar was secretive and partly because the movement was so small that it attracted little attention. But while Hedgewar did not write anything, his ideas are known from his followers, who regarded him with great veneration. He was succeeded by a series of leaders known as *sarsangchalak*, who, his followers insist, are in the great Indian tradition of leadership summed up in the familiar word, the guru. This reflects, they argue, not the cult of personality, a Western corruption, but the Indian understanding that followers willingly recognize the moral and spiritual truth embodied in the guidance their guru gives them. From such leadership comes the discipline that explains the success of the movement. To emphasize the personality of the leader, according to M. S. Gowalkar, the second leader, would show that Hindus were no better than Muslims and Christians.[74]

ORGANIZATION

The RSS is organized along fairly conventional lines, apparently modeled upon the territorial structure of the Indian National Congress, with an all-India assembly, then with the country divided into zones, states, divisions, districts, cities, and groups of villages, with small, manageable units at the bottom, the *shakhas*. Power flows downward from the *sarsangchalak* through regional leaders, known as *pracharaks*, defined in the RSS constitution as unpaid, full-time workers dedicated to the cause, and said to number in the thousands.

IDEOLOGY

The dictionary definition of ideology, as the manner or content of thinking characteristic of an individual or group, is being used here in commenting on some of the basic intellectual propositions of the RSS. The RSS leadership has always denied that it is either a political party or a religious organization, but it is, they claim, a cultural organization. This assertion must be taken seriously to understand its goals. RSS leaders rarely speak in terms of personal devotion to a deity, which is so central a part of various Hindu cults, but rather of dharma, the way of action and duty in social relations. Nor do they place much stress on the infinitely rich mythology of Hinduism, with the exception of Rama, the deity who has figured so largely in controversy over the destruction of the mosque at Ayodhya. In this incident, however, religious belief as such is not the issue, for Rama is treated as a historical figure, and destroying the mosque reclaims both actual Indian territory and Indian history.

The RSS rejects completely the tenet of secularism that religion is a private matter. "We make war or peace, engage in arts and crafts, amass wealth and give it away—indeed we are born and die—all in accord with religious injunctions."[75] The success of the RSS depends, to a considerable extent, upon the skillful appeal to the greatness of India's past, real or imagined, and the conditions, again, real or imagined, of the contemporary world. The task of the RSS, its leaders reiterate, is to define and defend the Hindu nation. Not the Indian state, it should be noted, but the Hindu nation. A distinction is being made between *raj*, state, and *rashtra*, nation. The *raj* is little more than the preserver of law and order, the function of the British Indian state, whereas *rashtra* encompasses all aspects of culture—language, literature, religion, the arts, territory, race. Hindu, then, is the adjective used for culture, not simply for religion, one of culture's components, which are all integrally related to each other.

The RSS from its beginning was critical of the Indian National Congress because of what it regarded as its failure to enunciate the true basis of Indian unity that was necessary if India was to be restored to its ancient power and glory. The Congress was pursuing a "phantom of unity" in trying to create a new sense of nationality based on secularism, thus denying the only real basis of unity, which was the Hindu nation, whose existence reached back to immemorial times. The RSS leaders would have agreed with the modern definition of nationalism as "an ideological movement for attaining and maintaining autonomy, unity and identity deemed by some of its members to constitute an actual or potential 'Nation.'"[76] What was needed was a passionate devotion to the Motherland and a reverence for the nation's ideals based on Hindu civilization. These ideals are succinctly summed up in the formal constitution of the RSS:

To eradicate differences among Hindus; to make them realize the greatness of their past; to inculcate in them a spirit of self-sacrifice and self-devotion to Hindu society as a whole; to build up an organized and well-disciplined corporate life; and to bring about the regeneration of Hindu society.[77]

This statement seems unexceptionable, and one in which many American Christians would be willing to substitute Christian for Hindu and call it their own, but yields a less mild reading when given a context. It is, in fact, a carefully phrased summary of the ideology known as Hindutva, which is so disliked and feared by secularists and members of the Muslim and Christian minority populations in India.

Hindutva, as shorthand for RSS ideology, has only in recent years become widely used by journalists and academics in India, but it had its origin in a remarkable book published in 1923 by V. D. Savarkar, a fiery nationalist who had been imprisoned in the Andaman Islands for terrorist activities. The title of the book was *Hindutva: Who Is a Hindu?* The answer to the question is that anyone is a Hindu whose ancestors have lived in India from ancient times, who acknowledge that their culture—their language, their religion, their understanding of the world—originated in India and nowhere else.[78] The people of India created a great and glorious culture, famous throughout the world for its achievements in all branches of the arts and sciences. But then comes the question that haunts so much of modern Indian history: If Indian culture was so glorious, why did it fall to invaders, first to the Turks and then to the British? The answer that runs throughout the book and much subsequent literature is simple and unqualified: internal disunity left the land open to the invaders. When Hindus are united through a true understanding of their history and culture, they will be able to build a new future. When they are united, bound together by common blood and culture, a day will come when they will be able to dictate their terms to the whole world.[79] It is easy to see how this kind of message as it was spread by the RSS would appeal to all sorts and conditions: to the young, the idealistic, the patriotic, who felt India had lost its rightful place in the world; it also appealed to those who felt marginalized and deprived by changes taking place in society; and also, inevitably, to ambitious politicians, for, in India as elsewhere, the margins of civil society in a democracy blend with those of political power.

ENEMIES OF THE NATION

All nationalisms need an enemy, something to define themselves against. The Indian National Congress had a real and visible enemy, the British government, but it was a peculiar sort of enemy, toward whom the nationalist leaders, especially Nehru and Gandhi, were strangely ambivalent. The leaders of the Congress, in the RSS understanding, wanted the British to leave so they could step into the structure of power in the state the British had created.

The enemies of the Indian—or Hindu—nation, according to the RSS, have in common the rejection, in some fashion, of the five components of the nation, which are territory, race, religion, culture, and language. The enemies are identified as: adherents of foreign religions, that is, Muslims and Christians, because they came as invaders, but not Parsis and Jews, who were invited to come to India; Communists and their sympathizers; Westernized Indian elites; and foreign countries, principally Pakistan and, more ambiguously, the United States, which has the virtue of being an enemy of Islam but which exports a corrupting culture to India.

The Partition of India proves for the RSS the enmity of Muslims for India, and wins them a hearing from many Indians who reject the main thrust of their ideology. Beyond this is the charge that Muslims possess an alien culture, forced on India by successive waves of destructive conquerors who set out to destroy Hindu culture by attacking its great symbolic structures, its temples and holy places, and converting the poor and ignorant by force and fraud. Building on these grievances, the RSS charges that both before and after independence, the Indian National Congress "pampered" Muslims by giving them favored treatment to win votes. Muslims then reciprocated by being pro-Pakistan and providing Pakistan with an effective fifth column for recruiting spies and saboteurs. How accurate these charges are in detail probably is unknown, even to the Indian intelligence and security forces, but that they are widely believed and have affected the positions of Muslims in India can scarcely be doubted. Coupled with the perception, fairly well founded, that Pakistan is the supporter of the insurgency in Kashmir against Indian rule, this generalized distrust of India's vast Muslim population of over 120 million is obviously of great significance for India's future social, economic, and political development.

Within civil society, a number of Muslim groups have found leadership to give them at least a partial voice in an unfriendly climate. Two of them have been particularly important in attempting to rally the Islamic community, although without notable visible success. The best known, the Jama'at-i-Islam, has a program, somewhat reminiscent of the RSS ideology, of seeking to create an Islamic state, which would follow Islamic law. It opposed the creation of Pakistan because its leaders, including Jinnah, were secularists, but after Partition its founder, Maulana Maududi, immigrated to Pakistan and became a force in its politics. Within India, they have sought to maintain the right to Islamic personal law and have opposed a uniform civil code for all Indian citizens. The other group, Tablighi Jama'at, was founded to unite all sections of the Islamic community through scrupulous observance of Islamic ritual observances, which would lead to a deepening of spiritual life. This emphasis on spiritual renewal has directed its adherents away from the common public sphere of civil society.[80]

Mushirul Hasan, a leading historian of Islam in India, emphasizes the perils to the Islamic communities of India and to India itself from such withdrawal. They are continuing, he argues, with the basic aim of many Islamic groups throughout the nineteenth and twentieth centuries, of seeking to preserve their religious and cultural identity in face of the pressures from both the intrusion of Western power and the revitalizing and reform movements within Hindu society. Thus, Muslim organizations within civil society have "insulated the community from the process of social change and modernization." Indian Islamic communities appear not to have been greatly affected by the radical Islamic movements elsewhere, possibly because of the very careful watch kept by the Indian intelligence services, but there is very great danger to them and to India from their growing alienation from the democratic and secular processes of the larger society.[81] While recognizing the force of Hasan's argument, the dispiriting truth is that the Muslim communities and their leaders are scarcely free to move toward more involvement in civil society, given the burden of being targeted as undifferentiated enemies by the RSS and its affiliates.

The other religious community that has been especially targeted for both physical and verbal attacks by the RSS and its affiliates are the Christian groups, which constitute a small minority, in comparison with the Muslims, of about twenty-two million. The charge made against the Christians by the RSS and its affiliates is that they are adherents of a foreign religion and are alien to Indian culture. The Christians are divided into three main groups, reflecting their historical origins. One group, quintessentially part of civil society, is found mainly in Kerala and Tamilnadu; they believe that their founder was the Apostle Thomas, who came to the region in the first Christian century. In liturgy and doctrine, they are related to the ancient Christian churches of the Middle East. They have survived through the centuries as a literate, reasonably prosperous group, having in their internal social forms some characteristics of a Hindu caste group in terms of marriage and commensality. A second group has its origins with the arrival of the Portuguese in the early sixteenth century, who, somewhat on the pattern they and the Spanish followed in the New World, began a program of officially sponsored conversion to Roman Catholicism of the indigenous people in the territory they controlled in Goa. The magnificent churches of Goa are one part of the legacy of this period; another is the large Roman Catholic Goan community, especially in Goa, Mumbai, and other urban centers. Descendants of these two communities make up probably half of the 22 million Christians in India today. The third group stems from the period that begins in the early nineteenth century, when the East India Company, having refused to let Christian missionaries into the territories it controlled, was forced in 1813 to admit them. Churches in Great Britain and the United States began sending workers, mainly from Protestant denominations, who during the next one hundred years established schools, colleges, hospitals, and numerous institutions that duplicated the social service endeavors that were part of civil society in the West. Few conversions followed from these institutions, although the workers known as evangelistic workers did win converts, mainly from the lower castes and tribal people. But considering the expenditure in resources, material and human, the effort was not cost effective, judged in terms of numbers. The greater effect was probably through the introduction of new patterns of educational and medical service. The RSS and other groups denounce all these efforts as using unfair inducements to conversion, and the extremely strong objection of Hindus to conversion can be understood in human terms, that it means breaking family relationships, but the fundamental objection of the RSS and many other Hindu groups is that conversions introduce an alien element into Indian culture. In essence, they see conversion as an attack on Indian nationalism by forces from outside the fabric of Indian civilization. A fourth phase of Christian activity began after 1947, when the Indian government, acting under pressure from many sources, not just from the RSS and its affiliates, began severely restricting the entry of foreign missionaries. After workers from the mainline churches in the West ceased coming to India, Christian communities in India began the kind of evangelistic work that foreign missionaries had once done, and with considerably more success, especially among Dalit and tribal groups. These were groups within Indian civil society, but they drew strenuous criticism from Hindu nationalists, culminating in violent attacks on churches and individuals in Gujarat in 1999, allegedly inspired by Hindu groups, especially the Hindu Vishva Parishad (VHP), which was also implicated in the much more serious attacks on Muslims. These incidents drew widespread attention in the foreign media, and in India itself they led to intense activity by groups in civil society that sought to expose the activity of the attacking groups, which also were drawn from civil society.[82]

Aside from the allegedly foreign religious groups, an internal enemy frequently mentioned as an enemy of Hindu nationalism are those Indians identified as belonging to the Westernized, English-speaking, intellectual elites, obviously a loosely defined category. They are described in the RSS literature as people ashamed to call their culture their own, who have adopted interpretations of Indian culture from British and other foreign sources. In fact, many of the RSS leaders come from the same class of society as the "de-Hinduized intelligentsia" they scorn, but the dividing line seems to be in their views of the modern, secular state and the RSS vision of a Hindu nation. Nehru is the great symbol of the Indian who, denying the values of the Indian tradition, turned for his models to Great Britain and the Soviet Union. "The Nehru mind is mostly abroad . . . and he never succeeded in catching the spirit of Indian culture at its best."[83]

Affiliated Organizations: The Sangh Parivar

The dedicated leadership, the persuasive ideology, and the disciplined cadres of the RSS finds expression in Indian society through a wide variety of organizations in civil society, often referred to as the "Sangh Parivar," or the family of the RSS. All of them cannot be enumerated here, but even a cursory treatment will indicate how the RSS has been successful in making an impact on Indian social and political development through the *swayamsevaks*, as its active members are called, numbering perhaps three hundred thousand.[84] In this, there is a curious resemblance to organizations for which the RSS has often expressed it enmity—the Communist Party and the Christian Church.

RSS members or sympathizers are found in positions of influence in many organizations that are not controlled by the RSS, such as schools, colleges, and other institutions throughout India as well as in the United States and Canada, but the central leadership itself, or its *pracharaks,* have supplied organizational skills or, in some cases, direct sponsorship. Neither of the two well-known parties, the Jana Sangh or the BJP, were direct creations of the RSS, but both drew support from its cadres, especially the BJP, whose two leading figures in the governments it formed, A. B. Vajpayee and L. K. Advani, had learned their political skills as *pracharaks* in the RSS. Although in its public manifestos the BJP has never clearly advocated the unequivocal Hindu nationalist positions as formulated by the RSS ideologues, the perception of the public, both in voting for the BJP or in opposing it, is that the BJP can be fairly described as a Hindu nationalist party.

There are a number of student movements founded by *pracharaks*, including one in Jammu and Kashmir, called the National Association, that according to RSS accounts not verified elsewhere had a significant part in saving Kashmir for India. When Pakistani tribesmen invaded Kashmir, it is alleged they killed Hindus and abducted thousands of Hindu women but the association held the Pakistan army at bay until the Indian army arrived.[85] Whether factually true or not, it fits into the myth of Hindu nationalism, with the brave young Hindu men defying the barbarous Muslims to save the honor of Hindu women. Another student organization sponsored by the RSS is the Akhil Bharatiya Vidyarthi Parishad (All India Students' Organization), with the special mission of saving tribal people from being converted by Christians.

The urban working classes were also of special concern to the RSS, and the Bharatiya Mazdoor Sangh was founded in Bombay in 1955. Unlike the unions supported by the Congress and the Communists, this group would seek to promote harmony between workers and employers, not confrontation, and spirituality, not materialism, as they marched beneath the saffron flag of the RSS. Further evidence of its Indian—or Hindu—cultural emphasis is shown by its having a festival dedicated to Vishvakarma, the architect of the universe, rather than one for May Day.[86]

The RSS and its affiliates have given the impression of being male dominated and even anti-women, but there is an RSS women's group, the Rashtra Sevika Samiti, founded in 1936 by Laksmi Bai Kelkar. Women had important roles in the Indian National Congress, but according to Kelkar's biographer, she found them only interested in driving out the British in order to take their place, not to build a new India. Kelkar also found the demands for equality and independence by the Congress's women members went against Indian tradition and religion. Hegdewar, the founder of the RSS urged her to start a women's organization, embodying its discipline, patriotism, and respect for Hindu values. An interesting innovation was the worship of what appears to be a new goddess, Devi Ashtabhuja, who was the symbol of "integrated society, woman's chastity, purity, boldness, affection, alertness."[87]

VISHVA HINDU PARISHAD (VHP)

Of all the organizations that owed the impetus of their creation to the RSS, the most powerful is the Vishva Hindu Parishad (VHP), formally organized in 1964. It is, in a very real sense, the public face of Hindu nationalism, an illustration of how potent a well-organized, well-funded instrument of civil society can be. There is evidence, according to some observers, that "a slow and subtle process has been taking place over the past few years—the eclipse of the RSS as the undisputed leader of the Sangh Parivar," with increasing power devolving to the VHP.[88] Whereas the RSS itself was secretive for a long time, the VHP uses all the instruments of the modern media to publicize its aim, which is to organize all the sects and divisions of Hinduism into a united front against the forces that threaten it. These are, according to its General Secretary, the three proselytizing religions: Christianity, Islam, and Communism. In language that foreshadowed Huntington's clash of civilizations, he announced its purpose as, "in this age of competition and conflict, to think of, and organise, the Hindu world to save it from the evil eyes of all the three."[89] Since Communism is no longer seen as a threat to the unity and integrity of India, the arena of conflict has concentrated on Christianity and Islam.

The Bajrang Dal, the youth wing of the VHP established in 1984, has been of particular importance in the arena of conflict, for its members have been active in many of the outbreaks of violence against Muslims and Christians. Ashish Nandy has described the Bajrang Dal as "lumpen gangsters" often defying organizational discipline,[90] but they have been credited with a major role in the destruction of the Babri Masjid at Ayodhya and the attacks on Christians and Muslims in Gujarat.

The VHP demonstrates the possibility of organizations within civil society effecting social and political change, even in a country like India, where the state had sought, with fair success, to abrogate the instrumentalities of power to itself, denying an autonomous space to civil society. Part of its success, aside from organizational skills obtained from dedicated RSS cadres, is the use it has made of three constituencies. One of these is the leaders of various Hindu sects and monastic orders, including many of the most revered figures, known as *shankaracharyas,* from famous holy places like Puri, as well as religious specialists of all kinds—popular gurus, Brahmin ritualists, priests from pilgrimage centers—who brought into the movement reputations of religious learning and piety that had not characterized the RSS itself.[91] The involvement of these leaders and many *sadhus* indicated, people felt, that India's vast reservoir of spirituality would at last be used for the unity of the country against the divisive forces that threatened it. The second important constituency for the VHP is the business community, many of whose leaders, like the Dalmias, Birlas, and Modis, have long been patrons of Hindu causes.

The third constituency that has been important for the influence of the VHP are Indians in what it likes to call the Hindu Diaspora, the prosperous, educated Indians living abroad, especially in the United States, where the VHP functions as the World Hindu Council.[92] As the U.S. government widened its investigations into Muslim charities suspected of supplying funds to terrorists abroad, one financed by Hindus in the United States came under suspicion. The India Development and Relief Fund has been accused by groups in both the U.S. and India of supplying funds to the RSS and VHP to support the violence against Muslims in Gujarat.[93]

The VHP's location and influence in civil society argues very strongly for a reexamination of the relation of institutionalized religion in modern India. It has long been customary to see religion being used by politicians for political ends, with the suggestion that communalism and its frequent attendant violence is not due to religion but to the abuse of religion. Tanika Sarkar, who has approached the subject of cultural nationalism in contemporary India by examining the shift in Bengal by the intelligentsia from a concern with liberal reformism in social customs and religious beliefs to Hindu revivalism at the end of the century, suggests that Hindu nationalist groups have "systematically tried to absorb the public and political spheres," which is, in fact, a return to a close connection between religion and the political processes that was broken during the British period.[94] Two great movements in civil society illustrate this thesis. The Brahmo Samaj in early-nineteenth-century Bengal concerned itself with very specific questions of private religious devotion and practice, whereas the Arya Samaj in Punjab at the end of the century, while having some of the same concerns, moved aggressively against Islam and Christianity, as well as what it regarded as evils in Hindu society. That many of its adherents became leaders of a militant variety of nationalism within the Indian National Congress is part of the attempt of Hinduism, through instruments of civil society, to reclaim a place in political space. It appears to have done so to a considerable degree in Gujarat.

Conclusion: Gujarat as an Arena of Conflict for Civil Society

"This is the home of Gandhi?" read the headline of an article in a Canadian newspaper after the riots in Gujarat in March 2002, when over a thousand people, mainly Muslims, were killed by Hindu mobs.[95] The massacres were allegedly in retaliation for a gruesome act of violence in which fifty-eight Hindus traveling by train were burned to death by a Muslim mob.[96] Gujarat is, indeed, the home of Mahatma Gandhi, the scene of some his most memorable campaigns, and is one of the most prosperous states in India because of its industrious farmers, energetic entrepreneurs, and great industrialists. It has some of the most magnificent Islamic architecture in India, dating from the time when it was the center of a powerful Muslim kingdom made prosperous by trade and agriculture. It has some of the best of modern India's architecture and some of her most prestigious cultural and educational institutions, reflecting a civil society with a record of philanthropy and organizations of all kinds engaged in social service.

The other side of Gujarat, however, is that it has been the scene of some of the worst communal violence, especially in the last twenty years. There have been many explanations given for this, but Professor Sunil Khilnani is surely correct when he attributes it to a combination of the success of the RSS and the VHP in creating a pride in Hindu nationalism and the political skill of the BJP in using this to build a Hindu vote bank, not just among the upper and middle classes but from among the large laboring class and the many small agriculturists.[97] They were united by an appeal to Hindu symbolism and a fear of enemies—the Christian and Muslim minorities and Pakistan.

Gujarat became an arena of conflict, in the literal sense of a bloody struggle between communities identified by religion and groups wracked by hatreds. It was also an arena of conflict between those who believed that the unity and integrity of India depended upon secularism and those who were convinced, deeply and passionately, that unity and integrity depended upon the recognition that Indian culture was Hindu culture, with the overwhelming majority of Indians rooted in that culture and loyal to it. According to a leader of the VHP, the massacre of the Muslims was necessary, as Muslims had to be taught a lesson. He added, "If they do not learn it will be very harmful to them."[98]

The lesson to be learned by the Muslims had been spelled out with great bluntness by Balraj Madhok, a leader and spokesman for the Hindu nationalist project and one of the founders of the Jana Sangh Party, in a book called *Indianisation*.[99] What is needed for the unity of the country is the "Indianisation" of the consciousness of the Indian people in every aspect of national life—in education, law, medicine, and the economy. Muslims and Christians should be brought into the mainstream of Indian life, and they should renounce their extraterritorial loyalties, symbolized by their use of foreign names instead of Hindu ones. The democratic process means that the culture of the majority should prevail, and that the adherents of alien cultures and religions, the Christians and the Muslims, are a threat to the nation unless in their behavior they show their complete identification with Hindu culture.

The idea that Gujarati Christians, a tiny, economically underprivileged minority, many of them from poverty-stricken tribal groups living on the margins of society, are a threat to the huge Hindu majority would be amusing if groups and individuals from the VHP and the Bajrang Dal, according to what seems trustworthy accounts, had not attacked the Christians, burning the small shelters they used as churches.[100] The anger and hatred displayed in these actions reflected the concern with unity and national integrity that is so frequently a reference point in Indian society. The attacks came from groups within Indian civil society and so did the protests against the attacks, especially when it became apparent that the police and other state authorities, if they were not actually involved, had done little to protect the Christians. Although the media, both Indian and foreign, reported on the violence, the only thorough investigation was started by a group called the National Alliance of Women. Although their normal sphere of action had to do with women, they became involved because of their commitment to marginalized and disadvantaged sectors of society and their concern for "a just, democratic and humane society." The Alliance established a

Citizens' Commission to investigate the persecution of Christians in the Dangs district of Gujarat.[101]

The Citizens' Commission's unequivocal conclusion was that the attacks on the Christians had the hidden agenda of raising concern about conversion of Hindus to Christianity by foreign missionaries. There were, in fact, no foreigners involved in evangelistic work, but Indian Christian groups had opened schools and dispensaries in the tribal areas, and this, it was argued, symbolized their anti-national activities in seeking to win converts through the bribes of education and health. This charge is very frequently believed by Hindus who otherwise are not at all favorable to the ideology of the RSS and VHP but who see conversion as an attack on the unity of India. The dislike of conversion is very deeply rooted among modern Hindus, undermining the frequent claim of Hindu tolerance of religious differences and indicating a reason for the appeal of Hindu nationalism. The fear of conversion in India is rather similar to the fear that many people in the United States once had of Communism—a force that undermines civilization.

Shortly after the fearsome massacres, state elections were held in Gujarat. Many supporters of secularism expected that the ruling party, the BJP, would lose the election since there had been well-founded allegations that the government had not only failed to take adequate measures to prevent the mob violence but that many officials had actively encouraged it. Furthermore, shortly after the killings, the Prime Minister of India, the leader of the BJP, seemed to blame the victims when he said that Muslims "don't like to live in co-existence with others . . . and instead of propagating their ideas in a peaceful manner, they want to spread their faith by resorting to terrorism and threats."[102] A reporter who heard this said he felt "a contaminating, nauseous sensation,"[103] but apparently the majority of the electors of Gujarat did not, as some months later they reelected the BJP with a sweeping majority.

"Who speaks for India?" was the question asked at the beginning of this essay, with Mahatma Gandhi's answer summarizing those of others: "Those in whose name we speak, we do not know, nor do they know us." I started with the suggestion that perhaps the authentic voice would come from civil society, yielding affirmation of a pluralistic democratic society, seeking unity and national integrity, through a multitude of citizens' groups engaged in the project of defining India as a nation. There is no question that there are many groups and individuals in civil society speaking for India, giving assurance of the reality of a national project affirming such a plural society, with special concern for secularism, with at least the minimum meaning that the nation's commitment to religious freedom, with no particular religion being privileged, represents a consensus. Looking at modern India's historic experience, however, there is no avoiding the conclusion that within civil society there is really no such consensus, and that very powerful groups are not enthusiasts for a pluralistic society but insist that a valid nationalist project be framed in terms of an Indian culture that is synonymous with Hindu culture. The idea that the Indian empire of the British contained two nations, one Hindu, the other Muslim, is usually associated with Muhammed Ali Jinnah, but the great Hindu nationalist Savarkar explicitly stated it when he wrote that "there are two antagonistic nations living side by side in India."[104] Despite the frequent denunciation of Jinnah's "two nations theory" by Hindu nationalists, the treatment in their literature of Muslims living in modern India is almost an implicit recognition that they, like Christians, are alien to the true Indian nation, constituting a separate nation.

The massacres of Muslims in India at the time of Partition, of Sikhs in Delhi in 1984 following Mrs. Gandhi's assassination, of Muslims in Bombay and elsewhere following the destruction of the Babri Masjid in 1992, and the attacks on Christians in Gujarat and elsewhere in 1998–99, and then the massacres of Muslims in Gujarat in 2002, demands an answer to the question, "Who speaks for India?" Is it the voices arguing for a pluralistic, secular democracy, or the louder, more insistent ones that argue that Hindu nationalism is the true voice of timeless Indian civilization? Many observers, not only Muslims, by any means, would, with foreboding, accept Sunil Khilnani's observation that Gujarat offers "the starkest image of what Hindu nationalism, should it ever gain unrestrained control of the Indian state, will mean for India's future."[105] The unanswerable question is, of course, how likely is that to happen? Social and political developments that might make it a reality depend upon imponderable factors, but the historical experience of the last fifty-six years suggests that it is a reasonable expectation, however unwelcome that may be to Indians and outsiders who see pluralistic, secular democracy as the best hope for India and mankind.

In 1977, during the Emergency, I wrote an essay attributing the apparent ease with which civil liberties were abrogated to what then seemed to be the weakness of civil society and the failure of what I then referred to, perhaps rather oddly, as the "ancillary institutions" of democracy to resist authoritarian power. I meant by the phrase those forms of corporate and community life that have sufficient independence from the state to have a considerable degree of autonomy, such as the judiciary, the universities, the media, trade unions, religious organizations, business groups, and professional societies.[106] In the end, some of them, especially the press and the judiciary, proved to have more resilience and power than they seemed to have when they were confronted by the swift, well-planned, and largely legal use of state power by Mrs. Gandhi and her close associates. Civil society was able to reassert itself, however, because of a consensus, even if nebulous, that authoritarian power could be blocked through the use of the existing constitutional and legal framework. The instrumentalities of civil society came into play in 1978 as they had in the first dangerous decades of the new nation. Article 19(1) of the Constitution, in stating the citizen's fundamental rights of freedom, comes close to defining civil society in India when it speaks of freedom of speech and expression, the right to form associations, and to assemble peaceably. The amendments of the constitution in 1976 that stress the duty of every citizen to promote harmony and the spirit of common brotherhood, to preserve the rich heritage of the composite culture, and to strive toward excellence in all spheres of individual and collective activity, seemed at the time no more than conventional phrases, meant to mask the realities of tyrannical power, but perhaps they did point to a consensus. It is possible that should civil rights once more be attacked, that civil society would be able to make use of the courts and its own institutions to preserve pluralistic democracy.

SEVEN

Hindu Nationalism and the BJP: Transforming Religion and Politics in India

Robert L. Hardgrave, Jr.

In 1998, in India's twelfth parliamentary elections, the Hindu nationalist Bharatiya Janata Party (BJP),[1] came to power at the head of a coalition, an inchoate alliance of diverse parties. A year later, the government in shambles, India again went to the polls, and the BJP, with Prime Minister Atal Bihari Vajpayee at the helm, led a more secure alliance to victory, forming the twenty-four-party coalition that governed India until its defeat in the May 2004 elections. The BJP had experienced a dramatic rise, from two parliamentary seats in 1984 to a position since 1996 as the largest single party in the Lok Sabha, the House of the People. The party's rise to power has been lauded as a triumph for Hindu nationalism, for an awakening and resurgent Hindu identity, and, at the same time, condemned as a threat to the secular state and to the rights and security of religious minorities. The volatile mix of religion and politics poses a fundamental challenge to Indian democracy, the nation's cultural diversity, and to Hinduism itself.[2] Although out of power at the time of this writing, the BJP remains a formidable force in Indian politics, and Hindu nationalism more generally has profound implications for India's future and its place in the world.

The roots of the Bharatiya Janata Party reach into the late nineteenth century to the emergence of a Hindu nationalism that, hearkening back to a Vedic golden age, sought the restoration of an imagined and idealized Hindu rule. Hindu nationalism developed essentially in opposition to the Indian National Congress, the movement under Gandhi and Nehru that led India to independence in 1947. Gandhi's decision to join with the Muslim

League in the Khilafat Movement (1919–21) alienated Hindu nationalists in the Congress, even as Gandhi's use of Hindu sentiment and symbols subsequently alienated the larger number of Muslims, including Jinnah (who led the Muslim League for the creation of Pakistan) in the Congress.[3]

Ideological Foundations of the BJP: Hindutva, the RSS, and the Sangh Parivar

Hindu nationalism took many forms, and elements of it—Hindu traditionalism—were embodied, both avowedly and unwittingly, within the Congress, but it is from the Hindu Mahasabha, founded in 1914, and the Rashtriya Swayamsevak Sangh (RSS), founded in 1925, that the BJP drew its Hindu nationalist form and character. At the core of its ideology is the concept of Hindutva ("Hinduness"), with its projection of a culturally Hindu India into which minorities—Muslims and Christians—will be integrated or to which they will be subordinated. The goals are a muscular Hinduism that overcomes the divisions of Hindu religion and society and a state that restores Ram Rajya, the ideal rule of the mythic Lord Rama.

Hindu nationalists sought to transform Hinduism, which, in their eyes, had become degraded, divided, and weak, but even as they demonized Islam and Christianity as threatening and alien, they sought to emulate these "muscular" religions to bring greater cohesion and strength to Hinduism.[4] To overcome the fragmentation of caste, sect, and language, the movement sought the consolidation of the Hindu *rashtra*, the Hindu nation. It sought to reclaim, through reconversion, those lost to the Hindu fold and to oppose those who refused to accept the preeminence of Hindu culture and identity. The call, in the words of V. D. Savarkar, a leader of the Hindu Mahasabha, was to "Hinduize all politics and militarize Hinduism." Savarkar's *Hindutva: Who Is a Hindu?* published in 1923, codified the ideology. Hindutva, for Savarkar, embodied a unity of geography, race, and culture, but it was the "common culture" of Hinduism that was the essential defining element. It was thus a *cultural* nationalism rather than a religious fundamentalism, but one in which culture was infused with Hindu religious traditions and mythologies. (In a series of decisions in 1995, the Indian Supreme Court, in effect, gave legal sanction to the Hindu nationalist concept of Hindutva, holding that it means essentially the Indian "way of life" and that it is not inherently religious.[5])

"Fundamentalism" is antithetical to the diverse nature of Hinduism, but efforts by Hindu nationalists to overcome division within Hinduism—in effect, to homogenize its traditions—give a quasi-fundamentalist character to Hindu nationalists in their expressions of religious zeal. This is most clearly evident in their focus on Lord Rama, mythic Hindu king and incarnation of the god Vishnu—but that Rama is not venerated by all Hindus (or in the same degree) underscores the diversity of Hinduism and, like emphasis on Sanskrit as a defining element of Hindu culture,[6] serves to limit the appeal of Hindu nationalist ideology among all those who consider themselves Hindu both in religion and culture. The challenge for the Hindu nationalist is to construct a united Hindu nation, to make the "imagined community" a social and political reality.

In 1925, to advance the cause of the Hindu nation, H. B. Hedgewar founded the RSS (Association of National Volunteers), the paramilitary organization that soon became the dominant force of Hindu nationalism.[7] In its hierarchical and disciplined structure, the basic unit of the RSS is the *shakha*, or local branch, where members, in khaki shorts, their distinctive uniform, gather early each morning for physical training, drill, and ideological indoctrination. The *shakhas* are directed by officers who, typically austere and celibate, devote themselves wholly to a "yoga of action" for the regeneration of the Hindu community. At the top of the pyramid of authority is the chief, "the Guide and Philosopher" of the RSS—first Hedgewar (1925–40), then M. S. Golwalkar (1940–73). Today, the RSS chief is K. S. Sudarshan.[8]

Although its membership, especially at higher levels, long came principally from the higher castes, particularly Brahmins, the RSS, open to all castes and committed to egalitarianism, sought to unite Hindus in one great "family" and to secure Hindus "as *the* nation of India." Building on Savarkar's Hindutva, Golwalkar argued that within India:

The foreign races [and those with alien beliefs] must either adopt the Hindu culture and language, must learn to respect and hold in reverence Hindu religion, must entertain no ideas but those of glorification of the Hindu race and culture . . . or may stay in the country, wholly subordinated to the Hindu nation, claiming nothing, deserving no privileges, far less any preferential treatment—not even citizens' rights.[9]

In contrast to the Congress's inclusive claim to represent all Indians, the RSS asserted a distinctly Hindu identity and, though vehemently opposed to the partition of India, was—ironically—the Hindu counterpart to the Muslim League in its concept of India as constituting "two nations," one Hindu, one Muslim. The RSS denounced Muslims for centuries of political oppression, for their denigration of Hindu traditions and desecration of Hindu temples, and with the creation of Pakistan in 1947, Muslims were held responsible for the vivisection of Mother India. In the wake of Partition, as some four million Hindu and Sikh refugees came across the newly created border (and as even more Muslims went the other way) with horrendous tales of atrocity and rape, Hindu nationalists attacked the Congress for acceding to the division of India and were infuriated by Gandhi's fast in January 1948 to stir "the conscience of all" and bring an end to the violence against Muslims. Near death, Gandhi gave up his fast only when the Indian government agreed to release to Pakistan its share of the assets of British India and when leaders of the Hindu and Sikh communities in Delhi agreed to "protect the life, property, and faith" of Muslims. Twelve days after he had broken his fast, on January 30, Gandhi was assassinated at the hand of a Hindu fanatic who had a background in both the Hindu Mahasabha and the RSS. The Mahasabha immediately suspended activity, and the government banned the RSS, arresting Golwalkar and more than twenty thousand RSS volunteers. The ban was lifted eighteen months later, but only after the RSS agreed to renounce political activity. No evidence tied the assassination to either the Mahasabha or the RSS, but the nation's revulsion at Gandhi's murder inflicted a terrible blow to Hindu nationalism and strengthened Prime Minister Nehru in forging the new India as a secular state.[10]

Secularism in India does not mean separation of church and state, much less hostility toward religion, but rather an official neutrality and respect for all religions, which are to be treated equally. The Constitution guarantees freedom of worship and the right of each religious group to establish and administer its own schools and to maintain its distinct traditions.[11] Accommodation of religion, however, quickly became a matter of intense controversy with the Hindu Code bills, which replaced Hindu personal law governing marriage, divorce, adoption, and inheritance with a uniform civil code that applied to all "Hindus" (including Sikhs) and exempted Muslims.[12] Hindu nationalists opposed the bills as interfering with traditional Hindu practice, but they were furious that Muslims were permitted to retain their own personal law while all other Indians were brought under the civil code. With the heightened insecurity of Muslims following Partition, the Congress government under Nehru sought to reassure Muslims that they were an integral part of one Indian nation and did so, ironically, by excluding them from what was to have been a uniform civil code. For Hindu nationalists, this was an anti-Hindu bias and a favoritism of Muslims—what was to become for the RSS and the BJP part of the recurrent theme of "pseudo-secularism."

The Hindu Code bills controversy came together with the campaign for cow protection and efforts to build a temple to Lord Rama at Ayodhya— what would become the explosive Ramjanmabhoomi issue—to give Hindu nationalists renewed purpose. They provided vehicles for Hindu mobilization and a target, Muslims, for vilification.

Hindus make up 83 percent of India's population; Muslims account for some 12 percent and Christians 2 percent. Sikhs, Buddhists, and Jains constitute distinct religious communities but are viewed by Hindu nationalists as within the Hindu fold. Islam and Christianity are seen as alien religions that through proselytization—and higher birth rates—threaten Hinduism. Indeed, though constituting an overwhelming majority, Hindus within India are portrayed as under siege—most critically from within, by distrusted Muslims, and from the outside, by world Islam and by Pakistan.[13] Hindus are vulnerable because they are divided, and the RSS—the vanguard of Hindu nationalism—takes as its mission "the spread of Hindu culture," as it works "to unite and rejuvenate [the Hindu] nation."[14]

In forging the Hindu nation, the RSS seeks to penetrate every aspect and level of society. It has placed increasing emphasis on social work, with literacy campaigns and projects for women's uplift. As it did immediately after Partition, in relief work among Hindus and Sikhs in refugee camps, the RSS has been active in flood and earthquake relief. Welfare schemes are directed to the lower castes, Dalits (untouchables), and tribal peoples within the Hindu fold. All of these efforts have been made to expand the influence and membership of the RSS, today estimated at more than 2.5 million members, with 40,000 *shakhas* throughout India. As the RSS has grown, its power has been extended through a web of some sixty affiliated organizations that constitute the RSS "family," the Sangh Parivar. The organizations include trade unions, students' and women's groups, and groups with a specifically Hindu religious orientation.

The Vishwa Hindu Parishad (VHP, or World Hindu Council)[15] was established in 1964 to provide the RSS a direct link to Hindu religious leaders and *sadhus*. The organization has three objectives:

1. To consolidate and strengthen the Hindu Society
2. To protect, promote, and propagate Hindu values of life, the ethical, and the spiritual in the context of modern times
3. To keep in touch with all Hindus living abroad, and to organize and help them in all possible ways in protecting their Hindutva[16]

Leaders of the VHP are almost all members of the RSS, but the majority of its members in some 3,500 branch units are not RSS cadres. Sanctioned by the RSS, the VHP has shaped its own family of organizations directed to social welfare work among untouchables, tribals, and the rural poor—those perceived as most vulnerable to religious conversion. Through its affiliates, the VHP operates student hostels, orphanages, vocational schools, medical missions, and temples. The VHP has gained prominence primarily through its campaigns to strengthen Hindu identity and solidarity, symbolized most dramatically by its leadership in the Ayodhya temple movement (discussed below).

In 1984 the VHP created the Bajrang Dal[17] as its "youth wing." Self-styled "warriors of the Hindutva revolution," the organization took its name, *bajrang* (strong and sturdy) for its association with Hanuman, the monkey god who led Rama's armies. The Bajrang Dal draws from a reservoir of poorly educated, often unemployed, and frustrated youth. Thuggish and undisciplined, they had no uniform until 1993, but were identified by their saffron headbands bearing the word "Ram." In 1993 they adopted blue shorts, white shirts, and a saffron scarf as a uniform and established a network of training camps modeled on the RSS.

The Bharatiya Jan Sangh

The BJP is an integral part of the Sangh Parivar and is the reincarnation of an earlier Hindu nationalist political party, the Bharatiya Jan Sangh (BJS, or simply Jan Sangh).

Following India's independence in 1947, Hindu nationalists had ties to Hindu traditionalists within the ruling Congress party, but for them, the Congress party, with its "pseudo-secularism," was political anathema. The RSS, as a "cultural" organization, was not directly involved in politics, but its leadership called for the formation of a new political party committed to the principles of Hindu nationalism. In 1951, Dr. S. P. Mookerjee, a former president of the Hindu Mahasabha who had broken with the declining party, organized the Bharatiya Jan Sangh with the object of rebuilding Bharat (India) on the basis of four "fundamentals"—one country, one nation, one culture, and the rule of law. The BJS embodied an eclectic mix of tradition and modernity, and although it proclaimed open membership, it had a distinctly communal character as a Hindu party. The Jan Sangh sought national unity by "nationalizing all non-Hindus by inculcating in them the ideal of Bharatiya Culture."[18] Although initially independent of the RSS, by the mid-1950s, the BJS had effectively been brought under the RSS umbrella as a member of the Sangh Parivar. The RSS provided the network of its organizational strength, and it was the principal source of its leadership, with RSS activists Atal Bihari Vajpayee and L. K. Advani soon rising to the highest levels of the new party. The Jan Sangh became the political agent of the RSS in party and electoral politics. The task it set for itself was long-term party-building rather than more immediate efforts to take control of government.[19]

As Christophe Jaffrelot portrays in his account of Hindu nationalism, the BJS "oscillated between a strategy of integration with legitimate politics and one of militant ethno-religious mobilization."[20] In the first, the party acquiesced to secular norms; formulated an economic program of centralization appealing to the merchant and trader, urban middle classes, and the rural land-owning peasantry; and asserted a nationalism that called for a strong defense and nuclear weapons capability. In seeking to "normalize" its position within the Indian political system, the Jan Sangh was, nevertheless, careful to insure that its fundamental identity as *the* party of Hindu nationalism was not diluted. Thus, the party, in oscillation with "normal" politics, engaged in periodic mobilization campaigns centered around such issues as cow-slaughter, and at its grass roots, the appeal to Hindu sentiment and the manipulation of Hindu symbols were central to its strategy of party-building.

The two strategies were symbiotic and, at the same time, contradictory, for the BJS leadership, with its electoral pragmatism, depended on an organizational base of RSS cadres, stalwarts of Hindu militancy. The tensions were a source of unresolved conflict within the party and between the party and its parent RSS, as they were to be in the Jan Sangh's successor, the Bharatiya Janta Party.

The social base of the Jan Sangh was among the middle classes and the upper castes. It was heavily urban in its electoral support, with some support among the rural peasantry and, surprisingly, among the Scheduled Castes (untouchables) and Scheduled Tribes, traditionally oppressed groups that had been courted by the RSS in various "uplift" efforts to secure them within the Hindu fold. The Jan Sangh's geographic base was concentrated in the Hindi-speaking heartland of North India, a confinement that reflected the party's commitment to Hindi as the sole national language of India—a stance that alienated non-Hindi speakers generally and South Indians particularly.

Between 1967 and 1971, the Jan Sangh participated in coalition governments in five states, and it intermittently controlled the Delhi Council. From its founding, the party gradually increased its strength to a peak of 9 percent of the vote in the 1967 parliamentary elections, with a decline to 7 percent in 1971.

In the spectrum of Indian political parties, the Jan Sangh, as a Hindu nationalist party, was situated on the right (along with the free-enterprise Swatantra Party), with the Socialist Party and the two Communist parties (CPI and CPI-Marxist) on the left. In the center was the ruling Congress Party, led after 1966 by Prime Minister Indira Gandhi, and an array of caste- and peasant-based populist parties (splinters from the Congress) and a growing number of regional parties, such as the Akali Dal in the Punjab and the Dravida Munnetra Kazhagam in Tamil Nadu, based in states outside the Hindi heartland. In the 1971 parliamentary elections, the Jan Sangh joined with three other parties in an alliance to remove Mrs. Gandhi, with the cry "Indira Hatao," a play on her campaign slogan "Garibi Hatao," "Abolish Poverty." The opposition was inundated in the "Indira Wave," and with the euphoria over India's defeat of Pakistan in the December 1971 liberation of Bangladesh, Indira Gandhi was popularly proclaimed "Empress of India."

But by the mid-1970s, with increasing discontent as economic problems deepened, and as Indira Gandhi aggrandized and personalized power, opposition mounted and came together in a mass movement led by Jayaprakash Narayan. The tempo of unrest heightened, with processions and demonstrations, and hardly a day passed without reports of a lathi (truncheon)-charge or police-firing somewhere in India. In June 1975 Mrs. Gandhi responded with the declaration of an Emergency, effectively suspending the Constitution and jailing leaders of the opposition who dared challenge her rule. Vajpayee and Advani of the Jan Sangh were among the leaders arrested, and the RSS, under an imposed ban, went underground. Thousands of RSS activists were jailed, but under the Emergency (1975–77) the RSS expanded its network and membership. In jail, leaders of the opposition, for all their political differences, found common cause. When Mrs. Gandhi, convinced that she would win and that her policies would be vindicated, lifted the Emergency in 1977 and called elections, the disparate opposition emerged as a united Janta Party. The results of the elections brought a stunning victory to the Janta and its allies. Vajpayee became Foreign Minister in the new government; Advani, Minister of Information and Broadcasting. The inclusion of the Jan Sangh within the party, however, had come with deep unease among its new partners, who saw it as communal— that is, Hindu—and feared its ties to the RSS. Within the Janta Party, the ex-Jan Sanghis retained their distinct identity, and in the wake of the party's collapse in 1979 from internal conflict, they formed the Bharatiya Janta Party. Formally inaugurated in April 1980, the BJP, with Vajpayee as party president, projected itself as the true heir of the Janta Party.

The Rise of the BJP

BJP leaders retained their RSS ties, and at the grass roots the new party depended on the RSS and its militant cadre. At the same time, however, the BJP sought to develop a wider, more "moderate" appeal. Over the years in its rise to power, the BJP, as the Jan Sangh before, has pursued two strategies, electoral pragmatism and Hindu mobilization, sometimes alternating, sometimes parallel, but always in tension with each other. Its goal was to present itself as the alternative to Congress rule.[21] In the early 1980s, to expand its geographic and social base, the party gave increased emphasis to economic and social interests, proclaimed its "openness," and signaled a readiness to enter into electoral alliances with other parties in opposing the Congress. At Vajpayee's initiative, the party appropriated the mantle of "Gandhian socialism" in projecting its program of economic decentralization, and it repackaged Hindutva as "positive secularism." This did not sit well with grassroots party activists or with the RSS leadership, and as a strategy it failed to reap electoral rewards.

The RSS cadre was the core of the BJP's organizational strength. In the

1983 assembly elections in Delhi and in Jammu and Kashmir, the RSS withheld support from the BJP, however, and in the 1984 parliamentary elections, elements of the RSS actively worked for the Congress Party. The *Organizer*, the RSS English-language weekly, gave its support to Rajiv Gandhi, who had succeeded to the prime ministership following his mother's assassination. The 1984 elections brought the BJP a stunning defeat. Contesting 229 seats, it secured 7.4 percent of the vote and only 2 seats, and BJP President Vajpayee was defeated in his home constituency. For all its losses, however, the BJP remained a major political force in North India, especially in Himachal Pradesh, Madhya Pradesh, Rajasthan, and Delhi, but the Congress had made deep cuts into the BJP's base of support among the urban Hindu middle classes.

In the wake of its electoral defeat, the BJP returned to its RSS roots and a more militant Hindu stance. Advani, with closer ties to the RSS, replaced the more moderate Vajpayee as party president. The change in party program and leadership was aided by sharpened communal tensions in India and by Hindu revivalism sparked by the conversion of Hindu untouchables to Islam, the Shah Bano affair (relating to Muslim personal law and a uniform civil code), the Ramjanmabhoomi issue at Ayodhya, and the movement for secession in Kashmir. These developments—conversion, Shah Bano, and Ayodhya, most saliently—reinforced the sense of insecurity— and anger—among Hindus and enhanced the appeal of the BJP in its efforts to strengthen Hindu identity and mobilize the Hindu nation under its political banner.

Hindu nationalists sought to heighten Hindu consciousness by arousing fears that India, as a Hindu nation, was under siege. They viewed with alarm the rise of Islamic fundamentalism in neighboring Iran, Pakistan, and Bangladesh, and what they perceived as aggressive proselytization by resurgent Islam within India. In 1981 more than one thousand Dalits had converted, en masse, to Islam in the South Indian village of Meenakshipuram. The RSS alleged that a "foreign hand" was behind the conversions and that the goal—political power—was to be achieved by expanding the numerical strength of the Muslim community in India. New mosques and Islamic schools, funded by "Gulf money," were seen everywhere, and Muslims were increasing in number, both by conversions and by having more babies. Various Indian newspapers published statistics that projected a Muslim majority in the Indian population by the year 2281, if not earlier.[22] The RSS, with other Hindu organizations, called for a ban on conversions to Islam and Christianity, and the VHP set out to reconvert the Dalits at Meenakshipuram and, more broadly, to bring Indian Muslims back into the Hindu fold.

Meenakshipuram energized the VHP, and as the principal voice of "Hinduism in danger," the organization drew numerous Hindu religious leaders and *sadhus* to its cause. The VHP conducted campaigns against untouchability, initiated new programs of social welfare, and undertook the construction of new temples. Central to its agenda was the promotion of Hindu unity, with the Bhagavad Gita as a sacred text comparable in its centrality to the Bible for Christianity and the Koran for Islam. The vehicle of mobilization for the VHP was the *yatra*, a grand procession or mobile rally, often covering great distances. Their impact was greatest in areas of communal tension, and they were often accompanied by incidents of Hindu–Muslim violence.

Shah Bano and the Uniform Civil Code

Hindu nationalists decried the government's "pampering" of minorities and denounced as "pseudo-secularism" state policies that accorded "special rights" to Muslims in matters of personal law—marriage, inheritance, and divorce.[23] The issue came to the fore in a 1985 Supreme Court case involving a seventy-three-year-old woman, Shah Bano, divorced by her husband in the traditional Muslim manner after forty-three years of marriage. The judgment granted her a monthly maintenance from her husband, whereas Muslim personal law would have required none. Muslim clerics, with the cry of "Islam in danger," attacked the decision as an interference in Shariat law and as a step toward a uniform civil code that would deny Muslims the right to follow the injunctions of the faith.

In an attempt to stem the loss of Muslim support from the Congress Party, Prime Minister Rajiv Gandhi (initially favorable to the Court's judgment) announced support for the Muslim Women (Protection of Rights on Divorce) Bill that would, in effect, scuttle the Supreme Court decision. Though welcomed by traditional Muslims, the bill came under immediate attack from more progressive Muslims, women, secularists, and Hindu nationalists. The bill became law in May 1986, "even though," as Ainslie Embree writes, "perhaps no other piece of legislation since 1947 had aroused such widespread and impressive opposition."[24]

The Shah Bano controversy was tailor-made for Hindu nationalist exploitation, and the RSS–VHP–BJP combine did so very effectively, for Shah Bano dramatized the dilemma of integrating a democratic constitution in a multicultural, multireligious society.[25] In this case, by according protection to Muslim rights in personal law, Muslim women were, in fact, accorded lesser protections under law than were enjoyed by all other Indian women. The Hindu nationalists' call for a uniform civil code, embodied in the platform of the BJP, now found wide resonance within India. For the Hindu nationalists, the government's response to the Shah Bano case was proof apparent that the Congress Party was courting the Muslim vote and that Indian "secularism" was a sham, that it was, in fact, anti-Hindu. The BJP, by contrast, stood for "genuine" or "positive" secularism—a secularism that embodied a Uniform Civil Code (albeit a Hinduized version), a purging of school textbooks that demeaned Hindu culture and tradition, and an end, more generally, to laws and practices that "privileged" minorities in a Hindu majority state.

The Road to Ayodhya: Mandal and Mandir

Hindu nationalist grievance was symbolized by the Babri Mosque at Ayodhya. In 1984 the VHP revived the Ayodhya issue and launched the movement to "liberate" Ramjanmabhoomi, the birthplace of Lord Rama.[26] At issue was the Babri Masjid, a mosque constructed in 1528 by the first Mughal emperor, Babur, on the site in Ayodhya, in Uttar Pradesh, where Hindus believe a temple (*mandir*) earlier stood marking the birthplace of Rama. Against a backdrop of nearly a century of conflict over the shrine, the government in 1949 had declared the premises a disputed area and locked the gates. The VHP reignited the dispute, and in 1986 a district judge ordered the gates opened to Hindu worshippers. Barred from entry, Muslims formed the Babri Masjid Action Committee and observed nationwide "mourning." As tensions sharpened between Hindus and Muslims, more than 300,000 Muslims gathered in Delhi in March 1987 to demand the return of the mosque. It was the largest rally of Muslims held since independence, and it was followed a month later by a massive Hindu rally organized by the VHP.

Undergirding the campaigns by the VHP was its effort to construct a "Hindu vote," a consolidated bloc that could be mobilized to exert pressure on government for the defense and promotion of Hindu interests and that could be drawn upon by the BJP as the base of its electoral support. And such a bloc, VHP leaders no doubt thought, would give them leverage with the BJP. From the mid-1980s, the BJP pursued a mixed strategy that combined an openness to alliance with mainstream opposition parties and mobilization campaigns focused on Hindu identity, most notably the campaign to build a Hindu temple at Ayodhya on the site occupied by the Babri Masjid.[27] The VHP had revived the Ramjanmabhoomi issue, and the BJP boarded its chariot.

The god-king Lord Rama had long been central to the ideology of Hindu nationalism, with its commitment to restore Ram Rajya, the ideal rule of the mythic age. In 1987–88 Rama gave renewed fervor to Hindu revivalism through the modern medium of television with the eighteen-month series of weekly episodes of the epic Ramayana that drew 100 million devoted viewers. The series was followed by the telecast of India's other great epic, the Mahabharata. Both served to displace local traditions and contributed to the emergence of the *national* Hindu identity long sought by Hindu nationalists.[28] But mythology entered the arena of politics most dramatically in the Ramjanmabhoomi–Babri Masjid dispute.

In 1989 the VHP launched the movement to demolish the Babri Masjid and "recapture injured Hindu pride" through the construction of a new Ramjanmabhoomi temple on its site. As Hindu devotees from all over India, each bearing a brick for the new temple's construction, made their way to Ayodhya, India witnessed perhaps its most serious Hindu–Muslim communal rioting since Partition in 1947. With the approach of the 1989 parliamentary elections, the VHP—probably at the behest of the BJP—called off its march on Ayodhya, but the BJP, linked to the VHP through the RSS, sought to make Ayodhya its own cause. Prime Minister Rajiv Gandhi, who earlier had stirred the communal pot in his bid for Muslim support in the Shah Bano controversy, now tried to use Ayodhya for Congress benefit but without success. The Congress went down to defeat on the issues of corruption, inflation, and Rajiv's ineffective leadership. In the elections, the BJP, with 11.4 percent of the vote, won eighty-five seats in the Lok Sabha, and it gained control of government in three North Indian states—Madhya Pradesh, Himachal Pradesh, and Rajasthan.

Hindu nationalism was a major factor in the BJP's expanded support after 1985. The 1989 electoral campaign of the RSS–VHP–BJP combine projected the transformation of the Hindu chariot into an irresistible juggernaut. Jaffrelot argues that "the invention of new rituals, the reinterpretation of the myth of Ram, the claim that Ayodhya was in some sense the centre of Hinduism, and the increased readiness to foment communal rioting represented what appeared to be a long-term policy of redefining the culture of the Hindus and their relationship with other communities. In immediate electoral terms, these techniques were partly responsible for the BJP's success."[29] Other factors, Jaffrelot recognizes, included the burden of corruption carried by the Congress, the BJP's populist appeals on socioeconomic issues, and, crucially, the electoral adjustments in contested seats between the BJP and the Janata Dal to insure a more united opposition challenge to the Congress.

In challenging the Congress, an amalgam of centrist parties, under the leadership of V. P. Singh, had come together as the Janata Dal, with its core support among the "backward" peasant castes of North India. In alliance with regional parties, the Janata Dal headed the National Front and entered into agreements with the BJP and the Communists on a constituency-by-constituency basis to maximize the number of "straight contests" between Congress and the opposition. Short of a majority in its own right, the new National Front government depended for its survival on "outside" support from both the BJP and the Communists.

The National Front government was riven by dissension, and to gain popular support and strengthen his own position within the Janata Dal, Prime Minister Singh announced that the government would implement the recommendations by the Mandal Commission to reserve 27 percent of all central government jobs for "Other Backward Classes" (OBCs), the lower, largely peasant castes that together make up some 52 percent of India's population. The announcement brought a firestorm of criticism, Singh was accused of starting a caste war, and a number of high-caste students immolated themselves in acts of protest. BJP leaders were incensed by what was, in their eyes, a cynical move to divide Hindus and undercut the BJP.

The BJP faced a dilemma, for to support the recommendation would alienate the party's upper-caste base of support, but with 52 percent of the population classified among the Other Backward Classes, it would forever lose the possibility of expanding its appeal among the lower castes and of securing a majority of votes. Rather than outright opposition, the BJP announced support for quotas on the basis of economic criteria rather than caste. To bridge the caste divide and galvanize Hindu unity, party president

L. K. Advani, in collaboration with the VHP, launched his Rath Yatra (chariot procession), a 10,000-kilometer journey in a van fashioned to look like a mythological chariot across the heartland of North India, from Somnath, in Gujarat, to Ayodhya, where on October 30, 1990, construction of the new temple was to begin. As the date neared, in growing communal tension, tens of thousands of Hindu militants led by Advani converged on Ayodhya. Prime Minister V. P. Singh, invoking the principles of secularism, warned that the state High Court's interim order to secure the status quo at the disputed site would be enforced and that the mosque at Ayodhya would be protected "at all costs." On October 23, as they were about to enter Uttar Pradesh in the drive to Ayodhya, Advani and other BJP leaders were arrested. The arrests and clashes at Ayodhya between government paramilitary forces and Hindus intent on destroying the mosque sparked a wave of violence that left more than three hundred people dead. Hindu militants withdrew from Ayodhya with the promise to return.

The incident had immediate political impact. Following Advani's arrest, the BJP withdrew its parliamentary support from V. P. Singh's National Front government, and on losing a vote of confidence, Singh submitted his resignation as Prime Minister.

The BJP fully exploited the Ayodhya controversy in the 1991 parliamentary elections. It doubled its popular vote from 11.4 percent in 1989 to 21.0 percent in 1991, and increased its seats in the Lok Sahba from 85 to 119. In the accompanying state assembly elections, the party gained power in Uttar Pradesh, India's most populous state.

BJP strength remained primarily in the Hindi belt of North India; in Gujarat, where, in its strongest showing, it captured more than 50.4 percent of the vote; and in Maharashtra, where the BJP was allied with the rabidly anti-Muslim Shiv Sena. In the South, where it was otherwise weak, the party made a reasonably strong showing in Karnataka, and it registered gains as well in eastern India. Both Mandal and Mandir (temple)—caste and religion—played to the benefit of the BJP. In Gujarat, where the RSS/VHP had been particularly active, Ayodhya had perhaps its greatest appeal, but the BJP also effectively exploited the Mandal reservations issue among the state's middle classes. In West Bengal and the Northeast, the BJP's issue was the illegal immigration of Bangladeshi Muslims.

If Mandal served to draw upper-caste support to the BJP, however, the party's stance on the reservation issue also served as a barrier to the BJP in

securing support among the "backward" castes, especially in those states, Bihar most notably, where the OBCs had been politically mobilized. With
OBCs accounting for 52 percent of India's population, the BJP could not afford to permanently alienate itself from so potent a political force, and over
the course of the 1990s, the party came tacitly to accept the Mandal reservations, as did all political parties with any aspiration for power, and by the
1996 elections, it had ceased to be an issue. Indeed, from 1993, the BJP
reached out to the OBCs by bringing members of the backward castes into
the higher ranks of party leadership and by putting them up as candidates.[30]

From the late 1980s, as the Indian economy opened under new policies of
liberalization and market reform, the middle class expanded, and the BJP
began to make inroads among the modern upper middle class—professionals and business people—where before its base had been principally among
the higher castes of the traditional urban middle classes—small traders,
shopkeepers, clerks, teachers, and civil servants. It reinforced its strength
among Brahmins and other higher castes but also among middle castes who
felt threatened by the specter of Mandal in the rise of the Other Backward
Classes. The sources of this expansion were socioeconomic, not religious. Indeed, the party's success in the 1991 elections was as much the product of
economic appeal as Hindu mobilization.

For all the gains enjoyed by the BJP, the 1991 elections brought the Congress again to power, under the prime ministership of Narasimha Rao. In
Parliament, the BJP was the largest opposition party. The Ayodhya issue
again exploded when the BJP and VHP vowed that on December 6, 1992,
they would begin construction of the temple to Lord Rama at the sacred
site. The Indian government had sufficient warning but deployed only
15,000 paramilitary troops to the area rather than the more reliable Indian
Army forces. Prime Minister Narasimha Rao took the Hindu leaders at their
word that they would not defy the Supreme Court order protecting the
mosque and would offer only "symbolic" temple construction. The leaders,
however, could not control the fervor of the devotees they had aroused, and
at the hour Hindu holy men had deemed propitious, some 200,000 Hindu
militants, with the Bajrang Dal in the lead, converged on Ayodhya, stormed
through the police barricades, and demolished the Muslim shrine. The police and paramilitary guarding the mosque offered no resistance.

The Prime Minister denounced the action as "a betrayal of the nation"
and attacked the BJP for exacerbating Hindu–Muslim tensions in a bid to

"grab power, whipping up communal frenzy to undermine the social fabric of the nation." In neighboring Pakistan and Bangladesh, Muslim mobs attacked and burned Hindu temples, and in Jiddah, Saudi Arabia, the fifty-nation Organization of the Islamic Conference expressed outrage at the Indian government's failure to protect the mosque from Hindu extremists. As reports of the destruction spread, Indian Muslims responded with attacks on Hindus and Hindu temples, and rioting erupted across India. In the following six days of violence, despite curfews, more than 1,200 persons were killed in rioting and police-firings—the vast majority of whom where Muslims. In Bombay, the riots—fueled by the Shiv Sena, the BJP's fascistic ally in Maharashtra—were the worst since India became independent in 1947.

The President dismissed the BJP-led state government of Uttar Pradesh and the legislative assembly and imposed President's Rule, thus bringing India's largest state under the direct control of the central government. Soon after, the Center dismissed the BJP state governments in Madhya Pradesh, Rajasthan, and Himachal Pradesh, on the grounds that "the Government of the State could not be carried on in accordance with the provisions of the Constitution." L. K. Advani, who had been on the platform with Hindu religious leaders at Ayodhya, resigned as leader of the opposition in Parliament, but other Hindu leaders remained defiant. Ashok Singhal, leader of the VHP, declared that any government efforts to impede construction of the Ram temple would result in "a confrontation of unimaginable magnitude."

Singhal, Advani, and Murli Manohar Joshi (the stridently Hindu nationalist who had succeeded Advani as BJP president in 1991) were among the hundreds arrested and charged with inciting the militants. The government banned for two years three Hindu communal organizations—the RSS, the VHP, and the Bajrang Dal—as well as two Muslim fundamentalist groups. At Ayodhya, troops cleared the site of Hindu devotees, leaving behind a temporary shrine to Rama. The BJP, like the VHP, remained committed to building a temple on the site, but the BJP sought to distance itself from the demolition of the mosque, declaring it a spontaneous and uncontrollable response to the government's "callousness" in dealing with the Ayodhya issue. The VHP and the Bajrang Dal clearly knew well what they were doing, and the BJP was implicated, even as it may have lost control over what happened. Vajpayee, who had not been present at Ayodhya, pronounced the demolition the "worst miscalculation" ever made by his party.

In 1993, the defeat of the BJP in a series of state assembly elections across North India brought the seemingly unstoppable Ayodhya wave to a halt and demonstrated the limits of religious mobilization. Ironically, the demolition of the mosque deprived the RSS–VHP–BJP combine of the symbol around which it had so successfully mobilized Hindu sentiment. Construction of the Ram temple at Ayodhya might remain the focus of the VHP,[31] but the destruction of the mosque and the violence that followed alarmed many among the BJP's middle-class supporters. Fearing both alienation of major segments in its base of support and domination by the increasingly militant VHP and Bajrang Dal, the BJP once again shifted emphasis in its strategies of pragmatism and mobilization. From 1993, in Jaffrelot's words, "the BJP decided to focus on issues that would help it recover its former respectability and strengthen its nationalist image; but it also realized that the Ayodhya policy had largely run its course."[32]

Kashmir and Article 370

The Uniform Civil Code and construction of the Ram temple at Ayodhya were the most prominent planks in the BJP's Hindutva platform. Another Hindutva theme involved Jammu and Kashmir, India's only Muslim-majority state. The BJP opposes the "special status" accorded Kashmir under Article 370 of the Constitution. The party calls for scrapping the provisions for autonomy, which were to have been temporary pending the state's full integration within the Indian Union.[33] Especially egregious in Hindu nationalist eyes is a Kashmir state law (often thought to be a provision of Article 370) that restricts the sale of immovable property to Indians who are not state subjects or permanent residents of the state, effectively limiting non-Kashmiri immigration into the state. Indeed, many Hindu nationalists would not only abrogate Article 370 and abolish the restrictive land-ownership law, but would ethnically "flood" the state by encouraging Hindus to move into Kashmir to alter the demographic balance. Efforts to dramatize the issue of Kashmir with an *ekta yatra*, a unity march from Kanyakumari, at the tip of India in the south, to Srinagar, capital of Kashmir, in 1991–92, came to little more than a fiasco,[34] but the insurgency in Kashmir, from 1989, and attendant cross-border terrorism, served to feed the Hindu nationalist demonization of Pakistan as intent on destabilizing and dismembering India. Downplaying more stridently Hindutva demands, the BJP could still use Kashmir and the plight of Brahmin Pandit refugees from the Valley of Kashmir in appeal to Hindu sentiment and do so in the secular garb of Indian nationalism.

Elections

In its shift to a more moderate approach, the BJP began to place greater stress on policy issues. Within the party, the leadership struggled to shape an economic policy with wide appeal. The more militant Hindu nationalists, backed by the RSS, called for *swadeshi*, self-reliance, a protectionist stance that opposed most foreign investment and opening India to global markets; against them were advocates of liberalization, who saw market reform as the engine of economic growth. The two were fused in the official statement of policy: "The BJP has long been an advocate of decentralization and deregulation but it has always maintained that internal liberalization should precede, not follow, the mad rush toward globalization."[35] The campaign slogan would be "Computer chips, not potato chips." Later, in power, even as the struggle over economic policy continued within the party, the BJP leadership pushed foreign investment, but with deference to a "level playing field" with a gradual opening to foreign competition.[36]

In the 1996 elections, the party held its core support, with 20.3 percent of the vote, and emerged as the largest single party in Parliament, with 161 seats—but far short of the majority needed to form a government on its own. The President invited the BJP, as the largest party, to form a government. It lasted only thirteen days, and the new Prime Minister, Atal Bihari Vajpayee, was forced to resign when it was clear that the party was isolated and would be unable to win support from other parties to secure the requisite majority. The BJP government was replaced by a United Front coalition of fourteen parties that lasted eighteen months.

Determined to avoid the isolation and humiliation that led to the fall of its thirteen-day government in 1996, the BJP entered into a series of alliances with over a dozen regional parties in preparation for the 1998 Lok Sabha elections. The elections, however, produced a fractured mandate and another "hung" Parliament. The BJP, with 25.6 percent of the vote, was again the largest single party, but with 182 seats it was well short of a majority even with the additional 40 seats won by its electoral allies. Following a brief period of maneuvering, bargaining, and uncertainty, the President finally decided to ask the BJP to form a government. Vajpayee, sworn in as Prime Minster on March 19, succeeded in cobbling together a shaky coalition of more than a dozen parties and a handful of independents, and won a vote of confidence, 274 to 261.

The BJP in Power

The BJP's success in the 1998 elections was based on Vajpayee's personal popularity, a toned-down Hindutva program, a split in the anti-BJP vote between the Congress and the United Front, and, most critically, the party's alliance strategy. The formation of the government was not cost-free, for to hold the fractious coalition together the BJP was forced to make substantial compromises in its program.

The National Agenda for Governance developed by the BJP and its coalition partners demonstrated how far the party leadership was prepared to compromise its Hindutva agenda in an effort to expand its base and strengthen its electoral appeal. The National Agenda made no mention of the three most distinctive features of the BJP manifesto—the commitment to repeal Article 370 of the Constitution, which gives special status to the state of Jammu and Kashmir; the promise to construct a Ram temple at Ayodhya; and the pledge to enact a Uniform Civil Code that would be applicable to all religious groups. For the RSS, this was apostasy, but for all its willingness to shelve its own program and govern in the spirit of consensus, the BJP was hostage to the potential that the withdrawal of even one partner could bring the government down. The day of reckoning came in April 1999 when Jayalalitha's AIADMK of Tamil Nadu withdrew support. After thirteen months in power, the government lost a vote of confidence by one vote, 269 to 270, and Vajpayee submitted his resignation as Prime Minister.

The President asked Vajpayee to remain as "caretaker" pending the formation of a new government. Efforts by the Congress to forge a new majority failed, and the President, acting on the advice of the Prime Minister, dissolved the Lok Sabha and called new elections—the third national election in three years. Despite predictions of voter fatigue, the turnout was an impressive 60 percent of some 600 million eligible voters.

As in 1998, there were three basic groupings, though the pattern of alliances was modified as parties split or shifted allegiance. The BJP's skill in forging the new National Democratic Alliance (NDA) expanded the number of parties committed to Vajpayee's leadership to twenty-four. The BJP, setting aside its own Hindu nationalist agenda in favor of a "common program," was at the core of the alliance that included regional parties as disparate and ideologically incompatible as the Hindu chauvinist Shiv Sena of Maharashtra and the pragmatic, secular Telugu Desam of Andhra and DMK of Tamil Nadu. The two other major groupings were the Congress, led by Rajiv's Italian-born widow Sonia Gandhi, with its regional allies, and the National Front/Left Front combine, principally the Communist Party of India (Marxist), various Janata Dal splinters, and a handful of regional parties.

The main electoral arena pitted the BJP against the Congress, and the campaign had something of the character of an American presidential election, with Vajpayee and Sonia Gandhi projected over parties or issues. The BJP immediately made Sonia's foreign origin an issue and contrasted the *videshi* (foreign) with its own *swadeshi* (home-grown) credentials. The BJP also sought to capitalize on Vajpayee's successful handling of the Kargil war in Kashmir (May–July 1999), but although both Sonia and Kargil played a part in the decision of some voters, as did sympathy for Vajpayee generated by the manner in which his government had been brought down, the most critical factors in deciding the elections were at the state level and related to caste and to the performance of state governments. Generally favorable economic conditions, with low inflation, a good monsoon, and an upturn in industrial growth, added some boost to the BJP, but the economic factor figured principally in terms of local bread-and-butter concerns. Market reforms were not a significant issue in the elections, reflecting the near consensus among political parties in support of economic liberalization. And religion had receded as a salient issue: the BJP had muted Hindutva and its opponents were unable to tar the BJP with responsibility for communal violence as they had in the wake the destruction of the Babri mosque at Ayodhya.

The election results brought Vajpayee's National Democratic Alliance a majority in India's 545-seat Lok Sabha, with 299 of the 597 seats contested and 41 percent of the vote. The alliances forged by Vajpayee were the key to victory. The BJP won 182 seats, the same number it had won in 1998, but its allies bagged another 117 seats. The Telugu Desam Party of Andhra Pradesh came back with 29 seats; the Shiv Sena won 15; the DMK of Tamil Nadu won 12. Especially important for prospects of political stability was that, despite the number of parties upon which the new government was dependent, it was less vulnerable to the kind of extortion that had brought down the previous Vajpayee government.

The BJP secured 23.7 percent of the vote, slightly below its 25.6 percent in 1998, but in deference to its allies, the BJP had contested far fewer constituencies than in 1998—339 seats, down from 388 in the previous election. But if the BJP roughly held its own nationally in seats and votes, it suffered a major setback in India's largest state, Uttar Pradesh, where voters passed a negative judgment on the BJP state government's poor performance. The BJP won only 29 of the state's 85 parliamentary seats—down from the 57 seats it won in 1998.

On October 13, 1999, the Bharatiya Janata Party's Atal Bihari Vajpayee, leader of the National Democratic Alliance, took the oath of office as Prime Minister of India, heading a twenty-four-party coalition with a seventy-member Council of Ministers. Widely respected and viewed as the force of moderation within the BJP, Vajpayee held the coalition together through its five-year term. But in parliamentary elections in May 2004, the BJP fell to a Congress-led alliance and took its place once again in opposition.

In its policies, from 1999 to 2004, the Vajpayee government largely pursued a centrist, mainstream approach. It sustained and extended, albeit cautiously and sometimes erratically, the course of economic reform. In social policies, the BJP-led government sustained continuity with the basic approach of previous governments—save in one area, education, where the coalition yielded, perhaps unwittingly, to the RSS. Murli Manohar Joshi, Minister of Human Resources Development and ardent Hindu nationalist, sought to "correct discrepancies" in school textbooks, to eradicate their Marxist orientation, and stress "ancient Indian [Hindu] values." The BJP had long sought the rectification of school history texts, to purge them of left-wing and pro-minority (Muslim) bias,[37] and in states where the BJP has come to power, schoolbook revision has been a major priority. Now at the Center, Joshi directed the National Council of Educational Research and Training to revise books and formulate a new National Curriculum Framework of School Education. The moves provoked controversy and unease among those who fear that textbook and curricular reforms could be the means by which the BJP, the VHP, and the RSS capture India's schools and the minds of the next generation.

If education had been at least a potential enclave for Hindutva, foreign policy under the Vajpayee government reflected a more broadly consensual approach. Out of power, foreign policy had been a relatively low priority for the BJP, but the party platform had called for "genuine nonalignment" and "improvement of relations with our immediate neighbours." The party had long favored India's acquisition of nuclear weapons, and in 1985 it called for the government to "take immediate steps to develop our own nuclear bomb." With the BJP in power, in May 1998 India conducted a series of nuclear tests, bringing India into the nuclear weapons club, but Congress governments had prepared the way, and had it not been for the U.S. surveillance satellite discovery of Indian test preparations in 1995, India might well have "gone nuclear" at that time. The timing of the 1998 tests, arguably, may have been influenced in part by BJP political considerations, but the compelling determinants were strategic and a widely held judgment that India's security environment had significantly deteriorated.[38] The decision to cross the nuclear Rubicon was supported across the political spectrum. Indeed, the BJP's foreign policy reflects a broad consensus within India and has not been communalized.[39] It surely views Pakistan as illegitimate, but it does not seek to undo Partition, whatever the Pakistanis may think, and has largely approached Pakistan and the Muslim world in terms of policies pursued rather than their Islamic identity. The BJP takes a hard line on Pakistani support for Kashmiri insurgents and its sponsorship of cross-border terrorism, but so too do the Congress and other Indian political parties. Significantly, however, Prime Minister Vajpayee actively pursued improved relations with Pakistan and is believed to have wanted his legacy to be, above all, peace with Pakistan and a settlement of the Kashmir crisis—something the 2004 election defeat denied him.

There are those within the RSS and among more extreme Hindu nationalists within the BJP who subscribe to Huntington's "clash of civilizations,"[40] but the party leadership has resisted pressure to align *Hindu* India with the West against Islam. The BJP-led coalition pursued good relations with numerous Muslim states; supported the cause of a Palestinian state even as it favored closer ties to Israel; and the BJP government opposed the Bush administration's push for war against Iraq. In all of this, there was little to distinguish the BJP from other parties and previous governments.

Even as Indian foreign policy retained a high degree of continuity, however, there were, in belated response to the collapse of the Soviet Union and the end of the Cold War and to the rise of economic globalization, significant changes in Indian foreign policy under the BJP. Nehruvian idealism was supplanted by pragmatic realism; relations with the United States improved and deepened; ties to post-Soviet Russia were rejuvenated; rapprochement with China moved forward and trade expanded; more extensive ties with the nations of Southeast Asia were pursued; and, perhaps more consequentially, India sought a more coherent strategic doctrine and placed a greater emphasis on force.[41]

Indian foreign policy under the BJP was an expression of *Indian* nationalism. But, as in other policy areas, the BJP had a Janus face. If Hindutva had become the ideological and policy thrust of the government, India's role in the world would likely have become more an expression of *Hindu* nationalism, with its strongest impact on relations with Pakistan and Bangladesh and perhaps the Muslim world more broadly. The Hindu zealots of the RSS and VHP, however, were held in check by a BJP leadership in foreign policy that was moderated both by the constraints of coalition government and its own commitment to a realpolitik that put national interests above sectarian or ideological design. Here, Prime Minister Vajpayee was crucial. L. K. Advani, his likely successor to the prime ministership had the BJP been returned to power in 2004, surely projects a "hardline" Hindu nationalism, but the realities of governance in India would have held him in check as well and underscored the contradictions within the Bharatiya Janata Party.

Conflicts, Contradictions, and the Implications of Gujarat

In July 2002 Vajpayee appointed Home Minister L. K. Advani as Deputy Prime Minister, a position hitherto vacant, formally according him recognition as second in command. Vajpayee and Advani reflect two faces of Hindu nationalism, one more moderate, the other more militant, but as Jaffrelot cautions, they do not represent "opposed groups or even ideological tendencies."[42] It is more a division of labor in the mixed strategy of the BJP. At the same time, conflict and contradiction has been endemic within the BJP, as it was earlier in the Jan Sangh, and they have been inevitably exacerbated in the exigencies of elections and in holding power. Power, too, brought opportunism and corruption.

Conflict between the BJP and more militant stalwarts of the RSS, VHP, and Bajrang Dal has been sharpened. And the BJP's alliance with the Shiv Sena has been strained by the Sena's violence and virulent anti-Muslim rhetoric and by the Sena's anti-Dalit stance. Problems between the BJP and VHP deepened after the BJP took power at the helm of the coalition government, and in the fall 2002 assembly elections in Jammu and Kashmir, the VHP set up its own party to contest seats in predominantly Hindu Jammu. The VHP was vocal in its criticism of the government's failure to move on the construction of the Ram temple at Ayodhya, and the BJP opposed the VHP's campaign to "liberate" temples at Varanasi (Kashi) and Mathura, where they believe, as at Ayodhya, mosques stand on sites of earlier temples.[43]

In October 2002, the RSS publication *Panchajanya* denounced the BJP-led National Democratic Alliance government and criticized both Vajpayee and Advani for "failure on all fronts."[44] Advani responded by saying, "The BJP is committed to cultural nationalism and we have not deviated from our ideals while supporting the programmes and policies of NDA,"[45] but tensions deepened in November when Advani, in a statement in the Lok Sabha, said that India can "never be a Hindu state." The VHP president saw relations between the BJP and the VHP as near the breaking point. And Bal Thackeray, leader of the Shiv Sena, lamented that until now Hindus had looked to Advani "as a strong votary of Hindutva." Why, he asked, "did Mr. Advani betray Hindus, Hindutva and the nation?"[46]

Contradictions within the BJP and conflict with the RSS and VHP sharpened in the wake of Hindu–Muslim violence in Gujarat in February 2002. On February 27, returning by train from Ayodhya, Hindu pilgrims who had earlier provoked local Muslims at Godhra were reportedly met by a mob of frenzied Muslims who set fire to two railroad cars, killing fifty-eight people, many women and children. In the following three days, Hindus in Gujarat retaliated with an anti-Muslim pogrom that left as many as two thousand people dead. The Bajrang Dal led lumpen elements in murder, rape, and arson, but middle-class people—women and children included—joined in to cheer and take part in the looting of Muslim shops and homes. The police stood by, defending themselves by saying, "We had no orders to save you." Gujarat's BJP Chief Minister, Narendra Modi, described the violence as "a spontaneous reaction"—but he surely did nothing to put out the flames. Indeed, at the height of the carnage, he declared, "The five crore [fifty million] people of Gujarat have shown remarkable restraint under grave provocation."

In its account of the events in Gujarat, Human Rights Watch reported,

The state of Gujarat and the central government of India initially blamed Pakistan for the train massacre, which it called a "pre-meditated" "terrorist" attack against Hindus in Godhra. The recent revival of the Ram temple campaign, and heightened fears of terrorism since September 11 were exploited by local Hindu nationalist groups and the local press which printed reports of a "deadly conspiracy" against Hindus by Muslims in the state. On February 28, one local language paper headline read: "Avenge blood for blood." Muslim survivors of the attacks repeatedly told Human Rights Watch that they were told to "go back to Pakistan."[47]

The horror of what had happened and the involvement of the state BJP and Sangh Parivar organizations in fomenting the violence rebounded on the national leadership of the BJP and was compounded by the Center's own failure to intervene more rapidly. Vajpayee, who did not go to Gujarat until April, condemned the massacres as a "blot on the country's face," and stated that the attack on the train at Godhra was "condemnable," but that what followed was "madness."

In the months that followed, with Gujarat assembly elections on the horizon, the state was volatile, and Chief Minister Modi and his VHP cadre were determined to exploit the widespread feeling among Hindus that these Muslims "got what they deserved." Modi, for example, called the relief camps for Muslims left homeless by the riots "baby producing centres." The terrorist attack in September 2002 on a temple at Gandhinagar, the state capital, left thirty people dead, but this time Modi acted to impose order and claim praise for Hindu restraint.

Vajpayee and Advani wavered back and forth, distancing themselves from Modi and his inflammatory rhetoric only to reverse course and embrace him. For whatever embarrassment—indeed, shame—Modi may have caused the national leadership of the BJP, Advani made it clear that winning the December 2002 election in Gujarat would be an "acid test" in the buildup to the 2004 parliamentary elections.[48]

In the campaign, Modi fused religion and politics and, as a spur to anti-Muslim sentiment, made Islamic terrorism and its ties to Pakistan a central plank in the BJP platform. Posters portrayed a defiant Modi silhouetted against the backdrop of the burning train at Godhra, proclaimed by the VHP as Hinduism's "Pearl Harbor."

In the Gujarat elections, held on December 15, the BJP, with Modi at the helm, returned to power with an unprecedented two-thirds majority in the legislative assembly. The VHP, the engine of mobilization in Gujarat, claimed the victory for Hindutva and put the national BJP leadership on notice that Gujarat would be the model for state assembly elections coming in 2003 and for the parliamentary elections in 2004. VHP leader Praveen Togadia proclaimed that only those who talk of Hindu interests can rule the country and that Muslim "fundamentalism and extremism cannot be finished till Pakistan is dismembered."[49] The Gujarat verdict, in the words of BJP President Venkaiah Naidu, had given the clear message that "Hindu-bashing" would not be tolerated. "We shall replicate our Gujarat experience everywhere."[50]

For their part, Vajpayee and Advani wavered as they sought to retain their Hindu nationalist base and, at the same time, allay the fears of their National Democratic Alliance partners. Both attended the ceremony in which Modi took the oath of office, but each sought to take the edge off inflammatory rhetoric. Advani said that India was already a Hindu society and that the BJP did not seek a theocratic state. Hindutva, he said, was to be understood as "cultural nationalism," a phrase that the BJP has taken as its preferred mantra. Vajpayee, invoking the Supreme Court's characterization of Hindutva as the Indian "way of life," emphasized the tradition of Hindu tolerance, stating that Hindutva and extremism can never go together.[51] This was kerosene to the fire of the VHP, which struck out at both Advani and Vajpayee, slamming the Prime Minster for "pseudo-Hindutva" sentiments. Even as RSS leaders sought to bring peace to their feuding family, the VHP warned that it would not deviate from the Hindutva cause and that it would confront the government on the construction of the Ram temple at Ayodhya.

Looking to the parliamentary election in 2004, the BJP faced a series of state assembly elections in 2003. The first was in Himachal Pradesh, in February, where Hindutva appeals failed to find resonance, and the incumbent BJP lost to Congress, in part, as a result of party infighting. (The BJP was not a player in the subsequent Meghalaya, Tripura, and Nagaland elections in India's Northeast.) The next round of state elections came in December—Chhatisgarh, Madhya Pradesh, Rajasthan, Mizoram, and Delhi—

where the national BJP leadership sought the high ground, stressing development and stable government, and distanced itself from "the Gujarat model" even as, at the grass roots, stalwarts of the Sangh Parivar invoked Ayodhya and stoked anti-Muslim sentiment. Hindutva ultimately played a comparatively minor role in the campaigns, and Vajpayee's "moderate" approach was vindicated in the BJP's dramatic victories in Chhatisgar, Madhya Pradesh, and Rajasthan. In Mizoram, its ally, the Mizo National Front, retained power. Only in Delhi did the BJP fail to dislodge the Congress.

The BJP was now on a roll. Buoyed by good monsoons, a high rate of economic growth (7 to 8 percent), and new hope for peace with Pakistan, the BJP and its coalition partners looked to early parliamentary elections. On February 6, 2004, at the request of Prime Minister Vajpayee, President Abdul Kalam dissolved the Lok Sabha, the lower house of Parliament, and called for new elections. With adjustments in party membership, the BJP-led National Democratic Alliance faced a Congress Party that had learned its lesson in electoral strategy by its defeat five years earlier. Now, for the first time, the Congress entered into a broad alliance with a number of regional and state parties, but few observers, including those within the Congress itself, thought the ascendant BJP could be dislodged from power. Confident of victory with Vajpayee at the helm, the BJP accentuated the positive in a "feel good" atmosphere with the slogan "India Shining." Its campaign focused on economic growth, political stability, good governance, military strength, and opposition to cross-border terrorism. Negatively, the BJP portrayed Congress leader Sonia Gandhi as a "foreigner" unfit to be prime minister, and, sotto voce, it pursued the theme of "cultural nationalism." At the state level, local cadres, hand-in-hand with the VHP, followed a more aggressive Hindutva line as conditions permitted.

The results of the May 2004 parliamentary elections came as a stunning surprise. Congress and its allies bettered the BJP's National Democratic Alliance by some thirty seats. Though just short of a majority in the Lok Sabha, the Congress alliance had the support of the communist Left Front and, as Sonia Gandhi stepped back in favor of former finance minister Manmohan Singh to become Prime Minister, the Congress took power, ending India's six and one-half years of government under the BJP. Various factors account for the BJP defeat, many peculiar to individual states. The BJP's "India Shining" slogan may itself have highlighted economic disparities, for all Indians and all regions had not benefited equally in the boom of India's economic growth. The sun simply did not shine as brightly in rural areas and on those in the cities left in the economic shadows. The vote may also have registered reaction against the BJP for the Gujarat atrocities of February 2002. "Anti-incumbency" was a factor in a number of states (though by no means in all), but it was not always directed against the BJP or its allies, like the Telegu Desam in Andhra; the Congress government in Karnataka—like Andhra, one of the showcase states in the information technology (IT) revolution—lost its majority.

The key factor in the Congress victory at the Center, however, was its new willingness to enter into a broad pre-election alliance—just as the BJP had done in securing its 1999 victory. From 1999 to 2004, the actual vote for the two parties shifted only marginally. The Congress, going largely alone in 1999, secured 28.3 percent of the vote for 112 seats in the Lok Sabha; in 2004, the Congress, yielding a number of constituencies to its allies, got 26.7 percent of the vote, with 145 seats. Where the BJP had gotten 23.8 percent of the vote in 1999 (and 182 seats), it got 22.2 percent of the vote (and 138 seats) in 2004. It was the pattern of alliances in both elections that determined whether it would be a BJP- or a Congress-led coalition in power.

The BJP has, as it has risen in power, oscillated between pragmatic moderation and Hindu mobilization. From a political "pariah," isolated from the mainstream by its communal politics and Hindutva ideology, it has broadened its social base from the upper castes to include the expanding middle classes, the rising "backward" castes, and, at the bottom of the Hindu hierarchy, Dalits and tribals. It has expanded geographically as well, reaching from the heartland of North India into Western India and, more tentatively and less fully, into the South, East, and Northeast. Its strength remains principally concentrated in the North, but it has all-India aspirations.[52] The BJP's alliances strengthened its electoral power but limited its geographic expansion as the party yielded extensive areas of the country to party allies. Now out of power, the BJP will likely seek to expand its geographic base.

Electorally, the BJP has stabilized (perhaps stalled) at just under 25 percent of the vote, making alliances with other parties essential in any strategy to attain and secure power at the Center and in all but a few states. Its core is Hindu nationalist, and the party remains dependent at its roots on the organization and cadre of the RSS, the VHP, and the Sangh Parivar as a whole. The 2004 defeat of the BJP is likely to strengthen the hand of the stalwarts of Hindutva and a strategy of mobilization, with construction of the Ayodhya temple again at the forefront. But the party faces a fundamental dilemma: the BJP's ability to garner wider electoral support, enter alliances, and lead coalition governments depends on moderating the Hindutva ideology upon which it is grounded.

The contradictions within the BJP are inherent and remain unresolved, but in the course of its rise, the party and its RSS/VHP associates have brought religion into the mainstream of Indian politics, and they have, at the same time, politicized Hinduism. Ayodhya and the various campaigns to mobilize Hindu sentiment politically were a major factor in the rise of the BJP, but they also underscore the limits of Hindu nationalist appeal in a culturally diverse society. Hinduism is itself heterogeneous, but under the aegis of mass communication and political mobilization, a national, homogenized Hinduism is beginning to emerge. Hinduism is being transformed, and, albeit slowly, Hindu nationalists are the likely beneficiary.

EIGHT

Hindu Ethnonationalism, Muslim Jihad, and Secularism: Muslims in the Political Life of the Republic of India

Barbara D. Metcalf

At Oxford [in 1919] I did Modern History . . . and the [special] subject I selected was The Practice and Procedure of the House of Commons. My friends were surprised that I should select a subject so remote from India and Indian conditions. . . . [The reason was that] I hoped one day to join a legislature in India, and that a knowledge of the procedure of the parliament in England would be very helpful.
—Mahommedali Currim Chagla, *Roses in December: An Autobiography*[1]

If the Muslims want to see their future bright, then it is their duty that by their actions and character they prove their importance and usefulness. The more they will be useful for the country, the more respect they will have. . . . Today the Muslims remember the word jihad, but have forgotten that against the enemies of Islam and the Muslim community, like those of the [non-Muslim] residents of Makkah, patience and steadfastness, self-control, and high morals are considered *jihad-i akbar* (the greater jihad). In this jihad-i akbar there is no need of any sword or daggers, but only the strength of character and good deeds, which are more effective.
—Maulana Husain Ahmad Madani, Presidential Address to the Jamiat Ulama Hind, Bombay, 1948[2]

In the aftermath of the destruction of the World Trade Center, *New York Times* columnist Thomas Friedman, reviewing the politics of Muslim countries, made what was to him an astonishing discovery: the eschewal of any militancy or even fringe militant jihad activity on the part of what is probably the world's second largest Muslim population, the Muslims of India, roughly 12 percent of the total population and estimated conservatively to number some 120 million people.[3] Couching his report as "Today's News

Quiz," Friedman reached the conclusion that the key to this was over half a century of participation in a secular, democratic political system. This discovery served to confirm his recurrent theme that militancy and the absence of democracy (above all, in the Middle East) go hand in hand.[4]

The epigraphs above illustrate two central themes in what in fact have been the orientations of India's Muslims (leaving aside Kashmir, whose situation is wholly different from that of the rest of the Muslim population). The first epigraph, a comment by an enthusiastic young Muslim Indian student at Oxford right after World War I at the dawn of mass politics in India, points to the long-cherished dream of educated Indians under colonialism, including Muslim Indians, to create their own parliamentary system. The second epigraph quotes an Islamic religious scholar who has relentlessly fought side by side with Gandhi and other Congress leaders in the independence movement. He is speaking in 1948, in the immediate aftermath of independence, which had come with the horrific partition of the country along religious grounds, something he and most of the Muslim religious leadership had opposed. He makes clear that Muslims in this context had now to focus on service to the new country, not on militancy but on *moral* jihad. The long tradition of commitment to liberal democracy along with widespread movements to encourage individual adherence to Islamically sanctioned behavior are distinctive and significant characteristics of India's diverse and scattered Muslim populations. This orientation needs to be emphasized, given the glib assumption, reinforced in India's case by Hindu nationalist organizations, of endemic Islamic "fundamentalism" and militancy.

The dual thrusts of "secularism" and "jihad" need to be understood in their historical context. The commitment to secularism has turned out to be a struggle against the assumption, subtly reinforced in such diverse domains as the law, classical music, and film, that the real citizen in India is the Hindu. In addition, the focus on moral jihad, propagated by a range of Muslim voluntary associations, has come to represent in part a culturally defensive, inward-looking enhancement of Muslim self-consciousness that, while understandable, also facilitates imagining Muslims as "the Other." Clearly, assertions of Hindu ethno-religious pride, on the one hand, and Muslim self-protective isolation, on the other, are challenges to the liberal democratic order in which India rightfully takes pride.

The first part of this paper, on the legacy of the colonial period, focuses on the growth of what could be called "Hindu ethnonationalism." This is a theme within Indian nationalism, not only, as usually imagined, in contrast to it. In the Indian context, it is called religious "communalism." Underlying this mentality is a narrative that vilifies Muslims as, historically, marauders who violated a peaceful India, and, more recently, as the sole cause of Partition and a subsequent fifth column. The Prime Minister's speech, in April 2002, the more shocking for coming after an anti-Muslim pogrom in western India that left thousands dead, repeats these old images:

Wherever Muslims live, they don't like to live in co-existence with others, they don't like to mingle with others; and instead of propagating their ideas in a peaceful manner, they want to spread their faith by resorting to terror and threats.[5]

A goal of this essay is to historicize these assumptions and show the extent to which—contrary to stereotypes current not only in India—Muslims themselves have been made the victim through discrimination and violence. To this end, the paper describes the Muslim "minority" that emerged after independence, emphasizing, above all, the economic and political weakness of most Muslims in the country and reviewing the pattern of Muslim political activity over the past half century. The concluding section of the essay speculates on why the Muslims emerged as a salient target of Hindu nationalism at the end of the twentieth century, and is followed by a final comment on the potential danger of this nationalism to India, and, indeed, beyond India's borders, as well as the future directions Muslims may take.[6]

This tale of discrimination and violence is, of course, not at all the whole story. Actual anti-Muslim violence has been endemic primarily in the urban areas of the western and northern sections of the country.[7] Muslim Indians do play a role in public life. For the third time, a Muslim has held the largely ceremonial position of president. And, whatever the ambiguous relation of the ruling Hindu nationalist party, the BJP, to the tragedy of Gujarat, the party, like the Indian National Congress before it, officially proclaims its commitment "to ensure that communal violence is never repeated" and insists that it "remains" committed to secularism.[8] There are, furthermore, articulate Indian voices, non-Muslim as well as Muslim, raised in outrage over recent developments; over two dozen citizens' human rights and community service organizations, for example, documented the horrors that took place in 2002 in Gujarat. This is a tribute to the vibrancy of India's civil society.

The Colonial Legacy

No historian today questions the importance of British colonialism in creating a context in which religiously defined sub-nationalism, or "communalism," emerged. The British colonial framework created "official" identities that were, particularly in the era of mass politics that was initiated with electoral reforms after World War I, translated into what could be called a "political" identity that shaped individual lives.[9] No aspect of colonial practice in this regard was more important than separate electorates initiated in 1909 that encouraged Muslim politicians to speak exclusively to a Muslim audience. This separation was further enhanced by a colonial "arithmetic" that fostered competition over the number of reserved seats in councils, schools, and government employment, as well as the potential for drawing boundaries of more Muslim provinces. Influential British actors throughout welcomed opportunities to "divide and rule," and at no time more than in the immediate pre-Partition period, when Congress and other leaders were imprisoned because of their opposition to the war while Jinnah and his Muslim League allies were free. Peter Hardy, who has written the classic history of the Muslims of British India, speaks of the "idiom" of British rule that shaped official policy in terms of caste and religious community.[10]

Conventional analysis, from scholarship to political rhetoric to films, lays the "blame" for Partition on Muslims. New scholarship questions this story in several ways. To start with, Mohammad Ali Jinnah (1876–1948), typically vilified for destroying Indian unity, should in fact be seen as a "devoted Indian nationalist" whose goals for the degree of protection granted to Muslim interests differed only in degree and not in kind from the goals of those who were, in the final decades, his rivals in the Indian National Congress.[11] All parties to nationalist negotiation with the British, not just Jinnah and the Muslim League, participated in the logic of colonial arithmetic in relation to the putative religious communities. Ayesha Jalal even has argued that the goal of a separate Pakistan, only adopted by the Muslim League in 1940, was no more than a bargaining chip.[12]

Other scholars have persuasively argued that at the national level Congress leaders like Nehru were influenced in favor of Partition by the fear that otherwise their goal of a strong centralized state would be compromised by politicians favoring provincial authority, which was understood to secure both Muslim and regional political interests. Nehru in particular, moreover, also distrusted the aristocratic leadership of the League that he feared would be an obstacle to his development goals.[13] In Bengal, some among the Congress leadership saw advantages to their own dominance in re-creating the first Partition of Bengal (1905) that cut off the Muslim majority hinterland.[14] These arguments challenge the singling out of Jinnah as the single architect of Partition, but the Muslims of India have been tainted by that accusation.

Other scholars have unveiled in surprising ways the extent to which in the decades preceding independence even those committed to Muslim participation in political life in a united India espoused ideas about Muslims and Indian civilization that are central to Hindu nationalism. These ideas permeated mainstream nationalism and even areas not assumed to be political at all. Two examples will suffice. First, the Congress Party. Even Nehru—whose secularism is anathema to Hindu nationalism—in a work like *The Discovery of India* (1944) imagined an organic Indian civilization for which the coming of Muslim dynasties, far from being seen as conducive to the kind of more complex economic life and more integrated polity one would assume a modernist like him would value, represent instead "new problems." Similarly, key Congress socialists, usually thought of as "the Left," in fact often had close connections to Arya Samaj and Hindu cultural revivalism. One such figure, Sampurananad in the United Provinces, for example, espoused an organic view of Hinduism like that of the extreme Hindu nationalists of the time. An even more striking example of the pervasiveness of the place of Hinduism in the emerging nationalist public sphere is the case of music, where upper-caste Hindu sacrality and piety increasingly excluded the Muslim musicians who had been at the center of musical performance and creativity in favor of the myth of "rescuing" music and recovering its pristine origins.

Underlying this was a narrative of the nation that posited Muslims as foreign invaders and marauders. The "naturalness" of that narrative, which flourishes in the present, is such that, as the anthropologist Peter van der Veer has written, "It is so entrenched as to be unassailable." This narrative is nowhere represented better than in the self-interested introduction to the multivolume excerpts of translations of historical documents from the Muslim dynasties of precolonial India, explicitly introduced by their colonial compiler to illustrate the tyranny and oppression of Muslim monarchs from which the British, as they hoped others would agree, had providentially saved India.[15] As Gyan Pandy argues, "By the end of the nineteenth century, the dominant strand in colonialist historiography was representing religious bigotry and conflict between people of different religious persuasions as one of the more distinctive features of Indian society, past and present." Vernacular novels in Bengali and Marathi, too, as well as British writing, imagined a past of heroic Hindu peoples defying Muslim tyrants.

Professional historians have questioned the meaning of "foreign" in a period before the idealized homogeneity of the modern nation-state. They have pointed to the basic difference of premodern polities based on dynastic loyalty in which the religious and cultural lives of subjects was fundamentally irrelevant. They have demonstrated that no Muslim monarch in the Indian subcontinent ever had a program of conversion. They have shown that temples and other sites of worship were not destroyed randomly but only when they were perceived as symbols of treason or conquest. Thus, Aurangzeb, most vilified of the Mughals, in fact patronized some Hindu temples while destroying those associated with rebels. Shaivite rulers historically acted no differently toward Vaishnava opponents.[16] Historians have documented, further, the fact that alliances and loyalties were not defined by religious ties, so that this same Aurangzeb, for example, depended on Hindu generals, and his defiant son turned to Hindu Maratha allies.

A corollary view in the nationalist imagination is that the presence of Muslims, and secondarily, Christians, is the product of violent coercion, whether physical or economic. In this view, "being a Hindu" is taken as the natural identity. In fact, a historian could argue, the presence of today's Hindu population is as much linked to the activities of saints, traders, and soldiers among nomads and tribals (who were not "Hindu" to begin with) as is the presence of Islam.[17] Despite the existence of a constitutional right to proselytize and convert, in 2002 the government of Tamil Nadu introduced a law banning "forced" conversion, and in 2003 the government of Gujarat announced the same intention. Van der Veer argues that the issue of conversion is "the most contentious issue in India today." Some have seen an analogy to anxieties over conversion in the fear of communism in America after World War II.

Hindu nationalists in the colonial period identified "recovery" of an "authentic" pre-Muslim past as a solution to current problems. This mentality has continued. The project that won mass support for the BJP and its allies in the late 1980s was the campaign to destroy a sixteenth-century mosque allegedly built on the precise spot of a Ram temple that had been destroyed so that the mosque could be built. The destruction of the temple, on December 6, 1992, was taken as a triumph of Hindu "pride." The subsequent violence against Muslims was carried out with the slogan that Muslims belonged properly in either "Pakistan" or "*qabaristan*" (the graveyard). Physical violence has been coupled with attempts to erase the historical past, whether through ongoing attempts to take over other religious sites; assaults on textbooks, called by opponents the "saffronization" of history; or the erasure of names, so that Ahmadabad, for example, no longer reflects the name of its fifteenth-century dynastic founder (the Muslim name, Ahmad) but simply appears on road signs and elsewhere as "Amdavad."

An emblematic event stands out from the early years of independence as an indication of the power of the dominant historical narrative and the extent to which Indian identity was conflated with a modern Hindu nationalist identity. This was the presence of Rajendra Prasad, the president of India, at the dedication of the rebuilt temple of Somnath (raided by Ghaznavi in the early eleventh century) in Gujarat in 1951. Prime Minister Nehru and other dignitaries worried that this event would contradict India's stated vision of being a modern secular nation-state. K. M. Munshi, the leading figure in the rebuilding, who argued that he spoke for the "collective subconscious" of India, prevailed. In a path-breaking study, Richard Davis has shown the shifting and contested meaning of this site over history, a far different story from the simplistic modern one that posits "a schematized, Manichean historical vision of ancient harmony, foreign invasion and disruptions, and brave indigenous resistance eventually overcoming the invaders to restore order."[18]

A final, and challenging, legacy of the colonial period is personal law. The most significant issue in the 1950 Constitution of newly independent India that impacted the future of its Muslim citizens was the protection afforded the separate personal law for Muslims dealing with such matters as marriage, divorce, maintenance, adoption, and some aspects of inheritance.[19] The colonial administration had fostered some degree of homogeneity and a high degree of rigidity that made "Muslim" law, like "Hindu" law, a product of colonial modernity and not, as it was typically understood, the preservation of some pristine "tradition." To be sure, among the "Directive Principles" of the Constitution, intended not as law but as goals, was that of establishing a Uniform Civil Code for all Indians (Article 44).

Muslim Indian leadership, however, made the preservation of a separate law a symbol of their cultural and political status, successfully excluding reform of Muslim personal law from the purview of Parliament and forestalling implementation of the directive principle of the common civil code. This meant that while Muslim states like Pakistan and Tunisia successfully legislated reforms of family law in the 1960s, Muslim personal law in India went unchanged.

The continuation of Muslim personal law became a particular grievance for the Hindu Right, which deplored this provision as a "privilege" indicative of the "appeasement" of a "pampered" minority. In contrast, Hindu law was subjected to parliamentary reform. The irony of this argument could not be greater. Why, one might ask, is there any advantage in preserving codes that were arguably both contrary to the spirit of contextually based Islamic legal tradition as well as detrimental to the real interests of Muslim women and men? Indeed, for liberals, a great tension in relation to legal reform in India, at no point more evident than in what became the sensational debate over the Shah Bano case in 1986, was that between sympathy for what many Muslims saw as their cultural rights, on the one hand, and the conviction that Muslims and all Indians would be better served by a common civil code, on the other. In this case, in which an elderly divorcée sued for maintenance, a Hindu judge used the occasion to denounce Muslim personal law. The Congress Prime Minister, in what was seen as a crass bid for Muslim votes ("appeasement"), sponsored a parliamentary law preventing Muslim women, unlike any other Indian women, from having maintenance adjudicated (as it had been, in this case) under the article of the common criminal code intended to prevent destitution and vagrancy.[20] Liberal Muslims, among others, deplored this legislation.

Conflicts between what are seen as "cultural rights" and what some see as "human rights" have been apparent elsewhere, for example, on such matters as the right of Muslim French schoolgirls to wear foulards. In the case of India, however, to intervene on the side of opposition to Muslim law in favor of a common code was particularly fraught because it was identified with the position of the Hindu Right, who were not seen as fundamentally committed to Muslim interests or well-being. To criticize the substance of Muslim law, in particular in relation to the treatment of Muslim women, appeared, moreover, to risk repeating the colonial denunciations of the treatment of Indian women, generally, which had served simultaneously to deflect attention from Britain's own "woman question" and justify a colonialism, as Gayatri Spivak famously wrote, that imagined white men saving brown women from brown men.[21]

The irony of seeing Muslim personal law as "appeasement" has, however, a further dimension. The decision to amend Hindu law in the Hindu Marriage Act and other parliamentary actions beginning in the 1950s enshrined Hindu law as *the* Indian code. Far from harmful to Hindus, one might argue, this very process generated a key component of creating "Hindu" as the default, unmarked identity that in fact broadly defined the Indian citizen. Thus, Muslims and Christians seemed faced with a choice that either branded them as outside the mainstream of national culture, on the one hand, if they held on to separate legal codes, or absorbed them into Hindu cultural forms, on the other, if they gave them up.

Whatever the reasons that certain colonial constructions on offer were internalized and reshaped, whatever the reasons that from this cultural repertoire extreme Hindu nationalism became newly salient at the end of the twentieth century, the fact remains that in India today, the "common sense" is widespread that Muslims violated India in the past; are less than fully Indian today; and that their presence is a problem to be solved. From this unsupported foundation there is what should be seen as an extraordinary leap to imposition of collective and historical Muslim "guilt," so that Hindus have the right to extract recompense for the past as well as revenge for any offense presumed to have been committed by any Muslim today from any other Muslim, be they man, woman, or child. At the time of the killing of some two thousand Muslims in Gujarat in 2002, Chief Minister Narendra Modi spoke of the violence (which followed the fatal attack on a train at Godhra, allegedly by Muslims being harassed by VHP activists) as a "natural reaction."[22] In India, as in other contexts of ethnonationalism, chilling phrases like "We need to teach 'them' a lesson" reverberate.

Muslim Indians as a "Minority" since 1947

It is important not to take notions of "Muslim community" and "minority" as natural and uncontested. The word "minority" in independent India invariably means a religious minority and implies that presumed religious identity trumps all else. The ideal of liberal democracy recognizes only individual citizens in relation to the state, citizens who may combine and re-combine to press varied interests—regional, class, cultural, and so forth. Instead, in this case, religious community is imagined, with the legal under-pinning of a separate personal law, as a permanent corporate body, and it becomes the category through which individual citizens are perceived. The label is one that may have little meaning for any given Muslim who, no matter how observant, may not wish to make religious commonality his or her total identity. There are some who explicitly resist the attempt, whether by Muslims or Hindus, who, like the British before them, claim to speak for or of monolithic "communities."

Partition was devastating for Muslims in India, both in real terms and in saddling them with suspicion. The percentage of the Muslim population in the total population was more than halved, from 25 percent to about 10 percent. The two Muslim majority areas in West Punjab and East Bengal were gone. In India's 356 districts there were only two, one in Kerala and one in West Bengal, left with majority Muslim populations, and only 30 with more than 30 percent Muslim population.[23] Many of those who left represented the more well-to-do business, professional, and service classes, thus decimating the number of Muslims represented in government service and other leadership positions. Not all who left did so by choice. Some Muslims simply found themselves in Pakistan. Yet others were wholly unswayed by ideology but were virtually driven out of their homes by RSS and other anti-Muslim forces.

It was partly the occasion of the fiftieth anniversary of the state that occasioned substantial scholarship on 1947, much of which yielded sobering accounts of the costs of that horrific event. In relation to Muslims, Mushirul Hasan traced many examples of discrimination and, in many cases, forced expulsion recorded in British and other memoirs, in the correspondence of government officials, including Nehru, and in reports in the Indian press.[24] The current dispute over illegal Bangladeshi infiltrators, who are distinguished only with difficulty from other East Bengali Muslims, makes clear that Partition should not be seen as an event that ended in 1947.[25] Despite the intervention of Gandhi and others on behalf of Muslims, for example in the case of the Meo population (southwest of Delhi) documented by Shail Mayaram, the scars of Partition were deep.

The Meo case, in the two princely states of Bharatpur and Alwar, bears scrutiny. The Muslim population of this area appears not to have identified with a larger Muslim population in India but imagined themselves as culturally integrated with a range of local practices (including the Krishna cult). Both states were modernizing in the decades before Partition, in terms of the level of control they sought to exercise, and both used cultural forms to bolster their authority, including, in both cases, ties to Hindu nationalist organizations. Meo peasant activism had been strong in the area and continued to seek cross-communal participation in support of Congress. In fact, what is particularly poignant in this case is the history of class-based organizing, reflecting "a vision of intercommunal solidarity and a decentering of power," strongly resisted by both the colonial and the princely states. But by the time of Partition, the rest of the community apparently saw Meos only in their identity as "Muslim." Muslim League activism in the area contributed to this, but the Hindu communalist organizations, including the Mahasabha, the Sanatan Dharma Sabha, and the RSS, in the interwar period, had also undertaken substantial military and political organization. Bharatpur, moreover, increasingly imagined itself as a Jat state, in which an agricultural caste stigmatized as low caste by the Rajputs (with their military and ruling ideals) would dominate. Despite earlier class-based solidarities, anti-Muslim violence increasingly held out the promise to groups like the Jats of control, self-esteem—and access to land. What happened instead, in part owing to press misrepresentation of Muslim aggression, was a campaign of mass extermination with state complicity. Three themes in this tragedy would periodically reappear in the decades to come: the misrepresentation of Muslim actions by the press, the failure of the state to maintain a disinterested role in preventing violence, and the displacement of issues of socioeconomic status and interests on to religious rivalry. Being anti-Muslim could enhance social standing. As for the Meos, after 1947 enhanced numbers participated in the quietist, inward-looking, Islamic pietistic movement, Tablighi Jamaat, discussed below.

Muslims in India run the gamut of mother tongue, socioeconomic status, and form of religiosity true of other Indians, with most of them, like most Indians, dependent on agriculture.[26] Muslims across the country are poor, "just slightly better off than the Scheduled Castes."[27] Poverty explains far more than "religion" about the lives of most Muslims, including Muslim women, who are popularly assumed to be particularly disadvantaged by religion. An important India-wide survey of Muslim women reported in 2002, however, linked poverty and discrimination, not Islam or, specifically, Muslim personal law, to the lack of education and very low levels of employment of Muslim women. It also challenged stereotypes about divorce and polygamy among Muslims, showing rates to be the same across religious groups.[28]

In 1996 a journalist writing in the *Times of India* suggested content for a speech that should be given by the BJP leader, Atal Bihari Vajpayee, who had commented that "Hindus were a majority with a minority complex," that is, that they were fearful of Muslims and even Christians. The journalist's dream speech would have had Vajpayee acknowledge the weakness of Muslims, their political marginalization as indicated by their numbers in Parliament, which are minute, and their overall insignificance in the "nation's life, economic, social [and] administrative."[29] In short, to think that the Muslims of India are a threat is illusory. Nonetheless, the theme of Muslims as menace continues unabated, for example, in the anxiety over conversion.

Underlying this anxiety is the presumed link of Muslim Indians to Pakistan. Laiq, in the "letter" cited above, aptly described Pakistan as "a petty, moth-eaten state."[30] Indeed, Pakistan continues to be rent by provincial antagonisms, sectarian violence, weak governance, a military culture that undermines both democracy and social development, and a population that is a small fraction of India's. But since that "letter" there have been two key changes that have escalated anxiety about Pakistan. First is the fact that Pakistan reacted in kind to India's testing of nuclear weapons in 1998. Second, after the U.S. declared a global "war on terrorism" in 2001, Indians now label what is happening in Kashmir as "international terrorism." In fact, it is, much as it had been throughout the 1990s, a small number of Pakistan-based militants crossing into Indian Kashmir. Pakistanis, moreover, are blamed for two serious attacks within India: the attack on the Indian Parliament on December 13, 2001, and the shooting at the Akshardham Temple in Gujarat in 2002. On both occasions the perpetrators were shot dead, thus preventing a formal inquiry. Although the official position is that foreigners, not Muslim Indians, are responsible for such events, in fact, in many contexts, Muslims are viewed as natural Pakistanis. The rhetoric of the post-pogrom elections in Gujarat in 2002, as many commentators pointed out, was waged by the BJP not against the Congress but against "Mulla Musharraf," the prime minister of Pakistan, implying that Congress was a party "soft" on Muslims—and Muslims were proxy Pakistanis. The election in December 2002 gave the BJP a landslide victory, yielding two-thirds of the provincial seats.

Muslim Political Participation

What, given this level of economic disadvantage and political marginality, should Muslims do, in terms of political participation? First off, and in contrast to virtually every other Muslim population in the world, there are, to underline the point made above, no extremist Islamic parties in India. In the words of an Indian English-language journal in early 2003:

The Vishwa Hindu Parishad (VHP) and the rest of its parivar ["the family" of Hindu nationalist organizations] may still be on a relentless hate campaign against the "minorities," but . . . at the end of a year when US investigators and their allies have left no stone unturned in their hunt for Al Qaeda terrorists, experts have reached an interesting conclusion: while the Islamic terror network has been found to exist in Africa, Europe and Asia, Indian Muslims have not been attracted by the jihad ideology. This, despite the country having the world's second largest Muslim population (140–50 million).[31]

Various other nationalities involved with Jehadi International have been identified, but Indians don't figure on the list. In the words of Ajai Sahni of the New Delhi-based Institute of Conflict Management: "The (absence of) jehadi culture here is best illustrated vis-à-vis Kashmir. In the over 10 years of terrorism in the state, there hasn't been a single non-Kashmiri (Muslim) from any other part of India involved in the so-called jehad or militance." The explanation for the absence of Islamic militancy, for Ranjit Bhushan (as for Friedman, quoted above), is democracy.

Contrary to abstract reasoning along the lines "Islam and democracy are incompatible," the vast number of the Muslims of India have actively participated in democratic life for over half a century. They have made use of three available strategies: a minor stream of separate Muslim parties; support of other parties; and involvement in public life through participation in debates, community, and educational service.

With the abolition of separate electorates and reserved seats defined by religion in the independent state, there were only a few localities in which Muslim parties were likely to be effective. The remnant All India Muslim League, tarred in India with leadership of the Pakistan movement, disbanded, although some members reorganized as the Indian Union Muslim League, with strength in Kerala, where Muslims constitute 20 percent of the population; the party also has had some success in scattered pockets elsewhere. In addition to the IUML, there have also been Muslim parties in other southern states, notably in the Hyderabad area of Andhra Pradesh, where the pre-independence Majlis Ittihad-ul-Muslimin (the Assembly of the Union of Muslims), which had opposed integration of the princely state of Hyderabad into independent India, was revived in 1957. In this last case, the party has clearly "filled up the space (vacuum) created by the perceived withdrawal of the state as the protective, benevolent institution." In this sense, its platform, in contrast to its earlier incarnation, became one of secular gains in modern life.[32] All these parties operate in coalition, they espouse the fundamental give and take of moderation, and they should be seen as Muslim parties in the sense of parties committed to the interests of Muslims, not to the "Islamist" restructuring of society. They are, broadly speaking, comparable to caste and other ethnically defined parties.

Most Muslims, however, voted for parties, not limited to Muslims, that they found sympathetic. Muslims after independence, like most other Indians, long voted primarily for the Congress Party. A key moment of alienation came under the prime ministership of Indira Gandhi, with her campaigns for slum clearance and sterilization and abrogation of human rights during the "Emergency" (1975–76), which seem to have been carried out with particular harshness toward Muslims. The election of 1977 marked a watershed in terms of Congress loyalty for many Muslims, and Indians in general.[33] For the last several decades, Muslims have voted for those they regarded most likely to provide security, education, and economic opportunities in particular local contexts.

What would seem one of the most promising trends among Muslims has been an alliance with disadvantaged non-Muslim groups on a shared socioeconomic agenda. There have, in fact, been efforts to secure recognition of some groups of Muslims as Dalit, with the benefits that come to those formerly known as "untouchables." An organization formed in Patna in 1994, for example, the All-India Backward Muslim Morcha (AIBMM), which argues that 90 percent of Bihar's Muslims are "backward," has attempted to forge links to similar disadvantaged populations.[34] The trajectory half a century ago in Mewat, described above, however, has echoed tragically in places like Gujarat, where cries of Hindu solidarity and pride have brought tribals and Dalits into murderous alliances with the upper castes and have seemingly severed the potential for class-based collaboration that there, too, had seemed incipient as recently as the 1980s.[35]

In addition to the political parties, there have also been several organizations that speak for Muslim interests publicly while not themselves contesting elections. The most enduring institution to speak for Muslims in public life in India is the Jamiat Ulama-i-Hind, an organization that emerged in the course of the Khilafat movement (a short-lived movement to protest the treatment of the Ottomans after World War I, and specifically the abolition of the caliphate). This movement marked the entry of the traditionally educated Islamic leadership into national political life and the beginnings of mass politics generally. Jamiat leaders, like Husain Ahmad Madani, quoted above, worked closely with Congress in the independence movement, priding themselves in their stories of the opposition to British exploitation on the part of Islamic leaders from the earliest days of colonialism. They never imagined themselves as a separate political party, a decision that was confirmed after independence. The organization strongly opposed Partition (as well as the minor stream of "Islamist" ideology, discussed below), articulating instead a vision of "composite nationalism" and loyalty to a territorially defined secular nationalism.

Maulana Madani served as president of the organization from 1940 to 1957 (a role his son has played from 1973 to the present). His comments above, emphasizing the responsibilities of Muslims to their new nation, the need for Muslims to bear suffering with forbearance, and the priority to be given to "the greater jihad" continue central to the organization. This jihad entails commitment to bolstering, through meetings and publications, individual adherence to Islamic teachings. Although nowhere explicit in their statements, the organization's leadership has been inclusive of Sunnis only and closely associated, in particular, with the "reformist" scholars of Deoband who abjure what are seen as deviant customary practices.[36]

The Jamiat undertakes a range of community service, relief work, and educational programs.[37] The organization speaks out actively to defend Muslim safety and interests in relation to violence, places of worship, and the defense of Muslim personal law. Although the organization as such does not ally with any political parties, individual members participate in political life actively and support different parties. The current president has been elected to the upper house of Parliament several times. The Jamiat leaders imagined that they would speak for the entire Muslim population after independence, but neither they, nor any other group, have played that role.

Two organizations in particular subsequently sought the mantle of leadership. In 1964, a group in Lucknow formed the All India Muslim Majlis-e-Mushawarat (the Muslim Consultative Assembly), distinguished by being led by secularly educated professionals but intended to coordinate a range of existing organizations, including the Jamiat-ul-Ulama, the Jamaat-i-Islami (discussed below), and the Muslim League of South India, as well as include individuals in Congress and other parties. The Majlis was formed in part to respond to communal riots that began more than a decade after independence. The organization, however, made issues of the general welfare of Indian society part of its program. It also focused on the preservation of a separate civil law as the platform on which to unite its varied participants. It was to be a nonpartisan pressure group supporting individual candidates.[38] The current head, Syed Shahabuddin, a former member of the Indian Foreign Service, issues articulate and persuasive statements on matters of concern to Muslims, but the organization as such has not had significant influence.[39]

The second organization, the All India Muslim Personal Law Board, was formed in 1972, precisely, as its name makes clear, to defend the one issue on which apparently all Muslim Indian organizations agree. The first head was the revered rector of the important Deoband seminary, Qari Muhammad Tayyab Qasimi, followed by Maulana Abul Hasan Ali Nadwi, rector of a second distinguished seminary, the Nadwat ul Ulama, in Lucknow. Maulana Nadwi was a prolific scholar, widely known in the Middle East and elsewhere, and highly respected within India. The Board now addresses other serious issues that impact Muslims, like the Babri Masjid demolition and the Gujarat carnage. It has interacted with Indian heads of state and is regarded by many as the most effective voice for Muslims, in part because of the popular conception that only religious leaders spoke for Muslims.[40]

India in the years before Partition gave birth to one of the world's leading ideologists of "Islamist" politics, Abul'l-A'la Maududi (1903–79). Maududi held out the theory that the goal of political action should be to establish governance shaped by Islamic doctrine in all aspects of corporate life, an Islamic "system" characterized by systems of Islamic economics, Islamic justice, Islamic political organization, and so forth. His works have been widely translated and are known to Muslims throughout the world. In principle, the party was opposed to the whole concept of nationalism in favor of a utopian polity founded on the transnational morality of Islam. Maududi founded an organization, the Jamaat-e-Islami (Islamic Party) in 1941, intended as a party of elite fully committed to a specific ideology of creating an Islamic "system," or "*nizam.*" Its totalizing system and its cadre-based vision of the influence of a small elite resonated with the contemporaneous twentieth-century movements of Fascism and Communism.[41]

Maududi opposed both the independence movement of the Indian National Congress, on the grounds that Hindus were in control, and the movement of the Muslim League, on the grounds that its leadership, while concerned with Muslim security and interests, had no commitment to the creation of an Islamic polity. After Partition, the party split into separate nationalist organizations (including an organization in Kashmir separate from the Indian, Pakistani, and, subsequently, Bangladeshi Jamaats). The separate movements pragmatically took on the style of the political culture in each setting, with the Pakistani Jamaat acting as a political party and the Indian Jamaat engaged in Islamic education, community service (with its relief work not limited to Muslims), and pressure to protect Muslim lives and interests. Until 1985, its members were encouraged to withdraw from political life in order "to remove the extraordinary [post-1947] prejudice the non-Muslim majority has against Islam," although that position was marked with ambiguity, given the participation, noted above, in the Majlis.[42] Members now may vote, but the Jamaat does not participate in elections itself.

To discuss this movement at some length may give the misleading impression that it has been influential in India. It in fact has been a very minor element among Muslim organizations, but it is imagined to be central. Discussion of the organization often serves to illustrate a theoretical spectrum of possible political positions held by Muslims, with this party positioned at the Right, or "fundamentalist," extreme. When the RSS has periodically been banned in India, for example, during the Emergency and the Bombay riots of 1992–93, the Jamaat has been banned as an equivalent. The comparison is misleading for several reasons. Jamaat ideology is not predicated on the kind of "psycho-drama" in which Hindus, in this case, would be posited as an "Other" to Muslim individual and community identity, nor does it provide a distinctive nationalist ideology. The Jamaat is not part of a larger "family" that includes a political wing. It has no paramilitary tradition. And its numbers are dramatically fewer.[43] Its resolutions at a recent annual meeting vowed to work toward "building a society where human rights are secured, life and property of all are protected, men not exploited by other men and where people are not discriminated against on the basis of their creed, region or language." Only vegetarian food was served as a courtesy to the estimated 5,000 non-Muslims attending.[44]

There is no question but that the Jamaat favors the spread of Islam and the renewal of Islamic faith among nominal Muslims. In the words of a spokesman, "We are thoroughly convinced that the solution to all human problems lies in reverting towards Allah. It is only when man forgets God, he plunges into problems, with morality being the most affected aspect."[45] While the Jamaat is typically discussed in relation to politics in India, as noted above, its place is more properly understood in the context of its sectarian orientation rather than as a political party.[46]

Far more significant in terms of numbers are a range of politically quietist movements focused on the jihad of the regeneration of the moral and spiritual life of Muslims. These groups are explicitly apolitical, in the sense that they do not enter into electoral or other public arenas. Of them, the largest in terms of numbers is Tablighi Jamaat, which hopes to turn each Muslim into a preacher and teacher of other Muslims, exhorting others (and thus teaching him or herself) to faithful Islamic practice on such matters as worship, dress, and everyday behavior. The Tabligh movement grew out of the same group of reformist 'ulama, the Deobandis, represented by Maulana Husain Ahmad Madani, discussed above.

A grassroots movement with no public face at all, male Tablighi participants in small groups fan out in their localities, throughout India, and, when they are able, throughout the world, to meet fellow participants and attract nominal Muslims to what is now a transnational movement.[47] All participants are volunteers, and there is no salaried staff. There is a pyramidal organization, with leaders chosen through consultation. Periodic annual meetings are held. In Bangladesh and Pakistan a single annual meeting draws in the range of two million participants. In India, in part seeking less visibility, there have been smaller regional meetings. Nonetheless, the meeting in Bhopal in December 2002 drew an estimated one million participants. The large numbers may have been encouraged in part by the sobering landslide election of the BJP in Gujarat, which seemed to reward anti-Muslim violence.

A second proselytizing movement represents the other major trend within modern South Asian Sunni Islam, focused on the teaching of Maulana Ahmad Riza Khan Barelvi (d. 1921) and popularly known after him as the Barelvi movement. The Dawat-e-Islami similarly seeks to disseminate correct teachings. Its focus on devotionalism makes the anniversary of the death of Ahmad Riza a major event, but the movement also holds annual meetings. In contrast with the Tabligh movement, which insists on face-to-face contacts, it enthusiastically embraces the Internet, not just for information and audio broadcasts, but for interactive answers to questions, dispensing of amulets, offers of greeting cards, and even granting of discipleship. In an often-noted, uncanny coincidence, its founder shares the name, Muhammad Ilyas, of the Tabligh founder.[48]

Movements like these provide clear sociality and psychological satisfactions to their participants. The movements also appear to receive benign support in terms of permits, facilities for annual meetings, and so forth from official agencies. They increase isolation from political activities, and they reinforce inward-looking cultural isolation. It is also true, of course, that Hindu cultural movements similarly enhance intensified cultural distinctiveness.

The Roots of Hindu Rage

In writing about Muslims today, Bernard Lewis, in a widely quoted phrase, has focused on "the roots of Muslim rage," directed as he sees it against "the West."[49] Judging from the violence that has been visited on Muslims in parts of India in recent years, and the emotion that has been focused on destruction of Muslim mosques, it would not seem misplaced to speak of a "Hindu rage" for some segments of the population, in this case, directed against Muslims. As I have argued, it is clear that competition between religious "communities" has a historical genealogy rooted in the colonial period, but why religion emerged as a crucial fault line at the end of the twentieth century remains to be explained. At least two kinds of arguments have been forcibly made for this development.

One argument, as befits the word "rage," is primarily psychological. In this regard, the work of Paola Bacchetta, an anthropologist who has studied both men's and women's organization within the Hindu "family," is particularly important. In her work, these movements represent a quest for self-esteem, which was damaged in the colonial period and in the harsh realities of socioeconomic life generally. To put her argument schematically, the gendered dimensions of constructing a Muslim "Other" are clearly central in

Sangh ideology, with Muslim men represented as virile rapists, raping the nation and the nation's emblematic "woman." Mosques in particular become the mark of Muslim penetration and national violation. Muslim women, in contrast to Muslim men, at best are available for protection and conversion. It is in confronting Muslims that Hindu men can potentially assert or recover their virility and masculinity, and, at the same time, that both women and men can make claims on social status, new skills, pride in service to the nation, and meaningful social solidarities.[50] No sociological or historical disquisition on the actual "facts" about Muslims could challenge such intimate constructs that become part of individual identity and social belonging.

The question still remains, despite the power of these arguments, of why emotions about Muslims so rose to the fore in the 1980s. Clearly, one critical dimension of this change has been the impact of the liberalized open economy and capitalist, market-oriented policies, coupled with a move away from state-controlled development, that began in the 1980s and accelerated in the 1990s. This unleashed all kinds of socioeconomic dislocations. The gap between rich and poor increased. The fact that some Muslims profited from employment in the Gulf and elsewhere, particularly in the 1980s, identified them as unfairly privileged and made them an easy target. In Gujarat in the 1990s economic change meant widescale closure of mills and factories and competition among those at the bottom of society, now left unemployed. It also impacted small-scale entrepreneurs and traders. Violence has given some businessmen, including bootleggers and other illegal operators in Gujarat, an opportunity to wipe out competitors. Others have found violence an opportunity to get rid of unwanted tenants at a time of rising property values.[51]

At the same time, Indian democracy has brought new political power to lower castes and classes, whose parties have made noticeable strides, for example, in such states as Uttar Pradesh and Bihar. That potential class-based strife has been displaced onto a religious faultline seems incontrovertible. The contemporary "tradition" of anti-Muslim violence that has emerged in Gujarat was initiated by violence occasioned by plans to enhance the number of places "reserved" for lower-caste employment and education in Gujarat in 1985; this violence soon was transformed into anti-Muslim violence.[52] Similarly, the national focus on destroying the Ayodhya mosque followed immediately on protests against the central government plan to en-

act the Mandal Commission recommendations for increased job reservations at the federal level for lower-castes. The protests that followed in the
summer of 1990 closed down entire cities and included self-immolation on
the part of higher-caste protesters. This was followed in October of 1990 by
the great *rath yatra*, the brilliantly organized nationwide procession that
ratcheted up the determination of the Hindu Right to tear down the Babur
mosque and build a temple in its place, an issue that continues to stir popular agitation.

It is this context of socioeconomic change that makes well-meaning films,
whether a Bollywood blockbuster like *Bombay* (1996) or a film like Aparna
Sen's *Mr. and Mrs. Iyer* (2002) so poignant. To be sure, romantic encounters
across religious boundaries, like the one in the latter film between a Tamil
Brahmin woman and a Muslim Bengali man on a bus, can forge warm personal relationships, but the larger structural context of conflict remains.
That conflict is rooted in social and economic rivalries and aspirations. But
it is fueled by a nationalism that, as the passionate concern with conversion
makes clear, equates Hindu and nationalist.

Muslim Indians, in Vali Nasr's memorable phrase, are unique for not having bitten "the apple of Islamic militancy."[53] For all the canards that Muslim
Indians cheer on the Pakistani cricket team, they in fact for the most part
have evinced little interest, let alone irredentism, in relation to India's neighbor.[54] But as simple a usage as "Indian Muslim" rather than the less common
"Muslim Indian," implying the priority of religious affiliation, denies Muslims the relation to the nation assumed for others.[55]

Final Thoughts on Secularism and Jihad

Secularism in the Indian context prohibits discrimination on grounds of religion (Article 15 of the Indian Constitution); it guarantees equality of opportunity in public employment irrespective of religious identity (Article
16); and it guarantees freedom of religion (Articles 25–30), including "freedom of conscience and free profession, practice and propagation of religion"
(Article 25). One way for a state to be secular is, in Thomas Jefferson's frequently quoted words, by "building a wall of separation between church and
State."[56] In India, in contrast, instead of such disengagement there has been
secularism in a different sense, namely, in principle, equal respect for all but

not necessarily "a wall." Thus, the state regulates and restricts a range of economic and political activities that may be associated with religious practices. For example, official agencies, both federal and state, manage religious properties and provide financial and logistical support to large *melas*, meetings, pilgrimage facilities, and so forth.[57] Given that degree of involvement, not surprisingly the state itself has been a central player, for example, in sponsorship and adjudication of contested sites.

Arguably, that role, as it did in colonial days, offers those who wish it an arena that allows for religious disputes and offers official sanction for those who win. For example, the placing of an idol at the Babri Mosque in 1949 violated an archaeological site and, since it was not treated as a criminal act, gave an edge to demands of those who wanted to build a temple and did not meet official resistance.[58] A new dispute in Karnataka (over the Baba Budhan Dada Hayat Qalandar Dargah) risks, in the words of Yoginder Sikand, being "a second Ayodhya." In December 2002, extremist Bajrang Dal activists defied the court rulings on legitimate practices at the shrine and introduced Hindutva symbols and Hindu objects without any action from police or the local administration, who claimed that they were helpless in the face of threats of violence. Such acquiescence on the part of officials, acts of "commission and omission," as Sikand puts it, points to what would seem inevitable ambiguity on the part of a state that is both secular and interventionist.[59] Interventionist secularism makes the need for vigilance in relation to equity and criminal acts particularly acute.

Just as puzzling as is this interventionist style to those accustomed to a principle of state disengagement in religious matters is the insistence by Muslim spokesmen that secularism requires the protection of a separate Muslim personal law. The biggest mobilization of Muslims since independence came over the Shah Bano crisis in 1986–87—though it is worth noting that this coincided with the escalation of anti-Muslim violence in Gujarat. As violence against Muslims has increased, Muslims seem to have grown ever more defensive. Liberal Muslims have had little success in challenging what seems an unquestioned acceptance of religious leaders—who, in some cases, seem to have more journalistic exposure than any genuine support— as spokesmen for Muslims.[60] This, in turn, feeds the stereotypes and discrimination, which, in circular fashion, reinforce Muslim defensiveness. The defense of personal law and moral jihad are not necessarily the same, but together they enhance an inward-looking stance and would not seem sufficient to serve Muslims well. Nor would apathy. In the words of the journalist B. G. Verghese, "Muslim Indians must not shrink back into the ghetto or opt out after Gujarat."[61]

Fears for life and livelihood, and, in some areas, increased residential ghettoization, encourage thoughts of a separate Muslim party, but to date those have had little influence.[62] Other voices, as noted above, have yet to gain as much attention but question the authority of religious leaders like Madani or the oft-quoted Imam of Delhi's Jami' Majid to speak for all Muslims. They insist that the interests of Muslims would be far better served by class-based alliances that, far from national, would deliberately address regional interests. Given the regional nature of much of Indian political life, this would seem to be a strong position to push.[63]

The narrative of Muslim politics in pre-Partition India is often told as one of lost opportunities, with Muslims, particularly peasants, initially finding common cause across religious lines only to be forced into religious alliances almost beyond their control.[64] To this end, the attempts in recent years to build links with other economically disadvantaged Indians would seem particularly important, the more so at a time like 2004 when India's economic growth overall is so promising and some, at least, are conscious of the millions left behind. It is the trio of education, jobs, and security that most Muslims, like most Indians, want. For example, when the Chief Minister of Uttar Pradesh, representing a party ostensibly based on the interests of the dispossessed,[65] recently announced that Friday afternoons would be a holiday for schools and intermediate colleges, presumably to show his secularism as against the Hindu nationalism of the BJP, Muslim leaders were not impressed. When contacted, Muslim Personal Law Board member Kamal Farooqi said: "This posturing isn't going to help us. . . . We need more schools, not an order that will be used by communal forces to attack us." To which Syed Shahabbuddin, a former diplomat and Member of Parliament, added "Nobody asked for it. You can always offer *namaz* during lunch break."[66]

Until the larger society in India undertakes its own "jihad" against anti-Muslim prejudice and the conditions that underlie it—fulfilling the promises of constitutional entitlements to all that majoritarian sentiment otherwise threatens—the moral jihad of the minority and the secularism of the entire polity will continue in uneasy tension.[67] An important dimension of that anti-Muslim prejudice is the pernicious rhetoric implying that Muslims are a fifth column of "proxy Pakistanis" within the body politic. Muslim politicians have, throughout India's history, often to observers' surprise, never linked their interests to Pakistan nor attempted to intervene in issues of India–Pakistan relations. It is not clear, however, whether objective changes in India's relations with Pakistan, like the dramatic thaw evident since early 2004, can impact majoritarian attitudes toward Muslims, but moments of crisis surely make them worse. Given the power of the "Bollywood" cinema culture in India, the disappointing audiences in early 2004 for *LoC Kargil,* a film that had been expected to capitalize on India's success against Pakistan's crossing of the Kashmir Line of Control in 1999, would seem an encouraging sign for popular acceptance of improved relations.[68]

Finally, the situation in India should have implications for U.S. foreign policy. The United States responded to the attack by al-Qaeda on September 11, 2001, by declaring a global "war on terrorism" that would focus, above all, as it happened, on extremist Muslims. A case can be made, however, for including some branches of the Hindu nationalist "family" of organizations (Sangh Parivar), led by the Vishnu Hindu Parishad (VHP, the World Hindu Congress), as "terrorist," in that they have targeted innocent civilians for their violence. They have not only been associated with anti-Muslim violence but with anti-Christian violence in such places as Gujarat and Orissa as well. The Hindu organizations have not been seen as a threat, presumably because their activities have been internal to countries in South Asia. Quite apart from the inconsistency in American foreign policy that this stance suggests, however, in the words of journalist Husain Haqqani, it may be a "grave miscalculation" to suggest that Hindu extremism does not have international ramifications, not least because it stimulates recruitment for extremist Islamists, even if not, so far, in India, in places like Pakistan and, at least potentially, Bangladesh.[69] At the least, the United States should apply its concern with identifying people in the U.S. providing material aid to terrorist organizations to those who transmit money to the organizations central to the Gujarat outrages,[70] just as they have done in relation to those supporting militant Palestinians.[71] The United States has not brought pressure in defense of the human rights of Muslim Indians, either on humanitarian grounds or to defend an environment in which Muslims have participated in the democratic practices the U.S. claims to want to foster among Muslim populations. This is not only in conflict with its moral claims but profoundly shortsighted in achieving its own goals.

NINE

Jammu and Kashmir in the Indian Union: The Politics of Autonomy

Chandrashekhar Dasgupta

Jammu and Kashmir is one of the most culturally and linguistically diverse states in India. Six major languages are spoken on the Indian side of the Line of Control. On the Pakistani side, there are at least three major linguistic groups. Taking the state as a whole, the largest linguistic group—the Kashmiri—accounts for only 37 percent of the total population and is found almost exclusively on the Indian side of the Line of Control. The western sector of the Line of Control broadly follows a linguistic divide between the mainly Punjabi-speaking population of "Azad," or "Pakistan-occupied," Kashmir on one side and the Kashmiri, Dogri, and Hindi speakers on the Indian side. In the northern sector, Balti is the major language on both sides of the Line of Control in the Kargil area, and the Shina linguistic area spills over the line to include a small pocket on the Indian side. On the Pakistan side of the Line of Control the population consists almost entirely of Muslims. On the Indian side, Muslims constitute a majority in a mixed population, which also includes a substantial minority of Hindus, Sikhs, and Buddhists.[1]

The term "Kashmiri" is all too frequently used to refer to any subject of the state of Jammu and Kashmir, without appreciating the distinction between the Kashmiri-speaking people of the Valley and other ethnic groups in the state. In Britain, for instance, it is often assumed that the large community of immigrants from Mirpur—Punjabi-speakers with traditional ties to Pakistani Punjabis—share the interests and voice the sentiments of the Kashmiri-speaking community on the Indian side of the Line of Control. To avoid such confusion, we need to recall the cultural and linguistic diversity of the state and the existence within its boundaries of multiple ethnic identities.

An analysis of the internal politics of the Indian side of the Line of Control in Jammu and Kashmir must take into account the aspirations of the different ethnic groups in the state. Bearing in mind that shared cultural identity can be used as a vehicle of political mobilization, we note that the 1981 census shows that of a total population of just under 6 million, Kashmiris account for a little over half (53.2 percent), Dogris for almost a quarter (24.3 percent), and Hindi (including Gujari-speakers) for another 16.92 percent. The Kashmiri speakers are concentrated mainly in the Kashmir Division and the Doda area of Jammu Division. Dogri, the major language of Jammu Division, accounts for a little over half of the population of that division and, as noted, just under a quarter of the total for the state. Ladakhi (also called Bodhi) is the principal language of sparsely inhabited Ladakh, though Balti-speakers constitute a majority in the Kargil area. Muslims constitute 95 percent of the population in Kashmir and a little under 30 percent in Jammu. Hindus account for 67 percent of the inhabitants in Jammu and 4 percent in Kashmir. In sparsely inhabited Ladakh, Buddhists constitute a majority.

Jammu and Kashmir has a special position in the Indian Union by virtue of the autonomy it enjoys under Article 370 of the Indian Constitution. In common with other states, the article gives Jammu and Kashmir a place in the Indian Union and reserves for the Union Parliament the right to legislate on matters corresponding to those covered by the terms of the state's accession to India (namely, foreign affairs, defense, and communications). However, Article 370 enables state authorities to determine the extent to which provisions of the Indian Constitution should apply to Jammu and Kashmir in other matters. Jammu and Kashmir is the only state to have its own constitution, and elections to the state legislature are held under the provisions of this constitution.

The autonomy provisions accommodated the sense of a Kashmiri identity, or Kashmiriyat, which was also a feature of the political mobilization of the Kashmir Valley under the leadership of Sheikh Abdullah since the 1930s. The actual extent of autonomy has fluctuated widely in different periods, with greater autonomy usually favored by Valley-based groups, while also being challenged, particularly by constituents outside the Valley, such as political parties in Jammu and Ladakh.

The political history of Jammu and Kashmir since 1947 is characterized by five periods: 1947–53—high autonomy; 1954–74—successively greater integration with the Indian Union; 1975–89—wider political participation based on a compromise formula on autonomy; 1990–96—disruption of civic society and electoral politics due to insurgency and cross-border terrorism, followed by a strengthened central government role; and 1996 to date—restoration of the political process through democratic elections. The elections of 2002, followed by the installation of a new government seeking to give a "healing touch," holds out promise of a new chapter based on a wider dialogue between the Center, the elected representatives of the people, and a number of insurgent groups.

1947–53: Maximum Autonomy

As in the case of the other princely states that joined the Indian Union, the letter of accession signed by the Maharaja of Jammu and Kashmir covered three subjects—defense, foreign affairs, and communications. The princes soon agreed to give up political authority on the understanding that they would retain their titles and receive fixed privy purses. Thus, the provisions of the Indian Constitution in their entirety applied to the whole country, with a partial exception in the case of Jammu and Kashmir, where identity based on language and culture was particularly strong. As noted earlier, this was the rationale of the temporary provisions incorporated in Article 370 of the Indian Constitution. In 1952, details of the state's special position were worked out in the Delhi agreement between Nehru and Sheikh Abdullah. This provided for the abolition of the hereditary monarchy; vesting of residuary powers in the state; continuation of certain special state rights concerning property ownership, employment, etc. for "state subjects" (vis-à-vis other citizens of India); a separate flag for the state (but with the national flag in a "supremely distinct place"); and, subject to certain limitations, the application to the state of the provisions of the Indian Constitution relating to fundamental rights, emergency powers, and jurisdiction of the Supreme Court.[2]

The National Conference government under Sheikh Abdullah subsequently carried out a peaceful political and economic revolution in the state. The Maharaja was divested of all powers and sent into virtual exile outside the state. Hereditary rule was abolished. Land ownership was limited to a ceiling of 22.75 acres. Surplus land was expropriated without compensation and redistributed to the tillers. The abolition of the feudal order and land reforms were carried out much more speedily in Jammu and Kashmir than in the rest of India. The Abdullah government was able to expropriate land without paying any compensation only because the state was exempted from application of the provisions of the Indian Constitution requiring compensation in such cases.

In inter-regional terms, these developments led to a dramatic shift of power from Jammu to Kashmir. Jammu was the seat of the Dogra monarchy and, before the reforms, Jammu-based landlords owned much of the cultivated land in the Kashmir Valley. Thus, while the reforms boosted Abdullah's popularity among the Kashmiris and also among the mass of the Jammu peasantry, they drew a strong reaction from the dispossessed Dogra landlords. The Dogra gentry, supported by the communalist Hindu RSS organization, launched a Jammu-based opposition party, the Praja Parishad, to campaign for full applicability of the Indian Constitution and full integration with the Indian Union. The Praja Parishad drew its main support from a narrow social base, but it was able to capitalize on the fact that Jammu had been denied due representation in the Abdullah cabinet, which comprised four ministers from Kashmir and only one from Jammu (vis-à-vis its population share of 45 percent). The reforms also drew protests from Ladakh, where land belonging to Buddhist monasteries was expropriated, depriving them of their means of support. The Ladakh Buddhist Association thus set its face against autonomy, calling for a closer relationship between Ladakh and the rest of India.

Despite his vast popularity, arising from his struggle against Dogra feudalism, and contrary to his democratic reputation, Abdullah had a markedly authoritarian streak. No believer in political pluralism, he maintained that the people of Kashmir wanted "one organization, one program, one voice."[3] In the elections to the state constituent assembly, held in 1951 under the auspices of his government, the ruling National Conference Party won all seventy-five seats, seventy-three of them uncontested. The Praja Parishad boycotted the elections after the nominations of forty-five of its forty-nine candidates were rejected on apparently flimsy grounds.

Within months of concluding the Delhi agreement, Abdullah changed course on autonomy, describing the agreement as only a temporary arrangement, thus veering toward full independence—despite having earlier spelled out the impracticability of this option. In his inaugural address to the state constituent assembly, Abdullah had observed that "it is not easy to protect sovereignty and independence in a small country which has not sufficient strength to defend itself on our long and difficult frontiers bordering so many countries. . . . Can we find powerful guarantors among them [neighbors] to pull together always in assuring us freedom from aggression? . . . From August 15 to October 22, 1947 our state was independent and the result was that our weakness was exploited [by Pakistan]. . . . The state was invaded. What is the guarantee that in future too we may not be victims of a similar aggression?"[4] In July 1953, however, he appeared to shift course; at any rate, New Delhi believed it had evidence that Abdullah had begun to work for an independent Kashmir. The U.S. archives show that Abdullah sought American support for an independent Kashmir.[5]

Two different (but not mutually inconsistent) reasons have been advanced to explain Abdullah's apparent about face. It has been suggested that the independence option was Abdullah's response to the Praja Parishad agitation and what he regarded as a lack of unqualified Central support for his stand against the Jammu agitation. Though New Delhi condemned the agitation in strong terms, it earned Abdullah's displeasure when it pleaded with him to release demonstrators who had been put into prison.[6] The alternative explanation is that the arrival of the Cold War in the subcontinent aroused Abdullah's hopes for finding a powerful foreign ally for an independent Kashmir.[7] His approaches to the United States have already been noted. Abdullah's moves split his own party and gave rise to deep concern in New Delhi. Three of Abdullah's four cabinet colleagues were strongly opposed to any secessionist move. Alarm in the central government led to Abdullah's detention on secessionist charges and his replacement as head of the state government by his deputy, Bakshi Ghulam Mohammed.

When subsequently the Jammu and Kashmir constituent assembly voted unanimously to ratify the state's accession to India, Abdullah rejected the decision. He encouraged his close associate, Mirza Afzal Beg, to form a new party, the Plebiscite Front. Though he did not become a formal member, Abdullah extended his patronage to the new party, which called for a plebiscite to decide the future of the state.

Three themes may be discerned in the politics of Jammu and Kashmir in the first period following its accession to India. First, because of regional linguistic and cultural differences, autonomy tended to cause internal tensions within the state in the absence of power-sharing arrangements between the regions. Thus, the total concentration of power in the Kashmir-based National Conference led to the alienation of Jammu and Ladakh. Second, since autocratic tendencies persisted in the state government, autonomy was not necessarily conducive to democracy. The Abdullah government's intolerance of opposition, its tight control over the press, and its failure to distinguish between party and government was possible only because autonomy made it immune to the checks and balances operating elsewhere in the country. Finally, Abdullah's reactions to the Center's position on the Jammu agitation and, later, to his detention illustrate a tendency on the part of Kashmiri politicians to raise secessionist demands when denied Central support or when excluded from the political process. These themes have been recurrent features of the political scene in Jammu and Kashmir.

1954–74: Years of Integration

The new Premier, Bakshi Ghulam Mohammad, led the state into closer integration with central political and administrative institutions. In February 1954, the Jammu and Kashmir constituent assembly unanimously confirmed the state's accession to India. In April, the customs barriers between the state and the rest of India were removed. In May, the Center passed the Constitution (Application to Jammu and Kashmir) Order. Under its terms, and at the request of the state authorities, the jurisdiction of the Center was extended to cover all subjects in the Union list. (However, the exclusive rights of "state subjects" to ownership of immovable properties, the special status of the Kashmir High Court, and some of the special powers of the state legislature were not affected.) In 1957, Jammu and Kashmir was brought on a par with other states in financial matters, thus enabling the state to receive its due share of Central funds. In 1958, the jurisdiction of the Central election commission and the All India Services was extended to the state.

Bakshi's administrative drive and the increased flow of Central funds led to rapid economic and social development. During the decade of his rule, the budget allocation for education increased tenfold and capital expenditures on health registered a sixfold increase. The first engineering, agricultural, and medical colleges in the state were established during these years.

Literacy rates, as well as higher education, registered impressive advances. The construction of the Banihal Tunnel, providing an all-weather road link with the rest of India, gave a major boost to the economy.

Bakshi's administrative skills were not matched by a dedication to liberal values. Intolerant of opposition, he did not hesitate to denounce other pro-India parties as "instruments of Indian interference" in Kashmir. Thus, when a breakaway faction, the Democratic National Conference, demanded that the jurisdiction of the Supreme Court and the Election Commission be extended to the state, it was accused of "trying to sell Kashmir to India."[8]

Bakshi's regime was also authoritarian and corrupt and lost popularity as a result. No tears were shed when he decided to step down from office in 1963, together with many other Indian leaders, under the Kamaraj plan.[9] It is important to note, however, that popular disenchantment with the Bakshi administration did not lead to alienation from the Indian Union. As a result, Pakistan miscalculated in 1965, when it launched a clandestine invasion of Kashmir, expecting to receive popular support. Kashmiris actively cooperated with the Indian army in flushing out the infiltrators.

Ghulam Mohammed Sadiq, who became prime minister of the state in 1965, carried the policy of integration to new heights. The provisions of Articles 356 and 357 of the Indian Constitution, empowering the president to take over the governance of a state in an emergency, were extended to Jammu and Kashmir. Central labor and trade union laws were made applicable in the state. Members of Parliament from the state were to be directly elected, as in other states, and not nominated by the state assembly. It was decided to redesignate the Sadr-e-Riyasat as Governor and the Prime Minister as Chief Minister, as in other states.

Particularly in the initial period of his term of office, Sadiq made a bold attempt to run state politics on liberal lines, instill institutional values, and reduce corruption. He disbanded Bakshi's Peace Brigade, which had gained notoriety for employing strong-arm methods on behalf of the party. Political detainees were released and curbs on press freedom lifted. Civil liberties were protected to an extent earlier unknown and a degree of fairness introduced in official appointments and promotions.[10] Though he failed to press on with reforms and fell short of his goals, Sadiq's achievements were nevertheless remarkable.

Kashmir achieved marked progress in political and economic terms under Sadiq. Yet he lacked charisma and the political skill of manipulating images and symbols. Sadiq committed a blunder in carrying the process of integration to the point of actually merging the National Conference with the Congress Party in the state. Despite its shortcomings, Kashmiris associated the National Conference with their political struggles and achievements. It was *their* party in a sense that the Congress could not match. In the words of a veteran Kashmiri observer: "The National Conference enjoyed glorious local traditions, a name and a past which evoked sentiments of patriotism, sacrifice and self-respect in the Kashmiris. . . . For Kashmiri Muslims it had a special attraction. It was a symbol of their political achievements, cultural advance and national existence."[11] Within a few years of Sadiq's untimely death in 1971, the National Conference was revived and the state sought a new balance in the distribution of powers with the Center.

Before turning to these events, we must note an act of political short-sightedness on the part of the ruling Congress which was to have tragic consequences in later years. In order to deny political space in the Valley to the rump National Conference, the Congress decided during the 1972 elections to encourage the fundamentalist Jamaat-i-Islami, which sought incorporation into Pakistan as a first step toward universal Muslim unity.[12] This was the same myopic and unprincipled policy that led the Congress to extend covert support to Bhindranwale in the Punjab against the Akali Dal. The same tragic consequences ensued. In 1990, the Jamaati cadres would organize themselves into the Hizbul Mujahidin (Army of Holy Warriors) and spread terror in the state.

1975–89: Compromise on Autonomy and Revival of the National Conference

By 1972, Sheikh Abdullah had come to the conclusion that the demand for a plebiscite would lead nowhere. The possibility of using the Pakistan factor to gain leverage in negotiations with New Delhi faded after the Bangladesh liberation war and the Simla agreement of 1972. Abdullah decided to bring the plebiscitary chapter of his politics to a close. He recognized that the state's accession to India, as ratified by the Jammu and Kashmir constituent assembly, was no longer subject to challenge, and he sought a new understanding with the Central government on the basis of at least partial restoration of the state's autonomy. "Our dispute with [the] Government of India," he said in March 1992, "is not about accession but it is about the quantum of autonomy."[13]

The outcome was the Delhi agreement of November 1974. The accord recognized that Jammu and Kashmir was a "constituent unit of the Union of India." The Indian Parliament would retain its legislative powers over subjects included in the Union list. Residuary powers would remain with the state legislature, but Parliament would continue to have legislative powers concerning prevention of activities directed against the territorial integrity of India. The Central election commission would continue to exercise its functions in the state. The accord authorized the state government to review laws made by the Union Parliament or extended to the state after 1953 on matters falling within the concurrent list (on such subjects as cultural matters, personal law, etc.) and to decide if these required amendment or repeal. The Delhi agreement promised that the "President's assent to such legislation would be sympathetically considered." Following the accord, Abdullah dissolved the Plebiscite Front, revived the National Conference, and formed a government with Congress support. Kashmir's most popular politician was back at the helm of affairs.

The honeymoon with the Congress did not last long, however. The Congress pressed for an electoral understanding; Abdullah responded by calling on the Congress Party in the state to merge with the National Conference. In March 1977, the Congress withdrew support for the Abdullah government. In the ensuing election campaign in 1977, the National Conference revived the demand for greater autonomy. From his sickbed, Abdullah issued a stirring, taped appeal to the electorate, in which he noted that "Kashmiri nationalism cannot be undermined by conspiracy" and that "only the people of Kashmir can decide about their future."[14] The outcome was that the National Conference won 42 seats, the Janata Party (which had, in the meantime, ousted the Congress at the Center) 13, and the Congress, 10.

Abdullah made a serious but only partly successful effort to combat the Jamaat-i-Islami's religious extremism. In 1975 he imposed a ban on Jamaat-i-Islami *madrasahs* for "spreading communal poison." The impact of the move was, however, limited, since the *madrasah* teachers were absorbed into government schools and thus provided a new platform for propaganda. It would also appear that the Jamaat was able to continue its infiltration of the provincial civil services and police.[15] However, at the level of electoral politics the National Conference did succeed in marginalizing the role of the Jamaat. Thus, in the 1977 elections the Jamaat was able to secure only one seat, compared to the five it had won in 1972.

On assuming office in 1975, Abdullah pledged to "make sincere efforts to ensure that all three regions not only have equal opportunity for full and speedy development but that the people in every part of the state have a full participation in the political affairs of the state."[16] As in the past, however, he paid little more than lip service to regional equity. Not surprisingly, agitations flared up once again in Jammu and Ladakh.

In 1978 the All-Party Jammu Action Committee demanded a devolution of powers to the regional, district, block, and *panchayat* levels. Abdullah rejected the demand, alleging that the movement was directed against the Kashmiris. Fortunately for him, the Jammu movement petered out because of lack of unity of purpose among its leaders.

In January 1981 the Ladakh Action Committee launched an agitation for divisional status, larger development allocations, and the reservation of seats in professional colleges. It condemned the state government's policy of allocating development resources on the basis of population, ignoring Ladakh's backwardness, territorial size, and scanty population. It pointed out that the state government itself pressed the Center to allocate resources on the basis of area, rather than population, but reversed the formula when it came to allocating resources within the state. Violent clashes broke out for the first time in Buddhist-majority Ladakh.

Abdullah sought to pacify agitators by appointing a commission under a retired supreme court judge, Justice Sikri, but did nothing to implement its recommendations. Once again, in the absence of remedial institutional arrangements, the concentration of power in a party drawing its support almost exclusively from the Kashmir Valley resulted in political discontent in Jammu and Ladakh. The return to power of the charismatic Abdullah helped to consolidate political stability in the Kashmir Valley, but it also compounded the regional grievances of Jammu and Ladakh.

Sheikh Abdullah, the Lion of Kashmir, passed away in 1982. His departure from the scene precipitated a new power struggle between the Congress and the National Conference, which resulted in the frittering away of most of the gains of Abdullah's second term in office. Indira Gandhi, restored to power at the Center by the 1980 general elections, pursued a narrow policy of seeking an enhanced role for the Congress Party in Jammu and Kashmir, without appreciating the political compulsions of the National Conference.

She tried to prevail on the young Farooq Abdullah, who had succeeded his father as chief minister, to enter into an electoral alliance that would guarantee the Congress some seats in the Valley. Farooq rightly rejected the proposal, which would have dented the image of the National Conference as the defender of "Kashmiri identity" vis-à-vis the Center. Farooq's defiant stand drew enthusiastic support in the Valley and greatly enhanced his political stature. Carried away by his success in the state, Farooq decided to take the fight against the Congress to the national level by joining hands with non-Congress governments in other states in order to mount a challenge to the Congress at the Center. Though its legitimacy cannot be questioned, this was an unwise move. Apprehending a threat to her own position, Indira Gandhi decided to destabilize two of the offending state governments—the National Conference government in Jammu and Kashmir and the Telegu Desam government in Andhra Pradesh. In July 1984 she encouraged G. M. Shah, the head of a disaffected faction in the National Conference, to defect from the party and form a new government with Congress support. The newly appointed Governor Jagmohan obliged by dismissing the Farooq Abdullah government without giving it an opportunity to test its strength on the floor of the assembly. This unprincipled ouster of a popular government was deeply resented by the Kashmiri electorate as an unjust interference in state politics and as the imposition of a chief minister on the state by the Center.

Farooq committed a second blunder in 1986 when, in order to return to office, he decided to give in to the Congress demand for an electoral alliance. The National Conference–Congress alliance was to have disastrous consequences for Jammu and Kashmir, as it destroyed the raison d'être of the two parties in the state. The Kashmiri electorate saw the National Conference as a regional party that had traditionally acted as the champion of the interests of the Valley vis-à-vis the Congress-run Center, while Jammu voters turned to the Congress (and other All-India parties) to defend their interests against a state government run by the National Conference. Each party played a balancing role against the other. The electoral alliance went against the logic of their separate roles. Secondly, the alliance between the dominant parties in Kashmir and Jammu, respectively, deprived other parties of effective political space. Through seat-sharing arrangements, the National Conference and the Congress could virtually monopolize the political space in state politics.[17]

The consequences of the alliance became clear in the 1987 elections. The main opposition to the National Conference–Congress alliance came from a broad coalition of religious parties called the Muslim United Front (MUF). MUF was united in rejecting secular politics but was divided between those (like the Jamaat-i-Islami) who rejected the state's accession to India and those (like the Ummat-i-Islami) for whom the issue was not accession but "restoration of democratic rights of Kashmiri Muslims." Participation in the elections was very high, with 75 percent of the electorate exercising their right to vote. Out of a total of 76 seats, the National Conference secured 40, the Congress 26, and BJP 2, while the other 8 seats were won by "Independent" candidates (of whom four belonged to MUF). The National Conference–Congress alliance thus won a resounding victory, but the polls were marred by widespread allegations of malpractice.

There can be little doubt that malpractices did occur in a number of Valley constituencies and their impact cannot be known for certain, but it seems unlikely that these materially affected the outcome in most contests. The National Conference–Congress combine would have won convincingly in any case. The "first-past-the post" electoral system gives an advantage to larger parties and coalitions in multi-cornered contests. The average number of candidates in a constituency was just under seven in the 1987 elections. Thus, the National Conference and the Congress were able to secure as much as 87 percent of the seats though they received only 53 percent of the votes cast, while candidates affiliated with the MUF, with 20 percent of the votes, was able to get only 5 percent of the seats. This weak correlation between votes and seats was not unusual in elections in other states. The evidence suggests that malpractices in some constituencies in the Valley were magnified in the people's perception on account of a failure to understand the mathematical reasons for the divergence between numerical support for a party and the seats obtained by it.[18]

In politics, perceptions are sometimes more important than realities. The 1987 elections marked a political turning point because they were perceived by Kashmiri opposition parties as fraudulent and illegitimate. Many opposition candidates drew the conclusion that democratic politics offered no channels for redressing their grievances. Among those who decided in the wake of the 1987 elections to forsake electoral politics were future militant leaders like Abdul Ghani Lone, Yasin Malik, and Syed Salahuddin. Lone later reflected: "It was this that motivated the young generation to say 'to hell with the democratic process and all that is about' and they said 'let's go for the armed struggle.' It was the flash point."[19]

1990–96: Terrorism and President's Rule

By the 1980s, the rapid expansion of educational institutions, the growth of the press, and the advent of television, together with the example of healthy democratic institutions in other parts of India, had created a new generation of Kashmiris who were much more conscious of their political rights than previous generations. They sought more effective participation in the political process.[20] The National Conference–Congress alliance and the electoral malpractices of 1987 denied them the political space they wanted, creating a sense of deep frustration with constitutional politics.

Internal failures were responsible for the alienation of Kashmiri youth, but they do not explain the speed with which this sense of alienation was converted into an armed movement, nor the subsequent conversion of a largely indigenous struggle into a movement run increasingly by foreign terrorists. Drawing inspiration from its success in running the clandestine Mujahedin operations in Afghanistan, Pakistan decided in the early 1980s to step up its operations in Kashmir. In 1984, well before the National Conference–Congress pact or the allegedly fraudulent election, the Pakistani military had approached the Pakistan-based Jammu and Kashmir Liberation Front (JKLF) to make preparations for an armed struggle.[21] The disillusioned Kashmiri youths who crossed over the Line of Control after the 1987 elections found that arrangements were already in place for training, arming, and financing a militant movement.

Pakistan's involvement in clandestine operations in Jammu and Kashmir is, of course, as old as the Kashmir problem itself.[22] The operations that were now launched, however, were conducted on a far grander scale in terms of both the numbers and relative sophistication of the weapons supplied. For the first time, Kalashnikovs, grenades, and rocket launchers appeared in the hands of Kashmiri militants. The police, armed at most with antiquated rifles, were hopelessly outgunned. The militants were able in a short time to paralyze the state law-and-order machinery by a systematic campaign involving assassination of policemen. They proceeded to render political institutions dysfunctional by assassinating National Conference leaders and seeking to enforce a boycott of the electoral process.[23] Thus, in the 1989 parliamentary bye-elections, they set polling stations on fire and threatened to kill anyone exercising the right of franchise. Predictably, the voter turnout was very low in militancy-affected areas.

The problem was compounded by the Central government's decision to send Jagmohan back to the state as governor. The decision was pushed by Farooq Abdullah's old rival in Kashmir politics, Mufti Mohammed Sayeed, who had recently been appointed as the Union Home Minister. Jagmohan, it will be recalled, had taken the dubious decision to dismiss Farooq in 1984. On Jagmohan's reappointment in January 1990, the National Conference government registered its protest by tendering its resignation. The state was brought under Governor's Rule for a six-month period and, since elections could not be held at the time on account of the terrorist threat, President's Rule was proclaimed later in the year. For the first time since 1947, control over the state passed out of Kashmiri hands.

The first wave of militants consisted of local Kashmiris, mainly youth from the Valley. The leading militant organization in the initial stage, the JKLF, stood for an independent Kashmir—a goal very different from that of its Pakistani patrons. In early 1990, however, Pakistan decided that the pro-independence movement had served its purpose. Assistance was diverted from secular, pro-independence groups to Islamic militants seeking accession to Pakistan.[24] The major beneficiary was the Hizbul Mujahedin, a militant group closely linked to the Jamaat-i-Islami. The Hizbul Mujahedin, however, found very limited support among the Kashmiris. A vast majority of Kashmiris subscribed either to a secular view of their identity, based on the shared values of Kashmiriyat, or to a Muslim Kashmiri (as distinct from pan-Islamic) view of their identity. The militant movement came to be plagued by declining support, factionalism, and internecine clashes.

New Delhi was totally unprepared for the outbreak of militancy. After an initial period of confusion, in which unprepared central authorities were working at cross-purposes, the militants were gradually made to give ground by the employment of army and paramilitary forces. By 1995, the militancy had been contained.

From the early 1990s, Pakistan decided to replace the ebbing indigenous militancy with foreign jihadis and mercenaries, including many veterans of the Afghan jihad. The Kashmiri militant increasingly gave way to the cross-border terrorist.[25] The shift was accompanied by a further escalation in the level of weaponry supplied by Pakistan. In 1995, for the first time, RDX explosives were seized by security forces from terrorist groups operating in the state. The induction of foreign terrorists was accompanied by two further developments. First, there was a growing criminalization of the movement in the Valley, with many cases of rape and robbery against the local people. Second, terrorism spread from Kashmir to Jammu and other non-Muslim areas, with an increasing number of jihadi attacks against civilian targets. In general, the induction of foreign jihadis led to a progressive shrinkage of support for the militant movement.

1996 to Date: Restoration of Electoral Politics and a Change in Government

By 1996, the situation was sufficiently under control for the Central government to hold parliamentary bye-elections in the state. Efforts were made to persuade the major political party, the National Conference, to contest the elections, but the party, seeking a program to present to the electorate, asked for the restoration of full autonomy on the basis of the 1952 agreement as a condition for participation. Though the National Conference stayed out of the contest, as many as 152 candidates defied assassination threats from the terrorists to contest the six parliamentary seats.

This paved the way for holding elections for the state assembly after a lapse of nine years. Recognizing the risk of losing its political base if it stayed out of the contest, the National Conference entered the fray this time. In a direct response to secessionist violence, the National Conference mobilized the people of Jammu and Kashmir as an integral part of India. "We are a part of India," Farooq Abdullah emphasized. "It is only with India that we will progress and our Kashmiriyat survive."[26] In the 1996 state assembly elections, the National Conference secured 59 out of 87 seats.

The 1996 elections renewed the political process and restored power to Kashmiri leaders. As competitive politics gathered strength, a new party, the People's Democratic Party (PDP), made its appearance in 1999. Founded by Mufti Mohammed Sayeed, a former Congress leader and a Union minister in the Janata regime, the party posed a new secular and democratic challenge to the National Conference.

The ruling National Conference failed to draw the correct conclusions from the history of the previous decade. Seeking a close link with the Center, the National Conference joined the National Democratic Alliance (NDA) government in New Delhi, and the chief minister's son, the able and energetic Omar Abdullah, became a junior minister in the Union government. The intention was to secure the maximum possible assistance for the state's development, but the excessively close relationship with the Center did no good to the party's image of being the champion of Kashmiri causes against the Center. The fact that the NDA was led by the BJP, a party whose secular credentials were deeply distrusted in the Valley, was particularly damaging for its National Conference partner.

The National Conference strategy was to revive the demand for full autonomy in order to reestablish its image as the defender of Kashmiri interests. As in the past, lip service was paid to the interests of other regions. Soon after the elections, the Farooq Abdullah government set up two committees to make recommendations concerning state autonomy and regional autonomy, respectively. These reports were issued in 1999. The State Autonomy Committee, composed exclusively of National Conference members,[27] recommended a return to the level of autonomy obtaining in the immediate post-accession period. This was to be achieved through a number of legislative steps detailed in the report. Among other measures, it recommended that the jurisdiction of the Supreme Court and the Election Commission should be withdrawn from the state; that the Fundamental Rights provisions of the Indian Constitution should not apply to residents of Jammu and Kashmir; and that the All-India Civil Services should not be employed in the state. State-level institutions would take over the functions currently performed by the Supreme Court, Election Commission, and the All-India Services, respectively, and new provisions would be made in the state constitution in regard to fundamental rights.

These recommendations were promptly endorsed by the state government, only to be dismissed by the Center. The offhand rejection by the NDA government did little to enhance the standing of its National Conference partner in the Kashmir Valley.

The first significant step toward accommodating Ladakh's regional demands had been taken during the period of President's Rule, when political power had temporarily passed out of the hands of the Kashmiri elite. In 1995, an Autonomous Hill Development Council was created for Leh, but its subsequent functioning under the National Conference government belied Ladakhi hopes. The Regional Autonomy Report was supposed to address the concerns of Jammu and Ladakh, but it turned out to be a weakly argued document that failed to reflect the concerns of those regions. On the contrary, it merely proposed the creation of no less than eight new provinces without providing any justification. Serious procedural irregularities also marred the committee's functioning. The working chairman—who was the only non-National Conference member—resigned from the post, and the final report did not bear the signatures of many of the other members as well. Not surprisingly, political parties have shown little interest in the document.

The erosion of support for the National Conference became evident in the assembly elections held in 2002. The elections returned a mixed verdict, in contrast to previous polls. The National Conference obtained only 28 seats (of which 18 were in the Valley), a sharp decline from the 59 seats it had secured in 1996. Though short of a majority, the National Conference nevertheless emerged as the largest single party in the assembly. Congress secured 20 seats (including 5 in the Valley), and the recently formed People's Democratic Party (PDP), led by Mufti Sayeed, won 16 seats, all from Valley constituencies.

The 2002 elections have been widely hailed in the state as having been free and fair, unlike those of 1987. It is worth noting that the election commission inducted a substantial number of officials from other states to conduct the polling in 2002. These officials had no connections with local politicians and were fully under the control of the election commission. This evidently contributed to the general perception that the elections were conducted fairly, unlike some previous cases in which only local officials had acted as polling officers.

The PDP and Congress subsequently formed a government together with a number of Independents. Even though it had a larger number of seats, the Congress conceded Mufti Sayeed's claim to the post of Chief Minister. The new government is thus led by a Kashmiri from the Valley, though it has a balanced representation of all three regions.

The coalition government announced that its goal is to "heal the physical, psychological and emotional wounds inflicted by fourteen years of militancy, to restore the rule of law in Jammu and Kashmir state, to complete the revival of the political process . . . and to request the Government of India to initiate and hold . . . wide ranging consultations and dialogue, without conditions, with the members of the legislature and other segments of public opinion in all three regions of the state to evolve a broad-based consensus on restoration of peace with honor in the state."

Conclusion

This call reflected the deep yearning of the people for an end to terrorist violence, for good governance and economic development. A survey conducted in April 2002 by a leading independent British research organization, Market Opinion Research International, found that in order to bring peace in the state, 86 percent of respondents wanted an end to militant violence; 88 percent wanted infiltration of militants across the Line of Control to be stopped; 87 percent wanted direct consultation between the Indian government and the people of Kashmir; and 93 percent wanted economic development to provide more job opportunities and a reduction in poverty.[28]

Answering the call from Srinagar, New Delhi invited the leaders of the Hurriyat Conference to commence a dialogue. Most of the groups represented at the Conference responded positively to the invitation. However, because of the terrorist groups that reject peaceful negotiations, the anti-terrorism campaign will have to continue in parallel with the political dialogue.

When a dialogue does begin, it is likely to be an open-ended process. The question of autonomy is certain to figure largely in the dialogue, though perhaps not at the initial stage. The ruling coalition in the state will take time to work out its own positions on autonomy for the state as a whole and on the related issue of regional autonomy. Moreover, many of the militant groups will, at least initially, press secessionist demands. However, the dialogue will eventually center round the question of autonomy since that is the demand of the largest Kashmiri party, the National Conference, and also because this is the maximum demand that any government in New Delhi can possibly concede.

In light of the post-1947 history of the state, New Delhi would be well advised to accommodate Kashmiri demands for autonomy to the maximum extent compatible with the legitimate regional interests of Jammu and Ladakh and with the requirements of democracy and good governance in the state as a whole. The interests of Jammu and Ladakh can be protected by a mix of regional autonomy; devolution of powers to lower (district, sub-divisional, and *panchayat*) levels; and an equitable inter-regional revenue-sharing formula. A broad consensus should be sought on the linked questions of state autonomy and adequate protection of regional interests. It must also be remembered that the period of maximum autonomy, 1947–53, was characterized by a high degree of authoritarianism, and that the extension to the state of the jurisdiction of the Supreme Court, the Central Election Commission, and the Auditor-General has proved beneficial for democracy and good governance.

In other words, Jammu and Kashmir requires *optimum*, rather than *maximum*, autonomy. The optimal balance might evolve over time and the degree of autonomy might accordingly be adjusted from time to time. A new accord on autonomy should not be regarded as a permanent arrangement for all time.

It is important for the state government not only to be invested with a substantial degree of constitutional autonomy but also to be *seen* as acting independently of the central government. The National Conference has paid a stiff political price whenever it has ignored this reality. Thus, despite his many achievements, G. M. Sadiq lost political ground when he made the misjudgment of merging the National Conference with the Congress Party. The 1986 electoral pact with the Congress was another major misjudgment—for this and other reasons. In 1996, the party once again committed a political blunder by joining the BJP-led National Democratic Alliance coalition at the Center, and it paid a heavy price for this misjudgment in the 2002 elections. The ruling party in Jammu and Kashmir must maintain a fine balance between cooperation and opposition in respect to the ruling party at the Center. It should offer *conditional* cooperation with the ruling party at the Center in the National Parliament in order to obtain maximum assistance for the state's development. At the level of state politics, it needs to adopt a stance of *qualified* opposition to the same party, in order to maintain the image of a local party dedicated to advancing the interests of the state. The requirements of this dual policy of conditional cooperation at the Center and qualified opposition within the state should be fully understood in both New Delhi and Srinagar.

As a result of the national elections held in 2004, a Congress-led coalition came to power at the Center. Thus, the Congress Party once again finds itself in office in both New Delhi and Srinagar. At some future point in the dialogue between the Center and Kashmiri political groups, it is quite possible that the PDP will feel a need to carry its advocacy of local Kashmiri interests to a point that its Congress ally will find difficult to endorse. It may well become tactically necessary for the PDP to be seen as loosening its links with the ruling party at the Center. In certain situations, the Congress Party should even be prepared, in the larger national interest, to withdraw from the state government while extending its support to a PDP government from outside.

While autonomy will be the major component of an internal political settlement in Jammu and Kashmir, it will not by itself provide an answer to the bilateral tensions between India and Pakistan. However, if the two countries are prepared to accept a pragmatic, long-term approach, autonomy and democracy can provide the basis of an eventual solution. If autonomy and democracy are instituted on both sides of the Line of Control, the path will be open for a gradual, long-term convergence of political systems in the two parts of Jammu and Kashmir. This would also facilitate a progressive softening of existing borders. Freer movement of people and limited border trade could start as soon as terrorist infiltration across the Line of Control is halted. If there is a convergence of political systems, it is quite possible to conceive of a much closer relationship between the two parts of the state—and, indeed, between Pakistan and India as a whole. Thus, arrangements could be worked out not only for free trade, free capital flows, and free movement of people, but also for coordination of local laws and regulations, rights of residence, etc. Western Europe provides an excellent example of the way in which nations can resolve deeply rooted territorial and political issues in an overarching framework of cooperation and good neighborliness. It is not possible at this point in time to predict the extent of autonomy or the precise nature of the ties that may eventually emerge between the two parts of the state of Jammu and Kashmir. The point is that convergence based on autonomy and democracy, coupled with a progressive softening of borders, can effectively satisfy Kashmiri aspirations for self-rule and restoration of ties across the Line of Control.

A measure of vagueness about the final outcome is probably an essential element of a constructive approach to resolving the differences between India and Pakistan on the issue of Kashmir. These differences are currently so deep that it is simply impossible at this point in time to propose any clear-cut solution that would be acceptable to both countries. The most that can be realistically proposed is an approach or process that both countries can accept as being consistent with their respective long-term objectives and as representing possible movement in the direction desired by each. This requires an open-ended approach concerning the final outcome of the process accepted by the parties concerned.

*India's and Pakistan's Nuclear Doctrines
and U.S. Concerns*

TEN

The Stability-Instability Paradox, Misperception, and Escalation-Control in South Asia

Michael Krepon

The United States and the Soviet Union managed to avoid nuclear and conventional warfare during the Cold War while jockeying for advantage in a myriad of ways, including proxy wars and a succession of crises that became surrogates for direct conflict. International relations and deterrence theorists aptly described this tense standoff in which much blood and treasure were expended—but without direct conflict—as the "stability-instability paradox."

The stability-instability paradox was embedded in the enormity of the stakes involved in crossing the nuclear threshold. As posited by Western deterrence theorists, offsetting nuclear capabilities and secure, second-strike capabilities would induce special caution, providing the basis for war prevention and escalation control. Offsetting nuclear deterrents channeled the superpower competition into "safer" pursuits, the object of which would be to impose penalties on an adversary without inducing direct conflict.

The stability-instability paradox was identified rather early in the Cold War, as Western strategists weighed the consequences of a Soviet Union able to produce thermonuclear weapons. In 1954, B. H. Liddell Hart reflected a widely held view that, "to the extent that the H-bomb reduces the likelihood of full-scale war, it increases the possibility of limited war pursued by widespread local aggression."[1] One of the reasons for rolling out the nuclear doctrine of massive retaliation during the Eisenhower administration was to warn against such adventurism.

The U.S. doctrine of massive retaliation was quickly qualified and subsequently shelved as a declaratory policy because it could not deter the unwanted eventualities that prompted its articulation. Precisely because retaliation by the Soviet Union as well as by the United States could be so massive, this threat would be insufficient. Worse still, threats of massive retaliation invited a bluff that could be called. In Glenn Snyder's words, the Soviets could still engage in "a range of minor ventures which they can undertake with impunity, despite the objective existence of some probability of retaliation."[2] Massive retaliation gave way to the quest for nuclear war–fighting options and limited war doctrine, but these calibrations never really altered the fundamental precepts of the stability-instability paradox. Robert Jervis summarized this dilemma as follows: "To the extent that the military balance is stable at the level of all-out nuclear war, it will become less stable at lower levels of violence."[3]

The purpose of this essay is to explore the extent to which the stability-instability paradox is applicable to the subcontinent of South Asia, drawing upon the work of Western and South Asian strategists. One central tenet of the stability-instability paradox—that offsetting nuclear capabilities will increase tensions between adversaries—has already been amply demonstrated in South Asia. While India's difficulties in Kashmir are rooted in poor governance and domestic grievances, Pakistan's support for separatism and militancy in Kashmir has notably coincided with its acquisition of covert nuclear capabilities. Tensions between India and Pakistan have intensified further since both nations tested nuclear weapons in 1998. A nuclearized subcontinent has already produced a succession of nuclear-tinged crises and one conflict that was limited in time and space, as well as in the choice of weapons used.

This high-altitude conflict above Kargil in 1999 was less than a full-blown war but far more than the skirmishing elsewhere along the Kashmir divide. A review committee assessing this conflict established by the Indian government asked, "Did the nuclear tests conducted by India and Pakistan in May 1998 rule out a major conventional war between them?" Its answer constituted a partial acknowledgment of the applicability of the stability-instability paradox to a distinctly non-Western setting: "Possibly not; but only up to a given threshold, which margin was exploited by Pakistan."[4]

Whether the second central tenet of the stability-instability paradox—that despite increased tensions and severe crises, nuclear-armed adversaries will avoid a major conflict or a nuclear exchange—applies to the subcontinent cannot be answered at this juncture. So far, India and Pakistan, like the Soviet Union and the United States, have been fortunate to avoid a nuclear exchange. It is possible that this luck will hold and that New Delhi and Islamabad will make concerted, joint efforts to avoid crossing the nuclear threshold. And perhaps the applicability of the second tenet of the stability-instability paradox to South Asia will become more evident once India and Pakistan feel completely assured that they have acquired secure second-strike capabilities. This, however, will take time. The resumption of substantive dialogue in 2004 offers an earlier opportunity to transition from recurring crises to collaborative efforts to reduce nuclear risks.

Western experience suggests that constructive engagement between nuclear adversaries can follow the chastening experience of flirting with disaster. The Cuban missile crisis occurred fourteen years after the Soviet Union joined the United States as a nuclear-weapon state. Within twelve months, both nations implemented a "hotline" agreement and negotiated a nuclear test ban treaty. The Kargil conflict occurred perhaps ten years after both India and Pakistan covertly acquired nuclear weapon capabilities.[5] After Kargil, however, the leaders of both countries could not agree on a framework for resumed dialogue. During most of 2002, the subcontinent was poised for another war. Perhaps this chastening experience will provide the impetus to constructive engagement.

Two camps of deterrence theorists have formed over whether a nuclearized subcontinent will prevent a major conflict and foster escalation control.[6] One camp might be called deterrence optimists.[7] This camp naturally includes Indian and Pakistani strategists who chafed at Western efforts to prevent new members from joining the nuclear club and who draw directly from Western experience. As the former Minister of External Affairs of India, Jaswant Singh, wrote, "If deterrence works in the West—as it so obviously appears to, since Western nations insist on continuing to possess nuclear weapons—by what reasoning will it not work in India?"[8] Similarly, Vijai Nair, an early Indian advocate of nuclear weapons, pointedly noted that, "There has been no direct conflict between states of the Western world, endowed with nuclear power . . . while conflict has been the order of the day in the developing, non-nuclear Third World."[9]

Another early conceptualizer of India's nuclear deterrent, former Army Chief K. Sundarji, flatly predicted that nuclear deterrence

will add to stability and peace and that the only salvation is for both countries to follow policies of cooperation and not confrontation. . . . A mutual minimum nuclear deterrent will act as a stabilizing factor. Pakistan will see it as counteracting India's superior conventional power potential and providing a more level playing field. The chances of conventional war between the two will be less likely than before.[10]

Sundarji's optimism is reflected in Raj Chengappa's insider account of India's nuclear and missile decision-making, which is titled *Weapons of Peace*. In Chengappa's narrative, Prime Minister A. B. Vajpayee is portrayed as thinking that nuclear testing by India and Pakistan would mean an end to war on the subcontinent.[11] Similarly, Jasjit Singh, a leading Indian commentator on strategic affairs, has argued that, with the advent of offsetting nuclear capabilities on the subcontinent, "deterrence will continue, but on a higher level. I don't think we are going to see a slide toward instability. I don't think anybody will allow it to happen."[12]

This view was widely echoed in Pakistan. At a symposium convened by the Institute of Policy Studies in 1995, General K. M. Arif declared that "the nuclear option will promote regional peace and create stability,"[13] while Air Marshal Zulfikar Ali Khan opined that nuclear weapons "make wars hard to start."[14] The accomplished Pakistani diplomat, Abdul Sattar, concluded that "attainment of nuclear capabilities by Pakistan and India has helped promote stability and prevented dangers of war despite the crises that have arisen from time to time. . . . Self-interest itself should persuade Pakistan and India to exercise due restraint. Continuance of responsible conduct is likely also because it could gain greater tolerance of their nuclear policies."[15]

During this period, a former Chief of the Pakistan Army, General M. Aslam Beg, summarized the prevailing view in Pakistan, "It is the nuclear deterrent that has kept wars in South Asia at bay."[16] The "father" of Pakistan's nuclear program, Abdul Qadeer Khan, is reported to have told the *Times of Oman*, "Anyone will have to think [a] hundred times before they try to indulge in any misadventure against Pakistan. I don't care if somebody disagrees, but I consider nuclear weapons as weapons of peace"—echoing similar views within the Indian nuclear establishment chronicled by Chengappa. "A nuclear Pakistan," in A. Q. Khan's view, "means safety, security and peace of mind."[17]

Assessments of the stabilizing consequences of offsetting nuclear capabilities have not been confined to deterrence theorists in South Asia. According to Sumit Ganguly,

Despite this tension-ridden relationship and contrary to a number of dire warnings, it is unlikely that India and Pakistan are on the verge of another war, let alone a nuclear war. . . . The possession of nuclear weapons on both sides has, in all likelihood, introduced elements of caution among strategic elites in the region.[18]

Likewise, Devin T. Hagerty concluded, "There is no more ironclad law in international relations than this: nuclear weapon states do not fight wars with one another."[19] Nuclear weapons on the subcontinent, in Hagerty's view, "deters nuclear and conventional aggression, but not the unconventional military operations characteristic of guerrilla warfare."[20] Ashley Tellis's exhaustive review of India's emerging nuclear posture also concludes with an upbeat assessment: "A reasonably high degree of deterrence stability currently exists within the greater South Asia region. . . . It is not unreasonable to expect that the acknowledged presence of nuclear weapons on all sides would inhibit any interactive sequences that could lead to serious forms of deterrence breakdown in the future."[21]

Those who hold diametrically opposed views might be called deterrence pessimists. This camp works from very different assumptions and arrives at deeply troubling conclusions. In this view, the situation in South Asia, like that during the Cold War, is far from stable and could lead to inadvertent escalation. As Robert Jervis notes, "It is rational to start a war one does not expect to win . . . if it is believed that the likely consequences of not fighting are even worse. War could also come through inadvertence, loss of control, or irrationality."[22] A close observer of South Asia, Neil Joeck, argues that,

India's and Pakistan's nuclear capabilities have not created strategic stability [and] do not reduce or eliminate factors that contributed to past conflicts. . . . Far from creating stability, these basic nuclear capabilities have led to an incomplete sense of where security lies. Nuclear weapons may make decision makers in New Delhi and Islamabad more cautious, but sources of conflict immune to the nuclear threat remain. Limited nuclear capabilities increase the potential costs of conflict, but do little to reduce the risk of it breaking out.[23]

Similarly, V. R. Raghavan is far from sanguine about the trajectory of India–Pakistan relations:

The conclusions drawn in New Delhi from the Kargil experience are significant. Instead of seeking a stable relationship on the basis of nuclear weapon capabilities, Pakistan has used nuclear deterrence to support aggression. Kargil indicated that armed with nuclear weapons, Pakistan has increased confidence that it could raise the conflict thresholds with India. It demonstrated a willingness to take greater risks in conflict escalation.[24]

Raghavan concludes that "the probability of a nuclear war between India and Pakistan is high, in the event the two countries engage in direct military conflict."[25] Moreover, as P. R. Chari has observed, "The nuclearized environment in South Asia has not informed the leaderships in both countries to observe restraint in making provocative and inflammatory public declarations."[26] In this view, the combination of harsh rhetoric, provocative action, and the absence of trust and communication channels between Indian and Pakistani leaders invites destabilizing actions and escalation.

Nuclear pessimists can also be found within the ranks of veteran Pakistani observers of tension on the subcontinent. Talat Masood has written that "it would be dangerous for either country to presume that its nuclear capability provides a cover for high-risk strategies or gives immunity from an all-out conventional war."[27] Columnist M. B. Naqvi has concluded that "the point is that nuclear weapons, by their mere presence, have actually proved to be a deeply destabilizing factor."[28]

Several deterrence and international relations theorists straddle these camps. Henry Kissinger has written that "nuclear weapons have rendered war between countries possessing them less likely—though this statement is unlikely to remain valid if nuclear weapons continue to proliferate into countries with a different attitude toward human life or unfamiliar with their catastrophic impact."[29] John Mueller argues that "nuclear weapons neither crucially define a fundamental stability nor threaten severely to disturb it."[30] In Mueller's view, "What deters is the belief that escalation to something intolerable will occur, not so much what the details of the ultimate unbearable punishment are believed to be."[31] Some notable deterrence optimists with a deep understanding of tensions in South Asia have also introduced important qualifiers to their relatively upbeat assessment. Ashley Tellis, for example, notes that "weak state structures" and "deficient strategic decision making" skewed by "severe motivational and cognitive biases" could produce a breakdown in nuclear deterrence in a deep crisis.[32]

This author will not switch camps from deterrence pessimism to deterrence optimism until the governments of India and Pakistan commit to constructive engagement and make concerted and sustained efforts to reduce nuclear risks. To begin with, the earliest stages of offsetting nuclear capabilities between states with significant grievances are inherently the most dangerous. During this period, lines of communication tend to be unreliable and crisis management procedures are especially ad hoc. As Richard

Betts has noted, "Confusion can be used against an enemy by increasing his uncertainty and encouraging caution, but it also widens the range for miscalculation."[33]

In the early stages of developing nuclear arsenals, the size and disposition of each side's nuclear deterrent are mostly opaque to the other, which can prompt worst-case assessments during an intense crisis. Another core element of strategic stability identified by Western deterrence strategists—secure second-strike capabilities—is difficult to constitute during the early stages of a new nuclear rivalry. In this dangerous passage, the United States and the Soviet Union went eyeball-to-eyeball over Berlin and Cuba, and the two pairings of contiguous nuclear-weapon states—China and the USSR as well as India and Pakistan—both fought border clashes soon after these adversaries demonstrated offsetting nuclear capabilities.

The concepts of escalation control and stable nuclear deterrence presume rational decisions by rational actors, even in the deepest crisis. There are, however, extremist groups in Pakistan and India that would view the advent of crisis as an opportunity rather than as a problem to be contained. Western deterrence theorists never had to contend with religious extremism. Deterrence optimists also presume that "Murphy's Law" does not apply to nuclear weapons—at least not to the extent that an accident or a chain reaction of miscalculation, error, chance, or misuse of authority would lead to a crossing of the nuclear threshold. These presumptions were rather generous during the Cold War, as has been amply documented.[34]

Additional reasons for pessimism are rooted in the military balance in South Asia, which was stable in the past, but which is becoming less so over the past decade. With respect to the nuclear equation, it is hard for Indian and Pakistani officials to predict with accuracy the holdings of the other side. Because opacity is commonly viewed as essential to deterrence and because national technical means are mostly lacking, unduly optimistic calculations on one side could well be paired with the other's undue pessimism. Misestimates could be destabilizing as well as stabilizing. Even if both adversaries are aware of the nuclear balance and acknowledge its equality, there are no guarantees against adventurism.[35] Indeed, the first tenet of the stability-instability paradox predicts the opposite result.

Sumit Ganguly argues that the stability-instability paradox will hold for the foreseeable future in South Asia because "neither side has the requisite capability to pursue a decapitating first strike against the other."[36] Deterrence optimists presume that India's nuclear arsenal is secure from attack, given its large landmass. But India's national command authority could be subject to a decapitating strike since New Delhi has been tardy in taking steps to address this vulnerability. In addition, capabilities at this early stage in the nuclear competition are opaque, and intentions are not presumed to be honorable. A "recessed" deterrent or a "force in being"[37] that cannot be constituted or deployed because of a decapitating strike might be unusable. Much of Pakistan's nuclear arsenal and command-and-control hierarchy, on the other hand, could be subject to prompt targeting and preemptive strikes from India, at least in the theoretical calculations employed by nuclear strategists. The more New Delhi moves toward a ready arsenal, thereby addressing worst-case assessments regarding decapitation, the more Islamabad must contemplate—and compensate for—its nightmare scenario of preemption. One side's quest for stability at this stage in the nuclear competition is likely to feed the other's concerns over instability.

Meanwhile, the conventional military balance is also fluid, and changing markedly in India's favor. From 1995 to 1999, South Asian military expenditures grew more than for any region of the world, with India's growth rate three times that of Pakistan.[38] This disparity, which could enable the Indian military to employ new military tactics in future conflicts with Pakistan, has grown even more appreciably in recent years. Nowhere is the growing disparity in conventional military capabilities more apparent than with respect to airpower. From 1993 to 2002, India received or licensed production of 10 Mirage-2000s, 10 MiG-21s, 10 MiG-29s, 190 SU-30s, 4 TU-22s, 54 MiG-27s, 2 Harriers, and 52 Jaguars. During this period, Pakistan acquired or placed orders for 97 F-7s, 40 Mirage-5s, and 10 Mirage-3s. It is also working with China to produce domestically 150 FGA combat aircraft.[39] Growing Indian air superiority has ramifications for escalation control and for the stability of nuclear deterrence on the subcontinent in at least two major respects. First, the attrition of the Pakistani Air Force in air-to-air combat in a "limited war" scenario could constitute a "red line" that cannot be predicted with assurance. Second, Pakistani military planners would view Indian air power as the quickest and most accurate means for deep strikes against nuclear, as well as conventional, targets.

More reason for deterrence pessimism can be found in the absence of nuclear risk-reduction measures on the subcontinent. The author has argued elsewhere that ten key commandments of nuclear risk-reduction evolved over time to help keep the Cold War from becoming white-hot.[40] These commandments are:

- Don't change the territorial status quo in sensitive areas by use of force.
- Avoid nuclear brinksmanship.
- Avoid dangerous military practices.
- Put in place special reassurance measures for ballistic missiles and other nuclear forces.
- Implement properly treaty obligations, risk-reduction, and confidence-building measures.
- Agree on verification arrangements, including intrusive monitoring.
- Establish reliable lines of communication, between political leaders and between military leaders.
- Establish redundant and reliable command and control arrangements as well as intelligence-gathering capabilities to know what the other side is up to, especially in a crisis.
- Keep working hard on these arrangements. Improve them. Don't take anything for granted.
- Hope for plain dumb luck or divine intervention.

It is unsettling to note that none of the key elements of nuclear risk reduction (with the possible exception of good fortune) are now present in South Asia.[41] Instead, Pakistan remains opposed to the status quo in Kashmir, the contiguous territory that has sparked previous wars and almost daily friction between the Indian and Pakistani forces deployed along this divide. Both governments have resorted to brinksmanship over Kashmir, India by mobilizing and threatening war, Pakistan by initiating the Kargil incursion and by its commitment to a Kashmir policy that has relied on militancy to punish India and to leverage favorable outcomes.

In this sense, both countries seem to have copied a page from early Cold War playbooks on how to demonstrate resolve: "The best way, perhaps the only way, for us to avert not only defeat but unnecessary escalation is to demonstrate clearly that our readiness to take risks is not less than theirs."[42] Brinksmanship leads to dangerous military practices, which are a common occurrence along the Kashmir divide, including the overrunning of border posts and the "routine" use of small arms and mortars as well as artillery firing. Aerial incursions take place, notwithstanding signed "confidence-building" measures designed to end such activity.

Deterrence optimists argue that brinksmanship in South Asia is highly ritualized and even pragmatic. As Satu Limaye has written,

Pakistan and India's brinksmanship is not wild-eyed but designed to meet policy objectives. Pakistan, as the weaker state in the bilateral relationship, ratchets up tensions over Kashmir to garner external (mainly U.S.) pressure on India to come to the bargaining table. India uses coercive diplomacy to bring U.S. pressure to bear on Pakistan to halt support for militants and their infiltration into Kashmir. Both states seek to achieve their ends without war: Pakistan because it might lose, India because it might not win. . . . In using brinksmanship, both India and Pakistan ultimately want to be held back while having the United States push their interests forward.[43]

There is much insight in this analysis, but it presumes a high degree of control over events by national leaders. The "pragmatic," self-interested use of brinksmanship leaves much to chance. As Thomas C. Schelling cautioned, "Brinksmanship involves getting onto the slope where one may fall in spite of his own best efforts to save himself, dragging his adversary with him."[44] Responses to repeated instances of brinksmanship could change, and Washington's ability to broker satisfactory outcomes could be diminished from one crisis to the next. If any of the three parties decides to change the rules of the game, outcomes could be surprisingly different.

For both tenets of the stability-instability paradox to be in place, thereby preventing unintended escalation, lines of communication need to be reliable, and the messages conveyed over these channels need to be trustworthy. As noted above, the United States and the Soviet Union began to address this requirement after the Cuban missile crisis. In contrast, after the Kargil crisis, communication between India and Pakistan worsened, and then ceased altogether.

The absence of communication further impairs intelligence assessments. These judgments have been badly wrong in the past, resulting in severe consequences. Most notably, the initiation or outcome of wars—and sometimes both—have come as a surprise to one side or the other. For example, the outbreak of the 1999 high-altitude conflict above Kargil came as a surprise to India; its outcome came as a surprise to Pakistan. Robert Jervis and others reminded us during the Cold War that "deterrence succeeds or fails in the mind of the attacker."[45] But Indian and Pakistani leaders have repeatedly misestimated each other's intentions.

Escalation control requires a careful and correct reading of one's adversary. Regrettably, problems of misperception on the subcontinent *have grown* as the wall of separation between India and Pakistan becomes higher and thicker. One leading Indian strategic analyst, Raja Menon, acknowl-

edges this danger, while identifying its source as "the belief among some Indian academics in the exaggerated resolve of the Pakistanis."[46] In Menon's
view, "an escalatory spiraling out of control could only grow from a Pakistani initiative."[47] There is much room for misjudgment in this analysis.
The war on terrorism declared by Washington provides further grounds for
misjudgment by Pakistan and India. As Polly Nayak has noted, "Each has
misread its closer ties to the United States as evidence that Washington has
embraced its perspective. Each has treated the intense engagement and military presence of the United States as insurance against escalation to war."[48]
The ten-month-long twin mobilizations in 2002, during which the government of India demanded the cessation of acts of terrorism abetted by Pakistan and the handover of leading militants, ended without satisfaction on
either count. The resulting lessons learned in both countries could well increase confusion or misjudgments.

Within India and Pakistan, official postmortems predictably put a positive spin on the crisis.[49] President Musharraf declared, "We have defeated an
enemy without fighting a war." He then added that, if Indian troops "took
even a step across the international border or LoC, we will not only be in
front of them, we will surround them. It will not remain a conventional
war."[50] Prime Minister Vajpayee declared that the extended Indian troop
mobilization "sent [a] 'strong message' to Pakistan to end cross-border terrorism. . . . 'I can tell you that the message is working. We'll make sure that
it works.'"[51] The Indian Army Chief of Staff during the crisis, General S.
Padmanabhan, declared the mobilization "a boon for the armed forces in
upgrading training along with equipment availability." In addition, Padmanabhan noted that infiltration across the LoC had markedly declined,
and that a successful state election had been held in Jammu and Kashmir.[52]

Prominent strategists, retired military officers, and journalists in India
and Pakistan have differed sharply on the lessons learned from this extended
standoff. The national security establishment in Pakistan was mostly upbeat
after India's exercise in coercive diplomacy. According to Shireen M. Mazari,
the chair of the government-funded Institute of Strategic Studies in Islamabad, "The reason for the present dissipation of the military threat is primarily the result of Pakistan calling India's bluff and the major power realizing the need to move India away from its game of brinkmanship."[53] Some
Pakistani military officers viewed the Indian stand-down as evidence of cow-
ardice and as prompting serious morale problems in the Indian Army.[54]

Indian commentators offered a mixed assessment, with some seeing the glass half full. The influential editor of the *Indian Express*, Shekhar Gupta, took solace from the confrontation: "The Pakistani pledge to abjure terrorism now has some international guarantees. Their nuclear bluff has been called—finally we have shown we cannot be blackmailed as we were in 1990."[55] Similarly, the dean of Indian commentators on national security, K. Subrahmanyam, argued that India's extended troop mobilization was a success insofar as it served "to compel the United States to apply pressure on Pakistan to promise a visible and permanent end to cross-border terrorism."[56] In contrast, several retired military officers were scathing in their assessment of Indian coercive diplomacy, as was General Afsir Karim, editor of *Aakrosh* (and former editor of the *Indian Defence Review*), in a published interview:

The troops became mere pawns in the hands of politicians intent on pursuing their own agenda. . . . The troops sweated it out on the borders in extremely harsh environments while the rest of us went about its [*sic*] normal business of celebrating festivals and holding fashion shows. . . . The aim of coercive diplomacy is basically to demand a particular change in an adversary's policies with a real and credible threat of devastating punitive action in case of noncompliance. . . . India, for obvious reasons, posed no such threat to Pakistan. . . . Not surprisingly, cross-border terrorism continued unabated and Pakistan seemed far from being coerced.[57]

Outlook magazine's national security correspondent, V. Sudarshan, heard similar sentiments from prominent members of the Indian national security establishment. He described "seething anger" in the armed forces against coercive diplomacy that, in the words of one source, "achieved so little with so much." The recently retired Vice Chief of Staff of the Indian Army, General Vijai Oberoi, is quoted as saying, "Instead of terminating it as that point in the graph where the gains from mobilization were headed downwards, we carried it on like a Hindi film." Vijai Nair added, "The fact that you deployed the entire military and did not take punitive action against terrorists demonstrated to all that New Delhi does not have the political will to use the means it has deliberately created to secure India when the chips are down."[58]

These divergent views do not bode well for war prevention and escalation control. When both Indian and Pakistani leaders claim to have succeeded at brinksmanship, they may be inclined to continue such practices. Confidence in being able to stare down India appears widespread within the Pakistani national security establishment. At the same time, significant elements of the Indian national security establishment have expressed deep dissatisfaction with threats that are not backed up by the use of force. This juxtaposition could lead to consequential misjudgment, particularly when India's vibrant democracy will present Pakistani leaders with mixed messages about the wisdom of using force to deal with terrorism originating across the Kashmir divide. The initiation of war could again come as a surprise to one side. Since both military establishments express confidence in achieving their objectives in the event of another war relating to Kashmir, one will be proven wrong in the event of another war.

In this sense, Kashmir is indeed a "nuclear flashpoint," as Pakistani officials tirelessly repeat. Large concentrations of Indian and Pakistani forces continue to be deployed on both sides of the Kashmir divide, where they have regularly engaged in artillery exchanges and minor skirmishes. Pakistan's Kashmir policy has relied heavily on militant groups to punish India and to leverage a favorable outcome to this long-standing dispute. Consequently, escalation control on the subcontinent has depended heavily on two risky assumptions: first, that jihadi groups would refrain from such horrendous acts of violence as to spark a war; and second, that the Indian government would refrain from attacking Pakistan in response to lesser grievances. Nuclear stability cannot possibly rest on these two assumptions.

In the event of a crisis, the increased readiness of nuclear capabilities can be expected, including the movement of missiles to complicate targeting and to signal resolve. Nuclear capabilities that are in a high state of readiness or are in motion to reduce their vulnerability could become more susceptible to accidents, sabotage, or breakdowns in command and control. Deterrence optimists tend to discount accidents, inadvertence, and sabotage as contributing factors in crossing the nuclear threshold, but accidents happened during the Cold War. Fortunately, none produced a mushroom cloud. There were also decisions made by local commanders during deep crises that could have led to misjudgments and grave misfortune.[59] Accidents, inadvertent steps, and misjudgments during crises could also occur in South Asia. Moreover, the writings of deterrence optimists usually discount problems associated with the possibility of domestic turmoil and its impact on command and control. These concerns were not prominent during the Cold War.

There are additional reasons for concern about escalation control in the event of a catalytic act of terrorism. The government of India has publicly declared that, "nuclear retaliation to a first strike will be massive and designed to inflict unacceptable damage."[60] As Indian Defense Minister George Fernandes warned,

We have been saying all through that the person who heads Pakistan today, who is also the whole and sole in-charge of that country, has been talking about using dangerous weapons, including the nukes. Well, I would reply by saying that if Pakistan has decided that it wants to get itself destroyed and erased from the world map, then it may take this step of madness, but if it wants to survive then it would not do so.[61]

The government of Pakistan has not released a draft or official nuclear doctrine for public consumption, but one might reasonably infer from the statements of senior military figures that they, too, endorse a massive response to Indian strikes against sensitive targets or the crossing of Pakistani "red lines." During the ten-month-long dual troop mobilizations in 2002, President Musharraf traveled to the front and announced that "even an inch" of Indian incursion across the Kashmir divide "will unleash a storm that will sweep the enemy. . . . The people of Pakistan have always had faith in the ability of the armed forces to inflict unbearable damage to the enemy."[62] In his address to the nation on March 23, 2002, Musharraf declared, "By Allah's Grace Pakistan today possesses a powerful military might and can give a crushing reply to all types of aggression. Anybody who poses a challenge to our security and integrity would be taught an unforgettable lesson."[63] In a subsequent address to the nation on May 27, 2002, Musharraf announced, "We do not want war. But if war is thrust upon us, we would respond with full might, and give a befitting reply."[64]

One might dismiss these statements as hyperbole, but the speaker will be called into account if these remarks are mere bluff and if that bluff is called. The public declarations of Indian and Pakistani leaders endorsing massive retaliation are reminiscent of the tense Cold War standoff in the mid-1950s. These threats are likely to be as ineffectual on the subcontinent as during the Eisenhower administration. Massive retaliation does not provide an answer to the bloodletting in Jammu and Kashmir, nor to ambiguous cases that result in the release of radioactivity. The critique of massive retaliation by Henry Kissinger and other Cold War deterrence strategists still rings true:

Given the power of modern weapons, a nation that relies on all-out war as its chief deterrent imposes a fearful psychological handicap on itself. The most agonizing decision a statesman can face is whether or not to unleash all-out war; all pressures will make for hesitation, short of a direct attack threatening the national existence. . . . A deterrent which one is afraid to implement when it is challenged ceases to be a deterrent.[65]

As Thomas C. Schelling wrote, "When the act to be deterred is inherently a sequence of steps whose cumulative effect is what matters, a threat geared to increments may be more credible than one that must be carried out either all at once or not at all."[66]

A declaratory doctrine of massive retaliation seems particularly ill-suited to the circumstances surrounding a low-yield detonation whose source might not be easily ascertained. Such an event could be caused by an accident, a terrorist act, or an inadvertent strike executed by an air force pilot under orders to avoid known nuclear targets. Under such circumstances, parallel and reinforcing doctrines of massive retaliation constitute a severe impediment to escalation control. Joint adherence to massive retaliation doctrines during the early stages of the nuclear competition in South Asia could result, as Maria Sultan has noted, in deterrence that is based "not on the credibility of the second-strike capability of either side, but on the effectiveness of the first strike."[67]

The threat of massive retaliation could have utility when the crossings of red lines that would result in the use of nuclear weapons are clear and bright, but such clarity is elusive in international relations. Indeed, it is in the interest of national leaders not to be too precise about the actual location of red lines, since to do so could invite unwelcome actions that approach, but do not cross, these thresholds. Consequently, advertised red lines could be overdrawn and purposefully vague. Take, for example, the interview of Lieutenant-General Khalid Kidwai, Director-General of the Strategic Plans Division, by two Italian researchers. In this interview, Kidwai, a key overseer of Pakistan's nuclear deterrent, is reported to have said that Pakistan would resort to nuclear weapons use in the event that:

- India attacks Pakistan and conquers a large part of its territory
- India destroys a large part either of its land or air forces
- India proceeds to the economic strangling of Pakistan
- India pushes Pakistan into political destabilization or creates a large-scale internal subversion[68]

These red lines represent unacceptable thresholds relating to losses of territory, military capability, economic viability, and political stability. As such, they reflect obvious Pakistani sensitivities. How Indian authorities might translate these markers into war-fighting guidelines, however, is anything but obvious. For example, Pakistan's vital lines of communication run perilously close to its international border. India does not need to capture a large part of Pakistani territory in order to deliver a devastating blow. And what constitutes "large" losses of air power? The blockade of Karachi could take many weeks to have a severe impact on the Pakistani economy. When might this red line be crossed? The political-stability threshold is the most difficult of all to calibrate, since Pakistan could be destabilized either in the absence of, or resulting from, a war with India.

Rather than being clear and bright, red lines can be hidden from view. They could be inadvertently embedded in tactical operations that are not expected to result in the detonation of nuclear weapons. During the "quarantine" of Cuba in the 1962 missile crisis, a red line could have been crossed when a U.S. naval destroyer used depth charges to compel a Soviet submarine to the surface. This red line was avoided when one of three officers on board the sub refused to concur with unauthorized, ad hoc procedures to use a nuclear weapon in extremis.[69] Analogous events could be imagined in the context of the use of force for limited military objectives in South Asia.

During the Cold War, the non-viability of massive retaliation as a nuclear doctrine against less than all-out threats led the United States to explore the concept of limited war. For such contingencies, nuclear doctrine evolved to emphasize limited nuclear strikes, tactical nuclear weapons, and a wide range of employment options. Escalation control in the event of a crossing of the nuclear threshold was a conundrum that was never satisfactorily resolved. Some Western deterrence theorists found solace in the pursuit of escalation dominance: superior nuclear capabilities at each rung of the ladder and advantageous nuclear force ratios in the event of all-out war would presumably dissuade the Kremlin from escalating or persuade it to capitulate. Western deterrence strategists inferred a similar animus to the Soviet nuclear posture.[70]

Despite considerable intellectual effort, Western deterrence strategists found no politically acceptable or militarily plausible way out of the conundrum. It was hard to envision how, if the differences between the United States and the Soviet Union had risen to the point of nuclear detonations, the construct of escalation dominance could offer a satisfactory outcome. Instead, the pursuit of advantage would likely become an invitation to uncontrolled escalation between two nuclear superpowers. One side's victory or the other's surrender were unlikely to be mutually acceptable outcomes. If equilibrium could somehow be found between these extremes, it would depend far more on escalation-control measures than on dominant escalatory potential. The conundrum of escalation control was resolved during the Cold War by avoiding direct conflict and by engaging in the nuclear risk-reduction measures enumerated above.

The juxtaposition of India's nuclear doctrine of massive retaliation with a conventional war-fighting doctrine focusing on limited war presents quite different, but no less challenging dilemmas for escalation control. New Delhi's interest in limited war is borne, in part, out of frustration over Pakistan's use of unconventional methods to bleed India in Jammu and Kashmir. Frustration grew after the successful, but self-punishing, tactics used by Indian forces to repel Pakistani intruders from the heights above Kargil. As the Indian Army Chief during this conflict, V. P. Malik, later observed,

Though India and Pakistan are nuclear nations, it is not true to say there cannot be a conventional war between them. Kargil proved that. There is a threshold under which a conventional war is possible.[71]

General Malik's successor, General S. Padmanabhan, echoed these thoughts:

I am looking at the whole range that constitutes the spectrum [of conflict]. You have low-level conflict on the one end and on the other you have the nuclear war scenario. In between this spectrum is a whole amount of strategic space. This is the space in the middle for conventional operations. . . . Nuclear war fighting is perhaps the last thing in anybody's mind. What we are looking at is to get an optimal return from conventional warfare.[72]

The penalties of the stability-instability paradox have been borne disproportionately by India. Offsetting nuclear capabilities appeared to rule out full-scale conventional war, while facilitating Pakistan's support for militancy across the Kashmir divide. At the same time, India's declaratory policy embraced nuclear minimalism and deemphasized limited nuclear options. Can limited-war objectives be backed up by a doctrine of massive retaliation in South Asia? This is unexplored territory for both Western deterrence theorists and for Indian strategists.

The twinning of limited war and massive retaliation could become a very unstable mix. To begin with, limited-war objectives are inherently incompatible with maximal penalties. To risk all for modest objectives appears nonsensical. And if the penalty is not credible, risk-taking by one side will likely prompt risk-taking by the other. Backstopping limited war with the threat of massive retaliation would therefore appear to run the familiar risks of escalation control. Western deterrence strategists have dwelled at length on this dilemma. Neither adversary, as Robert Jervis has written, "can confidently move into an area of significant concern to the other without great risk of incurring very high costs—if not immediately, then as a result of a chain of actions that cannot be entirely foreseen or controlled."[73] Conceiving of nuclear weapons as a firebreak does not necessarily prevent escalation. As Bernard Brodie observed, "The more that confidence in the firebreak is built up, the less is each side restrained from committing larger and larger conventional forces within the limits of its capabilities."[74]

The government of India has been caught on the horns of this dilemma ever since the subcontinent was nuclearized. Opposed to endorsing limited nuclear options and the other paraphernalia of nuclear deterrence that drove U.S. and Soviet arsenals to dizzying heights, New Delhi has yet to find favorable military methods to counter Pakistan's tactics in Kashmir. The device chosen after the terrorist attack on the Indian Parliament—keeping battle-ready forces in the field for ten months—is not one that lends itself to repetition, unless one chooses to wage war. Otherwise, the credibility of the threat would be further devalued, while confirming Brodie's observation, above. And if the full mobilization of conventional forces is no longer credible, how can the threat of massive retaliation successfully alter an adversary's behavior? The frustrations prompted by these excursions have no doubt contributed to Indian interest in limited-war options, which coexist awkwardly with an unlimited nuclear threat. Because this juxtaposition is inherently unstable at this stage of the subcontinent's nuclear standoff, the possibility of unintended escalation is always present, lending further credence to the concerns of deterrence pessimists, especially under conditions where bilateral relations are strained.

One key element of escalation control, as Morton Kaplan wrote in *The Strategy of Limited Retaliation*, is the "ability of the opponents to see the legitimacy of each other's claims."[75] It has been very hard for Indian and Pakistani leaders to show such generosity of spirit toward one another since General Musharraf's incursion above Kargil. Escalation control also requires the ability to reign in wild men eager to pursue violent agendas. Western deterrence theorists never made the acquaintance of the Jaish e-Muhammed or the Lashkar e-Taiba. Jihadi wild cards are now mixed into the deck of India–Pakistan relations, along with Hindu chauvinists who abet the mass murder of Muslims and mosque demolition. Catalytic acts of terror can again place India and Pakistan at the knife's edge. Concerns over terrorists acquiring fissile material are present in South Asia, as elsewhere.[76] The dilemma of escalation control was avoided after the attack on the Indian Parliament largely because the Indian prime minister wished to avoid war. A future Indian prime minister, faced with another major provocation, might choose a different course of action.

In the fifteen years since acquiring nuclear weapons, India and Pakistan have experienced difficult times. The last five years of this stretch have been particularly rough. Before outsiders pass judgment on this record of brinksmanship, it is worth recalling that the first fifteen years of the nuclear standoff between the United States and the Soviet Union were also very harrowing. The two superpowers looked directly into the nuclear abyss during crises over Berlin and Cuba. After this extremely dangerous passage, Washington and Moscow were finally ready to take steps to reduce nuclear dangers. Only after the Cuban missile crisis did the superpowers agree to establish a "hotline" for secure communication in crisis, and negotiate an end to nuclear testing in the atmosphere. Thereafter, the nuclear rivalry between the United States and the Soviet Union was eventually tamed by a long and difficult process of negotiating confidence-building measures, arms control, intrusive verification, and finally, deep cuts in nuclear forces.

The leaders of India and Pakistan face a similar challenge to transition from recurring crises to nuclear safety. Deterrence optimists could be proven right: perhaps a period of sustained collaboration is in the offing. After all, India and Pakistan have experienced severe crises, but national leaders have studiously avoided a conventional war that could result in a crossing of the nuclear threshold. National leaders are well aware of the adverse economic consequences of limited warfare and of their responsibilities to avoid unintended escalation. In the event of another crisis, third parties will seek to intervene quickly, if they are given time to do so before hostilities erupt.

Nonetheless, deterrence pessimists are correct in warning that the political conditions for escalation control and nuclear risk-reduction are not in place. Much could go badly wrong on the subcontinent unless Pakistan's national security establishment reassesses its Kashmir policy and unless New Delhi engages substantively on Islamabad's concerns and with dissident Kashmiris. Even if these steps are taken, those opposed to reconciliation will attempt to blow up the process. The best chance of defusing nuclear danger and controlling escalation lies in sustained and substantive political engagement.

ELEVEN

Pakistan's Nuclear Doctrine

Peter R. Lavoy

This chapter develops the implications of an earlier publication, *Planning the Unthinkable: How New Powers Will Use Nuclear, Biological, and Chemical Weapons*, a central theme of which is that nuclear (and biological and chemical) weapons can have different uses for different actors at different times.[1] On the surface, this theme appears obvious. But it stands in sharp contrast to political realism, the dominant approach underpinning American analyses of international politics. U.S. officials and defense analysts from Bernard Brodie and Albert Wohlstetter to Ken Waltz and John Mearsheimer have considered the utility of nuclear weapons almost entirely in the context of deterrence. Scholarly and policy debates have been waged over the kinds, numbers, locations, and targets of the forces needed to deter, and the precise actions of the adversary that ought to be deterred. But Western observers have devoted precious little attention to understanding the other roles that nuclear weapons can and do play.[2]

I have argued elsewhere that because there is so much uncertainty over the political and military effects of owning, threatening to employ, and actually employing nuclear weapons, the beliefs, or *myths*, that political and military officials hold about these weapons become the crucial factor in explaining why these weapons are acquired and how and when they will be used (for example, there probably are vigorous debates in Iran over whether acquiring nuclear weapons would provide greater or less security, and in India there are debates over whether threatening nuclear use would improve or diminish its regional power and international standing).[3] This is true even in countries such as Pakistan, where consensus formed quickly and conclusively on the need for nuclear weapons.

Zulfiqar Ali Bhutto was the first Pakistani official openly to call for nuclear weapons. In 1965, when he was Foreign Minister in President Ayub Khan's cabinet, he proclaimed: "If India developed an atomic bomb, we too will develop one even if we have to eat grass or leaves or to remain hungry, because there is no conventional alternative to the atomic bomb."[4] Although every civilian and military leader that followed Bhutto has safeguarded Pakistan's nuclear weapons capability, there always has been a conspicuous ambiguity concerning the exact role this capability would play, beyond providing a "nuclear deterrent" against Indian conventional or nuclear attack.[5] When it comes to the specific political and military uses of Pakistan's nuclear weapons, however, Pakistani officials appear to be much more uncertain, innovative, and opportunistic than U.S. or Russian officials ever have been. The range of roles that Pakistanis believe their nuclear weapons can play is much wider than that envisioned by most other nuclear powers.

This paper describes how Pakistan's civilian and military officials view their country's nuclear weapons. In contrast to the nearly uniform conception held by U.S. and Russian officials and experts during the Cold War of nuclear weapons as instruments for strategic deterrence, Pakistani leaders have conceived of at least eight separate uses for Pakistan's nuclear capability. Militarily, Pakistan's nuclear weapons have been viewed as: (1) "last-resort" weapons to prevent the loss of Pakistan's territory or the military defeat of the Pakistan armed forces, (2) deterrents to Indian conventional military attack, and (3) instruments that permit and facilitate low-intensity conflict against India. Politically, they have been considered as: (1) instruments for nation-building, (2) tools for domestic political and civil–military competition, (3) symbols of defiance of Western influence and of Pakistan's leadership within groups of regional and Islamic states, and (4) devices to draw international attention to the Kashmir issue. Finally, there may be a more controversial "commercial" view about Pakistan's nuclear weapons, materials, and technology as potential goods to be sold or bartered for acquiring foreign exchange and/or for promoting the causes of friendly states or non-state movements. A ninth view might be the ability to access foreign assistance both to develop more sophisticated deterrent capabilities (which are technologically acquisitive) and to make sure that nuclear capability is accompanied by economic growth so that the chances of misuse or commercial sale are lowered. Below, I describe what prominent Pakistanis have thought and tried to do about the political, military, and commercial uses of their nuclear weapons. I also suggest several ways in which Pakistan's nuclear uses affect U.S. security interests.

Uses of Pakistan's Nuclear Weapons

A caveat is in order. Because of the secrecy in which it is shrouded, Pakistan's nuclear use doctrine is not easy to describe. In 2002, Zafar Iqbal Cheema observed: "Pakistan did not have a nuclear *declaratory*, deployment, or employment doctrine before May 1998."[6] Cheema maintains that the Pakistan military began formulating such plans only after the country's May 1998 nuclear tests. Although Pakistan subsequently disclosed the basic features of its nuclear command and control organization,[7] no official spokesperson has declared exactly how Pakistan plans to use its nuclear weapons. Pakistani Foreign Minister Abdul Sattar's assertion that "minimum nuclear deterrence will remain the guiding principle of our nuclear strategy" is about as much as any government official will reveal.[8] In fact, General Khalid Kidwai, director of Pakistan's Strategic Plans Division (SPD), the military organization created in 1999 to oversee the development and employment of nuclear weapons, affirmed to a pair of Italian physicists last year that Pakistan would not make public a nuclear doctrine, as India did in August 1999.[9] Therefore, what follows is an interpretive analysis of the uses Pakistanis have conceived for their nuclear arsenal—uses that serve personal, organizational, political, and military interests.

MILITARY USES OF PAKISTAN'S NUCLEAR WEAPONS

Pakistan's principal motivation for acquiring nuclear weapons was Prime Minister Zulfiqar Ali Bhutto's desire to have a means for ensuring Pakistan's national security against an increasingly powerful adversary without having to rely on Western military assistance, which during the 1965 and 1971 wars proved to be unreliable. Bhutto and senior Pakistani military officials believed that nuclear weapons could help Pakistan's armed forces overcome the growing disparity in conventional military capabilities with India. And they could be developed largely indigenously, with some financial support from Saudi Arabia and Libya and technical assistance from China and North Korea (the last having helped build Ghauri, Pakistan's first ballistic missile nuclear delivery system).[10] As the nuclear weapons development program progressed, and as Pakistan's strategic environment evolved, Pakistani military leaders devised at least three strategic uses for their nuclear arsenal.

Last-Resort Weapons to Prevent Military Defeat or Loss of Territory

If Pakistan were unable to deter an attack by Indian armed forces, its nuclear weapons would be used to prevent India from destroying Pakistan's armed forces and/or from occupying significant portions of Pakistani territory. This objective has been central to Pakistani nuclear policy for decades. As early as December 1974, Prime Minister Zulfiqar Ali Bhutto said: "Ultimately, if our backs are to the wall and we have absolutely no option, in that event, this decision about going nuclear will have to be taken."[11] More recently, General Kidwai reportedly stated that Pakistani nuclear weapons would be used only "if the very existence of Pakistan as a state is at stake." Kidwai elaborated: "Nuclear weapons are aimed solely at India. In case that deterrence fails, they will be used if:

a. India attacks Pakistan and conquers a large part of its territory (space threshold);
b. India destroys a large part either of its land or air forces (military threshold);
c. India proceeds to the economic strangling of Pakistan (economic strangling);
d. India pushes Pakistan into political destabilization or creates a large-scale internal subversion in Pakistan (domestic destabilization)."[12]

In April 2002, after Indian and Pakistani forces had mobilized for war, President Musharraf affirmed that Pakistan was ready to use its nuclear weapons if it came under serious threat from India. Musharraf stated in an interview published on April 7 in the German magazine *Der Spiegel*: "Nuclear weapons are the last resort. I am optimistic and confident that we can defend ourselves with conventional means, even though the Indians are buying up the most modern weapons in a megalomaniac frenzy." Nuclear weapons could be used, Musharraf said: "If Pakistan is threatened with extinction, then the pressure of our countrymen would be so big that this option, too, would have to be considered." In a crisis, he said, the atomic bomb also had to be part of the calculation.[13]

There should be no doubt that President Musharraf and every other senior Pakistan government and military official believes that the primary use for Pakistan's nuclear weapons is to prevent the destruction of Pakistan by India. Exactly what kinds of Indian actions these officials would interpret as posing an existential threat is more difficult to ascertain with certainty. General Kidwai's explanation that Pakistan would employ nuclear weapons if any of four existential threats (territorial, military, economic, and political) were to materialize seems credible. But it also is very vague. Kidwai almost certainly intended the vagueness so as to enhance Pakistani deterrence. If he, or other officials, were any more explicit, India could adjust the scope of its military operations accordingly. By not specifying the precise Indian actions that would cause Pakistan to use nuclear weapons, Pakistani planners are able to create uncertainty in the minds of Indian officials regarding how far they can press Pakistan on the battlefield.[14]

Deterrent to Conventional Military Attack

An often-stated objective of Pakistan's nuclear weapons policy is to deter conventional military attack by Indian armed forces. Faced with a two-to-one disadvantage in most categories of military capability, this is an understandable concern. A declassified 1984 U.S. intelligence report assessed that, immediately after India's first nuclear test, Pakistan calculated that nuclear weapons were required to deter Indian conventional military attack:

> In about 1974, the strategic implications of a Pakistani nuclear weapon were seriously addressed by the military, which reasoned that since Pakistan was extremely vulnerable to a perceived Indian nuclear weapons program, the mutual possession of nuclear weapons not only was an effective deterrent at the nuclear level but also would lead to the avoidance of war between states that possessed such weapons. Therefore, went the rationale, a small nuclear program would enable the Pakistanis to do in nuclear terms what their ground and air forces could not do in conventional terms: threaten to punish any Indian attack so severely that consideration of such an attack would be deterred from the onset.[15]

Pakistani military officials emphasize that effective deterrence is based on a clearly communicated capability and willingness to use nuclear weapons as well as a robust conventional military posture. In their view, one is ineffective without the other. In fact, current defense strategy seems to rest on the belief that nuclear weapons permit the conventional military deterrence of Indian aggression. According to this logic, if India attacks, Pakistan will counterattack with conventional forces, both sides will inflict damage on the other, and India will be forced to refrain from escalating the conflict out of a fear of Pakistan's nuclear response.[16] Former Army Chief General Mirza Aslam Beg summed up this strategic concept in a 1999 article:

Nuclear deterrence alone cannot ensure security to Pakistan unless it is backed by an ideological propriety, aggressive diplomacy, and a viable conventional capability enjoying an optimum correlation of forces with India and adjusted correctly to the required level of operational balance. . . . Whenever India has attempted to impair this operational balance in its favor, Pakistan had to quickly restore it. In other words, Pakistan's security hinges on the overall operational balance achieved through conventional and minimal nuclear deterrence.[17]

Pakistan's acquisition of nuclear weapons in the mid- to late 1980s actually permitted then Army Chief General Mirza Aslam Beg to pursue the more aggressive conventional military doctrine of "strategic riposte" (a quick and devastating counterattack) to deter Indian aggression. Beg believed that the deterrent effect of nuclear weapons made the risks of strategic riposte acceptable. Recently, Beg has argued that the riposte, or "offensive-defense" doctrine he introduced, "which made a radical departure from stereotyped maneuvers and the self-defeating concept of holding formations," provides for effective deterrence "even in an environment where they may be outnumbered."[18]

The widespread conviction that Pakistan's nuclear capability is required to augment its conventional military deterrence of Indian conventional attack is reinforced by the common perception among Pakistani elites that Pakistan's nuclear capability has deterred attacks by India on at least six occasions—in 1984–85, 1986–87, 1990, 1998, 1999, and 2001–2. Ghulam Ishaq Khan asserted on July 23, 1993, shortly after being forced out of the presidency by Prime Minister Nawaz Sharif, that Indian Prime Minister Indira Gandhi had ordered an attack against Pakistan in early November 1984, but that the attack had been deterred by Pakistan's nuclear capability (and complicated by Mrs. Gandhi's assassination, which occurred ten days before the planned attack).[19] In October 1999 former Foreign Minister Agha Shahi, current Foreign Minister Abdul Sattar, and retired Air Force Commander in Chief Air Marshall Zulfiqar Ali Khan wrote that nuclear threats had deterred India from launching conventional attacks on at least three occasions.

The first episode was the one reported by Ishaq Khan, when India had planned air attacks against Pakistan's Kahuta uranium-enrichment plant. The second was during India's BRASSTACKS military operation, in which the authors claimed India had planned military operations to sever Pakistan's southern Sindh state from the rest of the country. The third case was in April–May 1990 when, faced with a deteriorating security situation in

Kashmir, the Indian military had recommended air raids on militant training camps in Pakistan-held Kashmir.[20]

Shahi, Ali Khan, and Sattar also wrote that Pakistan's nuclear-deterrence posture helped prevent the 1999 Kargil conflict from erupting into general war, as had occurred in 1965: "In 1965, actions provoked disproportionate reactions, with each side raising the ante leading to a general war that neither had contemplated. In 1999 India did not open a new front even in Kashmir, Pakistan did not bring its air force into action and the armed forces refrained from general mobilization. The crisis was contained."[21]

Another case of "successful deterrence" that is not widely written about, but is discussed in conversations with Pakistani officers, occurred at the time of the May 1998 nuclear tests. During this period, Pakistani leaders evidently feared that India's new BJP government, which was willing to act on its election pledge to test nuclear weapons, might also try to carry out another election manifesto pledge to conduct "hot-pursuit" military operations across the Line of Control in Kashmir. In response, Pakistan evidently fielded its Ghauri missiles in the days prior to its own nuclear tests, both to deter a possible Indian preventive military strike against its nuclear facilities and to deter Indian forces from trying to seize ground in Kashmir. Because no Indian attack took place, some Pakistani observers regard this as another case of successful deterrence.

Similar claims, that Pakistan "deterred" Indian plans to attack in the early winter and summer of 2002, have cropped up in the Pakistani media.[22] This interpretation gains even more credibility in light of President Musharraf's statement, on December 30, 2002, that war with India was averted because of his repeated warnings that if Indian forces crossed the border, Pakistan's response would not be confined to conventional warfare. Musharraf did not specifically mention the threat of nuclear weapons in his speech to an army corps reunion in Karachi, but he did state that he had been prepared to take severe measures at the height of 2002 crisis: "In my meetings with various world leaders, I conveyed my personal message to Indian Prime Minister Vajpayee that the moment Indian forces cross the Line of Control and the international border, then they should not expect a conventional war from Pakistan." Musharraf added: "I believe my message was effectively conveyed to Mr. Vajpayee."[23] Despite the fact that war was only narrowly averted in 2002, Pakistani military planners now appear to have even more confidence in their ability to manage the risks of conventional nuclear deterrence.[24] The assertion that Pakistan's nuclear capability has deterred several Indian military attacks since 1973 does have some critics, including a few retired military officers,[25] but dissenting voices are few and far between.

Evidently concerned about Pakistan's plans to use nuclear weapons in response to Indian conventional strikes, India tried to undercut this option by announcing a policy of no-first-use of nuclear weapons in the summer of 1998 and encouraging Pakistan to do the same.[26] Because it relies on nuclear options to deter conventional attack, Pakistan refused to adopt a no-first-nuclear use policy, and instead raised the idea that India and Pakistan should agree to a "no first use of force" policy, to apply to conventional as well as nuclear strikes.[27]

Pakistan's military approach to employing nuclear weapons thus rests on a calculation of its vulnerability to India's conventional and nuclear forces, and even of India's possible use of non-military instruments to threaten Pakistan's territorial integrity, political stability, and economic viability. Armed with few viable defense options apart from its nuclear capability, and worried about such wide-ranging threats, Pakistan is likely to continue to embrace a flexible and non-specified doctrine for using nuclear weapons. Agha Shahi summarized the logic underlying this approach in February 2002:

Chief Executive General Musharraf has made it clear that Pakistan will resort to the use of nuclear weapons only as a last resort if its security is threatened. What would be the moment of last resort would be difficult to precisely define, given the asymmetry in conventional as well as nuclear arms in relation to its lack of geographic depth. Whether a limited war imposed by India would warrant Pakistan's nuclear response would turn on the scale and gravity of the threat to Pakistan's existence. In these circumstances . . . a policy of ambiguity would appear to be best for Pakistan's security. Spelling out its nuclear doctrine would detract from the imperative of uncertainty about when a nuclear strike is to be resorted to. Also, not precluding first strike as a last resort would . . . reinforce maximally credible nuclear deterrence by raising the threshold of Indian calculation of unacceptable nuclear risk.[28]

These remarks, presented by a former foreign minister to a quasi-official international conference, appear to be the most definitive statement of the Pakistan government's concept of military nuclear use.

FACILITATORS OF LOW-INTENSITY CONFLICT

Below I discuss how Pakistan has tried to "use" its nuclear weapons to draw international attention to the Kashmir dispute. Here, I describe a similar strategy: the use of Pakistan's nuclear capability to facilitate low-intensity military conflict in Kashmir. The difference is subtle but important. The political use described below is not necessarily associated with Pakistani military action. Here, Pakistani military action is made possible by its possession of nuclear weapons and the perception of India's reluctance to risk nuclear war over relatively minor stakes. The intended outcome of Pakistan's military maneuvers could be the internationalization of the Kashmir issue or it could be taking territory previously held by India. In the 1999 Kargil crisis, it apparently was both.[29]

In the case of Kargil, Pakistani officials evidently believed that their nuclear weapons could be used according to the logic of the stability-instability paradox, a theoretical proposition derived by U.S. defense analysts: If one (or both) of two nuclear-armed rivals believes that nuclear war cannot be fought to a meaningful victory, and if it deems that the other side would dare not risk nuclear retaliation over a relatively minor bilateral dispute, then it might be tempted to apply a small measure of military force in the hope of altering the territorial or political status quo.[30] In a December 1998 conference in Islamabad, Pakistani scholars and military officials told me quite clearly that they believed that the new strategic environment created in the wake of the Indian and Pakistani nuclear tests permitted the Pakistan armed forces to employ "a small measure of military force" to alter the political and territorial status quo in Kashmir.

Of course, such thinking is not new among Pakistani military planners. In his classic 1984 study of the Pakistan army, Stephen Cohen assessed that "a Pakistani bomb, besides neutralizing an assumed Indian nuclear force, would provide the umbrella under which Pakistan could reopen the Kashmir issue. A Pakistani nuclear capability would paralyze not only the Indian nuclear decision, but also Indian conventional forces, and a bold Pakistani strike to liberate Kashmir might go unchallenged if Indian leadership was indecisive."[31] The army's wishful thinking that Cohen described before Pakistan had a significant nuclear weapons capability became more of a strategic reality as both India and Pakistan took steps to weaponize their nuclear forces. A senior general of the Indian army explained why: "What the nuclear capability does is to make sure that the old scenarios of Indian armour crossing the Sukkur barrage over the Indus [River] and slicing Pakistan into two are a thing of the past."[32] If conventional war had become too risky due to the new nuclear reality in South Asia, as Pakistani military planners evidently concluded, then they were confronted with a historic opportunity to take direct but limited action to revise the territorial and political status quo in Kashmir. General Musharraf himself revealed this perspective in April 1999 when he was army chief. He stated that in the aftermath of the nuclear tests, the possibility of a conventional war was virtually zero, but that the possibility of a proxy war had increased.[33]

What precise political and military objectives Pakistani officials hoped to achieve in Kargil, how exactly they believed nuclear weapons would aid their cause, and what lessons were drawn in the aftermath of the Kargil conflict are questions to which we have no definitive answers. Therefore, it is impossible to discern how Pakistani views about the stability-instability paradox have changed and whether the Pakistan army's interest in using nuclear weapons to facilitate low-intensity conflict remains intact. Judging by the Musharraf government's public statements, however, it appears that some reassessment of the assumptions that led to Kargil has occurred.

POLITICAL USES OF PAKISTAN'S NUCLEAR WEAPONS

Nuclear Weapons and Nation-Building

It would be mistaken to suggest that Pakistan's nuclear weapons were developed for reasons other than to secure the sovereignty and territorial integrity of the state; but they have had many important secondary uses. Governing a country where the nation-building process is far from complete, Pakistan's civilian and military leaders often tried to play the "nuclear card" (as well as the "Kashmir card") to enhance national unity, patriotism, and support for the government. A long-time proponent of Pakistan's nuclear program, Zulfiqar Ali Bhutto often did so to strengthen his own political popularity and to promote national unity, goals which he often conflated.

Bhutto's outspoken support for Pakistan's nuclear weapons program predated his assumption of power in December 1971. As Minister for Fuel, Power, and Natural Resources in the early 1960s, Bhutto concluded deals for Pakistan's first nuclear research and power reactors and sent hundreds of Pakistanis abroad for nuclear training. Coupled with his efforts to establish Pakistan's nuclear industry, Bhutto also called attention to India's growing nuclear progress and proposed that Pakistan immediately undertake a nuclear weapons program. But when Bhutto pressed the issue with other members of the cabinet, their response was that "India was too poor to go nuclear." Bhutto reported: "The former president [Ayub Khan] even said that by the time India had a nuclear device, such weapons would be so common that it would be possible for Pakistan to buy it from the market."[34] Undeterred, Bhutto continued to "mobilize nuclear nationalism" in his struggle for power against President Ayub.[35]

When Bhutto assumed power, he highlighted Pakistan's nuclear program as a source of national pride and patriotism, sentiments that were in short supply after the loss of East Pakistan in the 1971 Bangladesh war. In fact, Bhutto initiated several large-scale industrial projects—the Karachi Steel Mill, the Indus Highway, the Lowari Pass Tunnel, the Bhutto Sports and Culture Institute, and the nuclear program—to instill national self-esteem and popular support for his policies. Bhutto had specific political objectives for each project, but together they were viewed as grand, populist "solutions" to Pakistan's political and economic problems.[36] Of all these initiatives, Bhutto boasted the most about the nuclear program, going so far as to promise, "Pakistan will have an atom bomb within two years."[37]

Bhutto's successor, General Zia ul-Haq, was more cautious with respect to providing public information about the nuclear program. He realized that because nuclear nonproliferation had moved to the top of the international political agenda after India's 1974 nuclear test, the completion of Pakistan's highly enriched uranium (HEU) development program required strict secrecy, although he consistently maintained that the acquisition of nuclear technology was a "matter of life and death for Pakistan."[38]

In contrast, Zia's successors, Benazir Bhutto and Nawaz Sharif, often raised the nuclear issue to heighten national unity and increase their hold on power. After India conducted a series of nuclear weapons tests on May 11 and 13, 1998 Prime Minister Nawaz Sharif decided to follow suit. Sharif probably had decided from day one to test, but sought to portray himself as undecided as a way to obtain more support from the United States. Sharif's carefully crafted "indecision" created the desired appearance that he was being forced to test because of domestic political pressures (and possibly to bring the leadership of the armed forces along with his decision). In a meeting with newspaper editors after the Indian tests, one Urdu-language daily editor reportedly told Sharif: "There is going to be an explosion soon. It will either be a Pakistani nuclear test or you being blown out of office!"[39] After Sharif approved Pakistan's nuclear tests, he played up the nuclear issue as much as possible, to strengthen the population's pride, unity, and support for his government.

Today, however, even though nuclear weapons remain a source of national pride, the Musharraf government has not brandished the nuclear card as a political instrument.[40] Musharraf's public approach to nuclear weapons became even more restrained after the 1999 Kargil conflict, and particularly after the military buildup that followed the September 11, 2001 terrorist attacks against the United States and the December 13, 2001 attack against the Indian Parliament in New Delhi.

Tools for Domestic Political and Civil–Military Competition

In the current political environment in Pakistan, the nuclear issue seems to have lost some of its political salience. Not only has the Musharraf government deliberately refrained from playing the nuclear political card, no opposition political party, with the exception of Jamaat-e-Islami, uses the nuclear issue to score points against either the government or rival political parties.[41] Of course, this was not always the case.

Zulfiqar Ali Bhutto used the nuclear issue to increase his personal popularity with the electorate and to strengthen his hand against the military, which was his main competition for control of the country. Although Bhutto did increase the country's conventional defense capability,[42] he "humiliated the army as a matter of state policy."[43] Bhutto moved some of the more important personnel functions from the Army General Headquarters to the Prime Minister's Secretariat, reorganized the Ministry of Defense, created a Joint Chiefs of Staff Headquarters, retired several officers prematurely, including the army chief, General Gul Hassan Khan, and in January 1972, placed the Pakistani Atomic Energy Commission under his direct control.[44] Establishing Pakistan's nuclear weapons development program as a civilian rather than military effort served Bhutto's general strategy of reducing the role of the military in strategic affairs and in domestic politics.[45] Bhutto played the nuclear card until the very end. In his last political testament, smuggled out of his death cell, Bhutto contended that General Zia ul-Haq had ousted him from power because of U.S. pressure to terminate Pakistan's nuclear weapons program.[46]

Upon assuming power in 1978, General Zia "de-politicized" the nuclear program and placed it under military control.[47] As described below, Zia's rare references to Pakistan's nuclear program were designed to serve national security interests—deterring Indian military attack and gaining U.S. assistance—rather than to achieve domestic political objectives. When civilian rule was restored in 1988, however, the nuclear program again became politicized. Although there is little public information as to whether or how the nuclear program was exploited in the struggles of Benazir Bhutto and Nawaz Sharif to increase their power relative to that of the military,[48] there is ample evidence that they used the nuclear issue as political ammunition against one another.

Both political leaders played the nuclear card in two ways when they were in the opposition. First, before internal audiences, they emphasized their own roles in stewarding the nuclear program and accused the governing party of accepting costly limits (for example, suspension of HEU production, hints of agreeing to a nuclear test ban) on the nuclear program under external pressure. This approach caused Bhutto some difficulty when she was out of power. The U.S. Assistant Secretary of State for Public Affairs Margaret Tutwiler asked how Bhutto, who was visiting the United States in February 1991, squared her criticism of the Sharif government for its willingness to accept safeguards on a small nuclear reactor provided by China with her pledge before a joint session of the U.S. Congress in 1989 that Pakistan neither possessed nor had any intention of acquiring a nuclear capability. Bhutto replied that her criticism was not so much against safeguards as against those in Pakistan who had castigated her in the past for contemplating safeguards but were now ready to open up Pakistan's nuclear facilities to international inspection.[49]

Second, to external audiences, opposition leaders portrayed the ruling leader and party as reckless and irresponsible or as lacking control over the country's nuclear program. Benazir Bhutto claimed that she had been ousted from power in August 1990 in a "nuclear coup" that had been orchestrated by Army Chief General Mirza Aslam Beg and President Ghulam Ishaq Khan.[50] In March 1991, Salmann Taseer, an opposition legislator with Bhutto's Pakistan People's Party (PPP) stated:

If we [PPP legislators] resign, the army steps in. And once the army is directly in control, it may explode the [nuclear] bomb. The Americans are terrified of that. They hate Mirza Aslam Beg and are maligning him by calling him another Saddam. They are certain to put pressure on Mian Nawaz Sharif to behave himself. There are already serious tensions between the army and the Nawaz-Ishaq combine over

Kahuta. The Americans want it dismantled, and Ishaq and Nawaz appear willing to reduce its uranium enrichment capacity. The army cannot allow that to happen, which means that any situation can develop anytime.[51]

When they were out of power, Nawaz Sharif and other Pakistan Muslim League officials made similar remarks.

After Pakistan returned to military rule in October 1999, nuclear weapons ceased to play the prominent domestic political role they had earlier under the country's various civilian leaders. There probably are three reasons for this. First, the military's bona fides on defense matters generally are not questioned; its domestic agenda is. Therefore, President Musharraf must invoke political, social, and economic symbols, rather than defense and nuclear symbols, to increase his popularity and support for his political agenda. Second, as a professional military officer, Musharraf should be less inclined to exploit the nuclear issue for personal gain; he almost certainly regards nuclear weapons as a national security asset, not a domestic political instrument.[52] Finally, as is discussed below, after the surprisingly harsh international reaction to Pakistan's Kargil episode, Musharraf appears to have become more cautious in using the threat of nuclear war to gain international political mileage. In light of the national elections conducted in October 2002, Pakistan's nuclear program once again might be used by opportunistic politicians in domestic political and civil–military struggles. This dynamic will have a serious impact on the willingness of any government to accept restrictions on Pakistan's nuclear weapons capability.

SYMBOLS OF SELF-RELIANCE AND DEFIANCE

Pakistan's civilian and military leaders have used the nuclear issue to promote not only their personal or organizational interests but also the interests of Pakistan in international settings—particularly when these various objectives coincide. Once again, Zulfiqar Ali Bhutto paved the way. Bhutto constantly sought to increase Pakistan's—and his personal—leadership regionally, in the nonaligned movement, and among the world's Islamic countries. Pan-Islamism was a particularly important theme to Bhutto. According to Dr. Leili Bakhtiyar, a college friend of Bhutto's, from early in his life Bhutto "had this fervor of pan-Islamism." He often spoke of his dream of turning a unified bloc of all Islamic nations into a "major force against the great powers." He was "fanatical about it."[53] During Bhutto's association with Pakistan's nuclear weapons program, from the early 1960s to 1977, the gap between the five nuclear powers and the rest of the world was pronounced and represented "nuclear colonialism" or "nuclear apartheid" to many in the developing and Islamic world. Bhutto was adept at speaking to these feelings of resentment, and he frequently emphasized Pakistan's nuclear weapons program—an area where Pakistan had a real comparative advantage over other developing states—as a reason for Pakistan to play the leading international role to which he aspired.[54]

Bhutto's aggressive efforts to carve out a regional or "Islamic" leadership role for himself and Pakistan, coupled with his outspoken views about the need to develop nuclear weapons, created concerns in the West about an "Islamic bomb." In his July 1978 political testament from his death cell, Bhutto wrote: "The Christian, Jewish and Hindu civilisations have this (nuclear) capability. The Communist powers also possess it. Only the Islamic civilisation is without it, but that position was about to change."[55] The claim that Western nonproliferation policies singled out Pakistan's nuclear program on religious or racial grounds has been a persistent theme in Pakistan since Bhutto made this statement. Abdul Qadeer Khan, who lately headed Pakistan's uranium enrichment effort, often made this allegation: "The Western countries . . . could not tolerate a Muslim country becoming their equal. . . . All Western countries including Israel are not only Pakistan's enemies but also enemies of Islam."[56] Associating Pakistan's nuclear weapons effort with the struggles of Islam, of "brown people," or of the Third World has become commonplace, although much less so under Pakistan's military rulers.

Zia continued his predecessor's policy of cultivating political support in the Islamic world, but in markedly different ways than Bhutto, especially with regard to the nuclear issue. Whereas Bhutto openly spoke of Pakistan's leadership role in the developing world and raised the specter of an "Islamic bomb," Zia refrained from any rhetorical posturing that would put an unwanted spotlight on Pakistan's covert nuclear weapons program. He was more interested in "quiet" cooperation with Saudi Arabia, the United Arab Emirates, and other Islamic states with which Pakistan had mutual political, social, and economic interests. Zia's emphasis on orthodox Islamization at home, and his own devout religious practices, endeared him to conservative Muslim leaders, who felt more comfortable with him than with Bhutto, whose hedonism and socialist rhetoric was not to their liking.

A strategy in which Zia followed Bhutto's lead, but much more effectively, was that of using Pakistan's nuclear program as bait to obtain U.S. military assistance. In response to India's 1974 nuclear test, Bhutto warned that if Pakistan failed to obtain "sufficient conventional weapons" to act as a "deterrent" against India's "nuclear blackmail," Pakistan would be forced to stop spending on conventional weapons and "make a big jump forward concentrating all its energy on acquiring the nuclear capability."[57] A few months later, as Bhutto was preparing to visit Washington to ask President Gerald Ford to lift the decade-long U.S. embargo on arms sales to Pakistan, he declared that Pakistan's nuclear weapons policy was "under constant review," the outcome of which would depend on U.S. assistance to help Pakistan obtain a conventional military capability sufficient to deter India.[58] Whereas Bhutto had won only a $100 million arms sales package, and had actually stiffened U.S. congressional and bureaucratic resolve to terminate Pakistan's bid to reprocess plutonium, Zia played the same strategy to perfection.

After the Soviet invasion of Afghanistan in December 1979 transformed Pakistan into a "frontline state," Zia exhibited his political mastery by persuading the United States to ignore Pakistan's nuclear program and to provide $3.2 billion in economic and military assistance to the anti-Communist nation. According to Zia's chief of staff, General K. M. Arif, U.S. Secretary of State Alexander Haig assured Zia that "Pakistan's nuclear program would not become the linchpin of the new relationship."[59] Rather than trying to exploit Pakistan's nuclear program to propel the country or himself into a leadership position, which was Bhutto's unremitting obsession, Zia was content to develop Pakistan's nuclear weapons capability, dispel U.S. concerns about this effort, and conclude deals that made Pakistan the third largest recipient of U.S. security assistance in the world. In this regard, President Musharraf shows every sign of following in Zia's footsteps.

Tools to Internationalize the Kashmir Issue

Concurrent with its drive to develop nuclear weapons, Pakistan has pursued various strategies to draw international attention to the political status of Indian-held Kashmir. In the aftermath of the 1971 India–Pakistan war and the ensuing 1972 Simla agreement, Pakistan introduced resolutions on Kashmir in various forums, including the United Nations, the Non-Aligned Movement, the Organization of Islamic Conference, and other governmental and non-governmental groups. Along with these diplomatic efforts, Pakistan has pursued two other strategies to internationalize Kashmir: direct support to Kashmiri political groups and militants, and political-military actions to introduce the threat of nuclear escalation into India–Pakistan crises over Kashmir. These two tracks came together in a dramatic way in the spring of 1990.

The law-and-order situation in Kashmir deteriorated drastically in the winter of 1989–90 and led to the partial mobilization of Indian and Pakistani forces along the Line of Control. In January 1990 Pakistan's foreign minister, Sahibzada Yakub Khan, traveled to New Delhi and issued what India's prime minister, V. P. Singh, and external affairs minister, I. K. Gujral, interpreted as a possible nuclear ultimatum.[60] Subsequent Indian intelligence reports indicated that "Pakistan had produced several nuclear weapons and that it would attempt to hit one or two targets in India with nuclear weapons at the very commencement of any armed conflict."[61] It cannot be established with available evidence how seriously Pakistan attempted to communicate a nuclear deterrent threat to India and "operationalize" its nuclear weapons at this time, but what is certain is that Pakistan initiated diplomatic and public affairs efforts to create the impression that Kashmir had become a nuclear flashpoint and that the West must become engaged in the Kashmir issue in order to avoid an eventual nuclear war.

One lesson that Pakistani officials evidently drew from the 1990 crisis was that the nuclear issue was their most effective device to attract international attention to Kashmir. Moeen Qureshi, who was Pakistan's caretaker prime minister in 1993, admitted forging a "close link between Kashmir and Pakistan's nuclear capability."[62] India clearly recognized this dynamic. A 1995 Indian intelligence report cited by India's Kargil Review Committee asserted that Pakistan had tried to "attract the attention of Western nations to the Kashmir issue using the threat of nuclear escalation."[63] Another Indian intelligence report prepared after the 1998 nuclear tests assessed: "Aware of the U.S. desire to secure the entry into force of the CTBT and their fear of a nuclear exchange which would further damage the nonproliferation regime, Pakistani strategists projected that in the post-test environment, Kashmir has emerged as the 'root' cause of tension, at the 'heart of the deteriorating situation' and the 'core' issue."[64] Although these assessments are not collaborated by official Pakistani sources, no evidence is available to discount them.

Although in the current environment President Musharraf still raises the prospect of nuclear war with India—as in his much-cited April 2000 interview published in Germany's *Der Spiegel* magazine—he has not associated this risk directly with the political status of Kashmir, as his civilian predecessors had done persistently. This apparent policy shift may result from his reading that the Bush administration is much less preoccupied with nuclear nonproliferation than was the Clinton administration, especially after the September 11 terrorist attacks. It probably also results from a lesson he drew from Pakistan's 1999 attempt to seize territory in the Kargil sector of Indian-held Kashmir, an action that Pakistani military planners apparently initiated to manipulate Western fears of nuclear escalation so as to prevent full-scale war from breaking out and to force international negotiations over the political status of Kashmir. A finding of India's Kargil Review Committee Report is that, "having failed to secure international mediation on Kashmir [in the wake of the 1998 nuclear tests], Pakistan seems to have resorted to adventurism. It committed aggression in Kargil by crudely violating the LOC, using its regular forces in civilian dress along with some Mujahideen. It was able to re-focus international attention on Kashmir but, much to its surprise, in a manner that was critical of its rash and unprovoked action in the wake of the Lahore Declaration."[65] If Musharraf drew the same lesson as the Kargil Commission reached, that "the international community is averse to allowing nuclear blackmail to alter the long-established status quo [in Kashmir],"[66] then this would explain Pakistan's newfound reluctance to engage in nuclear saber rattling over Kashmir, and, more generally, its shift in emphasis away from the political toward strictly military uses of nuclear weapons.

"COMMERCIAL" USE OF PAKISTAN'S NUCLEAR WEAPONS

The final potential use of Pakistan's nuclear weapons considered in this paper is one that troubles Western officials and analysts much more than their Pakistani counterparts: the provision of Pakistan's nuclear weapons, materials, and/or technology to foreign governments or non-state movements in exchange for money, military equipment, or other considerations. This potential use is also the one about which reliable information had been the most difficult to obtain. However, the revelations of late 2003 and early 2004 that Abdul Qadeer Khan, the popular "father" of Pakistan's nuclear bomb, had secretly provided multiple forms of nuclear assistance—including Pakistani designs for the fabrication of centrifuges (devices used to enrich uranium to bomb-grade levels), nuclear materials, and the actual blueprints for nuclear weapons—to Iran, Libya, and North Korea reveal the enormity of this problem.[67]

Even before the Abdul Qadeer Khan scandal became public knowledge, concerns about the proliferation of Pakistani nuclear capabilities had skyrocketed when it was reported that two Pakistani nuclear scientists had cooperated with Osama bin Laden's al-Qaeda organization and the Taliban. It was reported in March 2004 that a former Pakistani nuclear scientist suspected of links with Islamic extremists had met with Osama bin Laden twice in Afghanistan but had not revealed nuclear secrets, according to the man's son. Sultan Bashiruddin Mehmood, who worked for Pakistan's Atomic Energy Commission until his retirement in 1999, did not even tell his family about meeting Osama, his son, Dr. Azim Mehmood, claimed. The family had learned about the meetings, which occurred in 2000 and 2001, only after Pakistan security agencies detained Mr. Mehmood in October of 2001 to investigate possible ties with the al-Qaeda network and its efforts to obtain nuclear technology. U.S. officials reportedly had long been suspicious of Mr. Mehmood's contacts with bin Laden, according to Pakistani authorities.[68] As recently as December 30, 2002, Azim Mehmood reported that his father, Sultan Bashiruddin Mehmood, had been asked by Abu Bilal, an agent of Osama bin Laden, to come to Afghanistan to help al-Qaeda build nuclear weapons.[69] In April 2002, President Musharraf affirmed that there had been contact between his country's nuclear scientists and followers of Osama bin Laden. "But we know today that the scientists involved had only a very superficial knowledge and that the al-Qaeda terrorists did not come closer to their dream of building their own atomic bomb," he said.[70]

Conclusion

This essay has explained the different uses Pakistani officials have conceived for their country's nuclear weapons program. Five points stand out. Below, I summarize these points and offer my personal views as to how they affect U.S. security interests.

First, although many Pakistani politicians have played the "nuclear card" to enhance national unity, patriotism, and support for the government, their motivation almost always has been to increase their personal popularity. Nonetheless, the outcome of nearly four decades of these efforts is the close identification of pride, patriotism, independence, and even Islam with the country's nuclear weapons program. Although it is argued—correctly, I believe—that the popularity of nuclear weapons in Pakistan results from (1) a poorly informed public, (2) a succession of civilian and military governments that discouraged information sharing with the public on serious nuclear matters (such as their dangers or economic costs), and (3) repeated government assertions that nuclear weapons are vital to Pakistan's survival,[71] the fact remains that nuclear weapons are very, very popular in Pakistan. Even more than this intense popular support for a robust nuclear posture, the political uses of Pakistan's nuclear weapons also have served to redefine Pakistan's identity as the only Islamic state to possess nuclear weapons. My personal view is that this outcome is an understandable attribute of Pakistan's political culture and does not threaten U.S. security interests in South Asia.

Second, because of the salience of nuclear symbols among the population, Pakistan's civilian political leaders, whether in power or in opposition, will use the nuclear issue as a political instrument to gain power over one another and over the military. This makes it very difficult for any civilian leader to limit the nuclear program, or even to undertake commitments, such as signing the comprehensive test ban treaty, that could be portrayed as weak. For its part, the Pakistan armed forces are likely to play "nuclear politics" mainly when they believe the civilians are becoming soft on national defense. This dynamic is another understandable attribute of Pakistan's political culture, but it is more troubling from a U.S. perspective because it is one of the factors propelling the dangerous strategic arms race between India and Pakistan.

Third, because Pakistani elites—and many Western journalists and policy analysts—have claimed that nuclear weapons helped Pakistan deter attack in 1984–85, 1986–87, 1990, 1998, 1999, and 2001–2, this assertion is reinforced in the minds of the public, the military, and the political elites. This is completely understandable because nuclear deterrence is a "theory" that is easy to accept and difficult to falsify.[72] As a result, Pakistani officials are likely to maintain—if not increase—the prominence of nuclear weapons in their defense policy and to threaten nuclear use under a wide variety of conditions that could jeopardize Pakistan's national security. In this respect, it would be difficult to disagree with the Director of Central Intelligence:

"The chance of war between these two nuclear-armed states is higher than at any point since 1971. If India were to conduct large-scale offensive operations into Pakistani Kashmir, Pakistan might retaliate with strikes of its own in the belief that its nuclear deterrent would limit the scope of an Indian counterattack."[73] This certainly is a dangerous development from an American perspective. Strategic stability in South Asia will be shaped largely by the lessons political and military leaders draw about past crisis dynamics. Therefore, in order to formulate a potentially more accurate understanding of the operation of nuclear deterrence in recent India–Pakistan crises, a serious study or workshop involving American, Pakistani, and possibly even Indian analysts, could be of value.

Fourth, many Pakistani military officers and some civilian advisors apparently believed that nuclear weapons could be used to facilitate low-intensity conflict against India, as exemplified most prominently in the 1999 Kargil operation and in Pakistan's broader "forward strategy" in Kashmir.[74] Whether and in what way these beliefs may have been revised after the Kargil conflict and the 2001–2 military mobilization is unclear but incredibly important. Once again, this is of paramount importance to the future stability of South Asia. Here, also, it is advisable to examine in close detail the assumptions underpinning Pakistan's Kargil operation and the lessons drawn from that experience.

Finally, some well-placed Pakistanis who have access to nuclear weapons, materials, or know-how may conceive of a particularly troubling nuclear use. Motivated by either financial or ideological considerations (or both), they might help other states or non-state groups obtain nuclear weapons, materials, or technology. Because this "nuclear use" would jeopardize Pakistan's ability to employ nuclear weapons for its own national security needs, one hopes that the Pakistani government would be able to prevent such behavior. In my view, this is a most disturbing threat to U.S. security interests both in South Asia and globally, and every effort should be made to work with Pakistani authorities to reduce the likelihood of further nuclear proliferation emanating out of South Asia.

TWELVE

Coercive Diplomacy in a Nuclear Environment: The December 13 Crisis

Rajesh M. Basrur

The terrorist attack on India's Parliament on December 13, 2001, not only left a dozen dead (including five terrorists) and a nation horrified, but marked an important turning point in India's post-1998 strategic doctrine. The military buildup that India subsequently initiated on its border with Pakistan represented the emergence of a new dimension in its understanding of the role of nuclear weapons in shaping its conflict with that country. Adherence to the oft-stated maxim that nuclear weapons ruled out war was superseded by a determination to break out of India's perceived strategic paralysis and to exploit its nuclear capabilities effectively for a clear-cut political end. That end was to compel Pakistan to drop its support for terrorist groups fighting the Indian government in the Kashmir Valley. India's strategic doctrine as a nuclear-armed state was thus extended from a focus on deterrence alone to encompass compellence. This resort to coercive diplomacy was accomplished not by the posing of a direct nuclear threat, but by two other means: first, by asserting the military advantage India derived from a favorable nuclear-cum-conventional asymmetry; and second, by creating in a third party—the United States—sufficient fear of a nuclear war breaking out to induce it to intervene on behalf of Indian interests. Below, I trace the evolution of this two-pronged strategy and its practice in the December 13 crisis, evaluate its effectiveness in terms of the objectives it sought to achieve, and assess its implications for the future of the region.

Kargil, Terrorism, and India's Search for Strategic Space

In the pre-nuclear era India's fractious relationship with Pakistan—centered on the protracted tussle over Kashmir—encompassed three wars (1947–48, 1965, and 1971).[1] Following India's first nuclear test in 1974, the antagonists remained hostile, perhaps primarily on account of the change in the regional balance after the 1971 war, which cost Pakistan its eastern territory and more than half its population. However, tensions arose again in the 1980s, as Pakistan found two ways to overcome its relative weakness: the gradual development of its own nuclear capability, and covert support to secessionists (first in Punjab and later in Kashmir) who had launched a violent terrorist movement against the Indian government. Since then, the combination of creeping nuclearization and ethnic militancy has intertwined with the protracted India–Pakistan conflict to engender a series of crises, in 1986–87, 1990, 1999, and the one under discussion.[2] Though none of these crises has involved the use of direct nuclear threats by one to coerce the other, or even the serious threat of an imminent nuclear war, every crisis has had an inescapable nuclear element to it, ranging from the possibility of attacks on civilian nuclear facilities to that of an inadvertent nuclear war.

The Kargil conflict, the first military confrontation after the regional rivals officially declared their nuclear-weapon capabilities in 1998, had a profound impact on Indian thinking about the relationship between nuclear weapons and war.[3] In the aftermath of the 1998 tests, Indian leaders had tended to view the strategic situation in the region as radically altered by the establishment of mutual deterrence, which, in their view, overrode Pakistan's revanchist objectives and reinforced the subcontinental status quo. The Pakistani intrusion into Kargil and the extensive fighting that ensued came as a shock. Prime Minister Atal Behari Vajpayee of India had invested considerable political capital in extending an olive branch to Nawaz Sharif, his counterpart, and the knowledge that their joint Lahore Declaration (February 1999), which envisaged nuclear risk-reduction measures, had coincided with Pakistani infiltration into Kargil contributed strongly to a perception of being "stabbed in the back."[4] Subsequent attempts to work out a deal—notably at the Agra summit between Vajpayee and General Pervez Musharraf, whose overthrow of Nawaz Sharif was also a fallout of Kargil—failed to bring about a compromise. While India insisted that Pakistan cease its support for "cross-border terrorism," Pakistan was equally adamant that India acknowledge Kashmir as the "core issue" between them. Neither side would budge. In the meantime, Indian frustrations continued to rise. While at the military level, India and Pakistan deterred each other with nuclear weapons, at the sub-conventional level, Pakistan was in a position to exploit the "stability-instability paradox" to its own advantage through unremitting support for Kashmiri secessionists engaged in a rising tide of terrorist violence against civilian and military targets in India.[5] The hijacking of an Indian Airlines aircraft to Kandahar by Pakistan-based terrorists in December 1999 and the forced release of their associates from Indian jails was a particularly painful episode that added sharply to the perception of frustration and helplessness. To Indian eyes, it seemed that their country was strategically paralyzed and unable to counter the Pakistani strategy effectively.

Indian thinking struggled to define a strategic response that might enable India to break out of its strategic paralysis. The discourse steadily veered away from a search for political solutions to a quest for an appropriate means of projecting force against an intransigent Pakistan. The options aired included hot pursuit of terrorists into Pakistani territory, limited strikes or special operations missions against terrorist camps in Pakistan, and a vague and undefined conception of "limited war."[6] The last, by virtue of its open-ended implications, drew considerable attention. In January 2000, Defense Minister George Fernandes asserted that nuclear weapons "can deter only the use of nuclear weapons, but not all and any war," and that Kargil had demonstrated that Indian forces "can fight and win a limited war, at a time and place chosen by the aggressor."[7] While admitting that under the nuclear shadow there were "definite limitations if escalation across the nuclear threshold was to be avoided," Fernandes claimed that conventional war "has not been made obsolete by nuclear weapons."[8] The declaration that limited war was feasible was not entirely without portent. During the Kargil conflict itself, India had initiated initial mobilization for a possible war on a wider scale.[9]

Nevertheless, there were serious constraints that prevented recourse to conventional fighting on even a limited scale. In the backdrop was the constant awareness, expressed in Fernandes's statement above, that any fighting between Indian and Pakistani forces had the potential to escalate into nuclear conflict. Besides, Kargil had underscored what was widely referred to as the "sanctity" of the Line of Control (LoC) in Kashmir and, by implication, the entire border. If anything, India's circumspection in not crossing the LoC despite grave provocation had earned it much international support, whereas Pakistan's violation of the LoC had drawn worldwide criticism and strong pressure from the United States. Indeed, this had been one of the lessons of the Kargil conflict for both India and Pakistan.[10] Under the circumstances, it was difficult to envisage a serious violation of the LoC or the border without undoing the international goodwill obtained by India's restraint during the Kargil conflict. Thus, the tension between the unacceptability of strategic paralysis and the problems inherent in attempting to break out of it remained unresolved.

The emergence of a changed global environment and of more compelling regional circumstances pushed Indian thinking and action in a more assertive direction. The dramatic events of September 11, 2001, and the chain reaction they released around the world were instrumental in crystallizing the new Indian strategy that had germinated after the Kargil conflict. The new environment was dominated by a global revulsion against terrorism, which provided India with a general setting conducive to anti-terrorist action. Second, Pakistan itself was suspect in the eyes of many because of its role in bringing the atavistic Taliban to power in Afghanistan. Its own emergence as a center of radical Islam added to its negative image and strengthened India's case. Third, the U.S.-led war in Afghanistan facilitated India's shift to a proactive policy against Pakistan-sponsored terrorism. While the United States and its allies naturally worried about the risk of a nuclear conflagration, they could hardly deny that India's stand was not different from the cause célèbre that they themselves had come to espouse. Fourth, the local impact of September 11 was to generate an inspired intensification of terrorist activity in India.

Two specific events—an attack on the Jammu and Kashmir legislative assembly on October 1, and a similar attempt on the Indian Parliament on December 13—galvanized Indian decision makers into action. The December 13 attack provided not only the provocation, but the opportunity as well. The gravity of the attack is often underestimated: though no member of India's Parliament was harmed, the terrorists could have caused immense damage if they had been able to penetrate well into the building, which they came close to doing.[11] There were at the time some two hundred Members of Parliament inside, including the Vice President, the Speaker of the Lok Sabha (the lower house), the Home Minister, the Defense Minister, and other members of the cabinet. Besides, by attacking Parliament, the terrorists had struck at the heart of India's democracy and the primary symbol of its nationhood. As a result, India's commitment to retaliate was very strong. This was the proverbial last straw.

The military buildup that followed on the India–Pakistan border embodied a major strategic shift that had been in the making since Kargil. As C. Raja Mohan, a former member of the National Security Advisory Board (NSAB), observed: "There is a growing belief in New Delhi that the time has come to call Pakistan's nuclear bluff. If it does not, India places itself in permanent vulnerability to cross-border terrorism from Pakistan."[12] As one commentator noted some months later, India, too, was a state dissatisfied with the status quo, and it was ready to play the stability-instability game and try to reshape the rules in its own favor.[13] This required a conceptual shift in the way Indian decision makers thought about the utilization of armed force in a nuclear environment.

December 13 and the Practice of Compellence

The theory and practice of compellence, or coercive diplomacy, have been the subject of considerable discussion and debate. Analysts have investigated its diverse components, including its relationship with crises, deterrence, and escalation in the entire range of conflict relationships, and specifically in the context of nuclear dyads.[14] Investigation of the present case can draw valuable lessons from these and other writings. At the same time, it is important to bear in mind that there are elements of uniqueness here, notably the occurrence of military confrontation between two emergent nuclear powers and the use of a trilateral strategy of deterrence that draws in a third state in order to try and influence the outcome. Compellence is defined here as "an attempt by policy makers in state A to force, by threat and/or by application of sanction, policy makers in state B to comply with demands of state A, including but not limited to retract actions already taken."[15] The distinction between deterrence and compellence is important.[16] First, deterrence attempts to prevent an adversary's action, while compellence requires the adversary to retract or initiate an action. Second, and in reverse, deterrence does not require the state attempting it to initiate an action, but compellence does. Third, deterrence has no time frame, but is indefinite, whereas compellence involves, or at least implies, a deadline or short time frame.

India's post–December 13 strategy, which involved a massive conventional buildup reinforced by the assertion of nuclear asymmetry, involved elements of both deterrence and compellence. The basic thrust of the strategy, which backed the demand that Pakistan cease support for cross-border terrorism, was that India was ready to go to conventional war, in which it enjoyed an advantageous balance of forces, and that Pakistan could not take recourse to a nuclear first strike because of India's capacity to inflict far greater damage with its own nuclear forces. The compellence component of the strategy involved the demand for Pakistani action (reversing its support for terrorists) on pain of punishment, the Indian initiation of action (the military buildup), and the sense of urgency caused by the rapidity of the buildup (which approximated a deadline-based ultimatum).[17] Its deterrence component was the assertion that India's nuclear advantage ruled out a Pakistani first-strike and, since India adhered to a no-first-use posture, any nuclear conflict at all. A compellence threat can be projected either through a "try-and-see" approach, in which a state takes one step at a time and waits for a response each time, or by means of a "gradual turning of the screw," which escalates the threat by means of a rapid succession of actions.[18] The latter case involves the "decomposition" of the compellence threat into a series of calibrated actions accompanied by a parallel series of verbal statements designed to build pressure on the target state.[19] India utilized the "gradual turning of the screw" method.

BILATERAL COMPELLENCE: PAKISTAN

The ten-month-long military confrontation between India and Pakistan began late in December 2001 and concluded with India's decision to withdraw its forces in October 2002. The threat of war was high in the early stages (January–February 2002), subsided a little thereafter, and peaked again in the summer (May–June 2002). There followed another lull, as the confrontation stretched out until India conducted elections in Jammu and Kashmir (September–October 2002). On October 16, India announced its decision to withdraw forces from the border—but not from the LoC—though the euphemism employed was "redeployment."[20]

At the level of action, the first major move made by Indian leaders was to recall India's ambassador (December 22) and to end bus and train services between the two countries. Two days later, it was announced that the Indian

Army had "moved," but not "deployed," the nuclear-capable short-range Prithvi missile, normally stored at Secunderabad in the south, to the border region.[21] Another two days later, Defense Minister Fernandes said India had deployed fighter jets at bases along the border and that its missiles were "in position."[22] The following day, Pakistani civilian aircraft were prohibited from overflying India, and India ordered the strength of its mission in Islamabad, as well as that of the Pakistani mission in New Delhi, reduced by half. By this time, the Indian army was laying land mines, constructing bunkers, and positioning tanks and heavy field artillery—all signs of preparation for large-scale conventional conflict. Exchanges of fire were occurring regularly.[23] The ante was upped again on December 29, when "defense sources" (in an obvious official leak) told a news reporter that the Army was preparing for its biggest exercise in fifteen years and would be testing its capacity to thwart a nuclear attack.[24] On the same day, the *Washington Post* reported that an Indian naval task force, consisting of India's sole aircraft carrier, six other ships, and two submarines had been positioned within striking distance of Karachi, Pakistan's largest port.[25] The following day, it was reported that India had moved three more divisions to the front. As the rising graph of tension flattened out following President Musharraf's crackdown on terrorists, including those in Pakistan-held Kashmir, yet another nuclear signal from New Delhi, albeit an oblique one, came in the form of a missile test: on January 25, 2002, a Pakistan-specific version of the intermediate-range missile Agni, with a declared range of 700–900 kilometers, was tested.

Under pressure from Indian military moves and from the U.S., Pakistan responded by making concessions. In late December 2001, Musharraf arrested about fifty members of two Muslim fundamentalist groups which India held responsible for the terrorist attack on the Indian Parliament.[26] In a major speech in January, he denounced terrorism, and expressly stated: "No organization will be allowed to indulge in terrorism in the name of Kashmir."[27] Insisting on seeing the proof of the pudding, India refused to withdraw its forces. There followed a prolonged lull, during which terrorist attacks in India continued, first on a reduced scale, then with a rising tempo. In May, tensions again rose sharply following the so-called "Kaluchak massacre" in Kashmir, in which thirty-two people, mostly wives and children of Indian soldiers, were killed by terrorists.[28] India stepped up the pressure yet another notch and ordered its Eastern Naval Command fleet to join its Western fleet in the Arabian Sea.[29] The threat of imminent war was in the

air once more. Under renewed pressure, Pakistan promised that the reduction in cross-border infiltration would be "visible" and "permanent," as announced by American Secretary of State Colin Powell.[30] India then de-esca-
lated somewhat, reinstating Pakistani overflights and moving its ships back
from forward patrol positions.[31] Pakistan responded by reducing import duties on six hundred trade items from India.[32] But Indian troops remained in
position until October, officially awaiting evidence of Pakistani good faith,
but evidently in anticipation of further terrorist infiltration and violence in
the state of Jammu and Kashmir, where elections were scheduled that October. Following the successful conduct of the elections, the order to withdraw the forces was given in mid-October.

On the verbal plane, Indian rhetoric was aggressive. The consistent aim
was to drive home the point that India stood by its plank of no first use, but
that if Pakistan were to use nuclear weapons first, it would be devastated by
a counterstrike from India's larger arsenal. As a smaller country, Pakistan
would be much worse off. In short, Pakistan's nuclear capability would no
longer deter India from taking military action. The nature of India's military
action was left unspecified but, given the extent of its deployment, conceivably included a major conventional thrust. The threat of nuclear desolation
came regularly and from diverse sources. On December 25, Jana Krishna-
murthy, the president of the Bharatiya Janata Party (BJP), the main party in
India's ruling coalition, warned that if Pakistan attempted to use nuclear
weapons, "its existence itself would be wiped out of the world map."[33] On
the same day, Prime Minister Vajpayee declared: "We do not want war, but
war is being thrust on us, and we will have to face it."[34] On December 26,
another official leak made it known that one Indian option was to open the
gates of the Salal Dam on the Chenab River, just 20 kilometers upstream
from the border, and flood vast tracts of Pakistani land.[35] Though this obviously did not constitute a nuclear threat, it was just the sort of statement to
keep Pakistan on edge and compel its leaders to take the nuclear risk seriously. An official nuclear threat followed soon. On December 29, Defense
Minister George Fernandes repeated the BJP president's warning:

Pakistan can't think of using nuclear weapons despite the fact that they are not committed to the doctrine of no first use like we are. We could take a strike, survive, and
then hit back. Pakistan would be finished. I do not really fear that the nuclear issue
would figure in a conflict.[36]

Two days later, while acknowledging Pakistan's action in arresting the founder of the Lashkar-e-Taiba (Army of the Pure) leader, India again raised the stakes by demanding that twenty individuals accused of terrorist acts in India be handed over. On January 11, a senior Indian official repeated the nuclear warning to an American journalist: "They must be aware we could destroy their whole country."[37] On the same day, India's Army Chief, General S. Padmanabhan, repeated the threat rather more graphically and ominously, saying: "If we have to go to war, jolly good." Asked specifically how India would respond to a Pakistani first strike, he declared that "the perpetrator of that particular outrage shall be punished so severely that their [*sic*] continuation thereafter in any form of fray will be doubtful."[38] The rhetoric declined after Musharraf's initial promises led to reduced tension, but rose again when tensions grew in May. Word went out through unofficial channels that Indian forces had been given permission to undertake "limited" strikes against terrorists in Pakistan (but not against the Pakistan Army).[39] India threatened to scrap the Indus Waters Treaty, an action which would have seriously jeopardized Pakistan's water resources.[40] Even after the military confrontation had ebbed, Minister of State for Home Affairs I. D. Swami announced in September that war remained "one option."[41] The strength of the rhetoric in part reflects a style of combative discourse that outsiders, particularly Westerners, often fail to comprehend adequately. It also reflects, in my view, a psychological tactic designed to keep interlocutors off balance, targeting a combination of reason and emotion rather than reason alone; in short, a form of "strategic acupuncture."[42]

Many observers did see the whole exercise as a bluff, but the scale of India's military mobilization, combined with the heated rhetoric, had the effect of creating a level of uncertainty: one could never be sure. Inherent in the situation, whether intended or not, was the classic "threat that leaves something to chance."[43] The recipient of the threat could never be sure if the threatener did indeed have full control of events, with the implication that nuclear conflict might occur without it being intended. Even after discounting for both bluff and style, the aggressive rhetoric emanating from the Indian leadership would have accentuated the problem. As Schelling has pointed out, the less cool and collected one is, the greater the credibility of such a threat.[44]

The central point of the Indian threat was to show that asymmetry matters. It was not a simple case of affirming that nuclear asymmetry in itself is significant. Rather, it was an assertion that *the combination of nuclear asymmetry and conventional asymmetry matters.* The thinking seems to have gone something like this. Had the two sides been equal in nuclear terms, there would have been no question of expressing a threat to go to war, since the cost of war would have been proportionate. However, in this case, the cost of nuclear war was held to be disproportionate: India would survive, Pakistan would not. The assumption underlying this logic was that size does matter in two ways: India's larger arsenal would inflict greater absolute damage, and its larger size would mean the damage it experienced would be much smaller in relative terms. Ergo, Pakistan was not in a position to resort to a first strike. It was effectively deterred from nuclear use altogether. The nuclear stalemate, however, left India at an advantage because of its superior conventional force, which could be used to carry out operations without fear of a Pakistani nuclear first strike. Even in a conventional war, Pakistan would be continuously inhibited by the fear of a possible uncontrolled escalation leading to nuclear war. There was thus strategic space for a limited war to inflict costs on an economically and politically unstable Pakistan. So long as its core interests were not jeopardized, Pakistan would have no incentive to launch nuclear weapons.[45]

Built into this conception of nuclear-cum-conventional asymmetry was the implication that the role of nuclear weapons was not restricted to mutual *nuclear* deterrence. Rather, because nuclear asymmetry would restrain Pakistan from a nuclear response in a conventional conflict, it was now possible for India *to deter a sub-conventional threat* from that country. So long as India refrained from striking at Pakistan's core interests, the latter would not—dare not—launch its nuclear weapons, and India would retain the advantage. India, from this standpoint, now enjoyed escalation dominance.[46] The conception of strategic advantage arising from mutual nuclear deterrence that had enabled Pakistan to utilize a low-cost sub-conventional strategy, through the Kargil venture and through support to cross-border terrorism, stood reversed.

TRILATERAL COMPELLENCE: THE UNITED STATES

Apart from posing a direct compellence threat to Pakistan by its massive military buildup, India also projected indirect pressure on Pakistan via the United States. The politics of nuclear weapons has generally been understood in terms of bilateral relationships between nuclear-armed adversaries or between a nuclear-armed state and a non-nuclear state. In South Asia, however, the regional rivals have found a new use for nuclear weapons since they went nuclear officially in 1998. Both countries have engaged in a creative expansion of nuclear strategy *to invite outside intervention* in their conflict over Kashmir. Pakistan initiated this in 1999 by launching the Kargil conflict, a large-scale covert intrusion into Indian-held territory in Kashmir. India engaged in a similar, though not identical, strategic exercise through the mobilization of conventional forces in the post–December 13 buildup. In both cases, the belligerents attempted not so much to threaten the direct use of nuclear force as to *create a fear of nuclear war* in the global community, especially the United States, in the pursuit of their political ends. Each hoped thereby to harness American intervention for its own purpose, primarily to use the United States to pressure the other into making political concessions relating to the Kashmir dispute. In short, the strategic target of the implied threat of nuclear conflict was a third party. The objective, of course, was to stimulate that third party into action. In Kargil, Pakistan attempted to use the United States as a lever to compel India to negotiate on Kashmir. In the December 13 crisis, India compelled the United States to put intense pressure on Musharraf to abandon his support for Pakistan-based terrorist groups operating in Kashmir.

Unlike the Kargil episode, in which Pakistan was widely seen as an irresponsible nuclear power, India had the advantage of a more conducive global environment. World opinion was sympathetic because of the immediate provocation of the attack on the Indian Parliament and, earlier, on the Jammu and Kashmir legislative assembly on October 1. Besides, since the United States and its allies had justified military intervention in Afghanistan as a war against terrorism, the Indian reaction was difficult to oppose. At the same time, Pakistan's record of support to the Taliban and to a number of identified terrorist groups was well known. Despite its interest in ensuring Pakistani cooperation in the hunt for members of al-Qaeda and the Taliban, the United States had little choice but to bring pressure to bear on Pakistan to curb its association with terrorists active in India. From the Indian standpoint, the presence of American forces in Pakistan at the time made the possibility of a war very low.[47] Even if low-level border skirmishes had broken out, it was believed, the United States would have intervened rapidly, possibly by interposing some of its own forces in the area of confrontation. Yet, Indian military mobilization was sufficiently strong to evoke the fear of a conflict actually breaking out, and hence to compel the United States to put considerable pressure on Pakistan to reverse its support for terrorists based on its soil.

From the American standpoint, South Asia is a difficult region to deal with. Since the mid-1980s, the U.S. has increasingly found itself in the thick of India–Pakistan crises.[48] However, it has not been inclined to help forge solutions to what appears to be an intractable problem, especially given India's insistence on tackling its disputes with Pakistan bilaterally in accordance with the Simla agreement (1972). But since the advent of nuclear weapons, the U.S. has felt compelled to intervene whenever the regional barometer has gone up. In the first two major crises after the steady covert nuclearization of the subcontinent—the Brasstacks crisis of 1986–87 and the Kashmir crisis of 1990—the U.S. became involved in peacemaking.[49] Though neither of the crises actually took a nuclear turn, the possibility of that happening lent urgency to U.S. mediation efforts. In both cases, the U.S. was convinced that the risk of war was high, and that intervention was necessary for the return of normalcy. By intervening to pour oil on troubled waters, it left itself open to future manipulation by the regional rivals. Kargil was the first result, with Pakistan seeking to apply pressure on India through the U.S. The attempt backfired and the U.S. twisted Pakistan's arm, forcing Prime Minister Nawaz Sharif to call off the venture. The December 13 crisis was more problematic for the U.S., as we have seen, since India's motivation was similar to that of the U.S. in Afghanistan, and also because India did not transgress the border or the LoC.

The American response was driven primarily by the fear of a regional war between the two nuclear antagonists. U.S. officials feared a "major miscalculation" by either side, particularly because neither side "seems to have a great grasp of the other's doctrine or limits."[50] CIA Director George Tenet testified before the Senate Intelligence Committee to the Bush administration's concern that "a conventional war, once begun, could escalate into a nuclear confrontation."[51] Even if there was a feeling that India was merely "huffing and bluffing," as one commentator put it, the risks were too great for the U.S. to ignore.[52] The U.S. sent a number of senior officials, including its Secretaries of State and Defense, to both countries, and President Bush and other officials were frequently on the phone to the two South Asian leaders. The President's message to President Musharraf was sharp, asking him to take "strong and decisive measures" to curb terrorism.[53] The

U.S. itself formally declared two major Pakistan-based terrorist groups, the Lashkar-e-Taiba and the Jaish-e-Mohammed, as terrorist organizations.[54] Under pressure, Musharraf arrested about fifty members of two Muslim fundamentalist groups believed to have been responsible for the terrorist attack on the Indian Parliament.[55] As the crisis persisted, so did American pressure.[56] It seemed to have an effect, and, as noted above, Musharraf committed himself publicly to drop support for the terrorists. Following the revival of tensions in May, American diplomacy again came into play, and was instrumental in defusing the crisis. Bush asked Musharraf to demonstrate "results in terms of stopping people from crossing the Line of Control."[57] In June, Powell declared that the problem was not over, and that in spite of Musharraf's assurances, "we can still see evidence that it is continuing."[58] While urging calm on both sides, Bush, according to a White House official, used "very firm language" to insist that Pakistan cease support for the terrorists active in Kashmir.[59] Deputy Secretary of State Richard Armitage also made it clear to Musharraf that Pakistan must ensure that infiltration into India by terrorist groups stopped.[60] Clearly, the Indian strategy had succeeded in inducing the U.S., fearful of a potential nuclear conflagration in the subcontinent, to put considerable pressure on Pakistan to stop supporting cross-border terrorism.

From the evidence available, it appears that trilateral rather than bilateral compellence was the primary feature of Indian compellence strategy. Pakistan had set a precedent through the failed Kargil intrusion, which had been devised to induce American intervention in the Kashmir dispute. The aim was to create a crisis without officially crossing the LoC—that is, to obtain a military advantage while retaining deniability, evoke a general fear of escalation from sub-conventional to conventional to nuclear conflict, and thereby induce international intervention. In the December 13 crisis, India too observed the "red line" of the LoC and refrained from military action that would violate its "sanctity." While the threat was officially directed toward Pakistan, the underlying motivation is evident from the confidence that war would not occur because the U.S. would not allow it to. The physical presence of American military forces in the region was seen as an effective firebreak against escalation: it made war very unlikely, and if fighting did break out, the United States would immediately intervene and force a ceasefire.[61]

In a sense, the U.S. was a better target for coercive diplomacy than Pakistan. Whereas Pakistan had a deterrent option to stave off the Indian threat, the U.S. had perforce to intervene in order to prevent war. With every crisis, the U.S. has felt compelled to intercede and help make peace. In doing so, it has left itself open to exploitation by the region's rivals. Conceivably, it could walk away and refuse to referee the India–Pakistan conflict.[62] But realistically, it cannot. Apart from the immediate U.S. interest in eliminating terrorism in Afghanistan, there are at least six longer-term reasons for it to remain involved. First, the humanitarian dimension simply cannot be overlooked. A nuclear cataclysm in South Asia would not be a local problem, but a global one, and for this reason alone it cannot be ignored.[63] Second, from a practical standpoint, the extent of the fallout from a regional nuclear conflagration cannot be predicted. Depending on what exactly happens, and on weather conditions, radiation effects may be felt in neighboring countries, including American bases (perhaps in Pakistan itself, and in Afghanistan and Uzbekistan). Third, the actual use of nuclear weapons is likely to give a fillip to nuclear proliferation: with the long-standing nuclear taboo broken, fears that nuclear weapons have become usable again may motivate at least some states to rethink their abjuration of nuclear capability. Fourth, the United States has an enduring interest in South Asia as an emerging market for sales and investment and as a source of cost-effective software services. This will certainly be hit, though not immediately. Fifth, were a nuclear war to occur in South Asia, the world might see it as a failure of American leadership, and Washington's global role in maintaining stability might come to be questioned. Finally, thousands of American citizens in India and Pakistan could become casualties in a subcontinental nuclear exchange, a possibility that the U.S. government cannot ignore.[64] In the December 13 case, the last problem was underscored by the presence of considerable numbers of American forces in the region. Taken cumulatively, these factors produce a strong incentive for the U.S. to intervene in the region when nuclear risks rise.

Evaluation of India's Strategy

It must be admitted at the outset that an assessment of India's post–December 13 strategy at this stage can only be of a preliminary nature. Discussion over the Cuban missile crisis remains lively four decades after the event, for the enormous mass of information on that event leaves important questions still unanswered.[65] Nevertheless, the facts available may be harnessed to theory and logic to draw some useful conclusions on the efficacy of the strategy and its implications for the future. In the following section, I will try to appraise the strategy in terms of the objectives it sought to attain. Thereafter, I will weigh the costs and the risks of the strategy against the elements of stability evident from its evolution.

OBJECTIVES AND ACCOMPLISHMENT

Indian opinion as to the effectiveness of the ten-month-long campaign to coerce Pakistan into a less aggressive policy has been mixed.[66] Much of it does not clearly sort out the Indian government's stated and inferred objectives and the extent to which they were met or not met.

Cross-Border Terrorism

The most prominent Indian demand was that Pakistan put an end to cross-border terrorism. This has not happened. In June, after the second period of peak tension had subsided, Vajpayee claimed victory on the grounds that there were "clearly visible" changes on the ground, yet all but admitted that the problem remained, and that Pakistan was still guilty of abetting it.[67] In September, Foreign Minister Yashwant Sinha complained to the United States that terrorist activity had risen sharply.[68] In November, Defense Minister Fernandes acknowledged only a "minor reduction" in terrorist infiltration, adding, "Islamabad is continuing its negative and hostile attitude towards India."[69] India's refusal to negotiate with Pakistan after the crisis was over confirmed this. Fernandes's subsequent claim that India's mobilization had "succeeded" in forcing Musharraf to denounce "jihad" and that infiltration had been reduced by 53 percent merely underscored the fact that terrorist flows across the border were still rife.[70] The larger objective of controlling terrorist violence in all its manifestations remained unmet. The violence continued unabated. My own calculations from newspaper reports show that in the month of November 2002, terrorist attacks in eight major incidents in Jammu and Kashmir resulted in at least sixty-nine deaths, including an assault on the famous Raghunath Temple in Jammu City.[71] In December, Fernandes told Parliament that Pakistan had reopened terrorist camps close to the LoC and the border.[72]

The List of Twenty

A specific demand India made of Pakistan was to hand over twenty persons listed as wanted for major terrorist activities, such as the serial blasts that rocked Mumbai in 1993. This demand was never met. For Indian officials, it was particularly frustrating that, under American pressure, Pakistan not only handed over a number of terrorists to the U.S., but also began pushing back Uighur militants in deference to Chinese wishes, and also extradited two terrorists to Uzbekistan.[73] This was one objective that clearly remained unfulfilled at the time of the Indian withdrawal.

Obtaining Global Support

A long-standing objective had been to obtain global—and especially American—support for India's contention that Pakistan was the source of much of the terrorist activity in India, dating back to the insurgency in Punjab in the 1980s. Before September 11, the issue was not taken seriously, partly because the issue did not affect the U.S. directly, and partly because of American strategic interests in Pakistan. The Kargil conflict, Pakistan's association with the Taliban, and the events of September 11 changed the American perception of Pakistan considerably. During the December 13 crisis, the U.S. clearly interceded on behalf of Indian interests, and world opinion was generally supportive of India's position. Even critics of Indian policy have acknowledged that India's mobilization caused the U.S. to force Pakistan to renounce support for cross-border terrorism.[74] In June 2002, when the crisis had receded from its second and final high-pressure phase, Prime Minister Vajpayee claimed success on this score:

There's been an unprecedented change in the world's view on J&K. For the first time, the world says that whatever is happening in Kashmir isn't a freedom struggle but terrorism. Pak[istan] has been isolated like never before.[75]

But, from the Indian standpoint, there is a negative side to the enhanced foreign intervention. As one sympathetic observer has remarked, "A fundamental lesson from the current crisis is that India and Pakistan are no longer free agents to pursue their quarrels as they please."[76] While India continues to insist on a bilateral resolution of all outstanding India–Pakistan issues, its strategy has pushed the problem in the direction of external intervention.

Much to India's discomfiture, Secretary of State Powell in June highlighted the new difficulties thus created by calling on India to release political prisoners before the Jammu and Kashmir elections, and allow independent observers to monitor the elections.[77] American pressure on Pakistan is restrained by the continuing interest in retaining Pakistani cooperation in apprehending remnants of al-Qaeda and the Taliban that might be in hiding in the region astride the porous Pakistan–Afghanistan border and within Pakistan itself. Pakistan is seen as a "very stalwart ally" and hence not to be labeled a "terrorist state," as India has long called for.[78] On the contrary, Deputy Secretary Armitage asserted in August 2002 that Pakistan was not solely responsible for continuing infiltration, perhaps implying that India should accept some of the responsibility for allowing it to happen.[79] The U.S. also indicated its interest in ensuring General Musharraf's continuation in power as a bastion against radical chaos in nuclear Pakistan, which implied limits to the pressure it would impose on him.[80] During the crisis and after, India came under increasing pressure to engage in a dialogue with Pakistan. For instance, in May 2002 the U.S. expressed its unhappiness with India's expulsion of Pakistan's ambassador as it would "make it more difficult to have dialogue."[81] It also conveyed to India that terrorist infiltration could not be restrained fully unless there was a political dialogue.[82] Similar views were expressed by the European Union's president, Danish Prime Minister Anders Fogh Rasmussen, and by European Commissioner for External Relations Chris Patten.[83]

Conveying a Message to Pakistan

The sense of being paralyzed by Pakistan's strategy of sub-conventional conflict under the nuclear shadow was a powerful motivating factor. Indian policy makers were spurred by a growing perception that it was time to "call the bluff."[84] The mobilization of Indian forces was meant to convey a symbolic message that Pakistan would no longer be free to conduct its proxy war unhindered, and that India would respond forcefully.[85] The Indian action was a message to Pakistan conveying India's determination to break out of its "strategic paralysis." In effect, it was: Pakistan would have to pay a price. That message was undoubtedly successfully conveyed, and still stands, as the possibility of future military action of some kind remains. Arguably, it was also driven by a self-regarding urge to act: to rouse the self from a helpless giant syndrome, a negative self-image of "softness" and "permanent vulner-ability" in the face of repeated and grave provocation.[86]

The price, however, has to be paid by both sides. Certainly, General Musharraf had to curb terrorist activity in Pakistan, but this by no means constitutes a permanent change. In economic terms, the cost for Pakistan of its own mobilization was high, amounting to as much as 30 percent of its annual budget, or $3.3 billion, in the first six months alone.[87] But the cost to India was large, too. According to sources in the NSAB, the total cost of the deployment was about $1.6 billion.[88] The economy also came under pres-sure, as business clients avoided travel to the region, causing corporate and government managers to put pressure on the government to ease the con-frontation.[89] On the military side, the massive scale of mobilization put im-mense pressure on the readiness of the armed forces for the future. An armed force that has always fought short wars was subject to a prolonged mobilization, resulting in the degradation of men and material.[90]

In sum, a cost–benefit analysis shows that, in terms of the objectives that Indian policy makers sought to attain, the return on India's investment was relatively limited. While some gains were made in realigning world opinion and putting pressure on Pakistan to curb its support for terrorist activity in India, the overall result was far from satisfactory.

Problems Inherent in the Strategy

The literature on compellence in general shows a mixed picture.[91] Compel-lence may or may not work, depending on a wide range of factors in a spe-cific context. Between nuclear-weapon states, barring the India–Pakistan re-lationship, there have been only two serious crises that brought the adversaries to the verge of war: the U.S.–Soviet Cuban missile crisis of 1962, and the Soviet–China border clashes of 1969. In both cases, compellence seemed to work. The "weaker" side—the Soviet Union and China, respec-tively—appeared to have given in in a game of chicken. But the apparent gains of the "victors" were of dubious value. The outcome of the Cuban case, it turns out, was not a victory for the United States, but a compro-mise—American missiles in Turkey for Soviet missiles in Cuba—arising out of mutual deterrence and prudence.[92] In the other case, China backed down initially, but the eventual outcome was that it did not yield any disputed territory as a result of the confrontation.[93] That India did not make any substantial gains as a result of its troop mobilization comes as no surprise. Between nuclear states, compellence is difficult to achieve, for it carries intrinsic difficulties that are hard to surmount.

First, compellence is unlike deterrence in one important respect. In deterrence, the targeted state is required to refrain from a specific action or set of actions. In contrast, as Schelling points out, in compellence, "the very act of compliance—of doing what is demanded—is more conspicuously compliant, more recognizable as submission under duress, than when an act is merely withheld in the face of a deterrent threat."[94] Thus, while not doing something appears to be an absence of gain, reversing an action under pain of punishment is more obviously a loss. As prospect theory tells us, loss aversion raises commitment to a position and willingness to bear pain as well as take risks, and hence raises potential costs to one who is seeking gain.[95] Pakistan's resolve and tolerance of costs remained high despite tactical concessions at the time. There was too much to lose. As Musharraf later pointed out, "No government of Pakistan can leave or abandon the issue of Kashmir" and any leader who does so will be "eliminated."[96]

Second, between nuclear-weapon states, deterrence overrides compellence. A compellence threat can be "called," and a threatener required to follow up with action. In that case, when both have nuclear weapons, the state which has to act first and thereby bring both to the point of war is likely to find that act difficult in the extreme. Nuclear powers are compelled by the threat of devastation to stop two steps short of nuclear war, that is, at some point *below* the threshold between skirmishing or sub-conventional conflict and conventional war.[97] While there may be doubt as to what exactly constitutes the threshold, it seems fairly clear in the present case that the "sanctity" of the LoC (in terms of the movement of ground forces) and the international border had been tacitly agreed upon by India and Pakistan. This was in one sense violated when Pakistani forces crossed the LoC in 1999, but at the same time underscored because they did so in mufti, and because the subsequent conduct of military engagements maintained its "sanctity" at considerable cost to both sides. Pakistan did not respond to the Indian assault on its forces with a counterattack across the line, and Indian forces refrained from crossing it, or the international border, during their campaign. In the December 13 crisis, India was in the position of having to risk violating the LoC and the border and, particularly in light of the size of its mobilization, consequently launching a conventional war. That it did not do so was clearly because the risk was not worth it. Just as Pakistan was constrained in 1999, so was India in 2001–2. In effect, deterrence overrode compellence in both instances.

Pakistani actions reminded Indian leaders that they were confronting a nuclear power. Apart from a matching large-scale troop buildup, these included overt nuclear signals, notably at the second peak point of the crisis in May. On May 20, word was unofficially given through the press that Pakistan had deployed the nuclear-capable Shaheen missile (with a range of 750 kilometers).[98] Shortly thereafter, Pakistan conducted a series of missile tests, first for the medium-range Ghauri missile (1,500–2000 kilometers), the remaining two for short-range missiles.[99] To have escalated after this would have been to raise the risk of war enormously. After a point, then, with further escalation deterred, there was, as one analyst put it, "nowhere to go."[100] The stalemate persisted for a time. Eventually, with the Indian armed forces chiefs coming round to the view that Pakistan was no longer "responding," as one Ministry of Defense source expressed it, the whole exercise had to be called off.[101] Besides, as one astute observer has pointed out, an Indian march into Pakistani territory would have invited the same negative world reaction as Kargil did for Pakistan, again because of the risk of crossing the threshold. Again, the game was not worth the candle.[102]

Third, compellence confronts a serious difficulty with the problem of reversibility. The Soviet–China border conflict is instructive in this respect. The situation preceding the Sino-Soviet border clashes of 1969 at Damansky Island (or, as the Chinese call it, Chenpao) on the Ussuri River bears a remarkable resemblance to the recent South Asian confrontation.[103] As with the Kashmir problem, the border dispute between China and the Soviet Union had its roots in the colonial era. Like Pakistan today, China was in a state of considerable internal instability, the result of the Cultural Revolution. Minor skirmishes had occurred at other places in the region before the first Damansky incident on March 1, 1969. At the time the March 1 fighting broke out, the Soviet Union had overwhelmingly superior conventional as well as nuclear forces. Following the first clash, it mounted a massive mobilization of conventional forces and resorted to coercive diplomacy through a series of threats as well as actual military engagements. A series of short engagements took place between March and August 1969. Unlike the South Asian case, though, there were hints of a nuclear first strike. Eventually,

China dropped its earlier stand and agreed to come to the negotiating table, signed a one-year navigation agreement with respect to the disputed river, and dropped its insistence that the "unequalness" of the old treaties that had determined the Sino-Soviet border had rendered them worthless. The Soviet strategy seemed to have worked. But in the long run, it did not. Once the crisis had been resolved, the Chinese backed away from negotiations "they had no intention of carrying to conclusion on Soviet terms."[104]

Musharraf and his successors have the same option of reversing their position. Musharraf has already exercised it. In June, shortly after the December 13 crisis had abated, he reverted to his old position by asserting that Kashmir was in the throes of a "freedom struggle," not "cross-border terrorism." He went on to say that while at the time "nothing is happening across the Line of Control," that was not a permanent state: "I'm not going to give you an assurance that for years nothing will happen."[105] This also underscores the matter of commitment. The effectiveness of a coercive strategy depends considerably on the balance of commitments on both sides, for the calculus of costs relates to commitment.[106] It is evident that Pakistani leaders have a high level of commitment to the cause of Kashmir as one vital to national identity, and hence would be willing to pay a high price to retain it, if for no other reason than their own survival. In June, senior Pakistani military officers privately told the *Washington Post* that the militants remained a vital component of Pakistan's strategy.[107] The reversibility problem is already visible. Forethought would have shown that it was inherent in India's compellence strategy from the beginning.

A fourth difficulty is that the strategy of trilateral compellence is subject to the third party's interests being compatible with the state practicing it. When their interests diverge, the strategy may be adversely affected. In the present case, India had a common interest with the United States in curbing terrorism, but not its exact manifestation. India was concerned about terrorists operating in Kashmir, the U.S. primarily with al-Qaeda and the Taliban. On the nuclear issue, American interest lies in preventing a war and maintaining regional stability, but its view of regional stability does not necessarily coincide with India's. For the U.S., a negotiated settlement to prevent war is the overriding concern; for India, an end to Pakistan's role in Kashmir comes first. American involvement in both the Kargil conflict and the December 13 crisis has placed Pakistan on the defensive, but has also pushed the Pakistani agenda of negotiation on Kashmir forward.

A fifth problem for nuclear powers resorting to a coercive strategy is that of risk. Optimists tend to emphasize the rational consequence of nuclear possession, which is prudence and war-avoidance. Critics tend to stress its non-rational elements, citing all that can go wrong. The debate is often conducted in the context of proliferation, but much the same can and has been said of the bigger nuclear powers.[108] The non-rational involves, of course, a great many factors, such as accidents, organizational processes, psychological factors, and cultural predispositions.[109] Even if both sides behave rationally, there may still be loss of control resulting in war. A rational decision may be taken under a given set of circumstances, but that set may change—for one side in a conflict cannot control all that the other does—and bring about what appears to be an "irrational" outcome.[110] Thus, a crisis between nuclear-weapon states tends to contain both stable and unstable elements. The December 13 crisis is illustrative.

A basic stabilizing factor is that, unlike other nuclear powers, neither India nor Pakistan is known to have its nuclear weapons in active deployment, let alone on hair-trigger status. On the contrary, both have been content with a "non-traditional" deterrence characterized by limited testing and disaggregated weapons.[111] In addition, India's goals in the crisis were limited to stemming the terrorist tide, not to occupying territory or dismembering Pakistan. Indian forces were not in a position to launch a full-scale conventional war against that country, and Indian leaders were sensitive to the potential for a nuclear conflict if they did make such an attempt.[112] In two cases, action was taken against top commanders who indirectly incurred risks. In January 2002, Lieutenant-General Kapil Vij, commander of India's 2nd Corps, a strike corps, was abruptly removed from his post for positioning his forces too close to the border.[113] In March, Air Marshal V. K. Bhatia was transferred out of the LoC/border region after his aircraft strayed into Pakistani air space, was shot by Pakistani forces, and forced to make a distress landing at Leh.[114] On the negative side, both incidents represent what can go wrong in a crisis. There were other serious incidents. Prolonged armed clashes took place in July and August when Pakistani forces occupied the Loonda Post on the Indian side of the LoC, and India reclaimed it with the use of 155 mm heavy artillery, Mirage 2000 aircraft, and helicopter gunships.[115] Indian forces also undertook unspecified "special missions" across the LoC during the crisis.[116] The deployment of India's western and eastern fleets in the Arabian Sea also raised risks considerably. Maritime operations are particularly susceptible to escalation because of the absence of clear geographical "red lines" and the common use of tactics that cause opposing forces to come close and even mingle.[117]

Completely unanticipated events may also cause catastrophic results. During the crisis, American early-warning satellites detected an energy release equivalent to the Hiroshima bomb caused by an asteroid impacting on Earth's atmosphere. Such incidents occur regularly, and could—in the absence of very sophisticated sensors—be mistaken for nuclear detonations, thereby increasing the risk of war in a crisis.[118] Both optimists and pessimists are right in their respective arguments. On one hand, nuclear-weapon states invariably behave cautiously as they near the brink; on the other, rational behavior does not preclude accidents and unanticipated events and outcomes. Nuclear conflict has never occurred between nuclear powers because they are always sensible and prudent. But it could, because sense and prudence may not be enough. On which side do the scales of judgment then tilt? I believe they should tilt on the side of the pessimists. That nothing has happened so far does not rule out its happening in the future. In contemplating war between nuclear-weapon states, the weight of the potential cost is far greater than almost any gain other than preventing societal destruction. As Robert McNamara pointed out while reflecting on the Cuban missile crisis, there is no "learning period" with nuclear weapons: "You make one mistake and you destroy nations."[119] It is certainly conceivable that there could be a major conventional war in South Asia without either side taking recourse to nuclear weapons. It might even be possible that an initial use of nuclear weapons (through a demonstration effect or careful tactical use) would cause little relative damage, and that intervention or self-restraint would limit destruction. But one cannot wager the lives of millions on it.

Conclusion: Lessons Learned?

The December 13 crisis ended where it had begun, with India and Pakistan still at loggerheads over the twin issues of Kashmir and cross-border terrorism. The Indian exercise in compellence had succeeded in putting Pakistan under the spotlight and forcing it to retreat from its uninhibited use of terrorists to further its cause, but not in changing its policy completely. The Pakistani retreat was clearly tactical. With the outstanding issues that caused both the Kargil conflict and the December 13 crisis unresolved, the possibility of future crises cannot be ruled out. For some Indian critics, the withdrawal of forces was a sign of "weakness and lack of fortitude," and Prime Minister Vajpayee wasted an opportunity to carry out "punitive strikes" immediately after December 13.[120] From this standpoint, the military option remains open. The Kargil failure taught Pakistan that a military adventure is counterproductive; the December 13 mobilization has (presumably) taught India that coercive diplomacy does not pay adequate dividends. Resort to compulsion through the threat of war runs into the brick wall of deterrence. Compellence through a third party is inherently problematic because the interests of the third party tend to be its own, and these may be a drag on the compelling power. Concessions extracted from the target state are reversible, and the investment in projecting a coercive threat can be brought to naught whenever that state chooses. Still, a government under pressure may be tempted to use force in some other way, say, by means of hot pursuit of militants fleeing across the border, air or ground strikes against terrorist camps, or even by "salami slicing" as a means of bargaining. But if military options remain, then the risks identified above go with them. It is not yet clear what lessons Indian leaders have learned from the December 13 experience.

The December 13 crisis also carries disturbing implications for India's nuclear posture of minimum deterrence. If, as no less than its Defense Minister stressed, India enjoys the advantage of nuclear asymmetry, and that in turn can be the basis of coercive diplomacy, then the disadvantaged state has an inducement to catch up. In effect, Pakistan has an incentive to try and reach some sort of equivalence so as to be less susceptible to coercion. The same applies to India vis-à-vis China, which, after all, provided the raison d'être for India's official nuclearization. We have here the intellectual basis for arms races similar to that which motivated the main protagonists of the Cold War. Coercive diplomacy between nuclear powers goes directly against the grain of minimum-deterrence doctrine. This is not to say that Indian doctrine is likely to undergo a radical shift. Many factors will restrain such a change, such as a strategic culture antithetical to nuclear weapons, a long history of "non-traditional deterrence," the cost factor, and not least the experience of the December 13 crisis.[121] The last demonstrated, if anything, the strength of minimum deterrence. Finally, the crisis shows that, for India, there is no military solution to the "Pakistan problem." Since the December 13 attack on its Parliament, India has refused to negotiate with Pakistan before the latter ends its support for cross-border terrorism. That left the troubled relationship between the two countries at a dead end, and the situation for India still uncomfortable. Moreover, it was not entirely a consistent stand. India *has* dealt with terrorists on parallel tracks on a regular basis, using armed force to suppress them and at the same time keeping the door open for political solutions.[122] The Pakistan case is different, of course, since it involves a state. Issues of national sovereignty and identity appear far graver when the threat is from the outside. But the adversarial relationship being a nuclear one, the need for the politics of negotiation to take precedence over the politics of force is unquestionable.

An important question is whether Indian leaders have learned from the failure of compellence. There is reason to believe that they have. Terrorist violence in Kashmir had increased significantly a year after India called off its massive deployment, but Indian leaders did not respond with a renewed compellence threat or with talk of limited war. Instead, Prime Minister Vajpayee sprang a surprise in October 2003 with a proposal to revive transportation links and sporting ties with Pakistan. The latter responded positively, and a cautious but optimistic process of negotiation was set into motion yet again that has continued after the change of government in India. This appears to be a case of learning from experience. Whether the turn in the India–Pakistan relationship is likely to develop roots is as yet an open question. A measure of reflection on the recent crisis may well help produce a positive long-term outcome.

THIRTEEN

U.S. Interests in South Asia

Howard B. Schaffer

There are probably few areas where Washington's assessment of U.S. regional interests and the policies it judged necessary for promoting them have changed as markedly and in so many different directions as they have over the years in South Asia. At times, the United States has viewed the region and the circumstances of regional countries—India and Pakistan, in particular—as important, even highly important, to U.S. global interests. More often, Washington has considered South Asia a political, economic, and security backwater that it could safely ignore.

For the most part, objections to the positions successive administrations adopted have been muted. Capitol Hill, military and civilian foreign policymakers, and influential private American citizens and non-governmental organizations have generally accepted or acquiesced in them. This consensus has reflected the limited attention South Asia has ordinarily attracted. There have been some important exceptions to this general rule. Not surprisingly, these have mostly occurred when South Asia found its way into the headlines. The strong and widespread opposition to the policies the Nixon administration adopted to deal with the 1971 crisis over Bangladesh is probably the most memorable example of such dissent. Less dramatic and longer lasting has been the advocacy by influential figures outside the Executive Branch of a more positive approach to India despite New Delhi's differences with Washington on many international issues.

The changing dynamics of the Cold War and its aftermath have been important in shaping American perceptions of South Asia, as they have elsewhere. Probably more so than anywhere else, Washington's global concern about the spread of weapons of mass destruction and its determination to stem their proliferation have played an influential, sometimes crucial role in the way it has viewed and dealt with the region. Another determinant of Washington's views has been its long-standing worries about the implications for broad U.S. interests of armed conflict between India and Pakistan and other manifestations of instability in the subcontinent. These two interests have been increasingly connected since the 1970s when both countries embarked on nuclear weapons programs. More recently, the war on terrorism, the reform of India's economic policies, New Delhi's changing perception of its security role in East Asia and elsewhere, and a growing sense that India has the potential to become a truly major world power have become more significant in U.S. assessments and policy formulations. The growing political clout of the South Asian diaspora, especially the Indian American community, has helped put the region in a different perspective for American politicians and policy makers alike.

U.S. officials and individual Americans did not know much, or care much, about the subcontinent before the British quit their Indian empire in 1947 or in the early years of South Asian independence that followed. Before the Second World War, American interests in the subcontinent were very limited. They had never approached the level of the prewar political, economic, security, and social interests America had in the Far East. Relatively few Americans had visited the region, let alone developed important relations there. There was no equivalent in South Asia of the business organizations that had long traded with China and Japan, or of the well-publicized activities of American missionaries there. (There were some American missionaries in South Asia in those days, but their activities were largely confined to remote and backward tribal areas in British India, and to Ceylon, now Sri Lanka. They enjoyed limited support in churches at home and made few converts among influential Indian families.) Understandably, Americans saw South Asia as a British show. Even after 1947, Washington continued for some time to look to London for knowledgeable advice in its dealings with the area. In any event, in the late 1940s and early 1950s it had far more pressing concerns to worry about in Europe and Northeast and Southeast Asia.

If the United States had any major interest in that early stage of its relations with the newly independent South Asian countries, it was regional peace and stability. Reflecting this, Washington played a leading role in international efforts to resolve the India–Pakistan dispute over Kashmir, the former princely state where, contrary to occasional Indian charges, the United States had no strategic or other specific interests. But Washington paid only limited attention to the communal outbreaks that accompanied the partition of the British Indian Empire and the potential for conflict between India and Pakistan for which this bloodbath set the stage. Its concerns were minor when compared with those that more recent India–Pakistan confrontations have prompted.

This attitude is understandable. In those days before the Cold War had penetrated the subcontinent, India–Pakistan hostilities, however regrettable, were judged unlikely to spread beyond the bounds of the subcontinent. Nor, of course, could they have led to a nuclear conflagration. U.S. Kashmir policy was designed to help the two countries resolve their differences, not to avoid a wider, more dangerous war.

After 1949, Washington's subcontinental concerns increasingly focused on the perceived danger that India could become another Communist China, with major Cold War consequences for the East–West balance of power as well as for American domestic politics. (These had been famously roiled by the demagogic query, "Who Lost China?" "Who Lost India" could well have followed.) U.S. economic-assistance programs were largely designed with this dire possibility in mind. The United States had other reasons for providing aid to the South Asian countries, of course. But both the Truman (1945–53) and Eisenhower (1953–61) administrations found that arguments in favor of higher levels of aid that stressed the Communist threat were more effective in mobilizing congressional, bureaucratic, and public support than those emphasizing humanitarian concerns and the moral importance of relieving South Asia's terrible poverty through economic development.

Even so, until the mid-1950s, Washington did not consider the external threat from the "Sino-Soviet bloc" sufficiently daunting for it to supply the South Asian nations with American arms, or to try to persuade them to accept a U.S. military presence on their soil. Nor was there any significant public disagreement with this approach. Washington policymakers and other Americans continued to focus on threats to U.S. security interests elsewhere.

In those years (and later) Washington did have important, usually unproductive relations at international forums with Prime Minister Nehru and his assertive and talented Indian colleagues. But aside from the continuing problem of Kashmir, its diplomatic clashes with the Indians reflected the sharp conflict between the two countries' different approaches to foreign policy in the Cold War world. They had little to do with South Asia or U.S. interests there.

However, Nehru's promotion of non-alignment in the United Nations and elsewhere did have an important indirect impact on the way the United States viewed and dealt with the subcontinent. It made India seem more consequential and hence to be regarded more seriously. But by annoying, sometimes angering influential figures in the Executive Branch and on Capitol Hill, as well as the general American public, New Delhi's seemingly anti-U.S. policies limited the degree of cooperation and support Washington was prepared to offer it. For many Americans, India seemed to make a practice of biting the hand that might have fed it.

The Eisenhower administration's decision in 1954 to welcome Pakistan into the U.S.-led Western security system ushered in a new phase in American perceptions of its South Asian interests. The region, or at least Pakistan, now became important to U.S. containment strategy. Initially, Washington saw Pakistan as part of a shield of northern-tier powers that would help the United States and its Western allies safeguard "Free World" interests in the Near East. But it soon perceived the country's security and well-being as important to U.S. interests for their own sake.

The new policy received strong support in the United States. Pakistan and the other regional nations that joined to form the Baghdad Pact (later the Central Treaty Organization, CENTO) and the Southeast Asia Treaty Organization (SEATO), were seen as useful additions to the lineup of "Free World" nations opposed to the "Sino-Soviet bloc." Influential figures who challenged the wisdom of the new alignment, such as the former Ambassador to India Chester Bowles, found themselves in rather lonely opposition.

As Bowles and a few others forecast at the time, the new policy certainly did not promote the United States' abiding interest in subcontinental peace and stability. Declaring angrily that the new alliance structure had brought the Cold War to South Asia, Nehru abruptly ended efforts to resolve the Kashmir problem and improve India–Pakistan relations. Arguably, over the years, Pakistan's security ties with Washington have worsened, not bettered, these relations.

Nor did the entry of Pakistan into the Western camp further the stated purpose of the alliance: containing the Communist powers. The Indians turned increasingly to the Soviet Union as a counterweight to the United States–Pakistan alliance. Washington's idea that Pakistan and the other Baghdad Pact nations could serve U.S. interests in the Near East by acting as a bulwark against the spread of Moscow's influence there proved fallacious. The Soviets easily leapfrogged over the northern-tier countries and developed strong relations with Egypt and other Arab powers.

These setbacks did not lead to any serious reexamination in the Eisenhower administration of the relationship with Pakistan. American interests in South Asia remained what they had been before Pakistan became, as the Pakistanis themselves put it, "America's most allied ally in Asia." But they were not well served by policies that unwisely made that alliance the keystone of America's approach to the region.

The situation began to change a few years later. As it entered its second term, the Eisenhower administration maintained the links it had with Pakistan despite shortcomings the president himself recognized. Yet at the same time, it developed a different perception of U.S. interests in India (and with other major non-aligned powers it had scorned earlier). Suddenly alarmed that the Soviets were effectively using economic assistance and other inducements to influence these countries, it revised its unsympathetic, sometimes hostile approach to the Third World and adopted measures to counter Moscow's blandishments.

This redefinition of U.S. interests in India was not universally applauded. Though the administration cited anti-Communist objectives in justifying its new line, critics asked whether these worthy goals were furthered by large-scale American economic assistance to a country that seemed almost always to tilt toward the Communist powers on international issues. More generally, they were not satisfied that the administration's revised assessment of U.S. interests in India could be reconciled with its continuing interests in Pakistan.

These objections, from the Pakistan lobby and other quarters, did not unduly trouble the administration. Eisenhower, and even his cold warrior secretary of state, John Foster Dulles (who had only recently called non-alignment immoral), were still defining American interests in both these South Asian rivals largely in the context of broader U.S. Cold War concerns and objectives. The differing circumstances of India and Pakistan and the different way their relations with the United States had evolved required that Washington pursue these interests in different ways.

U.S. perceptions of its South Asian interests changed again in the early 1960s. Americans within and outside the government resented Pakistan's deepening relations with Communist China at a time when Beijing was widely considered the United States' most implacable foe. To put it mildly, and Washington found it increasingly difficult to do so, the new Sino-Pakistan ties were (quite rightly) considered irreconcilable with U.S. global containment interests. The relationship, which reflected the animosity toward India that the two countries shared, seemed to undercut these interests and reduce the importance of Pakistan to the achievement of American security goals. It also complicated U.S. interest in promoting India–Pakistan reconciliation. Washington continued to stress this interest in the 1950s and early 1960s while pursuing policies that signally failed to advance it.

At the same time, the growing enmity between Beijing and New Delhi that eventually led to the 1962 Sino-Indian border war dramatically changed Washington's assessment of U.S. interests in India. It now regarded India as a potential quasi-ally against Chinese communism not only in the Himalayas but also in Southeast Asia, where many believed Beijing played a key role in fostering insurgencies in Vietnam and elsewhere. This fresh interpretation of U.S. interests won broad support outside the administration. Its proponents were encouraged by the extremely hostile Indian attitude toward the Chinese following the debacle the Indian army had suffered in the border war. This perception of India's willingness to play such a broad anti-Beijing role was soon judged to have been wrong.

The Kennedy administration (1961–63) made a serious effort soon after the war to persuade India and Pakistan to come to terms over Kashmir through U.S.-sponsored negotiations, thus making South Asia safer for anti-Communism. These talks failed; both sides faulted the United States for the compromise proposals it had formulated. When the contending countries went to war two years later, the Johnson administration (1963–69) quickly recognized what some commentators had long suspected: their mutual antagonism would outweigh their support for major U.S. interests, especially the containment of global Communism, whenever the two issues seemed to New Delhi and Islamabad to be in competition. The administration, with widespread support on Capitol Hill and elsewhere, effectively declared a curse on both their houses (and on Kashmir as well).

South Asia consequently became for the United States a political back-water, especially in comparison to Southeast Asia, to which the administration now gave top priority. Perceived American interests in the subcontinent dramatically shrank; they came to focus primarily on economic development, now more for its own sake than as a tool to ward off external and internal Communist threats.

Few Americans questioned this sharp redefinition downward of U.S. South Asian political concerns. Even confirmed friends of India agreed that their vision of what would nowadays be called a strategic partnership between Washington and New Delhi had been badly flawed. India's role in the non-aligned movement, where it generally tilted toward radical members led by Castro's Cuba, heightened their disillusion.

The belief of President Richard Nixon (1969–74) and Henry Kissinger, his national security advisor, that the 1971 India–Pakistan confrontation over Bangladesh had global significance seemed to signal yet another change in U.S. interests and objectives in South Asia. Nixon and Kissinger were grateful to Pakistani President Yahya Khan for the key role he played in the historic U.S. opening to Communist China. They believed that Washington's support for Pakistan against India (which they saw as a Soviet ally, if not tool) was important to their goal of restructuring U.S. relations with Moscow and Beijing. They had made this the administration's overriding foreign policy interest. Their views gave Pakistan, and South Asia, a sudden new importance in Washington.

The administration's pro-Pakistan approach at a time when the Pakistan army was brutally suppressing a popular uprising in East Pakistan (soon to be Bangladesh) aroused the sharpest criticism of U.S. South Asia policy witnessed before or since. Most South Asia specialists within and outside the government flatly opposed the policy. They were joined by many other Americans, most of them largely unfamiliar with South Asia, who asked how U.S. interests were served by policies that favored a genocidal military regime seeking to suppress a popular call for freedom.

But this renewed administration perception that the United States had significant political and security stakes in the region and needed to be closely involved there proved to be a brief aberration. In the Nixon–Kissinger view, India and Pakistan were little more than pawns on the international chessboard. The president and his national security advisor were not seriously interested in South Asia as such and knew little about it. When, with the defeat and breakup of Pakistan, the global game moved elsewhere, their concern about the region largely evaporated.

South Asia consequently again fell to a low position on the list of U.S. international political priorities. Interest in regional peace and stability remained. But Washington soon concluded that this could best be promoted by the bilateral India–Pakistan arrangements the two countries spelled out in their 1972 Simla accord, rather than by multilateral efforts at international forums or U.S. unilateral initiatives. The administration enthusiastically welcomed the agreement and urged the two countries to fully implement it. Nixon's successors in the White House maintained this hands-off, cheering from the sidelines approach for almost two decades.

India's 1974 nuclear test ushered in yet another phase in U.S. perceptions of its South Asian interests. The name of the South Asia game now became non-proliferation of nuclear weapons. Other interests, including even economic development, were reduced in importance as Washington vigorously pursued this overriding policy concern with both India and Pakistan. Legislation passed during the Ford administration (1974–77) threatening both countries with sanctions if they pursued unsafeguarded nuclear activities underscored and heightened the government's non-proliferation interest. In accordance with these congressional mandates, nuclear cooperation with both countries was terminated and economic assistance to Pakistan briefly suspended.

During the 1980s, the Soviet occupation of Afghanistan quickly made non-proliferation a distant second to the removal of the Red Army in Washington's ranking of its interests in Pakistan. The Carter administration (1977–81) tentatively, and the Reagan administration (1981–89) in a more full-blooded way, recognized Pakistan as a front-line state in the armed effort to prevent the consolidation of Communist power in Kabul. Washington's interest in its renewed security relationship with Islamabad now overrode all other concerns. Some of these interests, such as Pakistani economic development, were given fresh support in the context of the cooperation of the government of President Zia ul Haq with Washington in the struggle in Afghanistan. The administration used waiver provisions to restore economic assistance programs that had been suspended because of Pakistan's violation of U.S. non-proliferation legislation. Under Reagan, these programs were greatly expanded. Other long-standing interests, such as concern about Pakistan's heroin production and trade, remained on Washington's agenda but were largely soft-pedaled.

Opposition to the revised interpretation of U.S. interests the Soviet advance into Afghanistan had inspired was led by those on Capitol Hill and elsewhere who deplored Pakistan's authoritarian government and its vigorous promotion of orthodox Islamic laws and values. Some critics also feared that Pakistan sought American weapons primarily to bolster its security against India, as it had done a generation earlier. Skeptics also worried that Pakistan was continuing to develop a nuclear weapons option despite its assurances to Washington to the contrary.

But the Reagan administration had little difficulty in overcoming such misgivings while the Soviets remained in Afghanistan and Pakistan was perceived as indispensable to the efforts of the Afghan Mujahedin freedom fighters to dislodge them. India's relaxed attitude toward the Soviet occupation made the administration's pro-Pakistan interpretation of U.S. South Asian interests easier to defend.

Non-proliferation never disappeared as an American interest in South Asia in the 1980s. But the Reagan administration did not pursue it vigorously despite increasing calls on Capitol Hill and elsewhere that it do so. Two events that many observers believe were related changed the way Washington ranked its interest in the issue. These were the Soviet withdrawal from Afghanistan in 1989 and the judgment the Bush administration (1989–93) made the following year that it could no longer certify that Pakistan was in compliance with U.S. non-proliferation legislation. This finding mandated the cutoff of the sizeable military and economic assistance Washington provided Islamabad when the Soviets were in Kabul. Non-proliferation of weapons of mass destruction had returned with a vengeance as a priority item on the U.S. list of its interests in South Asia.

It remained a major, and probably *the* major American interest in Pakistan and India in the 1990s. As it had earlier, the primacy Washington gave this interest during the decade prompted friction with the Indians. These tensions were relieved somewhat by U.S. satisfaction with India's economic reforms. For the first time, major American business concerns became seriously interested in India as a potential trading and investment partner. The more sympathetic positions India took on international issues following the end of the Cold War and the breakup of the Soviet Union were also helpful in promoting better bilateral ties.

By contrast, the U.S. view of Pakistan, now no longer influenced by Cold War considerations, became increasingly negative. Washington seemed much more concerned with the danger that Pakistan would move in directions harmful to U.S. interests than with the possibility that it could foster them. Reflecting these negative perceptions, Washington's policies in Pakistan often seemed to comprise a long list of "don'ts." "Don't develop missiles and weapons of mass destruction"; "Don't support the Taliban and al-Qaeda in Afghanistan"; "Don't assist the insurgency in Indian Kashmir"; "Don't permit narcotics manufacturing and trafficking"—all figured prominently in the dreary litany. Although the Pakistanis called Washington's attention to what it claimed were other important reasons for a more positive U.S. view of the country—its links with the newly independent states of Central Asia, the good example it set as a moderate Islamic state, its contributions to United Nations peacekeeping operations—their arguments did not significantly change Washington's perception that America's primary interest in Pakistan was to keep its policies and problems from becoming worse in ways that could be damaging to the United States.

Opposition on the part of South Asian specialists and others inside and outside the government to the primacy the Clinton administration and key members of Congress gave to U.S. non-proliferation interests in India and Pakistan became increasingly vocal in the mid-1990s. Critics accepted the importance of these concerns. But they argued that in focusing so much on them Washington was damaging other interests the United States had in South Asia. Their most important point was that the end of the Cold War offered America fresh opportunities to develop a stronger relationship with an increasingly powerful India. These opportunities, they said, could not be fully realized as long as the administration persisted in giving center stage to non-proliferation and remained hobbled by unrealistic non-proliferation legislation. Their arguments seemed to be having some effect when the Indian and Pakistani nuclear tests of May 1998 refocused attention on the WMD issue.

What are contemporary U.S. interests in South Asia now that India and Pakistan have tested nuclear weapons, declared themselves nuclear weapons states, and (especially Pakistan) become important players in the U.S.-led war against terrorism?

As the foregoing review of five decades of American relations with South Asia indicates, successive administrations have consistently held that U.S. interests were served by peace and stability in the region and within the individual South Asian countries. The same can be said about Washington's view of almost any other part of the world, except of course the nations behind the Iron Curtain in Cold War times. But in South Asia it has had special salience.

During the early Cold War decades, Washington believed that harmonious relations between the regional countries and tranquility within them were important in curbing perceived Communist threats. The force of this perception diminished over the years as it became increasingly evident that no South Asian country was likely to "go Communist." It strengthened again at the time of the Soviet invasion of Afghanistan, which some observers thought foreshadowed a move by the Red Army into Pakistan and its warm-water ports.

Perhaps equally important in generating American interest in South Asian stability was Washington's concern that a war between India and Pakistan could lead to a wider conflict because of the ties the two countries had developed with major, extra-regional powers, including the United States. The end of the Cold War and the breakup of the Soviet Union removed this concern, but replaced it with another, even more worrying one. This was Washington's recognition of the crucial importance to the United States of heading off a nuclear war in the subcontinent that an India–Pakistan confrontation could spark.

The threat of such a conflict has made the resolution or at least the effective management of the Kashmir dispute more urgent to Washington. It has also had a profound impact on the way the United States defines its interests in the dispute, still the key problem between New Delhi and Islamabad. The United States has now come to regard Kashmir less in terms of the equities of the issue—the lot of the Kashmiri people, the morality or immorality of the insurgency in the Kashmir Valley. Instead, it sees the dispute primarily as a tinder box that could be the flashpoint of a nuclear conflagration.

This redefinition is the primary reason the Clinton (1993–2001) and George W. Bush administrations (2001—) have insisted on the inviolability of the Line of Control and condemned cross-border activity by forces based in Pakistan. It is still no doubt in the interest of the United States to see the long-suffering Kashmiris enjoy better governance, greater prosperity, and more tranquility and dignity than they have had since the state was divided fifty-seven years ago. But this interest has been trumped by a much greater American stake in avoiding a nuclear war. Few Americans would disagree with these implicit priorities.

Washington's interpretation of its other interests in Pakistan has been massively reordered by its post–September 11 leadership in the war against terrorism with a global reach. This redefinition followed President Pervez Musharraf's landmark decision to reverse his government's pro-Taliban Afghanistan policy and throw in Pakistan's lot with the United States and the anti-terrorist coalition it was organizing. It recalls the changes in U.S. assessment of its stakes in Pakistan in the 1950s and 1980s, when Washington enlisted the Pakistanis in its Cold War efforts to contain and roll back Communist power.

It is obviously in the U.S. interest to have Pakistan's continuing assistance in blocking Taliban and al-Qaeda activity in the tribal areas along the Afghan–Pakistan border and in Pakistan itself. The rehabilitation and reconstruction of Afghanistan, major American concerns, require at least tacit Pakistani acquiescence in a broad-based regime in Kabul that is not dominated by Pushtuns, as Islamabad would no doubt prefer.

The events of 9/11 also greatly heightened U.S. interest in stemming Islamic political extremism and terrorist activities in Pakistan, and, by extension, in Indian Kashmir. Washington has put major pressure on the Musharraf government to adopt a tougher line with so-called Jihadists both inside Pakistan and in Kashmir, with mixed results. It has rightly concluded that Pakistan's status as a de facto nuclear weapons state that is a breeding ground for Islamic extremism and terrorism greatly heightens U.S. stakes in the country. There can be no doubt that it is in America's highest national interest to prevent Pakistan from emerging as the world's first nuclear-armed radical Islamic state. That would be a true nightmare.

Sometime after the Indian and Pakistani May 1998 nuclear tests, Washington decided (at least implicitly) to live with the two countries' self-proclaimed status as nuclear-armed states. It regretfully concluded that the long-standing U.S. goal of stopping, rolling back, and eventually eliminating nuclear weapons programs in South Asia had definitively failed. The genie was out of the bottle.

The United States consequently redefined its South Asian WMD interests. It now seeks to head off a nuclear arms race between two irrevocably nuclear-armed states by encouraging them to limit their nuclear arsenals and refrain from deploying these weapons against one another. This goal is accompanied, perhaps even outstripped, especially with regard to Pakistan, by U.S. interest in strengthened nuclear-missile export-control regimes that would prevent sensitive material and technology from falling into the hands of rogue states and terrorist non-state organizations. Similarly important is a U.S. interest in preventing the theft of nuclear material, again especially in Pakistan, and avoiding the danger of an accidental India–Pakistan nuclear war.

These issues have made more urgent another fundamental U.S. interest in Pakistan: the strengthening of the country's fragile civilian political, social, and economic institutions. American administrations have recognized this need from time to time in the past, but usually concluded, incorrectly, that any interest the United States had in a strong, stable Pakistan could be satisfied by military regimes. In the view of many American South Asia specialists, Washington needs to acknowledge that its fundamental interest in avoiding a nuclear-armed Pakistan falling into the hands of extremist elements requires stronger governing institutions than the Pakistan army can or will promote.

These and most other present U.S. interests in Pakistan will endure even after al-Qaeda remnants are rooted out of Afghanistan, the border areas, and the interior of Pakistan. Extremist Muslim political parties and organizations will doubtless continue to operate in Pakistan. America's stake in containing and weakening them will remain. And so, as suggested above, will U.S. interest in the resolution or effective management of the Kashmir issue, which is likely to stay closely linked to the problem of Islamic radicalism and the terrorism it can spawn.

U.S. interest in stemming Pakistan's narcotics production and trafficking will also persist in a post-al-Qaeda scenario. Ironically, a successful crackdown on producers and traffickers by a stronger and more secure Afghan government could make this interest more acute. Some of Pakistan's recent success in its U.S.-supported war against heroin has been attributed to a migration of the industry to Afghanistan, where narcotics operations have generally been tolerated. Tough measures by Kabul could change this and rekindle Pakistan's illicit drug industry. But such successful efforts seem unlikely, given the limited power of the Karzai government and the magnitude of the problem.

The United States has regional interests that embrace both India and Pakistan. Washington will continue to give fostering subcontinental peace and stability and limiting WMD dangers a high priority. But the United States also has interests in India that relate only marginally at best to its Pakistan interests (though the degree to which Washington achieves its objectives in Pakistan could have a profound impact on how it reckons the interests it has in India, and vice versa). Although 9/11 gave Pakistan fresh importance for the promotion of U.S. global interests, the disparity in India's favor in America's calculation of its comparative stakes in the two countries is likely to expand further once al-Qaeda, the Taliban, and extremist forces linked to them have been destroyed or marginalized in Afghanistan and Pakistan.

India's economic reforms have given the United States an interest in investment and trade there that was inconsequential in the years when New Delhi promoted a "license-permit-quota raj" that discouraged foreign private business firms from operating in the country. The frustrations many multinational and other foreign corporations experienced in the past decade have reduced some of the enthusiasm for commercial ties with India that potential American entrepreneurs and Washington policymakers shared when India began to reform its economic policies in the early 1990s. (The important IT industry is an exception.) America's primary economic interest in India now is the hastening of economic reforms at the federal and state level that will lead to the development of a genuine and viable liberal market economy. At the same time, India's growing economic strength has heightened American interest in cooperating with New Delhi in the WTO and other multilateral economic organizations in which it plays an important role.

U.S. interest in India's domestic political and social tranquility goes back much further, of course. The Indians seem to have worked out a viable system of coalition governments that has provided the country welcome political stability, at least at the national level. But the civil rights and liberties of its minorities have been increasingly threatened by militant Hindu organizations and a weakening of popular support for India's secular traditions. The United States has an interest in the reversal of this trend, not least because the further alienation and marginalizing of India's large Muslim community might prompt the emergence in the country of a dangerous Islamic extremist backlash that would provide grist for the mills of global terrorism.

From the earliest days of its relations with independent India, Washington has lauded the country's democratic political institutions. It has properly hailed them as a bright spot in a largely authoritarian Third World. But these glowing accolades had only limited operational consequences, except perhaps in the late 1970s. That was when Prime Minister Indira Gandhi, who had suspended Indian democracy during a year and a half "Emergency," was voted out of office and the Carter administration happily and with great fanfare embraced the restored democratic order under the leadership of Morarji Desai.

Indeed, the fact that the United States and India were "the world's two largest democracies," to use the popular (and hackneyed) phrase, arguably complicated bilateral relations during much of the Cold War period. Why, Americans asked, did professedly democratic India seem to prefer Soviet positions to U.S. ones on important international issues? And why, Indians would counter, did the United States side with authoritarian, theocratic Pakistan against democratic, secular India?

More recently, U.S. professions of interest in the well-being of Indian democratic institutions have become more genuine. Washington has come to recognize the importance for the United States of a flourishing democracy in a country of India's size, strength, influence, and political and economic potential. Many Americans outside the government concur with this position, especially liberals who are the spiritual descendants of the small pro-India lobby of the early decades in bilateral relations.

One of the most remarkable features of current U.S.–Indian relations is the cooperation of the two countries on security matters. For many years, Washington considered Indian military power and pretensions unhelpful to the pursuit of its interests in South Asia and adjacent areas. (New Delhi reciprocated this sentiment.) This has now dramatically changed. More so than any other, the administration of George W. Bush has concluded that the Indians can play an important, positive role that will promote U.S. objectives over a broad area, especially the waters to the east of the subcontinent. Washington also recognizes that New Delhi shares its interest in open seas and the free movement of goods and energy supplies through the Indian Ocean. (India is likely to be the world's second fastest growing energy market in the next twenty years.) Washington's new attitude has been reflected in a series of joint military exercises, as well as in combined naval operations, most notably in the Straits of Malacca at the eastern entrance to the Indian Ocean.

Whether this new and surprising security relationship will grow into a genuine broader strategic partnership cannot be predicted at this point. But many American observers, concerned about growing Chinese military power and aggressiveness, argue that the United States has an interest in an eventual linkage with India designed to contain Beijing's ambitions. This expression of U.S. interest in an anti-Chinese military relationship with India is in some ways a replay of the situation following the 1962 Sino-Indian border conflict, when American strategists looked to New Delhi to help contain Communist power in Vietnam and elsewhere in Southeast Asia. The updated concept finds special favor among right-wing commentators both in the United States and India. They often overstate the case, which in any event has not to this point been accepted by the administration.

U.S. interest in the security role India can usefully play in the Indian Ocean and Southeast Asia also reflects to some degree a belief that the country may soon emerge as a major power in international affairs. Some American commentators have long forecast that India would sooner or later achieve that status. They have maintained that Washington needed to take this into account when designing its global strategy. Although these analysts' predictions have not been borne out over the fifty years they have been making them, the possibility that they will eventuate now seems more likely than before.

India's aspirations to great-power status date back at least as far as the predictions that it would attain it. For many of its citizens, India is not only a great country, it is also a great civilization. New Delhi has long sought to play a leadership role in international organizations such as the United Nations, the Afro-Asian group, and the Non-Aligned Movement, which it helped found. It was especially successful in doing so during the government of Prime Minister Jawaharlal Nehru (1947–64). Nehru's standing in international councils as the de facto leader of the non-aligned nations of the Third World was remarkable since he achieved it at a time when India did not have the military clout or the economic strength that it subsequently attained. His successors have sought to follow in Nehru's footsteps with varying degrees of ardor and success. None ever achieved his stature, however. India's present claim to a permanent seat on an expanded United Nations Security Council reflects and underscores its great-power aspirations.

Whether India will fulfill these aspirations probably depends more than anything else on its economic progress. New Delhi has been handicapped by the fact that its economy has not so far measured up to those of its competitors for top international billing. If India proves able to sustain the economic advances it has made over the last decade, it will be taken more seriously. If it does not, it could find itself facing a lack of credibility abroad. Limited economic progress could also lead to social and political difficulties at home that would prevent it from playing a global role, or at least a positive one from America's point of view.

Meanwhile, India's worth to U.S. interests in such areas as information technology, the environment, global terrorism, international crime, narcotic production and trafficking, health, and scientific research has grown rapidly. Cooperation in these areas has rightly received major attention from Washington in recent years. This was underscored to Americans and Indians alike by President Clinton during his historic visit to India in the year 2000. U.S. interest in cooperation with India in these fields is likely to become even more important in the future.

If any single theme stands out in this review of America's South Asia interests, it is the roller-coaster nature of Washington's perceptions of the region's significance for U.S. global goals. At times, the United States has considered the subcontinent highly important, as it does now. At other times, it has concluded that South Asia could safely be put on its foreign policy backburner. The latter situation has been more typical.

A sustained appreciation of U.S. interests in South Asia would surely have been desirable for the United States and the regional countries alike. Whether this can be achieved is another question. Developments since the end of the Cold War, especially the greater importance the United States has come to attach to India and the more benign view India has taken of U.S. motives and intentions in the region and elsewhere, suggest that a less mercurial approach might be more possible now than before. But given the volatility of the area, and of the rest of the world, it would be foolhardy indeed to predict with any confidence that Washington's view of U.S. interests in the region and the way it goes about promoting them will become more consistent than they have been in the fifty years since America first developed relations with the newly independent countries of the subcontinent.

Appendix

The focus of this review has been on India and Pakistan. American interests in South Asia, whether positive or negative, have centered on these two rival states. This is likely to continue for some time.

But the United States also has a variety of interests in the smaller South Asian countries. These interests have been relatively limited except in unusual circumstances, such as serious domestic disturbances or major confrontations between these smaller countries and India. They largely reflect the way Washington has defined its global interests, especially political stability, economic development, good governance (notably curbing corruption), and, more recently, the war against terrorism.

U.S. stakes in each country have been different. In Sri Lanka, Washington has an interest in a resolution of the country's twenty-year civil war. This is not because the United States has any significant economic or security interests in the island. (It does not, contrary to occasional but thankfully no longer current Indian allegations.) Nor is Washington's position motivated by fear that the war might spread elsewhere. American interest seems instead to reflect a moral calculus that as a friendly country with considerable potential, Sri Lanka deserves better. It is also the result of the terrorist tactics of the Tamil Tigers. Washington finds these unacceptable, and has placed the Tigers on its list of international terrorist organizations. (Nonetheless, it supports Tiger participation in the peace process now underway.) Traditional U.S. opposition to the breakup of nations, though now muted following the dissolution of the Soviet Union and Yugoslavia, has also influenced Washington's thinking.

Washington has (wisely) preferred to play a limited political and military supply role in efforts to bolster the Sri Lankan government and help bring about an end to the war. It has accepted Norway as the indispensable third party in the peace negotiations. The Norwegians' experience in moving seemingly implacable opponents toward a settlement and the fact that they cannot be accused of having any ambitions in Sri Lanka or elsewhere in the region are important advantages, in the U.S. view. Interestingly, Washington did not follow this basically hands-off approach in the early 1970s, when it joined with other nations (including Communist China!) to help the Sri Lanka government put down a radical insurrection.

Before Sri Lanka became a "single issue" state, following the outbreak of the civil war in 1983, U.S. interests focused most importantly on its economic development. Difficult as it may now be to believe, the island was considered in the late 1970s and early 1980s a poster child for Third World countries to emulate in choosing sensible, free-market-oriented policies. These interests found concrete form in assistance programs unusually large in a small state that had no alliance relationship with Washington.

For years Sri Lanka pursued what was for a small Indian Ocean country an unusually active foreign policy. In this role, Colombo championed the idea of the Indian Ocean as a zone of peace from which armed vessels of non-littoral states would be barred. This formulation was anathema in Washington. The United States considered (and, of course, still considers) the security of the Indian Ocean a major interest, especially in the context of its Near Eastern and fuel transport concerns. A ban on a U.S. naval presence there would seriously jeopardize this interest in Washington's view. With the defeat of its leftist government in the late 1970s, Colombo began to soft-pedal its zone of peace crusade. The concept is now a dead letter, to U.S. satisfaction.

U.S. interest in Bangladesh has been limited since the bloody birth of the country, which the Nixon administration opposed. Since that time, its focus has mainly been on economic development, largely for humanitarian reasons in a nation that an American statesman famously termed a basket case. Bangladesh has never had any particular security importance for the United States, despite old Indian allegations that there, too, Washington sought naval facilities. At the same time, the United States has welcomed the major role that Dhaka plays in U.N. peacekeeping operations and has added this to its list of interests in the country. (Little persuasion is necessary. The Bangladeshis have found peacekeeping both prestigious and lucrative.)

As elsewhere in the region, Washington has an interest in Bangladesh's good governance, preferably through democratic political institutions and a strengthened civil society. It genuinely welcomed the overthrow in 1990 of Bangladesh's authoritarian military leader and the generally free and fair elections that have followed. It has demonstrated its interest in consolidating and expanding Bangladeshi democracy by engaging in active behind-the-scenes jawboning designed to persuade the losing side to accept the results of elections. The United States has also used its influence to persuade rival political parties to accept responsible roles in the governance of the country, with limited results. It has sought, again with meager results, to promote a greater degree of honesty and transparency in government that would weaken Bangladesh's world-class record for corrupt practices.

Washington has an interest in the independence and territorial integrity of Bangladesh and other smaller regional powers. Pursuing this interest, it has dealt with these countries as sovereign entities and has only on rare occasions been willing to accept Indian aspirations to a hegemonic role. At the same time, Washington has seen it in its interest to avoid any encouragement or support of these countries in their squabbles with New Delhi and has generally sought to avoid unduly antagonizing the Indians. It has enthusiastically welcomed the high priority some Indian governments have given to better relations with its smaller neighbors. This U.S. attitude reflects Washington's enduring interest in South Asian peace and stability as well as its concern for the region's economic advance, which inter-state tranquility promotes.

For the last decade, traditional U.S. concerns in Bangladesh have been rivaled by a new interest in the country's rich natural gas resources. Before then, American economic interest in the country had been focused on grant and loan assistance Washington provided directly or through international financial institutions and on regulating the exports of Bangladesh's burgeoning garment industry to the United States. A good deal of Washington's attention now goes to efforts to persuade the Bangladesh government to allow international energy companies to function on a sound commercial basis and to permit natural gas exports. (India is the most logical market.)

The United States has at least tacitly accepted New Delhi's claim that Nepal lies within its sphere of influence. Washington's interests in the Himalayan kingdom have usually followed the pattern found elsewhere in the region. Economic development has ordinarily had the highest priority. (Remarkably, the United States opened an aid mission in Kathmandu before it established a resident embassy.) Washington has consequently provided generous funding for development projects and other assistance measures. A large Peace Corps program has operated in Nepal since the Kennedy administration started the program four decades ago. Its alumni form a Nepalese lobby in the United States.

Political stability, and more recently, the strengthening of Nepal's faltering democratic institutions, have also been important for Washington. This U.S. interest now focuses on the danger posed by a major Maoist insurgency in the kingdom. The United States has an important stake in avoiding Nepal's becoming another happy hunting ground for international terrorists. Reflecting this, it has begun to provide military supplies to the Nepalese for the first time. Washington is cooperating with the Indians and the

British to help the Nepalese deal with the insurgency. The administration surely recognizes that even at a time of greatly improved U.S.–Indian relations, unilateral American efforts to shore up Nepal's internal security could arouse latent suspicions in New Delhi that Washington has a hidden agenda in the kingdom challenging to India's interests there.

Notes

Chapter 1

1. See, for example, Michael Kraig, "The Political and Strategic Imperatives of Nuclear Deterrence in South Asia," *India Review* 2, no. 1 (2003): 1–48.

2. Underscoring the concern that economic failure can effect radicalism, a high-level Chinese official is reported to have pointedly noted to President Musharraf in late 2003 that China has put economics above everything else.

3. Of course, China, which has supported Pakistan's nuclear program, will also matter in the outcome.

4. Pakistan attributes both the Kashmir problem and the weak socioeconomic condition of India's Muslims to Hindu radicalism, which it believes to be an endemic problem of the Indian state, pre-dating Islamic radicalism on the subcontinent and even causing it. According to the Pakistani view of India, India is a state that is intrinsically Hindu but falsely voices support for secularism to support its territorial ambition, which consists of "keeping" Kashmir and destroying Pakistan. This perspective is an important part of Pakistan's argument for the violence in Kashmir and the need for Pakistan to be involved in the solution. Ironically, members of the Hindu radical right would strongly agree with components of this argument: that the Indian state is intrinsically Hindu and that Muslims and Christians are foreigners who chose a religion and culture that, in their times, oppressed the Hindu masses. V. D. Savarkar, a prominent Hindu nationalist (1883–1966) pre-dated Mohammed Ali Jinnah, founder of Pakistan, when he wrote that Hindus and Muslims were "two antagonistic nations living side by side in India." By contrast, many commentators maintain that secularism is enshrined in the Indian constitution and is largely well protected. This faction attributes Muslim decline to social factors, and the Kashmir problem to the undermining efforts of Pakistan.

5. The one weak point that Nehru saw in the new Indian nation was Kashmir, a state with its own constitution and with a high degree of autonomy. He assiduously

cultivated Sheikh Abdullah, Kashmir's then prime minister, negotiating for Kashmir a special, quasi-autonomous status, that has continued despite its stated nature as a temporary law.

6. The cease-fire line was recognized as a Line of Control after the Simla agreement in 1972.

7. Azad Kashmir enjoys a higher literacy rate and general level of development than both Pakistan itself and Indian Kashmir.

8. The form of autonomy should not be the subject of open discussion by either side's representatives—a particularly difficult task for Delhi, given the range of political pressures that it faces, including during local and national elections.

9. Such actions include changing the status of the head of government from prime minister to chief minister and subjecting the legal decisions of Kashmir courts to review in Delhi-based superior courts. Likewise, in contrast to the pre-1989 situation, India views both the pro-Pakistan and pro-independence segments of the Kashmir population as working outside the sphere of institutionally sanctioned politics and therefore subject to criminal action.

10. The MMA won 53 of the 342 seats in the National Assembly; see http://www.electionworld.org/pakistan.htm.

11. See, for example, J. Juan Cole, "Why Those Election Results in Pakistan Are Frightening," History News Network, October 21, 2002, http://hnn.us/articles/1053.html.

12. The ITP and JAH were unable to win any seats in the National Assembly.

13. For example, the ITP and the JUI have battled each other violently on Shia–Sunni issues. Power can also overcome some doctrinal differences, it seems. When the JI criticized a JUI faction's candidate, Akram Durrani, for chief ministership of NWFP on the grounds that Durrani lacked a beard, he obliged the JI by growing one (International Crisis Group, "Pakistan: The Mullahs and the Military," Asia Report, no. 49, March 20, 2003 [full text available in pdf format at http://www.icg.org/home/getfile.cfm?id=306]).

14. And also partly because the doctrinally most dissimilar parties, the JAH and the ITP, failed to win any seats in the National Assembly.

15. International Crisis Group, "Pakistan: The Mullahs and the Military," 18.

16. Ibid.

17. The Pakistan People's Party fought under the banner of PPP Parliamentarians for the election.

18. The army's role was evident in pre-election malpractices, such as giving undue time to the MMA in television coverage, and in special rules, such as the requirement of a bachelor's degree (*madrasah* graduates qualified), as well as in post-election maneuvering, such as engineering a coalition between the army's favored party, the PML-Q, and the MMA in Baluchistan.

19. In most democracies, internal crises are handled through politics, but Pakistan may have to accept a role for the army in handling internal crises for some time.

20. Except for the 1980s when the crisis originated in Afghanistan, the other crises have either been internal or related to India. Despite Pakistan having begun both the 1965 and 1999 wars (although not the 1971 war over Bangladesh), the Indian record of victory in all three wars has led to the popular view that the country is under mortal threat from a superior neighbor (see, for example, William Dalrymple, "Murder in Karachi," *New York Review* 50, no. 19 (December 4, 2003), http://www.nybooks.com/articles/16823.

21. Its motives notwithstanding, the army is certainly not free of corruption either.

22. For example, in 1990 the army promoted an alliance between Nawaz Sharif's PML and the JI to oppose the PPP in the upcoming general elections. The JI later turned against the PML, in 1993, again at the military's behest (International Crisis Group, "Pakistan: The Mullahs and the Military," 9).

Chapter 2

1. Pervaiz Iqbal Cheemah, "The Kashmir Dispute and Peace of South Asia," *Regional Studies* 15, no. 1 (Winter 1996–97): 170–88.

2. See Barnett R. Rubin, *The Fragmentation of Afghanistan: State Formation and Collapse in the International System* (New Haven, Conn.: Yale University Press, 1995); Olivier Roy, *Islam and Resistance in Afghanistan* (New York: Cambridge University Press, 1986); Marvin Weinbaum, *Pakistan and Afghanistan: Resistance and Reconstruction* (Boulder, Colo.: Westview, 1994); Rasul B. Rais, *War without Winners: Afghanistan's Uncertain Transition after Cold War* (Karachi: Oxford University Press, 1994).

3. Jonah Blank, "Kashmir: Fundamentalism Takes Root," *Foreign Affairs,* November–December 1999.

4. Robert Wirsing, *India, Pakistan and the Kashmir Dispute: On Regional Conflict and its Resolution* (New York: St. Martin's Press, 1994).

5. Seyyed Vali Reza Nasr, *Islamic Leviathan: Islam and State Power* (New York: Oxford University Press, 2001).

6. Rounaq Jahan, *Pakistan: Failure in National Integration* (New York: Columbia University, 1972); Philip Oldenburg, "'A Place Insufficiently Imagined': Language, Belief, and the Pakistan Crisis of 1971," *Journal of Asian Studies* 44, no. 4 (August 1985): 715–23; Vali Nasr, "The Negotiable State: Borders and Power-Struggles in Pakistan," in *Rightsizing the State: The Politics of Moving Borders,* ed. Ian Lustick, Thomas Callaghy, and Brendan O'Leary (New York: Oxford University Press, 2001), 168–200.

7. Mumtaz Ahmad, "Islamization and the Structural Crises of the State in Pakistan," *Issues in Islamic Thought* 12 (1993): 304–10.

8. Seyyed Vali Reza Nasr, "State, Society, and the Crisis of National Identity in Pakistan," in *State, Society, and Democratic Change in Pakistan,* ed. Rasul B. Rais (New York: Oxford University Press, 1997), 103–30.

9. Mumtaz Ahmad, "Islam and the State: The Case of Pakistan," in *The Religious Challenge to the State,* ed. Matthew Moen and Lowell Gustafson (Philadelphia:

Temple University Press, 1992), 239–67.

10. Nasr, *Islamic Leviathan.*

11. Seyyed Vali Reza Nasr, *The Vanguard of Islamic Revolution: The Jama'at-i Islami of Pakistan* (Berkeley: University of California Press, 1994), 170–87.

12. Anwar H. Syed, *The Discourse and Politics of Zulfikar Ali Bhutto* (New York: St. Martin's Press, 1992), 205–24; Stanley Wolpert, *Zulfi Bhutto of Pakistan* (New York: Oxford University Press, 1993), 214–29; and Nasr, *The Vanguard of Islamic Revolution,* 179.

13. See Vali Nasr, "The Rise of Sunni Militancy in Pakistan: The Changing Role of Islamism and the Ulama in Society and Politics," *Modern Asian Studies* 34, no. 1 (January 2000): 139–80.

14. *Herald* (Karachi), October 1996, 54.

15. On Sunni politics in Pakistan, see Nasr, "The Rise of Sunni Militancy in Pakistan"; and Muhmmad Qasim Zaman, "Sectarianism in Pakistan: The Radicalization of Shi'i and Sunni Identities," *Modern Asian Studies,* 32, no. 3 (1998): 687–716. On Shi'i politics in Pakistan, see Nikki Keddie, *The Shi'a of Pakistan: Reflections and Problems for Further Research,* Working Paper no. 23 (Los Angeles: G. E. von Grunebaum Center for Near Eastern Studies, University of California, Los Angeles, 1993); Saleem Qureshi, "The Politics of the Shia Minority in Pakistan: Context and Developments," in *Religious and Ethnic Minority Politics in South Asia,* ed. D. Vajpeyi and Y. Malik (Delhi: Manohar, 1989), 109–38; Afak Haydar, "The Politicization of the Shias and the Development of the Tehrik-e-Nifaz-e-Fiqh-e-Jafaria in Pakistan," in *Pakistan 1992,* ed. Charles H. Kennedy (Boulder, Colo.: Westview Press, 1993), 75–93; Maleeha Lodhi, "Pakistan's Shia Movement: An Interview with Arif Hussaini," *Third World Quarterly* (1988): 806–17; and Munir D. Ahmad, "The Shi'is of Pakistan," in *Shi'ism: Resistance and Revolution,* ed. Martin Kramer (Boulder, Colo.: Westview Press, 1987), 275–87.

16. Mushahid Hussain, "Pakistan–Iran Relations in the Changing World Scenario: Challenges and Response," in *Pakistan Foreign Policy Debate: The Years Ahead,* ed. Tariq Jan (Islamabad: Institute of Policy Studies, 1993), 211–22.

17. Vali Nasr, "The Iranian Revolution and Changes in Islamism in Pakistan, India, and Afghanistan," in *Iran and the Surrounding World,* ed. Nikki R. Keddie and Rudi Matthee (Seattle: University of Washington Press, 2002), 327–54.

18. S. Jamal Malik, "Islamization in Pakistan 1977–85: The Ulama and Their Places of Learning," *Islamic Studies* 28, no. 1 (Spring 1989): 5–28.

19. S. Jamal Malik, "Dynamics among Traditional Religious Scholars and Their Institutions in Contemporary South Asia," *Muslim World* 87, no. 3–4 (July–October 1997): 216–17.

20. Nasr, "The Rise of Sunni Militancy in Pakistan."

21. *Herald* (Karachi), September 1992, 34.

22. Ibid.

23. Weinbaum, *Pakistan and Afghanistan.*

24. Mary Ann Weaver, "Children of Jihad," *New Yorker,* June 12, 1995, 46.

25. For more on the Pakistan military, see Parvaiz Iqbal Cheema, *The Armed Forces of Pakistan* (New York: New York University Press, 2003).

26. For more on the Jama'at, see Mumtaz Ahmad, "Islamic Fundamentalism in South Asia: The Jamaat-i-Islami and the Tablighi Jamaat," in *Fundamentalisms Observed,* ed. Martin E. Marty and R. Scott Appleby (Chicago: University of Chicago Press, 1991), 457–530; Rafiuddin Ahmed, "Redefining Muslim Identity in South Asia: The Transformation of the Jama'at-i Islami," in *Accounting for Fundamentalisms: The Dynamic Character of Movements,* ed. Martin E. Marty and R. Scott Appleby (Chicago: University of Chicago Press, 1994), 699–705; Kalim Bahadur, *The Jama'at-i Islami of Pakistan* (New Delhi: Chetana Publications, 1977); and Seyyed Vali Reza Nasr, *The Vanguard of the Islamic Revolution: The Jama'at-i Islami of Pakistan* (Berkeley: University of California Press, 1994).

27. Seyyed Vali Reza Nasr, "Islamic Opposition to the Islamic State: The Jama'at-i Islami 1977–88," *International Journal of Middle East Studies* 25, no. 2 (May 1993): 261–83.

28. Weinbaum, *Pakistan and Afghanistan.*

29. Rubin, *The Fragmentation of Afghanistan;* Roy, *Islam and Resistance in Afghanistan.*

30. Rubin, *The Fragmentation of Afghanistan.*

31. Sumit Ganguly, *The Crisis in Kashmir: Portents of War and Hopes of Peace* (New York: Cambridge University Press, 1997).

32. Ahmed Rashid, *Taliban: Militant Islam, Oil, and Fundamentalism in Central Asia* (New Haven, Conn.: Yale University Press, 2001); Peter Marsden, *The Taliban: War and Religion in Afghanistan* (London: Zed Books, 2002); William Maley, *Fundamentalism Reborn?: Afghanistan and the Taliban* (New York: New York University Press, 1988); Larry Goodson, *Afghanistan's Endless War: State Failure, Regional Politics, and the Rise of the Taliban* (Seattle: University of Washington Press, 2001).

33. *Far Eastern Economic Review,* March 9, 1995, 24.

34. *News International* (Karachi), March 4, 1999, 1, 4.

35. Ibid.

36. *Herald* (Karachi), December 1997, 64.

37. Vali Nasr, "Democracy and the Crisis of Governability in Pakistan," *Asian Survey* 32, no. 6 (June 1992): 521–37.

38. Owen Bennett Jones, *Pakistan: In the Eye of the Storm,* 2nd ed. (New Haven, Conn.: Yale University Press, 2003).

39. Nasr, *Islamic Leviathan,* 154–56.

40. Mushahid Husain, interview by author, Islamabad, October 1997.

Chapter 3

1. This treatment of "constitutional phases" closely follows my approach and treatment in Craig Baxter, Yogendra Malik, Charles H. Kennedy, and Robert Oberst, *Government and Politics in South Asia* (Boulder, Colo.: Westview, 2002), 184–93.

2. *Federation of Pakistan v. Moulvi Tamizuddin Khan*, All-Pakistan Legal Decisions (PLD) 1955 (Federal Court), 240.

3. Prior to the adoption of the One Unit Plan in 1955, the population of East Pakistan exceeded the population of West Pakistan by a ratio of approximately 55 to 45; but as East Pakistan constituted a single province and West Pakistan was divided into four separate provinces, the population of East Pakistan far exceeded that of any of the other provinces of the state.

4. The so-called Disturbances of 1969 (January–March 1969) was a mass movement spearheaded by sections of Pakistan's civil bureaucracy, East Pakistani dissidents, and the leftist-oriented student cadre of the Pakistan People's Party (PPP). Among other demands, the movement called for the resignation of Ayub Khan (see Charles H. Kennedy, *Bureaucracy in Pakistan* [Karachi: Oxford University Press, 1987], 75–78).

5. Hamid Khan, *Constitutional and Political History of Pakistan* (Karachi: Oxford University Press, 2001), 448–53.

6. *Begum Nusrat Bhutto v. Chief of Army Staff*, PLD 1977 (Supreme Court), 657.

7. Constitution (Eighth Amendment) Act, 1985, PLD 1986 (Central Statutes), 1.

8. The president's dissolution was upheld by *Ahmad Tariq Rahim v. Federation of Pakistan*, PLD 1991 (Lahore), 778; and *Ahmad Tariq Rahim v. Federation of Pakistan*, PLD 1992 (Supreme Court), 648.

9. *Mian Nawaz Sharif v. President of Pakistan*, PLD (Supreme Court), 473.

10. For a detailed discussion, see Charles H. Kennedy, "Presidential–Prime Ministerial Relations: The Role of the Superior Courts," in *Pakistan: 1995*, ed. Charles H. Kennedy and Rasul B. Rais (Boulder, Colo.: Westview Press, 1995), 17–30. Also see Khan, *Constitutional and Political History of Pakistan*, 753–58, 792–96, 805–13.

11. See text of president's speech to the nation, in *Muslim* (November 5, 1996). Also, see Mohammed Waseem, "Pakistan Elections 1997: One Step Forward," in *Pakistan: 1997*, ed. Craig Baxter and Charles H. Kennedy, (Boulder, Colo.: Westview Press, 1998), 4–7.

12. *Benazir Bhutto v. President of Pakistan*, PLD 1988 (Supreme Court), 388.

13. *Dastoor v. Federation of Pakistan*, PLD 1988 (Supreme Court), 1263; see also S. M. Zafar, "Constitutional Developments in Pakistan, 1997–99," in *Pakistan: 2000*, ed. Charles H. Kennedy and Craig Baxter (Karachi: Oxford University Press, 2001), 1–33. Another useful discussion is found in Khan, *Constitutional and Political History of Pakistan*, 820–31.

14. Found in *Dawn* (Karachi), October 30, 1997.

15. As per the Supreme Court's dicta in *Jehad Trust v. Federation of Pakistan*, PLD 1996 (Supreme Court), 324.

16. See Ayesha Jalal, *The State of Martial Rule* (New York: Cambridge University Press, 1990), 273–76.

17. Khan, *Constitutional and Political History of Pakistan*, 212.

18. Laws (Continuance in Force) Order, 1977, PLD 1977 (Central Statutes), 325.

19. Provisional Constitution Order, 1999, PLD 1999 (Central Statutes), 446.

20. *Federation of Pakistan v. Moulvi Tamizuddin Khan,* PLD 1955 (Federal Court), 240; Reference by HE the Governor-General, PLD 1955 (Federal Court), 435. See also the discussion in Paula Newberg, *Judging the State* (Cambridge: Cambridge University Press, 1995), 42–68; and Khan, *Constitutional and Political History of Pakistan,* 136–54.

21. *State v. Dosso,* PLD 1958 (Supreme Court), 533. See also the discussion in Newberg, *Judging the State,* 73–78.

22. The Sixth Amendment had permitted sitting Chief Justices of the Supreme Court and High Courts to serve beyond their normal age of retirement—sixty-five years and sixty-two years, respectively. The Fifth Amendment, among other things, had set the term limits for Chief Justices of the Supreme Court at five years and Chief Justices of High Courts as four years (Khan, *Constitutional and Political History of Pakistan,* 530–35, 538).

23. Justice Yakub Khan, a Bhutto appointee, had reached the age of retirement but had not completed his five-year term as Chief Justice of the Supreme Court (see note 22). The suspension of the Sixth Amendment forced him to retire and allowed the appointment of Justice Anwar-ul-Haq to the post of Chief Justice. The latter justice was to prove far more sympathetic to Zia-ul-Haq's assumption of power than Justice Yakub Khan was anticipated to be.

24. *Begum Nusrat Bhutto v. Chief of Army Staff,* PLD 1977 (Supreme Court), 657. See also Newberg, *Judging the State,* 167–70.

25. Oath of Office (Judge's Order), 1999, PLD 2000 (Central Statutes), 38. Musharraf seems to have borrowed the idea of forcing the superior judiciary to take a fresh oath of office from the ever-resourceful Zia-ul-Haq. In 1981, after Zia promulgated his own Provisional Constitution Order, he required the superior judiciary to take a fresh oath. Four Supreme Court justices (Chief Justice Anwar-ul-Haq, Maulvi Mushtaq, Dorab Patel, and Fakhruddin Ibrahim) did not take the oath and stood retired (see Khan, *Constitutional and Political History of Pakistan,* 649–51).

26. Those refusing to take the oath in the Supreme Court were: Chief Justice Saeeduzzaman Siddiqui, and Justices Mamoon Kazi, Khalilur Rehman Khan, Nasir Aslam Zahid, Wajihuddin Ahmad, and Kamal Mansur Alam. Justice Irshad Hasan Khan, who took the new oath, became the new Chief Justice.

27. *Zafar Ali Shah v. Parvez Musharraf, Chief Executive of Pakistan,* PLD 2000 (Supreme Court), 869.

28. Article 6 of the Constitution reads: "(1) Any person who abrogates or attempts or conspires to abrogate, subverts or attempts to subvert the Constitution by use of force or show of force or by other unconstitutional means shall be guilty of high treason. (2) Any person aiding or abetting the acts mentioned in clause (1) shall likewise be guilty of high treason."

29. Three "white papers" were issued, in six volumes, each published by the Government of Pakistan: *White Paper on the Performance of the Bhutto Regime* (3 vols.)—Vol. 1, "Mr. Z. A. Bhutto, Family, and Associates" (January 1979); Vol. 2, "Treatment of Fundamental State Institutions" (January 1979); and Vol. 3, "Misuse of the

Instruments of State Power" (January 1979); *White Paper on the Misuse of the Media* (August 1978); and *White Paper on the Conduct of the General Elections in March 1977* (July 1978). The latter volume was 1,449 pages. A 118-page *Summary of White Paper on the Conduct of the General Elections, March 1977* was also published.

30. *State v. Zulfiqar Ali Bhutto,* PLD 1978 (Lahore), 523.

31. *Z. A. Bhutto v. State,* PLD 1979 (Supreme Court), 53.

32. For details, see Charles H. Kennedy, "The Creation and Development of Pakistan's Anti-Terrorism Regime, 1997–2002" (unpublished manuscript, November 2002).

33. Anti-Terrorism (Second Amendment) Ordinance, 1999, PLD 2000 (Central Statutes), 8.

34. Anti-Terrorism (Third Amendment) Ordinance, 1999, PLD 2000 (Central Statutes), 78.

35. The trial was covered extensively by the major Pakistani dailies; see the Internet editions of *Dawn* (Lahore) and the *News* (Islamabad), at http://www.dawn.com and http://www.jang.com.pk, respectively.

36. *Dawn* (Karachi), December 10, 2000, http://www.dawn.com.

37. Murtaza Bhutto, politically estranged from his sister, had formed a rival faction of the PPP—the PPP (Shaheed Bhutto)—in alliance with their mother, Nusrat Bhutto. The PPP (SB) fielded candidates in the 1997 election.

38. Khan, *Constitutional and Political History of Pakistan,* 221.

39. Ibid., 660.

40. Ibid. Of course, the reported turnout was inflated. I visited three polling stations near my residence in Islamabad on election day in 1984. At mid-afternoon, the time of my visit to the respective stations, a total of only six people had cast their ballots. At one polling station, no one had cast a ballot.

41. International Crisis Group, "Pakistan: Transition to Democracy?" ICG Asia Report, no. 40 (Islamabad/Brussels: October 3, 2002), 20.

42. Ibid.

43. Basic Democracies Order, 1959, PLD 1959 (Central Statutes), 364.

44. See, for example, Ronald Herring, *Land to the Tiller: The Political Economy of Land Reform in South Asia* (New Haven, Conn.: Yale University Press, 1983).

45. Punjab Local Government Ordinance, 1979, PLD 1979 (Punjab Statutes), 101; Baluchistan Local Government Ordinance, 1979, PLD 1980 (Baluchistan Statutes), 26; Sind Local Government Ordinance, 1979, PLD 1980 (Sind Statutes), 1; and NWFP Local Government Ordinance, 1979, PLD 1980 (NWFP Statutes), 1.

46. Government of Pakistan, Chief Executive Secretariat, National Reconstruction Bureau, *Local Government (Proposed Plan): Devolution of Power and Responsibility Establishing the Foundations for Genuine Democracy* (Islamabad: May 2000).

47. Government of Pakistan, *Local Government Ordinance 2001—Promulgated by Provinces (13 August 2001)* (National Reconstruction Bureau), http://www.nrb.gov.pk. For a discussion of the process, see Charles H. Kennedy, "Analysis of Pakistan's Devolution Plan," paper prepared for the Department for International Development (U.K.) (September 2001).

48. Government of Pakistan, Chief Executive Secretariat, *National Reconstruction Bureau, Devolution: Local Government and Citizen Empowerment (14 August 2001)* (National Reconstruction Bureau), http://www. nrb.gov.pk.

49. For an analysis of the first phase of the elections, see Farzana Bari, *Local Government Elections December 2000 (Phase One)* (Islamabad: Pattan Development Corporation, 2001).

50. Government of Pakistan, Cabinet Secretariat, *Report of the Pay and Services Commission, 1959–1962* (Karachi: MPCPP, 1969).

51. Kennedy, *Bureaucracy in Pakistan,* 75–78.

52. Khan, *Constitutional and Political History of Pakistan,* 274–76, 245–47.

53. In 1972, Bhutto purged 1,828 officers of the bureaucracy and later introduced significant administrative reforms which targeted the bureaucratic elite (see Kennedy, *Bureacucracy in Pakistan,* esp. 80).

54. Ibid., 122–25.

55. During the author's affiliation with the Federal Shariat Court (1984–86), none of the FSC regular judges (non-ulema judges) had sought appointment to the Court.

56. The Lahore High Court had benches established in Bahawalpur, Multan, and Rawalpindi; the Sindh High Court in Sukkur; the Peshawar High Court in Abbotabad and Dera Ishmail Khan; and the High Court of Balochistan in Sibi (Khan, *Constitutional and Political History of Pakistan,* 643).

57. See note 25.

58. This is becoming an increasingly contentious issue subsequent to the election of a civilian regime in late 2002. The Prime Minister does not have the same scope for the provision of political patronage as did his predecessor civilian regimes. See, for instance, Irfan Husain [aka Mazdak], "Jobs for Boys," *Dawn* (Karachi), October 5, 2003, http://www.dawn.com.

59. See Zeeshan Siddique, "Judges Get Extension," *Dawn* (Karachi), January 5, 2003, http://www.dawn.com.

60. *United Bank, Ltd. v. Farooq Brothers,* PLD 2002 (Supreme Court), 800.

61. The Seventeenth Amendment purportedly amended Article 179 of the Constitution (the article which deals with the tenure of superior court judges). However, since this provision of the LFO was not validated, the Article was technically never revised.

62. Government of Pakistan, *Report of the Constitution Commission, 1961* (Karachi: MPCPP, 1961).

63. Between 1980 and 1985 provisions relating to the operation of the Federal Shariat Court were modified twenty-eight times through the mechanism of twelve separate presidential ordinances, and were incorporated into the Constitution in fourteen subsections. For details of Zia's Islamization policies, see Charles H. Kennedy, *Islamization of Laws and Economy: Case Studies on Pakistan* (Islamabad: Institute of Policy Studies, 1996).

64. *Dawn* (Karachi), August 13, 1983, http://www.dawn.com. Also, see Khan, *Constitutional and Political History of Pakistan,* 656–57.

65. Revival of Constitution of 1973 Order, 1985, PLD 1985 (Central Statutes), 456.

66. Government of Pakistan, Chief Executive Secretariat, National Reconstruction Bureau, *Conceptual Framework of Proposals on the Government of Pakistan on the Establishment of Sustainable Democracy: Package I (26 June 2002)*, and *Package II (14 July 2002)* (National Reconstruction Bureau), http://www.nrb.gov.pk.

67. Legal Framework Order, PLD 2002 (Supplemental Federal Statutes), 1604.

68. The promise was made in the August 13 address to the nation. Most likely, Musharraf felt that this announcement would demonstrate his sincerity for democratizing the political process to domestic and international critics.

69. Political Parties Order, PLD 2002 (Federal Statutes), 250.

70. "Text of 17th Amendment Bill," *Dawn* (Karachi), December 30, 2003, http://www.dawn.com. Also, see the useful analysis of the Seventeenth Amendment by I. A. Rehman, "Grand Deal 2003," in the January 5, 2004, edition.

71. Khan, *Constitutional and Political History of Pakistan*, 312. Hamid Khan's discussion of the 1965 election (pp. 301–19) is particularly useful.

72. There are numerous excellent sources that detail the foreign policy of Ayub Khan's regime. Among the best are: Lawrence Ziring, *The Ayub Khan Era* (Syracuse, N.Y.: Syracuse University Press, 1971); and Lawrence Ziring, *Pakistan in the Twentieth Century* (Karachi: Oxford University Press, 1997).

73. Khan, *Constitutional and Political History of Pakistan*, 377–78.

74. See Charles H. Kennedy, "Repugnancy to Islam—Who Decides? Islam and Legal Reform in Pakistan," *International and Comparative Law Quarterly* 41, no. 4 (October 1992): 769–87.

75. His plan, derived from the Ansari Commission Report, would have replaced Pakistan's four provinces with its twenty-odd divisions (see Government of Pakistan, Cabinet Division, *Ansari Commission's Report on Form of Government 24th Shawal 1403* [Islamabad: MPCPP, 1984]).

76. Ralph Braibanti, *Research on the Bureaucracy of Pakistan* (Durham, N.C.: Duke University Press, 1966), 310–29.

77. Respectively, (Benazir Bhutto dismissals): *Abdul Tariq Rahim v. Federation of Pakistan*, PLD 1992 (Supreme Court), 646; *Benazir Bhutto v. Farooq Ahmed Leghari*, PLD 1998 (Supreme Court), 388; (Junejo dismissal): *Federation of Pakistan v. Muhammad Saifullah Khan*, PLD 1989 (Supreme Court), 166; (Nawaz Sharif dismissal): *Mian Nawaz Sharif v. President of Pakistan*, PLD 1993 (Supreme Court), 473.

Chapter 4

1. It should be noted that these are not the only data available for Pakistan. Other important resources for researching trends in Pakistani public opinion include: "The Ten Nation Impressions of America Poll," conducted by Zogby International (April 11, 2002); "Connecting Futures Research," commissioned by the British Council (June 10, 2002) (available at http://www.connectingfutures.com/research/); and "What the World Thinks in 2002," conducted by the Pew Foundation (De-

cember 4, 2002) (available at http://people-press.org/reports/display.php3?ReportID = 165). We chose not to employ these data here as they provided too little insight into religious practice and belief. Rather, the data tended to focus upon views of the United States, the West, and on the events of September 11, 2002.

2. Gallup Organization, "The 2002 Gallup Poll of the Islamic World" http://www.gallup.com/poll/summits/islam.asp.

3. For more information on the sample construction or the conduct of the survey, see ibid.

4. "Musharraf's New Pakistan: What People Think," *Herald* (Karachi), February 2002.

5. These data were provided in a personal communication during a visit to the U.S. Department of State in July 2002.

6. U.S. Department of State, *In Pakistan, Musharraf Has Broad Public Support; Most Back His Anti-Extremist Reforms* (May 17, 2002) (provided by personal communication).

7. Zogby International also conducted a survey, following the Gallup effort. Their questions sought to disentangle perceptions of specific nations by asking respondents about their views of, among other things, a specific country's citizens, its foreign policies, and its domestic policies. To address the issues of contexts, they also included France and Venezuela. These countries were selected because France represents a nation that has frequently opposed U.S. policy in a number of international arenas. Venezuela, on the other hand, has tended to support the United States in multilateral forums. See Zogby International, "The Ten Nation Impressions of America Poll" (April 11, 2002), for more information.

8. One of the innovations of the Zogby data is that in addition to predominantly Muslim countries, they also include a nationally representative sample of respondents from France and Venezuela. The Pew data also include an exhaustive national representation.

9. C. Christine Fair, "Military Operations in Urban Areas: The Indian Experience," *India Review*, no. 2 (January 1, 2003).

10. Sayyed Vali Reza Nasr, *The Vanguard of the Islamic Revolution: The Jama'at-I-Islami of Pakistan* (London: I. B. Taurus, 1994).

11. Jerrold D. Green, "The Information Revolution and Political Opposition in the Middle East," *MESA Bulletin* 33 (1999): 21–27.

12. Rouleau, quoted in Green, "The Information Revolution and Political Opposition in the Middle East," 22.

13. Green, "The Information Revolution and Political Opposition in the Middle East," 22.

14. Sayyed Vali Reza Nasr, *The Vanguard of the Islamic Revolution: The Jama'at-I-Islami of Pakistan* (London: I. B. Taurus, 1994), xiii.

15. "Musharraf's New Pakistan: What People Think," *Herald* (Karachi), February 2002, 60. The *Herald* further elaborated that "most analysts agree that if quizzed in detail, most of the respondents may actually be satisfied with laws that are not in

direct conflict with those generally understood as 'Islamic' laws" (ibid.).

16. P. W. Singer, *Pakistan's Madrassahs: Ensuring a System of Education not Jihad* (Washington, D.C.: Brookings Institution [November 2001]); International Crisis Group, "Pakistan: Madrasas, Extremism, and the Military" (July 29, 2002).

17. It should be noted that many proscribed groups have simply reorganized under different names, making the ban rather ineffective and cosmetic. For example, the annual three-day *ijtimah* (convention) of the Jamatud Dawah (the new name for the political umbrella of the LeT) was still held in November 2002, even though the organization was supposedly banned in January 2002. This *ijitmah* (convened when the MMA prevailed at the polls) signaled that jihadi forces have not disappeared and, moreover, that the Jamatud Dawah is even more politically active than its predecessor, the LeT. In a further demonstration of its power, the Jamatud Dawah was able to secure the release of Hafiz Mohammad Saeed, the leader of the LeT, from an undisclosed agency on the eve of the *ijtima* (Arif Jamal, *News on Sunday*, November 10, 2002 [personal electronic communication]; and Paul Watson and Mubashir Zaidi, "Militant Flourishes in Plain Sight," *Los Angeles Times*, January 25, 2004).

18. "Six Islamic Militant Groups Banned by Government," *Asia News,* December 6, 2003, http://www.asianews.it/view.php?l=en&art=139.

19. Rafaqat Ali, "Constitution Revived after 41 Months," *Dawn* (Karachi), March 13, 2003, http://www.dawn.com/2003/03/13/top2.htm.

20. Muhammad Qasim Zaman, "Sectarianism in Pakistan: The Radicalization of Shi'i and Sunni Identities," *Modern Asian Studies* 32, no. 3 (July 1998): 689–716; S. V. R. Nasr, "The Rise of Sunni Militancy in Pakistan: The Changing Role of Islamism and the Ulama in Society and Politics," *Modern Asian Studies* 34, no. 1 (2000): 139–80; Vali Nasr, "International Politics, Domestic Imperatives, and Identity Mobilizations: Sectarian in Pakistan: 1979–98," *Comparative Politics* 32, no. 2 (January 2000): 171–90; International Crisis Group, "Pakistan: Madrasas, Extremism, and the Military" (July 29, 2002); and Mandavi Mehta and Teresita C. Schaffer, "Islam in Pakistan: Unity and Contradictions" (October 7, 2002), http://www.csis.org/saprog/islaminpakistan.pdf.

21. P. W. Singer, *Pakistan's Madrassahs: Ensuring a System of Education Not Jihad* (Washington, D.C.: Brookings Institution, November, 2001).

22. Vice-Ameer of Jamaat Islami, interview by authors, Jamaat-e-Islami Pakistan headquarters, Mansoorah, Lahore, January 2003.

23. Sairah Irshad Khan, "For the General Good," *Newsline* (Annual 2003), 19–27.

24. Ibid.

25. Talat Masood, "A Complex Transition," *Dawn* (Karachi), January 15, 2003, http://www.dawn.com/2003/01/15/op.htm#1.

26. See Ashley J. Tellis, C. Christine Fair, and Jamison Jo Medby, *Limited Conflicts under the Nuclear Umbrella—Indian and Pakistani Lessons from the Kargil Crisis* (Santa Monica: Rand, 2001).

27. Ibid.; C. Christine Fair, "The Role of Civilian Combatants in the Kargil Operation," in *Asymmetric Warfare in South Asia: The Causes and Consequences of Kargil,* ed. Peter Lavoy (Monterey: Naval Postgraduate School, forthcoming).

28. See Raja Asghar, "Opposition Takes Oath under Altered Text," *Dawn* (Karachi), March 13, 2003, http://www.dawn.com/2003/03/13/top1.htm; and Rafaqat Ali, "Constitution Revived after 41 Months," *Dawn* (Karachi), March 13, 2003, http://www.dawn.com/2003/03/13/top2.htm.

Chapter 5

1. Victoria Schofield, *Kashmir in the Crossfire* (New York: I. B. Tauris, 1996), 183.

2. Stephen Cohen, "The Compound Crisis of May 2002" (Washington, D.C.: Brookings Institution, 2003) (unpublished paper).

3. While noting that there are a good number of issues—such as Azad Kashmiri's exclusion from international agreements, the suspicion in Pakistan that many Kashmiri Muslims would prefer an independent Kashmir over their accession to Pakistan, Azad Kashmiri's resentment against interference by the Ministry of Kashmir Affairs, and the utter dependence of the Azad Kashmir government upon Islamabad for financial support—which are a continuing source of disaffection between Islamabad and Muzaffarabad, Leo Rose, nevertheless, concludes that "Pakistan's influence and control in Azad Kashmir is exerted primarily through the State's political units and leaders as well as the government. . . . What we hear about (occasionally) . . . are instances of Azad Kashmir kowtowing to Islamabad. What rarely ever gets reported are the equally numerous occasions that the Pakistan government has to make concessions to Muzaffarabad" (Leo Rose, "The Politics of Azad Kashmir," in *Perspectives on Kashmir: The Roots of Conflict in South Asia,* ed. Raju Thomas [Boulder, Colo.: Westview, 1992], 244).

4. In his recent analysis of the causal impact of the prevailing socioeconomic conditions of the ongoing insurgency in Indian-held Kashmir, Siddhartha Prakash states: "It is clear that the alienation of the Kashmiri people has been driven by sheer disillusionment in the state. Their ideals and aspirations have been thwarted by a series of rent-seeking governments, as well as the misguided policies of the Centre. Therefore, a genuine solution to the conflict depends on restoring Kashmir's confidence in a democratic and secular India with the creation of job opportunities (within the state and in other parts of the country), a clean administration and political freedom. The first step in that direction is to hold a plebiscite to enable the people of Jammu, Kashmir and Ladakh to determine their future either as part of India or Pakistan, or as a separate nation" (Siddhartha Prakash, "The Political Economy of Kashmir since 1947," *Contemporary South Asia* 9 (3) (2000), 332–33).

5. However, it is worth noting that since 1947, when Pakistan gained control over AJK, the latter has done very well in the field of education. The literacy rate in AJK is higher than its average in Pakistan. In 1947, there were only 286 educational institutions in AJK, with only three hundred students in attendance at all levels. By 1986, the number of educational institutions had increased to 4,096, and 92 percent

of the boys and 49 percent of the girls were attending primary schools. By 1995, 97 percent of the boys and 82 percent of the girls were receiving primary education. Similarly, despite Pakistan's control over the banking sector, there are more bank branches per capita in Mirpur than in Karachi, the commercial and financial capital of Pakistan (see *Pakistan: An Official Handbook, 1988* [Islamabad: Directorate General of Films and Publications, Ministry of Information and Broadcasting, Government of Pakistan, 1989], 521–27).

6. *Pakistan: An Official Handbook, 1995* (Islamabad: Directorate General of Films and Publications, Ministry of Information and Broadcasting, Government of Pakistan, 1996), 270.

7. Ibid.

8. Rose, "The Politics of Azad Kashmir," 240.

9. Tavleen Singh, *Kashmir: A Tragedy of Errors* (New Delhi: Viking, 1995), xvi.

10. According to Sir Albion Bannerji, an Indian Christian who served as senior member of the Council of the State of Jammu and Kashmir for two years from 1927 to 1929, the people of the State of Jammu and Kashmir labored under many disadvantages during Maharaja Hari Singh's rule. Disassociating himself from the Maharaja's misgovernment in 1929, Bannerji wrote: "A large Muhammeden population [is] absolutely illiterate, laboring under poverty and very low economic conditions of living in the villages and practically governed like dumb drive cattle" (quoted in Alastair Lamb, *Kashmir: A Disputed Legacy, 1848–1990* [Hertfordshire: Roxford Books, 1991], 88). In a similar vein, Victoria Schofield has pointed out: "No Muslim in the valley was allowed to carry a firearm, and they were not allowed in the army. The only Muslims who were recruited, normally under the command of a Dogra officer, were the Suddhans of Poonch and the Sandans from Mirput, culturally and linguistically distinct from the Kashmiris of the valley, the Maharaja believed he could depend on them to suppress whatever trouble might arise in the valley" (Victoria Schofield, *Kashmir in Conflict: India, Pakistan, and the Unfinished War* [London: I. B. Tauris, 2000], 17).

11. Following Mohammed Iqbal, the influential philosopher-poet who in his presidential address to the All India Muslim League in 1930 had called for the creation of a Muslim state comprising the Punjab, Sind, and the North West Frontier Province (NWFP), Chaudhry Rehmat Ali, a Muslim student at Cambridge in 1933, proposed that this new Muslim state should be named *PAKISTAN* (Land of the Pure). Acronymically, "P" stood for Punjab; "A" for Afghans along the frontier (in fact, the Pushtuns of the NWFP); "K" for Kashmir; "S" for Sindh; and "TAN" for Baluchistan. The inclusion of the predominantly Muslim state of Jammu and Kashmir in the new entity to be called Pakistan was indicative of the fact that "there was already a body of opinion which believed that the princely state should become part of Pakistan, if and when it could be achieved. After . . . the partition of the subcontinent took place this opinion held fast" (Schofield, *Kashmir in Conflict,* 21).

12. Lamb, *Kashmir,* 97.

13. Singh, *Kashmir,* xvi.

14. Ibid., 23.

15. Alastair Lamb, *Incomplete Partition: The Genesis of the Kashmir Dispute, 1947–48* (Karachi: Oxford University Press, 1997), 102–3.

16. There is an unending controversy over the role played by Lord Louis Mountbatten, Britain's last viceroy in India, in the events leading to the partition of the subcontinent in 1947. Some scholars accuse him of rigging the final boundary award in favor of India, while others defend him as a fair and "impartial" man who did his best to deal with a very trying situation. For a good discussion of these contending viewpoints, see Robert G. Wirsing, *India, Pakistan, and the Kashmir Dispute: On Regional Conflict and Its Resolution* (New York: St. Martin's Press, 1994), ch. 1, esp. 11–38. Regardless of Mountbatten's intentions, the fact remains, "If Gurdaspur in Punjab had been awarded to Pakistan, and not India, by the Boundary Commission, Kashmir could not possibly have come to India" (Singh, *Kashmir*, xvii).

17. Schofield, *Kashmir in Conflict*, 25.

18. Owen Bennett Jones, *Pakistan: Eye of the Storm* (New Haven, Conn.: Yale University Press, 2002), 63.

19. Mushtaqur Rahman, *Divided Kashmir: Old Problems, New Opportunities for India, Pakistan, and the Kashmiri People* (Boulder, Colo.: Lynne Rienner Publishers), 2.

20. Lamb, *Incomplete Partition*, 124–25.

21. Jones, *Pakistan*, 66.

22. Rahman, *Divided Kashmir*, 18.

23. Sudhans are a major martial group residing in Poonch. They claim Afghan ancestry.

24. Rose, "The Politics of Azad Kashmir," 236.

25. Following is the text of this important agreement, which continued to govern ties between Azad Kashmir and the Government of Pakistan until 1970:

A. Matters within the purview of the Government of Pakistan.

Defense

Foreign policy of Azad Kashmir.

Negotiations with the United Nations Commission for India and Pakistan.

Publicity in foreign countries and in Pakistan.

Coordination and arrangement of relief and rehabilitation of refugees.

Coordination of publicity in connection with plebiscite.

All activities within Pakistan regarding Kashmir such as procurement of food, civil supplies, running of refugee camps and medical aid.

All affairs of Gilgit–Ladakh under the control of Political Agent.

B. Matters within the purview of Azad Kashmir Government.

Policy with regard to administration of AK territory.

General supervision of administration in AK territory.

Publicity with regard to the activities of the Azad Kashmir Government and administration.

Advice to the honorable Minister without Portfolio with regard to negotiations with United Nations Commission for India and Pakistan.

Development of economic resources of AK territory.

C. Matters within the purview of the Muslim Conference.

Publicity with regard to plebiscite in the AK territory.

Fieldwork and publicity in the Indian occupied area of the State.

Organization of political activities in the AK territory and the Indian
occupied area of the State.

Preliminary arrangements in connection with the plebiscite.

Organization for contesting the plebiscite.

Political work and publicity among the Kashmiri refugees in Pakistan.

Advise the honorable minister without Portfolio with regard to the
negotiations with the United Nations Commission for India and
Pakistan.

26. Vernon Hewitt, *Toward the Future? Jammu and Kashmir in the 21st Century*
(London: Cambridge, 2001), 110.

27. Rose, "The Politics of Azad Kashmir," 238.

28. Hewitt, *Toward the Future?* 111.

29. Schofield, *Kashmir in Conflict*, 91.

30. Ibid.

31. Other members of the committee were the Secretary of Defense, the Director of the Intelligence Bureau, Chief of the General Staff, and the Director of Military Operations (General K. M. Arif, *Khaki Shadows: Pakistan, 1947–1997* [Karachi:
Oxford University Press, 2001], 47; also see Sher Khan Mazari, *A Journey to Disillusionment* [Karachi: Oxford University Press, 1999], 128).

32. Sher Khan Mazari, *A Journey to Disillusionment*, 128.

33. Ibid.

34. Ibid., 48.

35. Ibid., 128.

36. Ibid., 129. According to General K. M. Arif, Operation Gibraltar envisaged
that "small groups" should be "inducted in the Indian-held Kashmir (IHK) on a
broad front to destroy or damage military targets—bridges, ammunition and supply dumps, formation headquarters, lines of communications, military convoys—
to create panic, arouse hatred against the occupation power and encourage the oppressed people to rise in revolt. The aim was to take advantage of the anti-India
feelings nursed by Kashmiris. The infiltrators carried arms and explosives and a limited quantity of rations with them. Thereafter they planned to live off the land and
rely on local hospitality" (ibid., 49).

37. Brian Cloughley attributes this failure on the part of the inhabitants of the
Valley to take up arms against their "Hind master" as a function of their perceived
interests, which "lay more in tourists, woodcrafts, and papier mache than in aspiring to political freedom" (Brian Cloughley, *A History of the Pakistan Army: Wars and*

Insurrections [Karachi: Oxford University Press, 1999], 69). General Arif gives the following assessment of the conceptual and operational flaws besetting Operation Gibraltar:

- The operation was conceived on faulty political assessment and flawed assumptions
- The people of Kashmir had not been consulted or taken into prior confidence. They did not rise in a war of liberation fearing brutal reprisals by the Indian military forces
- The planning time was excessively telescoped and the plan was implemented prematurely
- Excessive secrecy prevented the flow of essential information to all concerned on a need to know basis
- Intelligence failure
- Lack of inter-service and inter-arm coordination
- Inadequate training for the specialized operation
- Inadequate attention to the diplomatic and psychological fields
- The Pakistan Army possessed limited and mostly theoretical expertise in launching a guerrilla operation or combating it. The prescribed institutions were bypassed and operational planning violated the prescribed channels. Some of the planning errors might have been corrected had the relevant institutions been consulted. (Arif, *Khaki Shadows*, 50)

38. Jones, *Pakistan*, 77.

39. Arif, *Khaki Shadows*, 54.

40. Iffat Malik, *Kashmir: Ethnic Conflict, International Dispute* (Karachi: Oxford University Press, 2002), 122.

41. The August 29 directive from President Ayub Khan Genera Mohammed Musa, Commander-in-Chief of the Pakistan Army, defined "political aim for struggle in Kashmir" as follows:

1. . . . to take such action as will defreeze Kashmir problem, weaken India's resolve and bring her to a conference table without provoking a general war. However, the element of escalation is always present in such struggles. So, whilst confining our action to the Kashmir area we must not be unmindful that India may in desperation involve us in a general war or violate Pakistani territory where we are weak. We must therefore be prepared for such contingency.

2. To expect quick results in this struggle, when India has much larger forces than us, would be unrealistic. Therefore, our action should be such that can be sustained over a long period of time.

3. As a general rule Hindu morale would not stand more than a couple of hard blows delivered at the right time and place. Such opportunities should therefore be sought and exploited.

(Quoted in Cloughley, *A History of the Pakistan Army*, 70–71)

42. Dennis Kux, *The United States and Pakistan, 1947–2000: Disenchanted Allies* (Washington, D.C.: Woodrow Wilson Center Press, 2001), 164.

43. Patricia Ellis and Zafar Khan, "Partition and Kashmir: Implications for the Region and the Diaspora," in *Regions and Partition: Bengal, Punjab, and the Partition of the Subcontinent*, ed. Ian Talbot and Gurharpal Singh (London: Oxford University Press, 2001), 278.

44. Quoted in ibid., 276.

45. Wirsing, *India, Pakistan, and the Kashmir Dispute*, 69.

46. Malik, *Kashmir*, 219.

47. Ibid., 234.

48. Robert G. Wirsing, "Kashmir Conflict: The New Phase," in *Pakistan: 1992*, ed. Charles H. Kennedy (Boulder, Colo.: Westview, 1993), 138.

49. *Northern Areas—Facts, Problems, Recommendations* (Islamabad: Institute of Policy Studies, October 2000), 18.

50. Rahman, *Divided Kashmir*, 18.

51. The package proposed the following measures: (a) the membership of the existing Northern Areas Council should be enhanced from eighteen to twenty-six, and members should be elected on the basis of adult franchise; (b) the Federal Minister of Kashmir Affairs would be the Chief Executive of the Council, with a Deputy Chief Executive to be elected by the Council; (c) three to five members of the Council would be taken as Advisors to the Chief Executive, with the status of provincial ministers; (d) the post of the Judicial Commissioner would be abolished and a three-member Chief Court would be constituted under the chairmanship of a retired judge.

52. *Northern Areas—Facts, Problems, Recommendations*, 21.

53. For a good discussion of some of the underlying factors that precipitated the Kashmiri Intifada, see Rahman, *Divided Kashmir*, ch. 5.

54. Schofield, *Kashmir In the Crossfire*, 24.

55. For a good discussion of Pakistan's offset strategy, see Jeffrey Lee, "Pakistan's Offset Strategy" (unpublished essay, Department of Political Science, Stanford University, December 2002).

56. Saeed Shafqat, "From Official Islam to Islamism: The Rise of Dawat-ul-Irshad and Lashkar-e-Taiba," in *Pakistan: Nationalism without a Nation?* ed. Christophe Jaffrelot (London: Zed Books, 2002), 138.

57. At independence, in 1947, there were only 137 *madrasahs* in Pakistan. In 1956 this number was estimated to be 244. But by 2000 it had crossed the 10,000 mark. Much of this astonishing growth of the *madrasahs* took place during the ten years of the Soviet–Afghan war (see *Pakistan: Madrasas, Extremism, and the Military* [Islamabad/Brussels: International Crisis Group, July 2002], 2).

58. Shafqat, "From Official Islam to Islamism," 139.

59. Hasan-Askari Rizvi, "Pakistan's Strategic Culture," in *South Asia in 2020: Future Strategic Balances and Alliances*, ed. Michael R. Chambers (Washington, D.C.: Strategic Studies Institute, 2002), 323.

60. Amelie Blom, "'The Multi-Vocal State': The Policy of Pakistan on Kashmir," in *Pakistan: Nationalism without a Nation?* ed. Christophe Jaffrelot (London: Zed Books, 2002), 284.

61. The membership of all jihadi groups and organizations within Pakistan and Azad Kashmir is estimated to be in the range of 7,000, and is made up of Pakistani, Kashmiri, and non-Pakistani militants in Kashmir itself (see *Kashmir: Confrontation and Miscalculation,* 7).

62. Ibid., 322.

63. The number of militant-inflicted causalities increased from an annual average of 608 deaths to over 760 fatalities a year between 1996 and 2000 (Peter Chalk, "Pakistan's Role in the Kashmir Insurgency," *Jane's Intelligence Review,* September 2001, 26).

64. Ibid.

65. For an excellent discussion of the 1990 crisis, see Devin T. Hagerty, *The Consequences of Nuclear Proliferation: Lessons from South Asia* (Cambridge: Mass.: MIT Press, 1998), ch. 6, and pp. 133–70.

66. George Perkovich, *India's Nuclear Bomb: The Impact on Global Proliferation* (Berkeley: University of California Press, 1999), 308.

67. Ibid.

68. Ibid., 309.

69. Ibid.

70. Michael Newbill, "English Media Commentary in India and Pakistan on Confidence-Building Measures, 1990–97," in *A Handbook of Confidence-Building Measures for Regional Security,* 3rd ed., ed. Michael Krepon et al. (Washington, D.C.: Henry L. Stimson Center, 1998), 156.

71. Wirsing, "Kashmir Conflict: The New Phase," 150.

72. Ibid.

73. *Washington Post,* February 7, 1992.

74. Perkovich, *India's Nuclear Bomb,* 326.

75. Dr. Rifaat Hussain, "Facing the BJP Challenge," *News* (Karachi), March 21, 1998.

76. According to official Indian statements, these tests ranged from sub-kiloton devices to 43-kiloton thermonuclear devices. The purpose of these tests was to generate additional data for improved computer simulation for design and for attaining the capability to carry out some critical experiments, if necessary. For text of these statements, see the *News* (Karachi), May 12 and May 14, 1998.

77. *News* (Karachi), May 13, 1998.

78. Ibid.

79. Mr. A. Singhal, head of the Vishva Hindu Parishad Party, declared that a "war would be a better step to teach Pakistan a lesson" ("A War Is Needed to Teach Pakistan a Lesson: Singhal," *Asian Age,* May 24, 1998). Similarly, the Home Minister of India, Mr. K. L. Advani, stated on May 19, 1998: "Islamabad should realize the change in the geo-strategic situation in the region and the world and roll back its

anti-Indian policy, especially with regard to Kashmir. India's bold and decisive step to become a nuclear weapon state has brought about a qualitatively new stage in Indo-Pakistan relations, particularly in finding a solution to the Kashmir Problem" (*News* [Karachi], May 20, 1998).

80. Syed Rifaat Hussain, "International Response to Nuclearization of South Asia," *Strategic Issue,* March 2000, 19.

81. Ibid.

82. Robert Jay Lifton and Richard Falk, *Indefensible Weapons: The Political and Psychological Case against Nuclearism* (New York: Basic Books, 1982), ix.

83. Charles L. Glasner, "The Security Dilemma Revisited," *World Politics,* October 1997, 189.

84. Dr. Rifaat Hussain, "The Colombo Summit: A Review," *News* (Karachi), August 2, 1998.

85. Umer Farooq, "Indian War Planes Intrude Pakistani Air Space as LoC Shelling Intensifies," *Nation,* August 2, 1998.

86. "Aggression Will be Foiled," *Dawn* (Karachi), August 2, 1998.

87. "India Taking South Asia to Brink of War," *News* (Karachi), August 3, 1998.

88. "India Warns Pakistan against Any Attack," *News* (Karachi), August 4, 1998.

89. Shaheen Sehbai, "Washington Concerned over LoC Fighting," *Dawn* (Karachi), August 4, 1998.

90. "China Appeals for Calm between India and Pakistan," *News* (Karachi), August 4, 1998.

91. "OIC Concerned over Kashmir Situation," *News* (Karachi), August 8, 1998.

92. "LoC Situation Requires Serious Dialogue," *News* (Karachi), August 6, 1998.

93. "Forces Not to Fail the Nation, Assures COAS," *Dawn* (Karachi), August 6, 1998.

94. "India Warns Pakistan against Any Attack," *News* (Karachi), August 4, 1998.

95. Hasan Akhter, "Full Restraint along LoC," *Dawn* (Karachi), December 3, 2000.

96. "Kashmir Cease-fire Comes into Force," *Dawn* (Karachi), November 28, 2000.

Chapter 6

1. Rabindranath Tagore, *One Hundred and One Poems,* ed. Humayun Kabir (New York: Asia, 1966), 173.

2. Pupul Jayakar, *Indira Gandhi: An Intimate Portrait* (New York: Pantheon, 1993), vii.

3. Jawaharlal Nehru, *The Discovery of India* (New York: John Day, 1946), 37–44.

4. M. K. Gandhi, *Hind Swaraj, or Home Rule* (Ahmedabad: Navjiwan, 1946).

5. I regret that I had not seen the important study by Rodney W. Jones, *Religious Radicalism and Nuclear Confrontation in South Asia* (Delhi, Media House, 2004), before I wrote this essay. Among the many discussions of the current idea of "civil society," the following are particularly relevant for looking at social and political de-

velopment in India: Carol A. Breckenridge, ed., *Consuming Modernity* (Minneapolis: University of Minnesota Press, 1995); Christopher Candland, "Civil Society," in *The Oxford Companion to Politics of the World* (Oxford: Oxford University Press, 2001); Partha Chatterjee, *The Nation and Its Fragments: Colonial and Post Colonial Histories* (Delhi: Oxford, 1994); Ernest Gellner, *Conditions of Liberty: Civil Society and Its Rivals* (New York: Viking Penguin, 1994); Graeme Gill, *The Dynamics of Democratization: Elites, Civil Society, and the Transition Process* (New York: St. Martin's Press, 2002); Goran Hyden, "Civil Society, Social Capital, and Development: Dissection of a Complex Discourse," *Studies in Comparative International Development* 32 (Spring 1997); Niraja Gopla Jayal and Sudha Pai, *Democratic Governance in India: Challenges of Poverty, Development, and Identity* (New Delhi: Sage, 2001); Sudipta Kaviraj and Sunil Khilnani, eds., *Civil Society: History and Possibilities* (Cambridge: Cambridge University Press, 2001); and Ashutosh Varshney, *Ethnic Conflict and Civic Life: Hindus and Muslims in India* (New Haven, Conn.: Yale University Press, 2002).

6. Quoted in S. Gopal, *British Policy in India, 1858–1905* (Cambridge: Cambridge University Press, 1965), 298.

7. Sir Thomas Raleigh, *Lord Curzon in India* (London: Macmillan, 1906), 486–87.

8. Partha Chatterjee, "Post-colonial Civil and Political Society," in Kaviraj and Khilnani, *Civil Society,* 171.

9. Varshney, *Ethnic Conflict and Civic Life,* 4.

10. Chatterjee, "Post-colonial Civil and Political Society," 174.

11. Selig S. Harrison, *India: The Most Dangerous Decades* (Princeton, N.J.: Princeton University Press, 1960), 3.

12. C. Rajagopalachari, *Our Democracy* (Madras: B. G. Paul, 1957), 17.

13. Vincent A. Smith, *The Oxford History of India,* 3rd ed. (Oxford: Clarendon Press, 1958).

14. Jack Snyder and Karen Ballentine, "Nationalism and the Marketplace of Ideas," in *Nationalism and Ethnic Conflict,* ed. Michael Brown et al. (Cambridge: MIT Press, 2001), 65.

15. Dadabhai Naoroji, *Poverty and Un-British Rule in India* (London: Sonnenschein, 1901); and R. C. Dutt, *The Economic History of India,* 2 vols. (New Delhi: Publications Division, 1963).

16. The capitalization conforms to the official printings in 1975 and 1976 of the Constitution and Amendments (New Delhi: Government of India, 1975, 1976).

17. Hafeez Malik, *Muslim Nationalism in India and Pakistan* (Washington: Public Affairs Press, 1963), 254.

18. E. T. Stokes, "The Administrators and Historical Writing on India," in *Historians of India, Pakistan, and Ceylon,* ed. C. H. Philips (London: Oxford University Press, 1961), 401.

19. Vincent A. Smith, *The Early History of India* (Oxford: Clarendon Press, 1957), 370.

20. H. W. Brands, *India and the United States: The Cold Peace* (Boston:

Twayne, 1990), 3.

21. Jawaharlal Nehru, *Independence and After* (New Delhi: Government of India, 1949), 7–9.

22. Ibid., 89, 4.

23. Ayesha Jalal, *The Sole Statesman* (Cambridge: Cambridge University Press, 1985).

24. Granville Austin, *Working a Democratic Constitution: The Indian Experience* (New Delhi: Oxford University Press, 2000), 53.

25. Ainslie T. Embree, "Nehru's Understanding of the Social Function of Religion," in *Perceiving India: Insight and Inquiry*, ed. Geeti Sen (New Delhi: Sage Publications, 1993), 165–82.

26. Quoted in M. J. Akbar, *Nehru: The Making of India* (London: Viking, 1988), 181.

27. Quoted in Mushirul Hasan, *Nationalism and Communal Politics in India* (New Delhi: Manohar, 1991), 285.

28. Jawaharlal Nehru, *The Unity of India* (London: Drummond, 1941), 406.

29. Ibid., 1.

30. Quoted in Embree, "Nehru's Understanding of the Social Function of Religion," 167–68.

31. Amartya Sen, "Secularism and Its Discontents," in *Secularism and Its Critics*, ed. Rajeev Bhargava (New Delhi: Oxford University Press, 1998), 484.

32. Inder Malhotra, *Indira Gandhi: A Personal and Political Biography* (Boston: Northeastern University Press, 1989), 168–69; and Jayakar, *Indira Gandhi*, 206–10.

33. *Lok Sabha Debates* (New Delhi: Government of India, February 1975).

34. H. H. Halperin and D. J. Scheffer, *Self-Determination in the New World Order* (Washington: Carnegie Endowment, 1992), 12.

35. Quoted in Charles Heimsath and Surjit Mansingh, *A Diplomatic History of Modern India* (Bombay: Allied, 1971), 97.

36. Quoted in Horst Hannum, *Autonomy, Sovereignty, and Self-Determination: The Accommodation of Conflicting Rights* (Philadelphia: University of Pennsylvania Press, 1990), 20.

37. *Twenty-Four Human Rights Documents* (New York: Center for the Study of Human Rights, Columbia University, 1992), 10–30.

38. Halperin and Scheffer, *Self-Determination in the New World Order*, 22–23.

39. S. C. Dev, *Nagaland: The Untold Story* (Calcutta: Gouri Dev, 1988), 1–3.

40. Ibid., 147.

41. Sanjib Baruah, "Confronting Constructionism: Ending India's Naga War," paper presented at the University Seminar on South Asia, Columbia University, February 10, 2003.

42. Sangat Singh, *The Sikhs in History* (New York: Self-published, 1995) is an impassioned statement of this position.

43. Bharat Wariavwalla, "Die Zestörung des Muslimtempels und die Problematik des Nationalstaats," *Comparativ*, Heft 6 (4 January 1994): 87.

44. Gill, *The Dynamics of Democratization*, 6.

45. Karl Marx, "The British Rule in India," in *The First Indian War of Independence, 1857–1859*, ed. K. Marx and F. Engels (Moscow: Foreign Languages Publishing House, n.d.), 20.

46. Asha Mukerjee, et al., eds., *Civil Society in Indian Cultures: Indian Philosophical Studies*, vol. 3 (Washington: Council for Research in Values and Philosophy, 2001).

47. Tapan Raychaudhuri and Irfan Habib, eds., *The Cambridge Economic History of India* (Cambridge: Cambridge University Press, 1982), 1:xii.

48. Gill, *The Dynamics of Modernization*, 6.

49. Tapan Raychaudhuri, "Inland Trade," in Gill, *The Dynamics of Modernization*, 345–47.

50. Burton Stein, *Vijayanagara*, vol. 1.2 of *The New Cambridge History of India* (Cambridge: Cambridge University Press, 1988), 74–75.

51. Quoted in C. Bayly, *Indian Society and the Making of the British Empire*, vol. 2.1 of *The New Cambridge History of India* (Cambridge: Cambridge University Press, 1988), 50.

52. Bernard S. Cohn, *An Anthropologist and the Historians and Other Essays* (Delhi: Oxford University Press, 1987), 250.

53. Aziz Ahmad, *Islamic Modernism in India and Pakistan, 1857–1964* (Oxford: Oxford University Press, 1967), 6–12.

54. Rammohun Roy, *The English Works of Rammohun Roy*, ed. K. Nag and D. Burman, 6 vols. (Calcutta: Sadharan Brahmo Samaj, 1945–58), 3:5–8, 4:11–12, 4:106–8.

55. Chidananda Das Gupta, *The Cinema of Satyajit Roy* (New Delhi: Vikas, 1980), 1.

56. Lester M. Salamon et al., eds., *Global Civil Society: Dimensions of the Non-Profit Sector* (Baltimore: Johns Hopkins Center for Civil Society Studies, 1999), 4.

57. Joseph E. Stiglitz, *Globalization and Its Discontents* (London: Allen Lane, 2002), 8.

58. Arjun Appadurai and Carol A. Breckenridge, "Public Modernity in India," in Breckenridge, *Consuming Modernity*, 1–22.

59. *Report of the Working Group on National Film Policy* (New Delhi: Ministry of Information and Broadcasting, 1980).

60. Pradip Krishen, Introduction to "Indian Popular Cinema: Myth, Meaning, and Metaphor," *India International Centre Quarterly* 8, no. 1 (1981): 4.

61. M. V. Kamath, "The Indian Ethos," in *Film India: The New Generation: 1960–1980* (New Delhi: Directorate of Film Festivals, 1981), 31–32.

62. Rosie Thomas, "Melodrama and the Negotiation of Morality in Mainstream Hindi Film," in Breckenridge, *Consuming Modernity*, 161–66.

63. Celia W. Dugger, "Gandhi's Dream and India's Latest Nightmare," *New York Times*, March 10, 2002, 3.

64. Tanika Sarkar, *Hindu Wife, Hindu Nation* (Bloomington: Indiana University

Press, 2001), 253.

65. This paragraph is based on Rushad R. Nanavatty, "War Minus the Shooting: Cricket, Nationalism, and Identity in the Subcontinent," unpublished paper, SAIS, Johns Hopkins University seminar, December 6, 2003.

66. Ibid.

67. Quoted in Austin, *Working a Democratic Constitution*, 557–58.

68. Ashis Nandy, "The Politics of Secularism and the Recovery of Religious Tolerance," in *Communities, Riots, and Survivors in South Asia*, ed. Veena Das (Delhi: Oxford University Press, 1990), 80.

69. T. N. Madan, "Secularism in Its Place," *Journal of Asian Studies* 46, no. 4 (November, 1987): 748–49.

70. Rajeev Bhargava, Introduction to *Secularism and Its Critics*, 27.

71. *RSS: Spearheading National Renaissance* (Bangalore: Prakashan Vibhag, 1985), 8.

72. Nana Deshmukh, *RSS: Victims of Slander* (New Delhi: Vision Books, 1979), 12.

73. Ainslie T. Embree, "The Function of the Rashtriya Swayamsevak Sangh: To Define the Hindu Nation," in *Accounting for Fundamentalism: The Dynamic Character of Movements*, ed. Martin E. Marty and R. Scott Appleby (Chicago: University of Chicago Press, 1994), 618.

74. M. S. Gowalkar, *Bunch of Thoughts* (Bangalore: Jagarana Prakashan, 1980), 512.

75. M. S. Golwalkar, *We, or Our Nation Defined* (Nagpur: M. N. Kale, 1947), 28.

76. Anthony D. Smith, *Myths and Memories of the Nation* (Oxford: Oxford University Press, 1999), 256.

77. Translation of Hindi original, in D. R. Goyal, *Rashtriya Swayamsewak Sangh* (New Delhi: Radha Krishna, 1979), 206.

78. V. D. Savarkar, *Hindutva: Who Is a Hindu?* (Bombay: Veer Savarkar Publications, 1969), 110–11.

79. Ibid., 141.

80. Barbara Metcalf, "Remaking Ourselves: Islamic Self-Fashioning," in Marty and Appleby, *Accounting for Fundamentalism*, 708.

81. Mushirul Hasan, *Islam in the Subcontinent: Muslims in a Plural Society* (New Delhi: Manohar, 2002), 384.

82. *Report of the Citizen's Commission on Persecution of Christians in Gujarat*, ed. Kamal Chenoy et al. (New Delhi: National Alliance of Women, 1999); and *Gujarat Carnage 2002: A Report to the Nation*, ed. Kamal Chenoy et al. (New Delhi, 2002).

83. M. S. Golwalkar, *Bunch of Thoughts* (Bangalore: Jagarana, 1980), xxxiii.

84. Estimate based on Christophe Jaffrelot, *The Hindu Nationalist Movement and Indian Politics, 1925–1900's* (London: Hurst, 1996), 238.

85. H. V. Seshadri, ed., *RSS: A Vision in Action* (Bangalore: Jagarana Prakashana, 1988), 25–29.

86. V. Venkatachalam and R. K. Singh, *The Political, Economic, and Labor Climate in India* (Philadelphia: Wharton School Industrial Research Unit, 1982), 84.

87. Preface to *Rashtra Sevika Samiti: An Organization of Hindu Women* (Nagpur: Sevika Prakashan, n.d.), 13, 4.

88. Manini Chatterjee, "Clout Gone, RSS Could Pull No Strings," *Hindu*

(Chennai), February 2, 2003.

89. Quoted in Jaffrelot, *The Hindu Nationalist Movement and Indian Politics*, 197.

90. Ibid., 178–79.

91. Lise McKean, *Divine Enterprise: Gurus and the Hindu Nationalist Movement* (Chicago: University of Chicago Press, 1960), 112–15. McKean's book is the most detailed account of the VHP.

92. Teesta Setalvad, presentation before the U.S. Government Commission on Religious Freedom, Washington, D.C., June 10, 2002.

93. Demetri Sevastopulo, "US Widens Probe to Charities Tied to Militants," *Financial Times* (London), February 14, 2003.

94. Sarkar, *Hindu Wife, Hindu Nation*, 271.

95. Sunil Khilnani, "This Is the Home of Gandhi?" *The Globe and Mail* (Toronto), March 20, 2002, A19.

96. *Gujarat Carnage 2002*; and Siddharth Varadarajan, *Gujarat: The Making of a Tragedy* (New Delhi: Penguin Books, 2002).

97. Khilnani, "This Is the Home of Gandhi?" *The Globe and Mail* (Toronto), March 20, 2002, A19.

98. Celia Dugger, "Hindu Justifies Mass Killings," *New York Times*, March 5, 2002.

99. Balraj Madhok, *Indianisation* (Delhi: Hind Pocket Books, 1970).

100. This summary account is based on reporting in the Indian and Western press and by the detailed *Violence in Gujarat: Report of the Citizens's Commission on Persecution of Christians in Gujarat* (New Delhi: National Alliance of Women, 1999).

101. Ruth Manorma, Foreword to *Violence in Gujarat.*

102. Quoted in Varadarajan, *Gujarat*, 451.

103. Ibid., 447.

104. Donald E. Smith, *India as a Secular State* (Princeton, N.J.: Princeton University Press, 1963), 459.

105. Ibid.

106. Ainslie T. Embree, "The Emergency as a Signpost to India's Future," in *Transfer and Transformation: Political Institutions in the New Commonwealth*, ed. Peter Lyons and James Manor (Leicester: Leicester University Press, 1983), 91.

Chapter 7

1. See official web site for the BJP at http://www.bjp.org/.

2. On religious nationalism in India, see Ainslie T. Embree, *Utopias in Conflict: Religion and Nationalism in Modern India* (Berkeley: University of California Press, 1990); Peter van der Veer, *Religious Nationalism: Hindus and Muslims in India* (Berkeley: University of California Press, 1994); Gerald J. Larson, *India's Agony over Religion* (Albany: State University of New York Press, 1995); David Ludden, ed., *Contesting the Nation: Religion, Community, and the Politics of Democracy in India* (Philadelphia: University of Pennsylvania Press, 1996); and Thomas B. Hansen, *The*

Saffron Wave: Democracy and Hindu Nationalism in Modern India (Princeton, N.J.: Princeton University Press, 1999).

3. Portions of the following discussion are adapted from analyses of Hindu nationalism and of the BJP in Robert L. Hardgrave Jr. and Stanley A. Kochanek, *India: Government and Politics in a Developing Nation*, 6th ed. (Fort Worth: Harcourt College Publishers, 2000), 185–92, 301–8.

4. Christophe Jaffrelot, in *The Hindu Nationalist Movement in India* (New York: Columbia University Press, 1996), 6, has characterized the process as "a strategy of stigmatisation and emulation."

5. See Brenda Cossman and Ratna Kapur, "Secularism: Bench-marked by Hindu Right," *Economic and Political Weekly* 31 (September 21, 1996): 1613–30. Also see Gary Jacobsohn, *The Wheel of Law: India's Secularism in Comparative Constitutional Context* (Princeton, N.J.: Princeton University Press, 2003). In the wake of the February 2002 violence in Gujarat, Justice J. S. Verma (Chairperson, National Human Rights Commission), who authored the Supreme Court's 1995 Hindutva ruling, sought to save face, saying that the judgment had been "misconstrued and misused by many for narrow interests by quoting it out of context" (lecture on "Humanism—The Universal Creed," India International Centre, New Delhi, May 22, 2002, http:nhrc.in/hruniversalcreed.htm).

6. For the BJP's earlier incarnation, the Bharatiya Jana Sangh, language—in the commitment to Hindi as the national language—was a prominent plank in its platform, but it was a major factor in the failure of the Jana Sangh to make inroads beyond the Hindi heartland of North India, and the BJP, as it sought an expanded base of support, effectively dropped Hindi from its program.

7. See RSS home page at http://www.rss.org/.

8. See Walter K. Andersen and Shridhar D. Damle, *The Brotherhood in Saffron: The Rashtriya Swayamsevak Sangh and Hindu Revivalism* (Boulder, Colo.: Westview, 1987), 83–98; Tapan Raychaudhuri, "Shadows of the Swastika: Historical Perspectives on the Politics of Hindu Communalism," *Modern Asian Studies* 34 (2000): 259–79; Pralay Kanungo, *RSS's Tryst with Politics: From Hedgewar to Sudarshan* (New Delhi: Manohar, 2002); and Jaffrelot, *The Hindu Nationalist Movement in India*, 33–41.

9. M. S. Golwalkar, *We, Our Nationhood Defined* (1939), 62, quoted in Jaffrelot, *The Hindu Nationalist Movement in India*, 56.

10. See Donald E. Smith, *India as a Secular State* (Princeton, N.J.: Princeton University Press, 1963).

11. The word "secular" was added to the Constitution by Indira Gandhi in 1976 as part of the Forty-second Amendment, formally recognizing the policy that had been established under Nehru.

12. In the substantial literature addressing the Hindu Code, see especially J. Duncan M. Derrett, *Religion, Law, and the State in India* (New Delhi: Oxford University Press, 1999).

13. Internal distrust and external fear are fused in the view of Indian Muslims as

a "fifth column," symbolized by the widespread belief among Hindus that Indian Muslims root for the Pakistani team when India plays Pakistan in cricket.

14. RSS home page, http://www.rss.org/.

15. See the official web site for the VHP at http://www.vhp.org/englishsite/sub-home.htm.

16. "The Origin and Growth of the Vishva Hindu Parishad," http://www.vhp.-org/englishsite/subhome.htm.

17. See the official web site of the Bajrang Dal at http://www.hinduunity.org/bajrangdal.html.

18. *Manifesto and Program of the Bharatiya Jana Sangh*, 1958, quoted in Smith, *India as a Secular State*, 471.

19. On the JBS, in addition to Jaffrelot (*The Hindu Nationalist Movement in India*), see Craig Baxter, *The Jana Sangh: A Biography of an Indian Political Party* (Bombay: Oxford University Press, 1971); and Bruce Graham, *Hindu Nationalism and Indian Politics: The Origins and Development of the Bharatiya Jana Sangh* (Cambridge: Cambridge University Press, 1993).

20. Jaffrelot, *The Hindu Nationalist Movement in India*, 156.

21. On the BJP, in addition to Jaffrelot (*The Hindu Nationalist Movement in India*), see Yogendra K. Malik and V. B. Singh, *Hindu Nationalists in India: The Rise of the Bharatiya Janata Party* (New Delhi: Vistaar Publications, 1994); Thomas B. Hansen and Christophe Jaffrelot, eds., *The BJP and the Compulsions of Politics in India* (Delhi: Oxford University Press, 1998); Partha S. Ghosh, *BJP and the Evolution of Hindu Nationalism: From Periphery to Centre* (New Delhi: Manohar, 1999); and Sunil K. Sahu, "Religion and Politics in India: The Emergence of Hindu National-ism and the Bharatiya Janata Party (BJP)," in *Religion and Politics in Comparative Perspective*, ed. Ted G. Jelen and Clyde Wilcox (Cambridge: Cambridge University Press 2002), 243–65.

22. Muslims as a percentage of the total population increased form 10.7 percent to 11.7 percent in 1991. The higher birthrate is no demographic conspiracy, as Hindu nationalists contend, but a product of their comparatively lower socioeconomic po-sition, especially in levels of female literacy (see Ghosh, *BJP and the Evolution of Hindu Nationalism*, 182–83; and Neil DeVotta, "Demography and Communalism in India," *Journal of International Affairs* 56 [Fall 2002]: 53–70).

23. That minorities—and Muslims particularly—are "pampered" is a recurrent theme among Hindu nationalists, but the socioeconomic data surely suggest other-wise. Levels of poverty and illiteracy are higher among Muslims than among Hin-dus, and Muslims are significantly underrepresented in higher education and in the elite Indian Civil Service (see Ghosh, *BJP and the Evolution of Hindu Nationalism*, 170–73).

24. Embree, *Utopias in Conflict*, 110. Among the many books and articles on the Shah Bano case, also see Asghar Ali Engineer, ed., *The Shah Bano Controversy* (Hy-derabad: Orient Longman, 1987).

25. See Robert L. Hardgrave Jr., "India: The Dilemmas of Diversity," *Journal of*

Democracy 4 (October 1993): 54–68, reprinted in Larry Diamond and Marc F. Plattner, eds., *Nationalism, Ethnic Conflict, and Democracy* (Baltimore: Johns Hopkins University Press, 1994), 71–85.

26. See Sarvepalli Gopal, ed., *Anatomy of a Confrontation: The Babri Masjid–Ramjanmabhumi Issue* (New Delhi: Viking, 1991); Asghar Ali Engineer, ed., *Babri Masjid–Ramjanmabhoomi Controversy* (Delhi: Ajanta, 1990); A. G. Noorani, "The Babri Masjid–Ram Janmabhoomi Question," *Economic and Political Weekly* 24 (November 4–11, 1989): 2461–66; "Ayodhya: A Symposium on the Current Crisis," *Seminar* (New Delhi) 402 (February 1993); and John McGuire, Peter Reeves, and Howard Brasted, eds., *Politics of Violence: From Ayodhya to Behrampada* (New Delhi: Sage Publications, 1996).

27. See Jaffrelot, *The Hindu Nationalist Movement in India*, 369–410.

28. On the Ram cult, see Jaffrelot, *The Hindu Nationalist Movement in India*, 388–92; and Sheldon Pollock, "Ramayana and Political Imagination in India," *Journal of Asian Studies* 52 (May 1993): 261–97.

29. Jaffrelot, *The Hindu Nationalist Movement in India*, 403.

30. See, for example, Ghashyam Shah, "The BJP and Backward Castes in Gujarat," in *Religion, Religiosity, and Communalism*, ed. Praful Bidwai, Harbans Mukhia, and Achin Vanaik (New Delhi: Manohar, 1996), 217–35.

31. The ownership of the property and the construction of a temple at Ayodhya is now in a judicial limbo before the Supreme Court.

32. Jaffrelot, *The Hindu Nationalist Movement in India*, 491.

33. In reality, Kashmiri autonomy has been deeply eroded by legal changes and by political chicanery. In the substantial literature on Kashmir, see especially Raju G. C. Thomas, ed., *Perspectives on Kashmir: The Roots of Conflict in South Asia* (Boulder, Colo.: Westview, 1992); and Sumit Ganguly, *The Crisis in Kashmir: Portents of War, Hopes for Peace* (Washington: Woodrow Wilson Press; Cambridge: Cambridge University Press, 1997).

34. See Ghosh, *BJP and the Evolution of Hindu Nationalism*, 233–34.

35. *Onwards to Ramrajya—A Statement on National Issues Before the Electorate in the Mini-General Elections* (1993), quoted in Jaffrelot, *The Hindu Nationalist Movement in India*, 492–93.

36. On the BJP's economic policy, see Ghosh, *BJP and the Evolution of Hindu Nationalism*, 279–312.

37. On the BJP's policy for revision of textbooks, see Ghosh, *BJP and the Evolution of Hindu Nationalism*, 235–52.

38. For a close examination of India's decision to "go nuclear," see Sumit Ganguly, "India's Pathway to Pokran II: The Prospects and Sources of New Delhi's Nuclear Weapons Program," *Journal of Strategic Studies* 23 (Spring 1999): 148–77; and Ashley Tellis, *India's Emerging Nuclear Posture: Between Recessed Deterrent and Ready Arsenal* (Santa Monica: Rand, 2001). On the issue of nuclear proliferation and India's program more generally, see Geroge Perkovich, *India's Nuclear Bomb: The Impact on Global Proliferation* (Berkeley: University of California Press, 1999).

39. On Indian foreign policy under the BJP coalition, see C. Raja Mohan, *Crossing the Rubicon: The Shaping of India's New Foreign Policy* (New Delhi: Viking, 2003); and the volume by BJP leader and former Foreign Minister Jaswant Singh, *Defending India* (New York: St. Martin's Press, 1999). On the BJP's foreign policy doctrine and practice, see Ghosh, *BJP and the Evolution of Hindu Nationalism,* 313–65.

40. Samuel P. Huntington, *The Clash of Civilizations and the Remaking of World Order* (New York: Simon and Schuster, 1996).

41. See Raja Mohan, *Crossing the Rubicon.* I am grateful to Sumit Ganguly for his insights, in conversation, in underscoring shifts in Indian foreign policy.

42. Ibid., 376.

43. Among its first acts, in 1991, the Congress government under Prime Minister Narasimha Rao secured passage of the Places of Worship Act. The act specifies that all religious places shall be maintained according to their status quo as of August 15, 1947—except for Ayodhya, which was before the courts and remains so today. For the VHP, the act is the embodiment of the secular "appeasement" they are determined to resist.

44. Reported in *Asian Age* (Mumbai), October 9, 2002.

45. *Asian Age* (Mumbai), October 10, 2002.

46. *Hindustan Times* (New Delhi), November 22, 2002.

47. "'We Have No Orders To Save You': State Participation and Complicity in Communal Violence in Gujarat," *Human Rights Watch Reports* 14, no. 3 (C) (April 2002), http://www.hrw.org/reports/2002/india/. On the Gujarat violence, also see M. L. Sondhi and Apratim Mukarji, eds., *The Black Book of Gujarat* (New Delhi: Manak, 2002).

48. *Hindu* (Chennai), December 1, 2002.

49. Quoted in *Hindu* (Chennai), December 18, 2002.

50. Naidu's address to the BJP National Executive meeting, December 23, 2002, as widely reported in the Indian press. Naidu subsequently said that he had been misconstrued and emphasized that "Hindutva and intolerance cannot go together" (Press Trust of India story, December 25, 2002).

51. "PM's Musings from Goa," January 1, 2003, BJP home page, "Newspaper Clippings," http://www.bjp.org/.

52. See Oliver Heath, "Anatomy of BJP's Rise to Power: Social, Regional, and Political Expansion in the 1990s," in *Parties and Party Politics in India,* ed. Zoya Hasan (New Delhi: Oxford University Press, 2002), 232–56.

Chapter 8

1. Chagla was a Gujarati who served as Chief Justice of the Bombay High Court, Ambassador, Minister of Education, and Minister of External Affairs.

2. Quoted, with minor editing, from Malik Rizwan, "Mawlana Husayn Ahmad Madani and Jami'yat 'Ulama'-i-Hind, 1920–57" [Status of Islam and Muslims in India], Ph.D. diss., University of Toronto, 1995, 324–26.

3. Population estimates are from http://www.cia.gov/cia/publications/factbook/index.html by country. India's population is given as 1,045,845,226 and 12 percent Muslim. Pakistan's population, 97 percent Muslim, is given as 147,663,429; Bangladesh, 133,376,684, 83 percent Muslim. Indonesia, with 231,328,092 people, had the largest Muslim population, some 88 percent.

4. Thomas L. Friedman, "Today's News Quiz," *New York Times,* November 20, 2001.

5. The prime minister, Atal Bihari Vajpayee, is quoted in Siddharth Varadarajan, "The Ink Link: Media, Communalism, and the Evasion of Politics," in *The Concerned Indian's Guide to Communalism,* ed. K. N. Pannikar (New Delhi: Viking, 1999), 451. Attempts after the fact to revise Vajpayee's statement gained little credibility.

6. Two important book-length treatments of this subject are Mushirul Hasan, *Legacy of a Divided Nation: India's Muslims since Independence* (New Delhi: Oxford University Press, 1997); and Umar Khalidi, *Indian Muslims since Partition* (New Delhi: Vikas, 1995).

7. This point has been argued by Ashutosh Varshney, who specifically identifies riot-prone sites as those lacking in cross-cutting Hindu and Muslim civic institutions (see *Ethnic Conflict and Civic Life: Hindus and Muslims in India* [New Haven, Conn.: Yale University Press, 2002]).

8. A. P. J. Abdul Kalam, "Address to the Joint Session of Parliament, Republic of India," February 17, 2003, http://meadev.nic.in/speeches/Presi-add-parl.htm.9.

9. These helpful categories are discussed in David Ludden, *India and South Asia: A Short History* (Oxford: Oneworld Publications, 2002).

10. Peter Hardy, *The Muslims of British India* (Cambridge: Cambridge University Press, 1972), 11. The genealogy for Hindu nationalism is typically drawn from Tilak, beginning in the late nineteenth century, through the creation of the Hindu Mahasabha early in the twentieth century, to the RSS, with its paramilitary overtones, which continues as a grassroots base for the Sangh Pariwar today. The key leadership of the BJP represents men formed in the RSS who took a vow of celibacy and belong to the highest ranks of the organization (see Javeed Alam, "Composite Culture and Communal Consciousness: The Ittehadul Muslimeen in Hyderabad," in *Representing Hinduism: The Construction of Religious Traditions and National Identity,* ed. Vasudha Dalmia and Heinrich von Stietencron [New Delhi: Sage Publications, 1995], 342–44).

11. This is the title of ch. 6, introducing the advent of Muslim dynasties and populations in Nehru's history of India, written in jail in 1944 as independence approached (Jawaharlal Nehru, ed., *The Discovery of India* [New Delhi: Oxford University Press, 1989]).

12. William Gould, *Hindu Nationalism and the Language of Politics in Late Colonial India* (Cambridge: Cambridge University Press, 2004).

13. Janaki Bakhle, "Two Men and Music: Nationalism, Colonialism, and the Making of a National Art," Ph.D. diss., Columbia University, 2001.

14. Richard M. Eaton, *The Rise of Islam and the Bengal Frontier, 1204–1760* (Berkeley: University of California Press, 1993); Van der Veer, "Traditions of Violence in South Asia."

15. Peter Van der Veer, "Traditions of Violence in South Asia," paper presented to the International Conference on "Living Together Separately: Cultural India in History and Politics," Jamia Millia Islamia, New Delhi, December 19–21, 2002.

16. Richard M. Eaton, "Temple Desecration and Indo-Muslim States," *Frontline* (India) 17, no. 26 (December 23, 2000–January 5, 2001: 70–77).

17. The mass conversions of Dalits to Islam in Meenaskhipuram in 1981, presented by participants as an escape from caste oppression, were interpreted by Hindu nationalists as a product of foreign money. The event has been frequently evoked by Hindu nationalists since. Conversion to Islam is invariably made by the new converts on grounds of social equality, thus replacing one legitimate if not legal, discourse, anti-conversion, with another, both legitimate and legal, namely, anti-caste.

18. Richard H. Davis, *Lives of Indian Images* (Princeton, N.J.: Princeton University Press, 1997), 186–221.

19. But see below for a discussion of a second constitutional provision, the decision to limit compensatory discrimination only to "untouchables" who were "Hindu"—a label contested by them before Partition. This suggested that the state's interest was limited to rectifying a flaw in Hinduism that justified compensation instead of addressing the needs of oppressed segments of society generally.

20. The law that passed was called (again, ironically) the Muslim Protection of Women Act (1986). The case arose out of an application for maintenance on the part of an elderly, impoverished divorced woman, Shah Bano, who had married her husband, an advocate, in 1932, borne five children, and been driven out of her home by unilateral divorce in 1985. In 1978, she turned to the court since her former husband had denied her demand for maintenance on the grounds that Muslim personal law required maintenance only during the short period required to ascertain possible pregnancy. The Supreme Court, following earlier precedent, took the position that the husband was obligated to pay maintenance under section 125 of the Criminal Procedure Code (designed to prevent vagrancy). The 1986 Act made the resort to the criminal code on the issue of maintenance subject to consent of both parties, thus protecting the Muslim husband's right to deny maintenance.

21. Gayatri Chakravorty Spivak, "Can the Subaltern Speak," in *Marxism and the Interpretation of Culture,* ed. Cary Nelson and Lawrence Grossberg (Urbana: University of Illinois Press, 1988).

22. Subsequent reports on the killings by human rights and non-government groups criticized Modi for failing to stop the violence. A British government report obtained by the BBC said the violence was planned months before by right-wing Hindu groups and had all the hallmarks of ethnic cleansing. It also accused Mr. Modi of being directly responsible (BBC News, "Godhra Braces for an Anniversary," February 27, 2003, http://news.bbc.co.uk/2/hi/south_asia/2802509.stm).

23. Umar Khalidi, *Indian Muslims since Partition* (New Delhi: Vikas, 1995), 16. See also the district-wise listing of Muslim population percentages in Hasan (*Legacy of a Divided Nation,* 329–40) to bring home how scattered the Muslim population is. I reiterate the point made at the outset that I exclude Kashmir from this discussion.

24. Hasan, *Legacy of a Divided Nation,* 169–87.

25. Concerning the dispute over "illegal Bangladeshi infiltrators," Satadru Sen has written: "Hindus who trickle across the Bangladesh border today are usually accepted as 'refugees', provided they are not shot by the BSF in the process of crossing the line. But if Muslims who come from 'that side' are automatically illegal, then perhaps the Indian state needs to come clean on where it stands on the Two-Nation theory. I do not mean an exercise in contemplative self-mortification; the complicity between Indian nationalism and the Hindu Self is too well established for that to be necessary, let alone productive. What I have in mind is an act of juridical honesty: a statement from the Supreme Court, perhaps, that will spell out the legal and ideological basis for these selective deportations. Surely the possession (and non-possession) of passports and visas cannot be the basis of citizenship in countries like India, Bangladesh and Pakistan. . . . The real reasons why people are being pushed back and forth between India and Bangladesh today, with barely an audible word of protest, have to do with our fundamentally warped conception of Indian citizenship, and our fatally colonised sense of ourselves, our states and our societies. The saving grace in all this are the villagers on the Indian side of the border at Satgachi, who—not being proper citizens—provided the 'foreign' snakecharmers [the occasion of the article was the deportation of two hundred snakecharmers] in the no-man's-land with some measure of comfort and sustenance" ("Border of Insanity: Deporting Bangladeshi Migrants," *Economic and Political Weekly* [Bombay], February 15, 2003).

26. Shail Mayaram, *Resisting Regimes: Myth, Memory and the Shaping of a Muslim Identity* (Delhi: Oxford University Press, 1997), 162–208.

27. One journalist offered these figures at the end of 2000: 57 percent of Muslims are below the poverty line; 58 percent are illiterate; 3 percent of Muslims are high school graduates; they represent only 2 percent of the armed forces and fewer in state police (S. Ubaidur Rahman, "Muslim Political Party: Necessity or Hypocrisy?" *Milli Gazette,* December 15, 2000).

28. Amulya Gopalkrishnan, "Gender Issues: Dispelling Myths," *Frontline* 20, no. 1 (January 18–31, 2003).

29. Javid Laiq, "Suggested Speech for Vajpayee on the Minority Syndrome," *Times of India* (Mumbai), June 22, 1996, reprinted in *The Maverick Republic: Thirty Years of Coverage* (New Delhi: Rolli Books, 1996), 98–101.

30. Ibid., 99.

31. Ranjit Bhushan, "No Virus in the Faithful," *Outlook* (India), January 13, 2003, www.outlookindia.com.

32. Javeed Alam, "Composite Culture and Communal Consciousness: The Itte-

hadul Muslimeen in Hyderabad," in *Representing Hinduism: The Construction of Religious Traditions and National Identity,* ed. Vasudha Dalmia and Heinrich von Stietencron (New Delhi: Sage Publications, 1995), 349, 356.

33. For a fictional account of this, see one of the most outstanding recent novels on India in English: Rohinton Mistry, *A Fine Balance* (1995); see also Theodore P. Wright, Jr., "Muslims and the 1977 Indian Elections: A Watershed?" *Asian Survey* 17, no. 12 (1997): 1207–20.

34. Yoginder Sikand, "A New Indian Muslim Agenda: The Dalit Muslims and the All-India Backward Muslim Morcha" (typescript, 2002).

35. The so-called KHAM alliance (Kshatriya, Harijan, Adivasi, and Muslim) was victorious in Gujarat in 1980 and 1985, but it was controlled by high-caste Hindu members of Congress (Umar Khalidi, *Indian Muslims since Partition,* 185).

36. The Jamiat explicitly targets only one minor sectarian group in their writings and speeches, the Ahmadiyya (pejoratively called "Qadianis"). Originating in the late nineteenth century in Punjab, this group has been declared non-Muslim by the Pakistani Parliament (1974) on the grounds of denying the finality of the Prophet Muhammad.

37. Jamiat Ulama-i-Hind, "Jamiat Ulama-i-Hind: Saga of Unfinished Struggle" (New Delhi, n.d.); Jamiat Ulama-i-Hind, "Gujarat Earth Quake Relief Projects" (New Delhi, n.d.); Jamiat Ulama-i-Hind. "Gujarat Carnage Victims Relief and Rehabilitation" (New Delhi, [2003?]).

38. Khalidi, *Indian Muslims since Partition,* 177; Zaheer Masood Quraishi, "Emergence and Eclipse of the Muslim Majlis-e-Mushawarat," *Political Science Review* (Jaipur) 10, no. 3–4 (1971): 1–16.

39. The failure of the Mushawarat to bring pressure on elected officials gave rise to a separate party, the Muslim Majlis in UP in 1968, but it had little success.

40. "Muslim Personal Law Board" (editorial), *Milli Gazette,* July 1–15, 2002, http://www.milligazette.com.

41. Charles J. Adams, "The Politics of Maulana Maududi," in *South Asian Politics and Religion,* ed. Donald Eugene Smith (Princeton, N.J.: Princeton University Press, 1966), 371–97.

42. Maulana Abu'l-Lais, quoted in Khalidi, *Indian Muslims since Partition,* 173.

43. At the time of Partition, only 240 members of the party remained in India. A recent study counts 4,000 members and 25,000 workers in the organization (see Frederic Grare, *Political Islam in the Indian Subcontinent: Jamaat-I-Islami* [New Delhi: Manor Publishers, 2001], 98–102).

44. The three-day meeting, in 1999, was held in Bangalore and reportedly drew about 70,000 participants from the region. A session on "India—Present and Future" included Hindu, Christian, and Muslim speakers, who deplored the deteriorating law and order in the country and specifically the violence against minorities. The resolution of the final meeting also pledged to strive "for the social and moral upliftment of people. It drew attention to the rights of women saying that women should have all human rights, dignity and their role in society. It accused the media

of corrupting the morality and character of the youth for business interests and condemned the anti-Muslim approach of the media which tended to project all Muslims as ISI [Paskistan intelligence] agents and anti-nationals" (G. Javed. "Against
Evils, For Peace: The Jamaat Meet, Attended by More than 70,000 Delegates,
Pledges to Strive for an Evil-Free Society," *Islamic Voice* 13-03, no. 147 [March 1999],
http://www.islamicvoice.com/march.99/jamat.htm).

45. Mohammad Javed, "Jamaat-e-Islami Hind Gearing up for South India Conference," *Islamic Voice* 13-02, no. 146 (February 1999), http://www.islamicvoice.com/
february.99/.

46. This is Khalidi's approach, since he lists the Jamat along with the Deobandi
Tablighi Jamaat, Ahl-i Hadith, and Barelwi sects (Khalidi, *Indian Muslims since Partition*, 5–6). Maududi can be understood as a theological modernist who emphasized a return to Quranic sources and prophetic tradition as against the mainstream
acceptance by the 'ulama—from whom he sharply distinguished himself by rejection of the traditional law schools (Adams, "The Politics of Maulana Maududi").

47. The historic focus on reaching nominal Muslims continues in India. Tab-
lighis in the West also address outsiders in what is often a more open environment.
See, for example, the guidebook, *Da'wah Etiquette* (Houston: Madina Masjid,
2002), which includes a long chapter on other religions, including Judaism, Christianity, and Hinduism, and reviews charged topics like the status of women, as they
see it, according to other religions.

48. The Dawat-e-Islami offical website, http://www.dawateislami.org/, is only
one of many Dawat-e-Islami sites. The center appears to be in Pakistan, where a
three-day meeting, seemingly modeled on the Tabligh pattern, is held in Multan.
Other active sites are in Britain, Canada, and the United States. Dawat-e-Islami
congregations have also been held in India; in late 1999 Urdu posters in Ahmadabad, for example, advertised an upcoming *ijtima* to be held in Bombay.

49. Bernard Lewis, "The Roots of Muslim Rage: Why So Many Muslims Deeply
Resent the West, and Why Their Bitterness Will Not Easily Be Mollified," originally published in *Atlantic* (September 1990) and available online at http://
www.theatlantic.com/issues/90sep/rage.htm.

50. Paola Bacchetta, "Communal Property/Sexual Property: On Representations
of Muslim Women in a Hindu Nationalist Discourse," in *Forging Identities: Gender,
Communities, and Nations*, ed. Zoya Hasan (New Delhi: Kali for Women, 1994),
188–225.

51. See Stanley J. Tambiah, *Leveling Crowds: Ethnonationalist Conflicts and Collective Violence in South Asia* (Berkeley: University of California Press, 1996), ch. 5,
for a parallel argument about the emergence of Sinhala–Tamil conflict in Sri Lanka.

52. Ornit Shani, "The Making of *EthnoHinduism* in India: Communalism,
Reservations, and the Ahmedabad Riots of 1985," Ph.D. diss., Cambridge University, 2002.

53. Spoken at the conference, "Prospects for Peace in South Asia," sponsored by
the Stanford University Asia/Pacific Research Center and the U.S. Army War Col-

lege Strategic Studies Institute, Stanford, Calif., January 21–22, 2003.

54. The observation about the lack of interest of Muslim Indians in Pakistan was made by U.S. Ambassador Howard Schaeffer, at the conference "Prospects for Peace in South Asia," sponsored by the Stanford University Asia/Pacific Research Center and the U.S. Army War College Strategic Studies Institute, Stanford, Calif., January 21–22, 2003.

55. The inversion of the phrase "Indian Muslim" is a cause taken up by the current president of the All India Muslim Majlis-e-Mushawarat, the former diplomat and Member of Parliament, Syed Shahabadin, in his journal *Muslim India*. In his farewell editorial, after twenty years with this journal, in February 2003, he optimistically wrote as follows: "*Muslim India* has recorded this transformation from 'Indian Muslim' to 'Muslim Indian' and monitored the evolving equation between religious identity and the nation-state reach a stable equilibrium, not only in form, but in substance, not in fear, but in freedom, as a declaration of faith, as a proclamation of Indianness, without claiming any special rights, without asking for anything in return, but acceptance as equal citizens" (http://www.islamicvoice.com/february.2003/community.htm#mis).

56. Thomas Jefferson, letter responding to the Danbury Baptist Association, January 1, 1802, http://w3.trib.com/FACT/1st.jeffers.2.html.

57. T. N. Madan, "Freedom of Religion," *Economic and Political Weekly* (India), March 15, 2003, http://www.epw.org.in.

58. More recently, the relevance of ancient history has been brought in to the Ayodhya dispute by the decision in March 2003 to excavate beneath the site of the mosque to see if there was a temple (Purnima Joshi, "Ayodhya: Sediments of Faith," *Outlook* (India), March 24, 2003, http://www.outlookindia.com). This arguably sets a troubling precedent, whatever the outcome, for what should properly be a matter of law and social justice for all citizens.

59. Yoginder Sikand, "The Baba Budhan Dada Hayat Qalandar Dargah Controversy: The Ayodhya of South India?" in *Qalandar* (March 2003), http://www.islaminterfaith.org.

60. Mushirul Hasan (*Legacy of a Divided Nation*, 319–27), for example, identifies alternate voices to those of the 'ulama and the law board.

61. B. G. Verghese, "India's Forgotten Gospel of Fraternity," *Outlook* (India), November 18, 2002, http://www.outlookindia.com.

62. In the wake of recent riots, "prominent Muslim leaders" at the 2003 meeting of the Jamiat Ulama-e-Hind called for Muslims to form their own party. In the words of the Syed Ahmed Bukhari, Imam of the Jama Masjid in Delhi, "Muslims have been foiled by all political parties. The Congress ruled the country for nearly 50 years but what have they done to empower Muslims? . . . Other secular and regional parties come to power with the help of Muslims but they use us only to gain power" (Nilofar Suhrawardy, "India: Muslim Groups Form a New Political Party," *Arab News,* March 10, 2003, http://www.arabnews.com). Maulana Ahmad Bukhari has urged this issue since at least 2000. To be sure, these efforts continue to espouse

a secular program with emphasis less on Islam than on Muslim rights.

63. In the words of one Muslim activist, "Whenever an issue arises that concerns Muslims, the media approaches certain name-sake and un-elected Muslim 'leaders' in Delhi, who do not have the confidence and support of the Muslims, and presents them as 'spokesmen' for the 150 million Muslims of India. I feel this quest for an All-India level Muslim leadership is not only futile, it is also counterproductive. Muslims in India are regionally divided, and are organizing at the regional level. I think this is a good thing, because the social conditions in different regions are different. Thus, for instance, in Tamil Nadu Muslims might seek to establish ties with the Dravidian movement, while in Bihar they have united with the Yadavs and the Dalits" (Yoginder Sikand, "Interview with Iqbal Ahmed Shariff," *Qalandar,* March 2003, http://www.islaminterfaith.org).

64. For examples of this, in Mewat, see Shail Mayaram, *Resisting Regimes: Myth, Memory, and the Shaping of a Muslim Identity* (Delhi: Oxford University Press, 1997); and in Bengal, see Pradip Kumar Datta, *Carving Blocs: Communal Ideology in Early Twentieth Century Bengal* (New Delhi: Oxford University Press, 1999).

65. The Samajawadi Party, whose core has been the so-called Other Backward Castes. The Chief Minister in 2004 was Mulayam Singh Yadav.

66. "Mulayam Draws Up a Friday Timetable," *Indian Express* (New Delhi), February 19, 2004, http://www.indianexpress.com/full_story.php?content_id = 41456.

67. For a list of specific risks that VHP ideology would yield should it prevail, see Prem Shakar Jha, "The Cost of Hindutva" (*Outlook* [India], January 20, 2003, http://www.outlookindia.com), which asks whether the BJP wants to join the largely Muslim category of "rogue state."

68. See "LoC Kargil Fails to Impress the Public," http://www.bollywoodblitz-.com/news/bollywoodnews.php?newsarticle=66. The failure may, however, also be a comment on a movie that failed to deliver the usual success formula of romance, music, etc., along with war.

69. Husain Haqqani, "The Politics of Hindutva in India," *Asian Wall Street Journal,* January 28, 2003.

70. But see the website for the protest against "non-resident Indian" (NRI) funding, the term used for Indian immigrants abroad, at http://www.stopfunding-hate.org, "a coalition of people—professionals, students, workers, artists and intellectuals—who share a common concern that sectarian hatreds in India are being fueled by money flowing from the United States. SFH is committed to an India that is open, tolerant, and democratic. As the first step, SFH is determined to turn off the money flow from the United States to Hindutva hate groups responsible for recurring anti-minority violence in India." The decision of the BJP government, the ruling party, to extend citizenship to NRIs would seem to make the opportunity for extremist expatriate involvement even greater. This was announced on January 8, 2003, and reiterated in the President's address to the joint session of Parliament (A. P. J. Abdul Kalam, "Address to the Joint Session of Parliament, Republic of India," February 17, 2003, http://meadev.nic.in/speeches/Presi-add-parl.htm).

71. In February 2003 an American of Palestinian origin was arrested not for any crime committed against the United States but on the grounds that he had helped funnel money to Palestinian militants (Anwar Iqbal, "Rights Groups Upset by Professor's Arrest," *Washington Times*, February 20, 2003, http://www.washtimes.com/-upi-breaking/20030220-060338-2208r.htm).

Chapter 9

1. For a detailed study, see K. Warikoo, "Language and Politics in Jammu and Kashmir: Issues and Perspectives," in *Jammu, Kashmir, and Ladakh: Linguistic Predicament*, ed. P. N. Pushp and K. Warikoo (New Delhi: Har Anand Publishers, 1992).

2. For details of the Delhi Agreement, see Sisir Gupta, *Kashmir: A Study in India–Pakistan Relations* (New Delhi: Asia Publishing House, 1966), 371–74.

3. Cited in Gupta, *Kahsmir*, 366.

4. For the text of Abdullah's speech, see Navnita Chadha Behera, *State, Identity, and Violence: Jammu, Kashmir, and Ladakh* (New Delhi: Manohar, 2000), 315–22.

5. Abdullah shared his views with Adlai Stevenson in 1953. B. P. L. Bedi, a person "closely associated with Abdullah," sounded Leach, first secretary in the U.S. Embassy (see Sten Widmalm, *Kashmir in Comparative Perspective* (London: Routledge-Curzon, 2002), 46, 167.

6. P. N. Bazaz, *Kashmir in a Crucible* (Bombay: Pearl Publications, 1967), 86.

7. For example, see Gupta, *Kashmir*, 382–83; and Behera, *State, Identity, and Violence*, 97–98.

8. Behera, *State, Identity, and Violence*, 109.

9. In 1963 the Congress Party adopted a plan proposed by K. Kamaraj, the chief minister of Madras, calling upon cabinet ministers at the Center and chief ministers in the states to voluntarily resign from their posts in order to devote themselves to the task of revitalizing the party. It was left to Prime Minister Nehru to decide whose resignations should finally be accepted.

10. Bazaz, *Kashmir in a Crucible*, 99–100, 103–4.

11. Ibid., 113–14.

12. Balraj Puri, *Kashmir: Towards Insurgency* (New Delhi: Orient Longmans, 1993), 49; Behera, *State, Identity, and Violence*, 141. For an account of the ideology of the Jamaat-i-Islami, see Yoginder Sikand, "Changing the Course of the Kashmiri Struggle," in *Kashmir: How Far Can Vajpayee and Musharraf Go?* ed. Karan B. Sahni (New Delhi: Peace Publications, 2001), 108–16.

13. Cited in Behera, *State, Identity, and Violence*, 128.

14. *Times of India* (New Delhi), July 2, 1977.

15. Behera, *State, Identity, and Violence*, 142.

16. Cited in ibid., 135.

17. The Farooq–Rajiv accord "blocked secular outlets of protest against governments both at the Center and at the State. Before the Accord was signed, the National Conference provided an outlet for the first and the Congress an outlet for the

second kind of protest. The Accord destroyed the raison d'être of both the parties and forced all types of discontent to seek fundamentalist or secessionist outlets" (Puri, *Kashmir*, 52).

18. For an in-depth analysis, see Widmalm, *Kashmir in Comparative Perspective,* 77–80, 186–89. See also Inderjit Badhwar, "A Tarnished Triumph," *India Today,* April 15, 1987.

19. Cited in Widmalm, *Kashmir in Comparative Perspective,* 80.

20. Literacy rates increased from 11.03 percent in 1961 to 26.37 percent in 1981; the number of college students expanded from 2,779 in 1950–51 to 34,000 in 1992–93; and the number of newspapers rose from 46 in 1965 to 254 in 1991 (see Sumit Ganguly, *The Crisis in Kashmir* [Cambridge: Cambridge University Press, 1997], 33, 34, 37, 60). Ganguly argues that a "dichotomy—the increase in political mobilization against a background of institutional decay— . . . best explains the origins of the secessionist insurgency in Kashmir" (ibid., 20–21).

21. This was revealed by the JKLF leader, Hasim Qureshi (see Behera, *State, Identity, and Violence,* 167). For further details of Pakistani plans in the 1980s, see Manoj Joshi, *The Lost Rebellion* (New Delhi: Penguin, 1999), 18–21.

22. For accounts of Pakistan's clandestine operations in 1947–48, see Akbar Khan, *Raiders in Kashmir* (Karachi: Pak Publishers, 1970); and C. Dasgupta, *War and Diplomacy in Kashmir: 1947–48* (New Delhi: Sage, 2002).

23. In 1990, 155 security personnel and 461 civilians were killed in terrorist attacks in the state, according to figures compiled by the Home Ministry, Government of India. Among the political personalities killed by terrorists in 1989–90 were Mohammed Yusuf Halwai, Ali Mohammed Bachroo, Anwar Khan, Sheikh Abdul Jabbar, Sheikh Mohammed Mansoor, Maulana Mohammed Syed Masoodi (all National Conference); Tika Lal Taploo (BJP); Ghulam Nabi Butt (Congress); and Abdul Sattar Ranjoor (CPI).

24. Victoria Schofield, *Kashmir in Conflict* (London: I. B. Taurus, 2000), 157; Robert Wirsing, *India, Pakistan, and the Kashmir Dispute* (New Delhi: Rupa, 1994), 122–23; Behera, *State, Identity, and Violence,* 176–77.

25. Indian Home Ministry figures show a sharp rise in the number of foreign militants killed in security operations from 1993 onward. Thus, only 12 and 14 foreign militants were killed in 1991 and 1992, respectively, as against 90 and 122 in 1993 and 1994, respectively. By 2001, the figure had risen to 625. For details concerning terrorist groups operating in the state, see K. Santhanam et al., *Jihadis in Jammu and Kashmir* (Thousand Oaks, Calif.: Sage; New Delhi: Institute for Defence Studies and Analyses, 2003).

26. Cited in Behera, *State, Identity, and Violence,* 201.

27. Dr. Karan Singh, the only member of the committee not belonging to the National Conference, resigned on account of differences with the chief minister.

28. http://www.mori.com/polls/2002/kashmir.shtml.

Chapter 10

1. Reprinted in B. H. Liddell Hart, *Deterrent or Defence* (London: Stevens and Sons, 1960), 23.

2. Glenn Snyder, *Deterrence and Defense* (Princeton, N.J.: Princeton University Press, 1961), 226.

3. Robert Jervis, *The Illogic of American Nuclear Strategy* (Ithaca, N.Y.: Cornell University Press, 1984), 31.

4. Kargil Review Committee, *From Surprise to Reckoning: The Kargil Review Committee Report* (New Delhi: Sage Publications, 2000), 22.

5. The best narrative of India's nuclear ambitions is George Perkovich, *India's Nuclear Bomb: The Impact on Global Proliferation* (Berkeley: University of California Press, 1999), 293–333. A companion volume for Pakistan's nuclear program has yet to be written.

6. For a clear exposition of these alternative views, see Scott D. Sagan and Kenneth N. Waltz, *The Spread of Nuclear Weapons: A Debate* (New York: W. W. Norton, 1995).

7. These terms are adapted and borrowed from Sagan, ibid.; and Peter R. Lavoy's review essay of the debate between Sagan and Waltz, "The Strategic Consequences of Nuclear Proliferation" (*Security Studies* 4, no. 4 [Summer 1995]: 695–753).

8. Jaswant Singh, "Against Nuclear Apartheid," *Foreign Affairs* 77, no. 5 (1998): 43.

9. Vijay Nair, *Nuclear India* (Hartford, Wis.: Spencer and Lancer, 1992), 79.

10. K. Sundarji, "Proliferation of WMD and the Security Dimensions in South Asia: An Indian View," in *Weapons of Mass Destruction: New Perspectives on Counterproliferation,* ed. William H. Lewis and Stuart E. Johnson (Washington, D.C.: National Defense University Press, 1995), 59.

11. Raj Chengappa, *Weapons of Peace: The Secret Story of India's Quest to be a Nuclear Power* (New Delhi: HarperCollins, 2000), 8.

12. Interview with Jasjit Singh, "One on One," *Defense News* (July 27–August 2, 1998): 22.

13. K. M. Arif, "Retaining the Nuclear Option," in *Pakistan's Security and the Nuclear Option,* ed. Tariq Jain (Islamabad: Institute of Policy Studies, 1995), 123.

14. Zulfikar Khan, "Pakistan's Security and the Nuclear Option," in Jain, *Pakistan's Security and the Nuclear Option,* 138.

15. Abdul Sattar, "Nuclear Issues in South Asia: A Pakistani Perspective," in Jain, *Pakistan's Security and the Nuclear Option,* 89.

16. M. Aslam Beg, *Indian and Pakistani Security Perspectives* (Rawalpindi: Foundation for Research on National Development and Security, 1994), 73.

17. "N-Arms Weapons of Peace," *Hindu* (Chennai), August 26, 2002, http://www.hinduonnet.com/thehindu/2002/08/26/stories/2002082603851200.htm.

18. Sumit Ganguly, "Nuclear Proliferation in South Asia: Origins, Consequences, and Prospects," in *The Asia-Pacific in the New Millennium: Geopolitics, Security, and Foreign Policy,* ed. Shalendra D. Sharma (Berkeley: Institute of East Asia Studies of the University of California, Berkeley, 2000), 252–53; also see Sumit Ganguly, "Indo-Pakistani Nuclear Issues and the Stability/Instability Paradox," *Studies in Conflict and Terrorism* 18 (1995): 325–34.

19. David Hagerty, *The Consequences of Nuclear Proliferation: Lessons from South Asia* (Cambridge, Mass.: MIT Press, 1998), 184.

20. Ibid., 39.

21. Ashley Tellis, *India's Emerging Nuclear Posture: Between Recessed Deterrent and Ready Arsenal* (Santa Monica: Rand, Project Air Force, 2001), 743.

22. Robert Jervis, "The Political Effects of Nuclear Weapons," in *Nuclear Diplomacy and Crisis Management,* ed. Sean M. Lynn-Jones, Steven E. Miller, and Stephen Van Evera (Cambridge, Mass.: MIT Press, 1990), 29.

23. Neil Joeck, "Maintaining Nuclear Stability in South Asia," Adelphi papers, no. 312 (Oxford: Oxford University Press for the International Institute for Strategic Studies, 1997), 12.

24. V. Raghavan, "Limited War and Nuclear Escalation in South Asia," *The Nonproliferation Review* 8, no. 3 (Fall–Winter 2001), 83.

25. Ibid., 82.

26. P. R. Chari, "Nuclear Restraint, Risk Reduction, and the Security-Insecurity Paradox in South Asia," in *The Stability-Instability Paradox: Nuclear Weapons and Brinksmanship in South Asia,* Report no. 38, ed. Michael Krepon and Chris Gagne (Washington, D.C.: Henry L. Stimson Center, June 2001), 20.

27. Talat Masood, "Our Multiple Challenges," http://www.dawn.com/2002/06/22/op.htm.

28. M. B. Naqvi, "Facts about Indo-Pak Impasse," http://www.jang.com.pk/the-news/mar2002-daily/06-03-2002/oped/o4.htm.

29. Henry Kissinger, "America at the Apex: Empire or Leader?" *The National Interest,* no. 64 (Summer 2001): 13.

30. John Mueller, "The Essential Irrelevance of Nuclear Weapons: Stability in the Post-War World," in Lynn-Jones, Miller, and Van Evera, *Nuclear Diplomacy and Crisis Management,* 3.

31. Ibid., 14.

32. Ashley Tellis, *India's Emerging Nuclear Posture,* 743–44.

33. Richard Betts, *Nuclear Blackmail and Nuclear Balance* (Washington, D.C.: Brookings Institution, 1987), 211.

34. See, for example, Scott Sagan, *The Limits of Safety: Organizations, Accidents, and Nuclear Weapons* (Princeton, N.J.: Princeton University Press, 1993); and Bruce Blair, *The Logic of Accidental Nuclear War* (Washington, D.C.: Brookings Institution, 1993).

35. Betts, *Nuclear Blackmail and Nuclear Balance,* 214.

36. Sumit Ganguly, *Conflict Unending: India–Pakistan Tensions since 1947* (New York: Columbia University Press, 2001), 108.

37. These terms have been borrowed from Jasjit Singh and Ashley Tellis, respectively.

38. India's military expenditures rose an average of 8.8 percent from 1995 to 1999; Pakistan's rose an average of 2.9 percent. In 1999, the last year for which official U.S. data are available, India spent $11.3 billion on military expenditures; Pakistan spent $3.5 billion (U.S. Department of State, Bureau of Verification and Compliance, *World Military Expenditures and Arms Transfers, 1999–2000* [Washington, D.C.: Library of Congress, 2002], 2–3).

39. Stockholm International Peace Research Institute, "Transfers and Licensed Production of Major Conventional Weapons: Exports to India," http://projects. sipri.se/armstrade/INDIA_MPTS_93-02.PDF; and "Transfers and Licensed Production of Major Conventional Weapons: Exports to Pakistan," http://projects. sipri.se/armstrade/PAK_MPTS_93-02.PDF.

40. Michael Krepon, "Nuclear Risk Reduction: Is Cold War Experience Applicable for South Asia?" in Krepon and Gagne, *The Stability-Instability Paradox*, 1–14.

41. Desmond Ball, Hans Bethe, Bruce Blair, and others compiled a shorter list of key measures: do not use deadly force against an adversary; do not force an adversary to choose between humiliation and escalation; do not use military forces to undermine an adversary in geographic areas he deems vital; do not use force against an adversary's ally; do not use force to dramatically alter the status quo in a sensitive region; and do not initiate horizontal escalation (*Crisis Stability and Nuclear War* [Ithaca, N.Y.: Cornell University Peace Studies Program, 1987], 62).

42. Bernard Brodie, *Escalation and the Nuclear Option* (Princeton, N.J.: Princeton University Press, 1966), 128.

43. Satu Limaye, "Mediating Kashmir: A Bridge Too Far," *Washington Quarterly* 26, no. 1 (Winter 2002–3): 159.

44. Thomas Schelling, *The Strategy of Conflict* (Oxford: Oxford University Press, 1960), 200.

45. Robert Jervis, Richard Ned Lebow, and Janice Gross Stein, *Psychology and Deterrence* (Baltimore: Johns Hopkins University Press, 1985), 125.

46. Raja Menon, *A Nuclear Strategy for India* (Thousand Oaks, Calif.: Sage Publications, 2000), 152.

47. Ibid., 230.

48. Polly Nayak, "Reducing Collateral Damage to Indo-Pakistani Relations from the War on Terrorism," *Policy Brief*, No. 17 (Washington: Brookings Institution, September 2002), 2.

49. See, for example, "Troop Withdrawal Vindicates Our Stance, says Musharraf," *Daily Times* (Lahore), October 26, 2002; "Objective of Army Deployment Achieved, says Fernandes," *Hindu* (Chennai), October 28, 2002; "Indian Troops Deployment Failed, says Yusuf," *Dawn* (Karachi), December 11, 2002.

50. "Warning Forced India to Pull Back Troops, says President," *Dawn* (Karachi), December 31, 2002. This statement was subsequently "clarified" by Pakistan's military spokesman as meaning "unconventional forces and not nuclear or biological weapons" ("Gen Shoots Mouth Off, Backfires," *Indian Express* [New Delhi], December 31, 2002).

51. "Troop Build-up Sent Strong Message to Pak: PM," *Indian Express* (New Delhi), December 13, 2002.

52. "Gen Shoots Mouth Off, Backfires," *Indian Express* (New Delhi), December 31, 2002.

53. "The Real Intent?" *News International* (Rawalpindi), July 24, 2002.

54. Interviews with author (names withheld to maintain confidentiality),

Rawalpindi and Islamabad, October 7–13, 2002.

55. "One Month after Kaluchak: Five Lessons We Learnt, Can't Afford to Forget," *Indian Express* (New Delhi), June 15, 2002.

56. "Premature Pullback vs. Army Fatigue," *Times of India* (New Delhi), October 29, 2002.

57. "Premature Pullback vs. Army Fatigue," *Times of India* (New Delhi), October 29, 2002.

58. "Mirage 2001–02," *Outlook* (New Delhi), October 28, 2002.

59. See Sagan, *The Limits of Safety*, ch. 2; James G. Blight, Bruce J. Allyn, and David A. Welch, *Cuba on the Brink: Castro, the Missile Crisis, and the Soviet Collapse*, 2nd ed. (Lanham, Md.: Rowman and Littlefield, 2002); Laurence Chang and Peter Kornbluh, eds., *The Cuban Missile Crisis, 1962: A National Security Archive Documents Reader* (New York: W. W. Norton, 1999). Also see "The Havana Conference on the Cuban Missile Crisis," press release from the National Security Archive, http://www.gwu.edu/~nsarchiv/CWIHP/BULLETINS/b1a1.htm.

60. "Cabinet Committee on Security Reviews Progress in Operationalizing India's Nuclear Doctrine," press release, Prime Minister's Office, January 4, 2003.

61. "Pak. Will Be Erased if it Nukes India: Fernandes," *Hindu* (Chennai), January 28, 2003.

62. "Musharraf Vows to 'Unleash a Storm' if India Attacks," *News International* (Rawalpindi), May 30, 2002.

63. Available online at http://www.infopak.gov.pk/President_Addresses/-Pres_23Marc.htm.

64. Available online at http://www.infopak.gov.pk/President_Addresses/presidentadress-27-5-2002.htm.

65. Henry Kissinger, *Nuclear Weapons and Foreign Policy* (New York: Harper and Bros., 1957), 133–34.

66. Thomas Schelling , *The Strategy of Conflict*, 42.

67. "Deterrence and Limited War," *News International* (Rawalpindi), June 3, 2002.

68. The wording of these thresholds is that of the Italian interviewers. See Paolo Cotta-Ramusino and Maurizio Martellini, *Nuclear Safety, Nuclear Stability, and Nuclear Strategy in Pakistan* (Como: Landau Network, January 2002), 5.

69. Kevin Sullivan, "One Word from Nuclear War," *International Herald Tribune*, October 14, 2002.

70. See, for example, Herman Kahn, *On Escalation: Metaphors and Scenarios* (New York: Frederick A. Praeger, 1965); Paul H. Nitze, "Assuming Strategic Stability in an Era of Détente," *Foreign Affairs* 54, no. 2 (January 1976): 208–32; Richard Pipes, "Why the Soviet Union Thinks It Could Fight and Win a Nuclear War," *Commentary* 74, no. 1 (July 1977): 21–34.

71. Rediff interview with General V. Prakash Malik, Part II: "Pakistan Thought the Indian Army's Back Was Broken," Rediff On the Net, July 27, 2001, http://www.rediff.com/news/2001/Jul/27inter.htm.

72. "Army Will Be Prepared to Tackle Nuclear Threat," *Hindustan Times*, September 29, 2000, cited in Tellis, *India's Emerging Nuclear Posture*, 44.

73. Robert Jervis, *The Illogic of American Nuclear Strategy* (Ithaca, N.Y.: Cornell University Press, 1984), 148.

74. Brodie, *Escalation and the Nuclear Option*, 124.

75. Morton Kaplan, *The Strategy of Limited Retaliation* (Princeton, N.J.: Center of International Studies, 1959), 3.

76. See Michael Krepon and Ziad Haider, eds., *Reducing Nuclear Dangers in South Asia*, report no. 50 (Washington, D.C.: Henry L. Stimson Center, January 2004).

Chapter 11

1. Peter R. Lavoy, Scott D. Sagan, and James J. Wirtz, eds., *Planning the Unthinkable: How New Powers Will Use Nuclear, Biological, and Chemical Weapons* (Ithaca, N.Y.: Cornell University Press, 2000).

2. A notable exception is Robert Jervis, *The Meaning of the Nuclear Revolution* (Ithaca, N.Y.: Cornell University Press, 1989), 174–225.

3. As I use the term, a "nuclear myth" is an unverifiable claim about the relationship between a nation's nuclear weapons and its national security, power, and welfare. Nuclear mythmakers assert these claims and try to persuade others of their validity. A key premise of this perspective is that nuclear myths can be believed but not necessarily "known." See Peter R. Lavoy, *Learning to Live with the Bomb: India, the United States, and the Myths of Nuclear Security* (New York: Palgrave Macmillan, forthcoming); and Peter R. Lavoy "Nuclear Myths and the Causes of Nuclear Proliferation," in *The Proliferation Puzzle: Why Nuclear Weapons Spread and What Results*, ed. Zachary S. Davis and Benjamin Frankel (London: Frank Cass, 1993), 192–212.

4. Zulfiqar Ali Bhutto, *Awakening the People* (Rawalpindi: Pakistan Publications, 1970), 21.

5. Written shortly after the 1965 war with India, Bhutto's *The Myth of Independence* (Karachi: Oxford University Press, 1969), 153, contains the rationale for a Pakistani "nuclear deterrent," which continues today as state policy.

6. Zafar Iqbal Cheema, "Pakistan's Nuclear Use Doctrine and Command and Control," in Lavoy, Sagan, and Wirtz, *Planning the Unthinkable*, 159 (emphasis added).

7. See Pakistan Ministry of Foreign Affairs, "Organisation of Pakistan's National Command Authority," http://www.forisb.org/NCA.html; and "National Command Authority Established," Associated Press of Pakistan, February 3, 2000, http://www.fas.org/news/pakistan/2000/000203-pak-app1.htm.

8. Cited in "Pakistan to Upgrade Nuclear Deterrent," *Dawn*, November 25, 1999.

9. See Paolo Cotta-Ramusino and Maurizio Martellini, "Nuclear Safety, Nuclear Stability, and Nuclear Strategy in Pakistan," *Concise Report of a Visit by Landau Network–Centro Volta*, January 21, 2002, http://lxmi.mi.infn.it/~landnet. The Draft Re-

port of the National Security Advisory Board on Indian Nuclear Doctrine can be found at http://www.meadev.nic.in/govt/indnucld.htm.

10. For background on Pakistan's nuclear program, see Joseph Cirincione with Jon B. Wolfsthal and Miriam Rajkumar, *Deadly Arsenals: Tracking Weapons of Mass Destruction* (Washington, D.C.: Carnegie Endowment for International Peace, 2002), 207–19.

11. Reported in the *Pakistan Times*, December 27, 1974, 1.

12. Pakistani military officials subsequently informed the authors of the Landau report that General Kidwai's remarks on what would trigger a Pakistani nuclear reaction were "purely academic." The officials stated: "These are matters which as elsewhere, are primarily the responsibility of the political leadership of the day. . . . The elaborate command and control mechanisms introduced with the establishment of the National Command Authority which is Chaired by the Head of State and assisted by political and civilian leaders . . . ensure the highest level of responsibility and due deliberation on all matters of strategic importance" (see Cotta-Ramusino and Martellini, "Nuclear Safety, Nuclear Stability, and Nuclear Strategy in Pakistan").

13. Roger Boyes, "Musharraf Warns India He May Use Nuclear Weapons," *Times Online* (London), April 8, 2002, www.thetimes.co.uk/article/0,3-260481,00.html.

14. Of course, the logic of Pakistan's declaratory doctrine is similar to that of the non-specified declaratory deterrence doctrine of other nuclear weapons powers, including the United States: "The United States will continue to make clear that it reserves the right to respond with overwhelming force—including through resort to all of our options—to the use of WMD against the United States, its forces abroad, and friends and allies" (President George W. Bush, *National Strategy to Combat Weapons of Mass Destruction*, December 2002, http://www.whitehouse.gov/news/releases/2002/12/WMDStrategy.pdf).

15. U.S. Defense Intelligence Agency, "Operational and Logistical Considerations in the Event of an India-Pakistan Conflict" (December 1984), DDB-2660-104-84, declassified document obtained in the U.S. National Security Archive, Nuclear Nonproliferation Collection.

16. For background, see Feroz Hassan Khan, "Pakistan's Nuclear Future," in *South Asia in 2020: Future Strategic Balances and Alliances*, ed. Michael R. Chambers (Carlisle Barracks, Pa.: U.S. Army War College, 2002).

17. Mirza Aslam Beg, "Deterrence, Defence, and Development" (Pakistan Institute for Air Defence Studies), 1–2, http://www.piads.com.pk/users/piads/beg2.html.

18. Beg, "Deterrence, Defence, and Development," 2.

19. See "Ex-Pakistan President Says Nuclear Program Deterred Indian Attacks," *Nucleonics Week*, July 29, 1993, 6.

20. Agha Shahi, Zulfiqar Ali Khan, and Abdul Sattar, "Securing Nuclear Peace," *News International*, October 5, 1999.

21. Ibid.

22. For example, see "Are Pakistani Nukes More Effective Than Indian?" *Daily*

Times (Lahore), December 13, 2002, http://www.dailytimes.com.pk/print.asp?page = story_13-12-2002_pg1_11.

23. "India Was Warned of Unconventional War," *News International,* December 31, 2002, http://www.jang.com.pk/thenews/dec2002daily/31122002/main/main2.htm.

24. Director of Central Intelligence George J. Tenet expressed this view early in 2002: "Both India and Pakistan are publicly downplaying the risks of nuclear conflict in the current crisis. We are deeply concerned, however, that a conventional war—once begun—could escalate into a nuclear confrontation" (see Senate Armed Services Committee, "Worldwide Threat—Converging Dangers in a Post 9/11 World," testimony of George J. Tenet, March 19, 2002, 107th Cong., 1st sess.).

25. A nuclear "hawk" that discounts the role of nuclear weapons in deterring war in the 1984–85 and 1986–87 crises is General K. M. Arif; see his *Khaki Shadows: Pakistan 1947–1997* (Karachi: Oxford University Press, 2001), 251, 276. For a similar interpretation from a rare retired military officer who is a nuclear "dove," see Lt. General (ret.) Mujeebur Rahman Khan, "Nuclear Deterrence is a Myth," *Dawn* (Karachi), December 5, 1992, 15.

26. See "India Evolves Nuclear Doctrine," *Times of India* (Mumbai), August 5, 1998.

27. Pakistani Foreign Minister Abdul Sattar, speech at the Carnegie International Non-Proliferation Conference, June 18, 2001, www.ceip.org/files/projects/npp/resources/Conference%202001/sattar.htm.

28. Agha Shahi, "Address to ICWA-ISS Seminar on Command and Control of Nuclear Weapons in South Asia," Islamabad, Pakistan, February 21, 2000.

29. Ejaz Haider, "Stable Deterrence and Flawed Pakistani Nuclear Strategy," *Friday Times* (Lahore), February 8–14, 2002.

30. The stability-instability paradox was articulated first by Glenn Snyder ("The Balance of Power and the Balance of Terror," in *The Balance of Power,* ed. Paul Seabury [San Francisco: Chandler, 1965]). See also Robert Jervis, *The Illogic of American Nuclear Strategy* (Ithaca, N.Y.: Cornell University Press, 1984), 29–34.

31. Stephen P. Cohen, *The Pakistan Army* (Berkeley and Los Angeles: University of California Press, 1984), 153.

32. The late General Sundarji was the general quoted in Shekhar Gupta and W. P. S. Sidhu, "The End Game Option," *India Today,* April 30, 1993, 28.

33. A. R. Siddiqui, "COAS Views on Relations with India," *Nation,* April 29, 1999.

34. Cited in Ziba Moshaver, *Nuclear Weapons Proliferation in the Indian Subcontinent* (New York: St. Martin's, 1991), 62. Whether Ayub actually said this is arguable. Zafar Iqbal Cheema observes that Ayub was far too experienced to believe he could purchase nuclear weapons (Zafar Iqbal Cheema, "Pakistan's Nuclear Policy under Z. A. Bhutto and Zia ul-Haq: An Assessment," *Strategic Studies* [Islamabad] 14, no. 4 [Summer 1992]: 5–6). Moreover, based on my interviews with Pakistani officials who were in Ayub's government, Ayub apparently did authorize a

serious study of the requirements for building nuclear weapons, but deferred the decision to do so. Thus, it appears that Bhutto used Ayub's reluctance to initiate a crash nuclear weapons program to score political points against the military ruler.

35. See Ashok Kapur, *Pakistan's Nuclear Development* (New York: Croom Helm, 1987), 57.

36. Shahid Javed Burki, *Pakistan Under Bhutto, 1971–1977*, 2nd ed. (London: Macmillan Press, 1988), 148–54.

37. Cited in S. A. I. Tirmizi, *Profiles of Intelligence* (Lahore: Combined Printers, 1995), 254.

38. *Morning News* (Karachi), August 31, 1979.

39. See Dennis Kux, *The United States and Pakistan, 1947–2000: Disenchanted Allies* (Baltimore: Johns Hopkins University Press, 2001), 346.

40. The official Government of Pakistan website (www.pak.gov.pk) contains no reference to Pakistan's nuclear weapons policy or program.

41. Point five of the six-point Jamaat-i-Islami national agenda reads: "Protection of nuclear capability: Protection of Pakistan's nuclear capability and the demands of the country's defense and security cannot be compromised. The target of Pakistan-hostile forces is before us quite clearly. This is now our duty to frustrate their conspiracies and acquire such a multi-dimensional military, economic, political, and moral strength to ward off every threat and deter the enemy from committing aggression" (www.jamaat.org). No mention of the nuclear issue is evident on the official websites of Pakistan's other political parties.

42. The Pakistan army ended the 1971 war with twelve divisions, having lost three in East Pakistan. Bhutto raised six divisions, which all were in place by 1973.

43. Arif, *Khaki Shadows*, 363.

44. See ibid.; and Burki, *Pakistan under Bhutto*, 102–4.

45. Ashok Kapur, *Pakistan in Crisis* (New York: Routledge, 1991), 157.

46. Zulfiqar Ali Bhutto, *If I Am Assassinated . . .* (New Delhi: Vikas, 1979), 135–38.

47. Political use of the nuclear issue continued out of the public's view. Under Zia, Munir Ahmad Khan, chairman of the Pakistan Atomic Energy Commission (PAEC), and Abdul Qadeer Khan, chairman of the Khan Research Laboratories (KRL), continued their struggle over government resources, public acclaim, and the nuclear program's technical orientation, with PAEC championing the plutonium reprocessing route to weapons development and KRL pushing the uranium enrichment route. The first public revelation of this rift was the unattributed article, "Reprocessing Leaves One Cold" (*Pakistan Economist*, October 21, 1978, 5–8). For background, see Kapur, *Pakistan's Nuclear Development*, 193–280.

48. Bhutto stated that although she was initially not "read into" the nuclear program, within a few months she managed to "push her way" into the nuclear policy circle which had been the exclusive domain of army chief, General Mirza Aslam Beg, and President Ghulam Ishaq Khan (see Kux, *The United States and Pakistan*, 299).

49. Editorial, *Friday Times* (Lahore), February 21–27, 1991. Nawaz Sharif also became caught in the same trap. During Bhutto's second term in power, opposition leader Sharif complained to the former foreign secretary Abdul Sattar (now Pakistan's Foreign Minister) that Bhutto was selling out Pakistan's nuclear program. Sattar replied that Sharif had no right to complain because he himself had continued the suspension of fissile material production initially imposed by Bhutto (Shahid-ur-Rehman, *Long Road to Chagai* [Islamabad: Print Wise Publication, 1999], 118–19).

50. For background, see Shahid-ur-Rehman, *Long Road to Chagai*, 107–11.

51. Cited by Aamer Ahmed Khan in the *Friday Times* (Lahore), March 22–April 3, 1991.

52. While serving as army chief under Nawaz Sharif, however, General Musharraf evidently tried to pressure the Prime Minister against signing the Comprehensive Test Ban Treaty by playing "nuclear politics."

53. As told to Stanley Wolpert (see Wolpert, *Zulfi Bhutto of Pakistan: His Life and Times* [New York: Oxford University Press, 1993], 28).

54. Then KRL Director A. Q. Khan has carried forth Bhutto's perspective: "Pakistan is the only Muslim country where there are such scientists and engineers who could get results in the nuclear field. This is why the success of Pakistan is the success of the whole Islamic world" (cited in Mohammad Aslam, *Dr. A. Q. Khan and Pakistan's Nuclear Programme* [Rawalpindi: Diplomat Publications, 1989], 100).

55. Bhutto, *If I Am Assassinated*, 137–38.

56. *Nawa-I-Waqt* (Lahore), February 10, 1984.

57. Cited in P. B. Sinha and R. R. Subramanian, *Nuclear Pakistan: Atomic Threat to South Asia* (Delhi, 1980), 70.

58. See Shirin Tahir-Kelhi, "Pakistan's Nuclear Option and U.S. Policy," *Orbis* 22, no. 2 (Summer 1978): 371.

59. General K. M. Arif, *Working with Zia: Pakistan's Power Politics 1977/1978* (Karachi: Oxford University Press, 1995), 341.

60. See Government of India, *From Surprise to Reckoning: The Kargil Review Committee Report* (New Delhi: Sage Publications, 2000), 65.

61. Ibid., 193.

62. *Times of India* (Mumbai), July 24, 1993.

63. Government of India, *From Surprise to Reckoning*, 199.

64. Ibid., 198–99.

65. Ibid., 208–9.

66. Ibid., 209.

67. For background on the A. Q. Khan episode, see Peter R. Lavoy and Feroz Hassan Khan, "Rogue or Responsible Nuclear Power? Making Sense of Pakistan's Nuclear Practices," *Strategic Insights* 3, no. 2 (February 2004), http://www.ccc.nps.navy.mil/si/2004/feb/lavoyFeb04.asp.

68. "Pak. Scientist met Osama," *Hindu* (Chennai), March 5, 2002.

69. "Scientist Says Osama Sought Nuclear Help," *Daily Times* (Lahore), De-

cember 31, 2002, http://www.dailytimes.com.pk/default.asp?page = story_31-12-2002_pg1_9.

70. Roger Boyes, "Musharraf Warns India He May Use Nuclear Weapons," *Times Online* (London), April 8, 2002, http://www.thetimes.co.uk/article/0,3-260481,00.html.

71. Zia Mian, "Pakistan's Fateful Nuclear Option," in *Out of the Nuclear Shadow*, ed. Smitu Kothari and Zia Mian (Delhi: Lokayan and Rainbow Publishers, 2001), 103–6; and Samina Ahmad and David Cortright, eds., *Pakistan and the Bomb* (South Bend, Ind.: University of Notre Dame Press, 1998).

72. Lavoy, "Nuclear Myths and the Causes of Nuclear Proliferation."

73. Senate Armed Services Committee, "Worldwide Threat—Converging Dangers in a Post 9/11 World," testimony of George J. Tenet, March 19, 2002, 107th Cong., 1st sess.

74. Haider, "Stable Deterrence and Flawed Pakistani Nuclear Strategy."

Chapter 12

I thank Itty Abraham, Stephen P. Cohen, Sunil Dasgupta, George Perkovich, Timothy Hoyt, Scott Sagan, and Teresita Schaffer for their comments and suggestions at various stages in the writing of this paper.

1. Arguably, there were two wars in 1965, since the first, in March of that year, was fought along the southern sector of the border, while the second, which broke out in September, was fought over a much wider theater.

2. On the first and the second crises, see Kanti Bajpai, Pervaiz Iqbal Cheema, Stephen P. Cohen, and Sumit Ganguly, *Brasstacks and Beyond: Perception and Management of Crisis in South Asia* (New Delhi: Manohar, 1995); Michael Krepon and Misha Faruqee, eds., *Conflict Prevention and Confidence Building Measures in South Asia: The 1990 Crisis* (Washington, D.C.: Henry L. Stimson Center, 1994); and Devin T. Hagerty, *The Consequences of Nuclear Proliferation: Lessons from South Asia* (Cambridge, Mass.: MIT Press, 1998). On all three crises, see Waheguru Pal Singh Sidhu, "India's Nuclear Use Doctrine," in *Planning the Unthinkable: How New Powers Will Use Nuclear, Biological, and Chemical Weapons,* ed. Peter R. Lavoy, Scott D. Sagan, and James J. Wirtz (Ithaca, N.Y.: Cornell University Press, 2000), 135–50.

3. For a detailed discussion of the shift in Indian thinking, see Rajesh M. Basrur, "Kargil, Terrorism, and India's Strategic Shift," *India Review* 1, no. 4 (October 2002): 39–56.

4. Harjinder Sidhu, "Ansari Arrest Proves Pak Hand: PM," *Hindustan Times* (New Delhi), February 11, 2002.

5. On the "stability-instability paradox," see Michael Krepon and Chris Gagné, eds., *The Stability-Instability Paradox: Nuclear Weapons and Brinkmanship in South Asia* (Washington, D.C.: Henry L. Stimson Center, June 2001). For the original formulation of the concept, see Glen Snyder, "The Balance of Power and the Balance of Terror," in *The Balance of Power,* ed. Paul Seabury (San Francisco: Chandler, 1965), 194–201.

6. "Hot Pursuit Option Still Open: Advani," *Hindu* (Chennai), October 25, 2001.

7. C. Raja Mohan, "Fernandes Unveils 'Limited War' Doctrine," *Hindu* (Chennai), January 25, 2000.

8. C. Raja Mohan, "Fernandes Unveils 'Limited War' Doctrine," *Hindu* (Chennai), January 25, 2000.

9. V. R. Raghavan, "Limited War and Nuclear Escalation in South Asia," *Nonproliferation Review* 8, no. 3 (Fall–Winter 2001): 89.

10. C. Raja Mohan, "Kargil Diplomacy," *Hindu* (Chennai), August 3, 2000.

11. Purnima S. Tripathi, "Capital Terror," *Frontline* (Chennai), December 22, 2001–January 4, 2002.

12. C. Raja Mohan, "Between War and Peace," *Hindu* (Chennai), December 12, 2001.

13. Michael Krepon, "Last-Minute Diplomacy," *Outlook* (New Delhi), April 29, 2002, 24.

14. For general discussions encompassing both conventional and nuclear weapons, see David Baldwin, "Thinking about Threats," *Journal of Conflict Resolution* 15, no. 1 (March 1971): 71–78; Daniel Byman and Matthew Waxman, *The Dynamics of Coercion: American Foreign Policy and the Limits of Military Might* (Cambridge: Cambridge University Press, 2002); Gordon A. Craig and Alexander L. George, *Force and Statecraft: Diplomatic Problems of Our Time* (New York: Oxford University Press, 1983), 189–204; Alexander L. George, *Forceful Persuasion: Coercive Diplomacy as an Alternative to War* (Washington, D.C.: United States Institute of Peace Press, 1991); and Walter J. Petersen, "Deterrence and Compellence: A Critical Assessment of Conventional Wisdom," *International Studies Quarterly* 30, no. 3 (September 1986): 269–94. On specifically nuclear contexts, see Desmond Ball et al., *Crisis Stability and Nuclear War* (Ithaca, N.Y.: Peace Studies Program, Cornell University, 1987); Richard K. Betts, *Nuclear Blackmail and Nuclear Balance* (Washington, D.C.: Brookings Institution, 1987); Daniel S. Geller, "Nuclear Weapons, Deterrence, and Crisis Escalation," *Journal of Conflict Resolution* 34, no. 2 (June 1990): 291–310; Paul Huth and Bruce Russett, "Testing Deterrence Theory: Rigor Makes a Difference," *World Politics* 42, no. 4 (July 1990): 466–501; Edward Rhodes, *Power and MADness: The Logic of Nuclear Coercion* (New York: Columbia University Press, 1989); Thomas C. Schelling, *Strategy of Conflict* (Cambridge, Mass.: Harvard University Press), 1960; and Thomas C. Schelling, *Arms and Influence* (New Haven, Conn.: Yale University Press, 1966).

15. Huth and Russett, "Testing Deterrence Theory," 475.

16. The best discussion on this is Schelling, *Arms and Influence*, 69–91. See also Huth and Russett, "Testing Deterrence Theory," 475–77.

17. Alexander George (*Forceful Persuasion*, 7) notes that a specified time limit may not always be appropriate.

18. George, *Forceful Persuasion*, 8.

19. On the decomposition of threats for greater effectiveness, see Schelling, *Strategy of Conflict*, 41–43.

20. Sandeep Dikshit, "Govt Orders Withdrawal of Troops from IB," *Hindu* (Chennai), October 17, 2002.

21. Vishal Thapar, "Prithvi Missiles Moved Near Border in Punjab," *Hindustan Times* (New Delhi), December 25, 2001.

22. Terrey Friel and Jane Macartney, "India Deploys Planes as Tensions with Pakistan Rise," *Washington Post*, December 26, 2001.

23. Celia W. Dugger, "India and Pakistan Add to War Footing," *New York Times*, December 28, 2001.

24. "Army Prepares for Exercise along Border," *Times of India* (Mumbai), December 29, 2001.

25. John F. Burns, "Pakistan Appeals to US as India Continues Border Buildup," *Washington Post*, December 30, 2001.

26. John F. Burns, "Pakistan Moves against Groups Named by India," *New York Times*, December 29, 2001.

27. "In Musharraf's Words, A Day of Reckoning," *New York Times*, January 12, 2002.

28. "Morning Terror in Jammu Casts Shadow on Days Ahead," *Indian Express* (New Delhi), May 15, 2002.

29. "Naval Ships Head West," *Hindu* (Chennai), May 22, 2002.

30. C. Raja Mohan, "Musharraf Vows to Stop Infiltration: Armitage," *Hindu* (Chennai), June 8, 2002. The assurance was given personally to Powell's deputy, Richard Armitage.

31. "Indian Warships Sail Away from Pak Waters," *Times of India* (Mumbai), June 11, 2002.

32. "Pakistan Slashes Duty on 600 Trade Items from India," *Hindustan Times* (New Delhi), June 18, 2002.

33. "Pak Would Be Wiped Out If It Uses Nuclear Bomb: BJP," *Hindustan Times* (New Delhi), December 26, 2001.

34. John F. Burns, "Pakistan Leader in Sharp Rebuke to Indian Threat," *New York Times*, December 26, 2001.

35. Parul Chandra, "India Can Breach Indus Waters Treaty to Flood Pakistan," *Times of India* (Mumbai), December 27, 2001. While there was no solid evidence to show that the threat was projected with the intention to actually carry it out, it seems very unlikely to have been more than a bluff, as indicated by conversations with officials, who pointed out that Indian leaders were well aware of the adverse consequences of breaching a long-standing treaty.

36. "We Could Take A Strike and Survive. Pakistan Won't: Fernandes," *Hindustan Times* (New Delhi), December 30, 2001.

37. Celia W. Dugger, "Following India's Brinkmanship, Ominous Preparations to Follow Through," *New York Times*, January 12, 2002.

38. Celia W. Dugger, "Indian General Talks Bluntly of War and A Nuclear Threat," *New York Times*, January 12, 2002. While an official hastened to say that the General's remarks had not been cleared by the Prime Minister's office, that

would have pertained to the actual form and style rather than the substance of what he said. In the context of civil–military relations in India, it is inconceivable that an Army Chief would have broached the subject of potential nuclear conflict without clearance from the political leadership.

39. "India Preparing for Limited Punitive Strikes in Kashmir: Analyst," *Hindustan Times* (New Delhi), May 21, 2002.

40. "India May Scrap Indus Waters Treaty: Minister," *Hindustan Times* (New Delhi), May 23, 2002.

41. "Option of War with Pak Open: Swami," *Hindustan Times* (New Delhi), September 29, 2002.

42. Michael Pillsbury, "Strategic Acupuncture," *Foreign Policy* 41 (Winter 1980–81): 44–61.

43. Schelling, *Strategy of Conflict*, 187–203.

44. Schelling, *Arms and Influence*, 36–43.

45. This logic was stated to a newsman by Uday Bhaskar, deputy director of a government of India think tank, the Institute for Defense Studies and Analyses (Rajiv Chandrasekharan, "For India, Deterrence May Not Prevent War," *Washington Post*, January 17, 2002). What, exactly, Pakistani core interests are, and whether these are truly knowable, is a far more problematic question. While the argument was, in a sense, logical, it assumed that a first strike was bearable for India, which was in complete contradiction of the basis of minimum deterrence. Like the threat to violate the Indus Treaty, this was clearly rhetoric designed to intimidate the adversary psychologically, since at a time of high tension the latter could never be sure that the threat would not be carried out.

46. Escalation dominance may be defined as "the ability to increase the threatened costs to an adversary while denying the adversary the opportunity to neutralize those costs or to counterescalate" (Daniel Byman and Matthew Waxman, *The Dynamics of Coercion: American Foreign Policy and the Limits of Military Might* [Cambridge: Cambridge University Press, 2002], 30). For a critical discussion, see pp. 38–44 in the same volume.

47. This point, though never officially articulated, was made twice by K. Subrahmanyam, an influential strategic analyst and former convener of the NSAB (see K. Subrahmanyam, "Containing Pakistan," *Times of India* [Mumbai], December 31, 2001; K. Subrahmanyam, "Indo-Pak Nuclear Conflict Unlikely," *Times of India* [Mumbasi], January 2, 2002). The view is echoed by another former NSAB member (see C. Raja Mohan, "Between War and Peace," *Hindu* [Chennai], December 12, 2001).

48. The United States did get politically involved in the 1971 war to the extent of tilting toward Pakistan at the time, but only from afar. American officials were not engaged in active diplomacy in the region at the time.

49. For detailed case studies of the two crises, see Hagerty, *The Consequences of Nuclear Proliferation.*

50. David E. Sanger with Judith Miller, "Bush Meets India's Envoy; Fears of Pak-

istan War Deepen," *New York Times*, January 11, 2002. See also Michael R. Gordon, "As Threat Eases, U.S. Still Sees Peril in India–Pakistan Buildup," *New York Times*, January 20, 2002.

51. S. Rajagopalan, "Risk of Indo-Pak War Highest since 1971," *Hindustan Times* (New Delhi), February 2, 2002, 1.

52. Nicholas D. Kristof, "This Is Not A Test," *New York Times*, December 28, 2001.

53. "Bush Leans on Pakistan's President," *New York Times*, December 29, 2001.

54. Peter Slevin, "Pakistan Groups Called Terrorist Organizations," *Washington Post*, December 27, 2001.

55. John F. Burns, "Pakistan Moves against Groups Named by India," *New York Times*, December 29, 2001.

56. Alan Sipress, "Musharraf Urge to Calm S. Asia," *Washington Post*, January 12, 2002.

57. "Show Results, Bush Tells Musharraf," *Hindu* (Chennai), May 27, 2002.

58. Sridhar Krishnaswami, "Infiltration Still On: Powell," *Hindu* (Chennai), June 1, 2002.

59. David E. Sanger and Celia W. Dugger, "Bush Intervenes in Effort to Stop Kashmir War," *New York Times*, June 6, 2002.

60. Dirk Beveridge, "U.S. Envoy Says Tension Easing in South Asia," *Washington Post*, June 7, 2002.

61. Schelling, *Arms and Influence*, 36–43.

62. Stephen Philip Cohen, "Aim for Peace—or the Exit Door," *Los Angeles Times*, January 11, 2002.

63. Arguably, large-scale deaths do not always attract as much international concern and involvement as they ought to, as in the case of the Rwandan genocide in the 1990s. But a nuclear holocaust has the potential to inflict far greater damage— possibly in the millions—than the Rwandan massacres.

64. I am grateful to George Perkovich for drawing my attention to the last two points in a personal communication.

65. For a thoughtful methodological discussion, see Len Scott and Steve Smith, "Lessons of October: Historians, Political Scientists, Policy-Makers, and the Cuban Missile Crisis," *International Affairs* 70, no. 4 (October 1994): 659–84.

66. For a positive estimation, see Pramit Pal Chaudhuri, "India Proves Adept at Diplomatic Jugglery," *Hindustan Times* (New Delhi), June 12, 2002; Salman Haidar, "Moving towards Détente," *Statesman New Delhi*, October 22, 2002; Prem Shankar Jha, "Empty Promises," *Hindustan Times* (New Delhi), June 21, 2002; Gaurav Kampani, "India's Compellance [*sic*] Strategy: Calling Pakistan's Bluff over Kashmir," Center for Nonproliferation Studies, Monterey Institute of International Studies, Monterey, Calif., June 10, 2002, http://cns.miis.edu/iiop/cnsdata?Action=1&Concept=0&Mime=1&collection=CNS+Web+Site&Key=pubs%2Fweek%2F020610%2Ehtm&QueryText=Kashmir&QueryMode=FreeText; Shekhar Gupta, "After Coercive, Now Diplomacy," *Indian Express* (New Delhi), October 19, 2002;

Maharajakrishna Rasgotra, "Piety Will Not Deliver," *Indian Express* (New Delhi), June 28, 2002; and Jasjit Singh, "Auditing Coercive Diplomacy," *Indian Express* (New Delhi), July 31, 2002. For negative assessments, see Amit Baruah, "Indian Diplomacy Runs Aground," *Hindu* (Chennai), September 29, 2002; Achin Vanaik, "Deterrence or A Deadly Game? Nuclear Propaganda and Reality in South Asia," *Disarmament Diplomacy* 66 (September 2002), http://www.acronym.org.uk/-dd/dd66/66op3.htm; R. S. Bedi, "Demobilisation of Armed Forces: How Far Was Their Deployment Justifiable?" *Tribune* (Chandigarh), October 26, 2002; and V. Sudarshan, "Mirage 2001–02," *Outlook* (New Delhi), November 4, 2002, http://www.outlookindia.com/full.asp?fodname=20021104&fname=Border+blunder+%28F%29&sid=1.

67. "We Won without Going to War," *Indian Express* (New Delhi), June 18, 2002. The admission and the accusation are clearly implicit in his statement that "until infiltration is stopped and terrorist camps in POK [Pakistan-Occupied Kashmir] are not [*sic*] destroyed, India won't accept any claims by Islamabad" (ibid.).

68. Glen Kessler, "Kashmir Incursions Increasing, India Tells U.S.," *Washington Post*, September 10, 2002.

69. "Minor Reduction in Infiltration from Pakistan: Fernandes," *Hindu* (Chennai), November 13, 2002.

70. "Armed Forces Mobilisation Met Objectives: Fernandes," *Hindu* (Chennai), November 21, 2002.

71. These numbers do not include those of terrorists killed, nor the figures for terrorist activity in other parts of the country. They correspond with Fernandes's statement regarding a halving of the killing rate, since the average number of killings in November 2002, again excluding those of terrorists themselves, was about half the average of 138 per month in 2001, when such killings peaked. See the chart, "Casualties in Terrorist Violence in Jammu and Kashmir (2000–2002)," South Asia Terrorism Portal, http://www.satp.org/satporgtp/countries/india/index.html.

72. "Pak Has Reopened Terrorist Camps: India," *Times of India* (Mumbai), December 18, 2002.

73. Udayan Namboodiri, "Pak Hypocrisy over Deportation of Terrorists Exposed," *Hindustan Times* (New Delhi), August 26, 2002.

74. P. R. Chari, "The Border Confrontation," *Hindu* (Chennai), July 11, 2002.

75. "We Won Without Going to War: PM," *Indian Express* (New Delhi), June 18, 2002.

76. C. Raja Mohan, "Drawing America into Kashmir," *Hindu* (Chennai), June 6, 2002.

77. Udayan Namboodiri, "Powell Delivers Tough Message to India, Pak," *Hindustan Times* (New Delhi), July 28, 2002.

78. "US Not to Declare Pak Terrorist State," *Hindustan Times* (New Delhi), July 19, 2002.

79. B. Muralidhar Reddy, "Pak Alone Not Responsible for Infiltration," *Hindu* (Chennai), August 25, 2002.

80. Atul Aneja, "India, U.S. Differ on Perceptions of Musharraf," *Hindu* (Chennai), May 18, 2002.

81. "US Not Happy with Decision on Envoy," *Hindu* (Chennai), May 21, 2002.

82. Pramit Pal Chaudhuri, "US Weak Link in India's Pressure Game," *Hindustan Times* (New Delhi), July 16, 2002.

83. Amit Baruah, "India, E.U. Differ on Kashmir," *Hindu* (Chennai), October 11, 2002; Dina Vakil, "EU Must Ditch Narrow Prism of Pak: Sinha," *Times of India* (Mumbai), October 10, 2002.

84. Raja Mohan, "Between War and Peace."

85. For an extended treatment of symbolism and interstate conflict, see Barry O'Neill, *Honor, Symbols, and War* (Ann Arbor: University of Michigan Press, 1999).

86. Former Indian Ambassador to the United States Naresh Chandra, cited in Celia W. Dugger, "In Kashmir Sequel, Seeking A New Ending," *New York Times*, January 2, 2002.

87. Jasjit Singh, "December 13: A Year After," *Indian Express* (New Delhi), December 16, 2002.

88. The figure stated was Rps. 8,000 crore (cited in Sood and Sawhney, *Operation Parakram*, 85). I have arrived at the dollar cost by converting the stated cost from crores of Indian rupees (1 crore = 10,000,000 Rps.) to U.S. dollars at an approximate rate of $1 = Rps. 49. The figures cited in this and the preceding note are drawn from official statements by the Indian and Pakistani governments and are not confirmed.

89. Saritha Rai, "India Success in Software Is Set Back by War," *New York Times*, June 6, 2002; Thomas L. Friedman, "India, Pakistan, and G.E.," *New York Times*, August 11, 2002.

90. Sudarshan, "Mirage 2001–02," *Outlook* (New Delhi), November 4, 2002, http://www.outlookindia.com/full.asp?fodname=20021104&fname=Border+blunder+%28F%29&sid=1.

91. Michael Krepon, "Last-Minute Diplomacy," *Outlook* (New Delhi), April 29, 2002, 24.

92. Scott and Smith, "Lessons of October," 669–70.

93. Thomas W. Robinson, "The Sino-Soviet Border Conflict," in *Diplomacy and Power: Soviet Armed Forces as a Political Instrument,* ed. Stephen S. Kaplan (Washington, D.C.: Brookings Institution, 1981).

94. Schelling, *Arms and Influence*, 82.

95. Ross McDermott, *Risk-Taking in International Politics: Prospect Theory in American Foreign Policy* (Ann Arbor: University of Michigan Press, 1998).

96. "No Pak Leader Can Abandon Kashmir: Musharraf," *Hindu* (Chennai), September 15, 2002.

97. Rajesh M. Basrur, "Nuclear Confidence-Building in the Post-Kargil Scenario," in *The Challenge of Confidence Building in South Asia,* ed. Moonis Ahmar (New Delhi: Har-Anand, 2001).

98. "Pak Deploys Shaheen," *Hindu* (Chennai), May 21, 2002.

99. "Pakistan Test Fires Nuclear-Capable Missile," *Hindustan Times* (New Delhi), May 25, 2002; "Pakistan Test Fires Second Missile," *Hindustan Times* (New

Delhi), May 26, 2002; "Pakistan Test Fires Third Missile," *Hindustan Times* (New Delhi), May 28, 2002.

100. C. Raja Mohan, cited in Vishal Thapar, "Troop Build-up Marks A First in Military History," *Hindustan Times* (New Delhi), October 18, 2002.

101. Vishal Thapar, "Troop Build-up Marks A First in Military History," *Hindustan Times* (New Delhi), October 18, 2002.

102. Premvir Das, "The War That Never Was," *Indian Express* (New Delhi), November 18, 2002.

103. Robinson, "The Sino-Soviet Border Conflict."

104. Ibid., 283.

105. "Musharraf: Here's What I'll Do" (interview), *Washington Post*, June 23, 2002.

106. See George, *Forceful Persuasion*, 77–78, for a discussion on this. "Asymmetry of motivation," which George identifies as a key ingredient of success, is the same as a favorable balance of commitment.

107. Karl Vick and Kamran Khan, "Pakistani Ambivalence Frustrates Hope for Kashmir Peace," *Washington Post*, June 29, 2002.

108. For the nonproliferation aspect, see Scott D. Sagan and Kenneth N. Waltz, *The Spread of Nuclear Weapons: A Debate Renewed* (New York: W. W. Norton, 2003); ch. 3 (pp. 88–124) is specifically concerned with the India–Pakistan relationship. Both authors have presented their positions in the larger context of all nuclear powers in separate writings (see Scott D. Sagan, *The Limits of Safety: Organizations, Accidents, and Nuclear Weapons* [Princeton, N.J.: Princeton University Press, 1993]; and Kenneth N. Waltz, "Nuclear Myths and Political Realities," *American Political Science Review* 84, no. 3 [September 1990]: 731–45). An early and neglected precursor to these debates may be seen in the differing positions taken by Bernard Brodie over a span of two decades. For a pessimistic view of nuclear weapons, though he still thought war possible (doubtless from the historical closeness of the Second World War), see his "Implications for Military Policy," in *The Absolute Weapon: Atomic Power and World Order*, ed. Bernard Brodie (New York: Harcourt, Brace, 1946). For a more optimistic view that limited nuclear war is feasible, see his *Escalation and the Nuclear Option* (Princeton, N.J.: Princeton University Press, 1966).

109. In addition to the works by Sagan cited above, see, for example, Paul Bracken, "Accidental Nuclear War," in *Hawks, Doves, and Owls,* ed. Graham T. Allison, Albert Carnsdale, and Joseph S. Nye, Jr. (New York: W. W. Norton, 1985); Robert Jervis, *The Meaning of the Nuclear Revolution* (Ithaca, N.Y.: Cornell University Press, 1989), 87–94; Richard Ned Lebow, *Nuclear Crisis Management: A Dangerous Illusion* (Ithaca, N.Y.: Cornell University Press, 1987); Jeffrey W. Legro, "Military Culture and Inadvertent Escalation in World War II," *International Security* 18, no. 4 (Spring 1994): 108–42; Rhodes, *Power and MADness*; and Hakan Wiberg, Ib Damgaard Petersen, and Paul Smoker, eds., *Inadvertent Nuclear War: The Implications of the Changing Global Order* (Oxford: Pergamon Press, 1993).

110. Robert Powell, "The Theoretical Foundations of Deterrence," *Political Science Quarterly* 100, no. 1 (Spring 1985): 75–96.

111. For the concept of "non-traditional deterrence," see Saira Khan, *Nuclear Pro-*

liferation Dynamics in Protracted Conflict Regions: A Comparative Study of South Asia and the Middle East (Aldershot, Hampshire, U.K.: Ashgate, 2002), 151–65.

112. Gaurav Kampani, "Placing the Indo-Pakistani Standoff in Perspective," *CNS Web Reports*, Center for Nonproliferation Studies, Monterey Institute of International Studies, Monterey, Calif., April 8, 2002, http://cns.miis.edu/pubs/reports/pdfs/indopak.pdf.

113. "Lt-Gen Vij Moved Forces 'Too Close' to Border," *Times of India* (Mumbai), January 21, 2002.

114. R. Prasannan, "Fall of A Star," *The Week*, March 17, 2002, http://www.theweek.com/22mar17/events2.htm; Sandeep Dikshit, "Air Marshal Bhatia Shifted," *Hindu* (Chennai), April 25, 2002.

115. Praveen Swami, "When Pakistan Took Loonda Post," *Frontline*, August 31–September 13, 2002, http:///.frontlineonnet.com/fl1918.19180220.htm.

116. "War-Time Awards Conferred for 'Special Missions,'" *Hindu* (Chennai), November 3, 2002.

117. Ball et al., *Crisis Stability and Nuclear War*, 64–65.

118. House Committee on Science, Space, and Aeronautics, Brigadier General Simon P. Worden statement on "Near-Earth Objects," 107th Cong., 2nd sess., October 3, 2002.

119. Cited in David Gonzalez, "At Cuba Conference, Old Foes Exchange Notes on 1962 Missile Crisis," *New York Times*, October 14, 2002.

120. Siddharth Srivastava, "Withdrawal of Troops Sign of Weakness: Parthasarathy," *Times of India* (Mumbai), October 19, 2002; Brahma Chellaney, "Perils of Crying Wolf," *Hindustan Times* (New Delhi), November 27, 2002.

121. On Indian strategic culture with respect to nuclear weapons, see Rajesh M. Basrur, "Nuclear Weapons and Indian Strategic Culture," *Journal of Peace Research* 38, no. 2 (March 2001): 181–98.

122. Indian strategy with respect to the long-standing secessionist movement in Nagaland in the Northeast is but the most recent example.

About the Contributors

Co-Editors

Rafiq Dossani, Senior Research Scholar at Stanford University's Asia-Pacific Research Center (A-PARC), responsible for developing and directing the South Asia Initiative. Research interests: Domestic politics and security policy interactions in South Asia, technology policy and the globalization of business services. His most recent book is *Telecommunications Reform in India*, Westport, CT: Greenwood Press, 2002. Dossani serves as an advisor to the Indian Ministry of Information Technology and the Pakistan Telecommunications Authority. Dr. Dossani has a Ph.D. in Finance from Northwestern University.

Henry S. Rowen, Director Emeritus of A-PARC. He is a senior fellow at the Hoover Institution and a professor of public policy and management emeritus at Stanford's Graduate School of Business. Rowen was assistant secretary of defense for international security affairs in the U.S. Department of Defense from 1989 to 1991. He was also chairman of the National Intelligence Council from 1981 to 1983. He served as president of the RAND Corporation from 1968 to 1972 and was assistant director, U.S. Bureau of the Budget, from 1965 to 1966.

His current research focuses on economic growth prospects for the developing world, political and economic change in East Asia, and the tenets of federalism. He recently wrote "Catch Up. Why Poor Countries are Becoming Richer, Democratic, Increasingly Peaceable, and Sometimes More Dangerous," published in August 1999 by A-PARC, and co-authored "Cool on Global Warming" with John Weyant for *The National Interest* (Fall 1999). He is the editor of *Behind East Asian Growth: The Political and Social Foundations of Prosperity* (London: Routledge Press, 1998). Among his numerous publications, his other noteworthy writings include "The Short March: China's Road to Democracy," *The National Interest* (Fall 1996); "Inchon in the Desert: My Rejected Plan," *The National Interest* (Summer 1995); "The Tide Underneath the 'Third Wave,'" *Journal of Democracy* (January 1995); *The Im-*

poverished Superpower: Perestroika and the Soviet Military Burden (1990), co-edited with Charles Wolf, and *The Future of the Soviet Empire* (1987), also co-edited with Charles Wolf.

Other Writers

Dr. Rajesh M. Basrur, Director, Centre for Global Studies, Mumbai, India. Research interests: minimum deterrence and Indian nuclear strategy, and on nuclear-terrorism threats to India. Publications: (edited) *Security in the New Millennium: Views from South Asia* (New Delhi: India Research Press, 2001); *India's External Relations: A Theoretical Analysis* (New Delhi: Commonwealth Publishers, 2000); and (edited) *Perspectives on India's Defense and Arms Control* (Mumbai: Mumbai University, 1999). He has a Ph.D. in Political Science from Mumbai University.

Chandrashekhar Dasgupta, Distinguished Fellow at the Observer Research Foundation, New Delhi. Dasgupta was a member of the Indian Foreign Service from 1962 to 2000, serving as ambassador/high commissioner to the European Union, Belgium, and Luxembourg (1996–2000); China (1993–96); Tanzania (1984–86); and Singapore (1981–84). Research interests: security policy in South Asia. Publications: *War and Diplomacy in Kashmir: 1947–48* (New Delhi: Sage, 2002).

Ainslie T. Embree, Professor Emeritus of History, Columbia University. Embree also teaches at the School of Advanced International Studies, Johns Hopkins University. Publications (books): *India's Search for National Identity; Imagining India: Essays on Indian History;* and *Utopias in Conflict: Religion and Nationalism in India.* He was Editor-in-Chief of the *Encyclopedia of Asian History* (4 vols.) and *Sources of Indian Tradition* (2 vols.).

C. Christine Fair, at the time of writing was a political scientist at RAND. At present she is a senior South Asia analyst at the United States Institute of Peace. Dr. Fair has accumulated several years living, working, and conducting research in Pakistan, India, as well as Sri Lanka and Nepal. At USIP she is working on a number of projects that seek to expose the roots and sources of militant Islam in Pakistan, including a critical translation of major publications of Jaish-e-Mohammad and Lashkar-e-Taiba. She holds an MA in Public Policy and a Ph.D. in South Asian Languages and Civilizations, both from the University of Chicago.

Robert L. Hardgrave, Jr., Temple Professor Emeritus of the Humanities in Government and Asian Studies at the University of Texas at Austin. He is a specialist in the domestic and international politics of South Asia. Publications (books): *The Dravidian Movement* (1965); *The Nadars of Tamilnad: The Political Culture of a Community in Change* (1969); *India Under Pressure: Prospects for Political Stability* (1984); and (with Stanley A. Kochanek) *India: Government and Politics in a Developing Nation,* now in its 6th edition (2000).

Syed Rifaat Hussain, Chairman of the Department of Defense and Strategic

Studies (DSS) at Quaid-i-Azam University in Islamabad, Pakistan. He also served as the Minister of Information at the Embassy of Pakistan in Washington, D.C. from 1994 to 1997. He has a Ph.D. in International Studies from the University of Denver.

Charles H. Kennedy. is a Professor of Political Science at Wake Forest University. He received his Ph.D. from Duke University in 1979. Professor Kennedy has written about South Asian comparative political and governmental systems since 1975, and has authored, co-authored, or edited sixteen books, which deal with South Asia. His most recent include: *Pakistan: 2004* (Oxford University Press, 2005), *Pakistan at the Millennium* (Oxford University Press, 2003), and *Government and Politics in South Asia* 5th edition (Westview Press, 2002).

Michael Krepon, Founder and President Emeritus of the Henry L. Stimson Center. Research interests: South Asia and the Kashmir dispute, nuclear risk-reduction and confidence-building measures, military space policy. Recent publications (books): *Global Confidence-Building: New Tools for Troubled Regions* (1999); *Cooperative Threat Reduction, Missile Defense, and the Nuclear Future* (2002); *Space Assurance or Space Weapons? The Case Against Weaponizing Space* (2003); *Escalation Control and the Nuclear Option in South Asia* (2004).

Peter Lavoy, Director of the Center for Contemporary Conflict at the Naval Postgraduate School, Monterey. Publications: *Planning the Unthinkable: How New Powers Will Use Nuclear, Biological and Chemical Weapons* (Cornell University Press, 2000). His next books are *Learning to Live with the Bomb: India, the United States and the Myths of Nuclear Security* (New York: Palgrave Macmillan, forthcoming 2005) and *Asymmetric Warfare in South Asia: The Causes and Consequences of the Kargil Conflict.* He is on the editorial board of *Asian Security* and *Defence Studies.* He has a Ph.D. in Political Science from the University of California, Berkeley.

Barbara D. Metcalf, Professor of History at the University of Michigan. Research interest: History of South Asian Muslims. Recent publications (books): *Islamic Contestations: Essays on Muslims in India and Pakistan* (New Delhi: Oxford University Press, 2004); (co-authored) *A Concise History of India* (Cambridge: Cambridge University Press, 2002), *Islamic Revival in British India: Deoband, 1860–1900* (Princeton: Princeton University Press, 1982 and 2nd edition, Delhi: Oxford University Press, 2002). She has a Ph.D.from the Department of South and Southeast Asian Studies, University of California, Berkeley.

Vali Nasr, Professor, Department of National Security Affairs at the Naval Postgraduate School, Monterey. Research interest: Political Islam and Middle Eastern and South Asian politics. Recent publications (books): *The Islamic Leviathan: Islam and the Making of State Power* (Oxford University Press, 2001), *The Vanguard of the Islamic Revolution: the Jama`at-i Islami of Pakistan* (University of California Press, 1994); and *Mawdudi and the Making of Islamic Revivalism* (Oxford University Press 1996).

Howard B. Schaffer, Director of Studies and Deputy Director, Institute for the Study of Diplomacy, Edmund A. Walsh School of Foreign Service, Georgetown University. Earlier he worked as a U.S. Foreign Service officer, served as U.S. ambassador to Bangladesh, political counselor in India and Pakistan, and deputy assistant secretary of state responsible for South Asian affairs. Publications (books, both biographies): *Chester Bowles: New Dealer in the Cold War* (Harvard University Press, 1993); *Ellsworth Bunker: Global Troubleshooter, Vietnam Hawk* (University of North Carolina Press, 2003). He has a B.A. from Harvard College and has done graduate work at Columbia and Princeton.

Karthik Vaidyanathan is a graduate student at the University of California at San Diego. Previously, he was a research assistant at RAND.

Index

Abbas, Ghulam, 111, 112, 116, 117

Abdullah, Farooq, 122, 249, 252, 253, 254, 384n17

Abdullah, Omar, 254

Abdullah, Sheikh Mohammad, 111, 112, 113, 240, 241–44, 246–48, 348n5, 383n5

Abu Talib Khan, Mirza, 162

Advani, L. K., 131, 365n79; and Bharatiya Janata Party (BJP), 194, 199, 201, 208, 210, 211; and Gujarat massacre, 210, 211; and Rashtriya Swayamsewak Sangh (RSS), 177, 191, 193, 209

Afghanistan: narcotics production in, 338; Pashtuns in, 13, 26, 27, 28, 100, 337; relations with India, 26, 137, 334; relations with Pakistan, 1, 7, 14, 19, 20, 24–29, 30, 32–33, 35, 71, 98, 99–100, 104, 108, 121–22, 137, 251, 304, 311, 316, 317, 333–34, 335; relations with United States, 1, 2, 7, 13, 16, 24, 32–33, 99–100, 103, 104, 121, 136–37, 295, 304, 311, 312, 314, 317, 333, 337, 338, 339; Soviet occupation of, 7, 22, 23, 24–25, 27–28, 30, 121–22, 251, 252, 295, 333–34, 336, 364n57; Taliban, 14, 19, 24, 27–29, 30, 32–33, 34, 88, 89, 97, 98, 100, 298, 304, 311, 316, 317, 321, 335, 339

Afro-Asian group, 341

Ahmadiyya, 379n36

Ahmad, Wajihuddin, 353n26

Ahmed, Sheikh Riaz, 62, 63

Ajmal Mian, 46

Akali Dal, 192, 246

Akhil Bharatiya Vidyarthi Parishad, 177

Aksai Chin, 111, 115

Alam, Kamal Mansur, 353n26

Al Badr Mujahideen, 122

Ali, Chaudhry Rehmat, 360n11

Ali, Chaudry Muhammad, 47

Ali, Muhammad Yakub, 50

All India Anna Dravida Munnetra Kazagham (AIADMK), 204

All-India Backward Muslim Morcha (AIBMM), 228

All India Muslim Majlis-e-Mushawarat, 230, 231, 379n39, 381n55

All India Muslim Personal Law Board, 230, 237

All Jammu and Kashmir Muslim Conference, 112, 113, 115, 116–17, 120

All Parties Hurriyat Conference (APHC), 132–33

All Parties Kashmir Committee, 118

All-Party Jammu Action Committee, 248

Anjuman-i-Islam, 112

Annan, Kofi, 134–35

Anwar-ul-Haq, Sheikh, 50, 60–61, 353nn23,25

Appadurai, Arjun, 164

Arif, K. M., 264, 295, 362n36, 363n37, 391n25

407

The authorized representative in the EU for product safety and compliance is:
Mare Nostrum Group
B.V Doelen 72
4831 GR Breda
The Netherlands

9 780804 750851